THE NARROW LAND

THE

Narrow Land

Folk Chronicles of Old Cape Cod

BY ELIZABETH REYNARD

FIFTH EDITION

WITH A FOREWORD BY ANDREW OLIVER

PUBLISHED BY

THE CHATHAM HISTORICAL SOCIETY, INC.

CHATHAM, MASSACHUSETTS

Also by Elizabeth Reynard

THE MUTINOUS WIND

CAHABA VERSES

PARTS OF YOUTH
Fragment of an Autobiography

FOREWORD

ELIZABETH REYNARD, the author of this volume, and her close friend Virginia C. Gildersleeve shared for much of their lives many common interests to which they devoted their not inconsiderable energy and ability.

They loved their profession, teaching, and their college, Barnard College, at which Miss Reynard was Associate Professor of English and Miss Gildersleeve, for thirty-six years, Dean. They were active throughout their lives in encouraging the participation by women in fields of endeavor long pre-empted by men, even including the military. During the Second World War Miss Reynard was Assistant Director of the Women's Reserve of the United States Navy (the WAVES) with the rank of Lieutenant Commander, and Miss Gildersleeve was Chairman of its Advisory Council. Not the least of their common interests, however, was Cape Cod, the "Narrow Land" about which this book was first written in 1934. For many years the author and Miss Gildersleeve shared a home in Chatham overlooking Nantucket Sound, whence Miss Reynard conducted her research and collected the tales recorded in this volume.

On her death in 1962, Miss Reynard, as a mark of the appreciation and affection she bore her old friend, provided by her will funds for the publication and free distribution to Barnard alumnae of a volume of essays written by Miss Gildersleeve. As a graceful return of the compliment, Miss Gildersleeve at her death in 1965 similarly provided by her will funds for the publication of a new edition of *The Narrow Land,* the royalties from which she bequeathed to The Chatham Historical Society.

It is a privilege as Miss Gildersleeve's Executor to carry out her instructions by the publication of this new edition of Miss Reynard's

The Narrow Land, and thus to record, in the very land of which they were both so fond, their long and fruitful years of friendship and common endeavor.

ANDREW OLIVER

June, 1968

PREFACE
TO THE FIRST EDITION

Around the long, thin, curving peninsula that is now Cape Cod, there has risen and ebbed away again through the years a ceaseless flow of folk tales, of myths and legends and tales of the sea that form a heritage of this unique Cape region, and a contribution to American folklore. In old Icelandic sagas, a story of Vinland the Good has slumbered since the thirteenth century; a tale of battle, murder, sea adventure off the American coast; but it is only by the wisdom of modern scholars that the scene of the story has at last been set. From musty records, from anthropological reports, and by word of mouth, Indian legends of the same region have come to light; tales of giants, pygmies, princesses and warriors. From town records, church records, letters, manuscripts, pamphlets, newssheets, broadsides, histories, genealogies, a lost lore has been accumulated; yarns of pioneers and pirates, of witches, ghosts and "seafarin' men" who lived on a Narrow Land.

To supply the detail necessary to these narratives, historical, antiquarian and oral sources have been invoked freely. The author is deeply indebted to all searchers into the past of Cape Cod, those who are with us and those who have gone. In an appendix acknowledgment is rendered for the written sources of each tale and also for certain of the oral sources.

A few stories have survived comparatively complete in content; others have had to be reconstructed from the most meager of fragments. The choice of traditions has perforce been arbitrary; many well-known tales are left untold; others have been presented in their less familiar versions. Although this rendition makes use of historical "embroiderings," it does not pretend to antiquarian infallibility; nor does it ask of the reader to accept other than an individual interpretation of selected chronicles rescued from oblivion.

Three wayfarers set forth to collect these tales. One of the three was not spared to aid in the completion of the task; but the first expression of personal gratitude goes to the memory of Nevett Steele Bartow who placed at my disposal his knowledge gleaned from years of Cape experience, who worked indefatigably for two years, after he was stricken with blindness and until his death, at the collecting of oral traditions. Few people could refuse him their utmost memories.

This collection could not have been completed without the cooperation, wise and unfailing, of Mabel Sears Bartow whose work has extended so far beyond the usual limits of research-assistant and typist that she should accept her responsibilities as collaborator.

To Miss Gildersleeve and the Department of English of Barnard College I am indebted for a leave of absence that permitted concentrated work. To Cape librarians and to the librarians of special collections, particularly to the staff of the Massachusetts Historical Society, I am indebted for many courtesies and privileges. To Mrs. Michael Fitzgerald, who contributed invaluable notes amassed and unused by her late husband, and who also gave me some of his books, I am happy to have an opportunity to express thanks. To Joseph C. Allen, Editor of the Edgartown *Gazette,* I am indebted for three Tall Stories. Somewhat "contracted," they are told in his own inimitable words. To all the Cape people at whose doors we knocked and who proved so responsive, helpful, kindly, no acknowledgment will ever express my debt of gratitude.

For individual contributions and assistance, I take pleasure in thanking Mr. E. J. Bliss, Jr., Miss Agnes Mary Claudius, Miss Rosamond Crompton, Miss Hildegarde FitzGerald, Mr. and Mrs. Frederick Gardner, Miss Sally Gehman, Mrs. Louis Harding, Mrs. Alexander Hinckley, Miss Mary F. Hoyt, Miss Gesine Jaeger, Mr. and Mrs. Charles Kendrick, Mr. Henry C. Kittredge, Dr. and Mrs. Alfred Meyer, Captain George Nickerson, Miss Elizabeth Nye, Mrs. Edward Read, Chief Red Shell of Mashpee, Miss Evelyn Rich, Miss Edith Howland Sears, Mr. William U. Swan, Mr. and Mrs. Theodore Swift, Miss Phoebe Atwood Taylor, Mr. Perry Walton, Chief Wild Horse of Mashpee, Mrs. Bartow Woodland.

E. R.

INTRODUCTION

The Chatham Historical Society is happy that it can now reissue Elizabeth Reynard's *The Narrow Land*. Since its first appearance in 1934 and its reprinting in 1962 this book has enjoyed a well deserved popularity, so much so that the number of remaining copies is again becoming very low. Our Society is grateful to the firm of Houghton Mifflin Company for most generously relinquishing its copyright to us. A new generation of readers can now enjoy what surely must rank as one of the most distinguished books ever written about Cape Cod, a book which so skillfully mingles the account of this area's historic and legendary past.

Ernest J. Knapton, Vice-President,
Chatham Historical Society.
For the Committee on Publication

Chatham, Massachusetts
28 September 1978

FOREWORD TO THE 1993 EDITION

The Chatham Historical Society is pleased to continue the publication of *The Narrow Land* by Elizabeth Reynard, with this Fifth Edition.

For the benefit of those reading this book for the first time, we want to mention other publications published by the Society.

Vital Records—Town of Chatham, Massachusetts 1696-1850 was published in 1991. Births, Marriages and Deaths, literally transcribed from original town records. 512 pages of listings in chronological order, with an Index in which names are alphabetized under familiar spellings, followed by variations.

Days To Remember by Joshua Atkins Nickerson 2nd was published in 1988. Mr. Nickerson, a Chatham native, recalls life in Chatham and on Cape Cod since the turn of the century. He dedicated the book to his grandson, Peter, so that he and other grandsons and granddaughters can have a better appreciation of their grandparents' time, and of their own position within the flow of never-ending thread that runs through and unites all our generations.

History of Chatham, Massachusetts by William C. Smith was initially published in four successive parts dated 1909, 1913 and 1917. Following his death, the Chatham Historical Society brought out in 1947 a fourth part comprising Smith's remaining manuscripts. In 1971 the Society reprinted the four parts as one volume, with an elaborate genealogical index compiled by Rachel Baker Napier. The book includes maps and illustrations, and numerous genealogical notes. The Fourth Edition was published in 1992.

The Chatham Historical Society, organized in 1923, provides an important service to the Town of Chatham in preserving its history.

The Museum in the Old Atwood House is one of the few spots on Cape Cod where so much of interest to so many may be seen so easily. Recent additions include The New Gallery, a display of tools and equipment, and the North Beach camp of Joshua Atkins Nickerson 2nd, built in 1946 and moved by barge to the mainland from North Beach, and trucked to the grounds of the Old Atwood House.

All who read *The Narrow Land* are cordially invited to visit Chatham's historical Museum.

Jay A. Ebel
Chairman, Committee on Publications

January 1993

CONTENTS

VI. GHOSTS WHO STILL WALK THE NARROW LAND

ILLUSTRATIONS

THE NARROW LAND

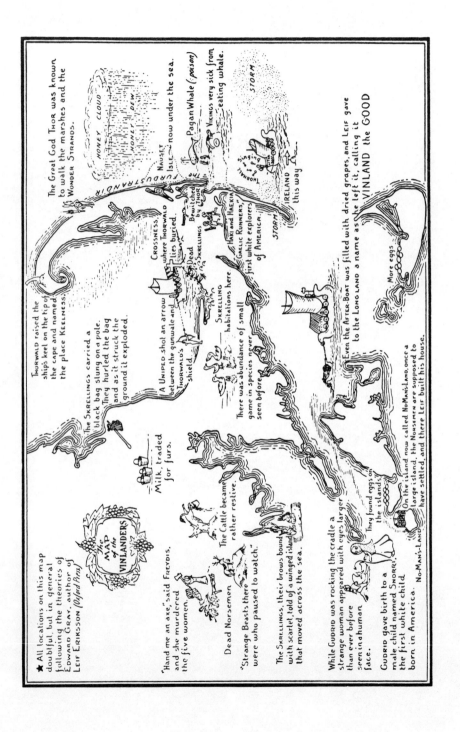

★ All locations on this map doubtful, but in general following the theories of EDWARD GRAY, author of LEIF ERIKSSON (Oxford Press).

THE MAP of the VINLANDERS

"Hand me an axe," said FREYDIS, and she murdered the five women.

Dead Norsemen

"Strange Beasts there were who paused to watch."

The SKRELLINGS, their brows bound with scarlet, told of a winged island that moved across the sea.

While GUDRID was rocking the cradle a strange woman appeared with eyes larger than ever before seen in a human face.

GUDRID gave birth to a male child named SNORRI, the first white child born in America.

They found eggs on the islands.

On the island now called No-MAN'S-LAND, once a large island, the NORSEMEN are supposed to have settled, and there LEIR built his house. NO-MAN'S-LAND.

The Cattle became rather restive.

Milk, traded for furs.

THORWALD raised the ship's keel on the tip of the cape and named the place KEELNESS.

The SKRELLINGS carried a black bag slung on a pole. They hurled the bag and as it struck the ground it exploded.

A UNIPED shot an arrow between the gunwale and THORWALD'S shield.

There was abundance of small game in species never seen before.

SKRELLING habitations here

CROSSNESS, where THORWALD lies buried.

Dead SKRELLINGS

Bewitched by THOR

HAKI and HAEKIA, "Gaelic Runners," first white explorers of AMERICA.

The Great God THOR was known to walk the marshes and the WONDER STRANDS.

HONEY CLOUD

HONEY DEW

NAUSET now under the sea.

THE FURDUSTRANDIR

PaganWhale (poison)

Vikings very sick from eating whale.

STORM

THORWALL singing

STORM

IRELAND this way

More eggs

Even the AFTER-BOAT was filled with dried grapes, and LEIF gave to the LONG-LAND a name as the left it, calling it VINLAND the GOOD

MIRAGE ON THE DUNES

A slim peninsula of white lies like a silver key thrust in the portals of a continent, a key that has, long since, unlocked a nation. Tall dunes cast shadows like the prows of ships whose moving figureheads are silhouetted from the bowing crests of dunes. Fluctuant sands wear occult veils of mirage. Winds are the voices of Indian giants, of shrill Pukwudgees, *of* Whistlin' Whales, *of the* Screechin' Hannah. *The moon is a witch familiar, and the stars are the* Chart o' God. *Once paradise of twenty thousand sailors, once rendezvous of half a thousand pirates, this port of whalers was, itself, born of a great ice whale. The vast Moby Dick of glaciers, pushing dark silt before it plowed homeward to the sea to die. With transparent lips it sucked the ocean, while its gaunt sides withered inward, leaving around them a narrow shroud rimmed by tallow-white beaches, plumed with blue fire of waves and flanged by the smoky sea.*

VINLAND THE GOOD

THREE BOYS and a little girl sat in the "Skali," or Great Hall at Brattahlid, and listened to tales of westward voyaging told by young Biarni Herulfson, who wintered at their home. Eric the Red, father of the children, discovered and colonized Greenland. They, in turn, longed to possess a sunny, forested shore. They filled the ears of Tyrker, their German tutor, with plans for expeditions. They pestered old Thorhall the Hunter, who listened to their talk in silence occasionally punctured by derisive speech. Hunter and fisherman in summer, in winter their father's bailiff, stout, overbearing, unpopular, he possessed a pessimist's curious enthusiasm for the negative, and made an excellent bulwark against which to amass argument.

The four children who clamored against him differed greatly in appearance and temperament; two of the boys upright, strong, handsome; the third a delicate dreamer and romantic; the girl, Eric's illegitimate daughter, wild, passionate, fearless, with the strength and ambition of a boy.

The Great Hall at Brattahlid buzzed with discussion of voyages. For fifteen years Eric the Red, thrice wanted for manslaughter, had found refuge in his pioneer settlement in Greenland. In the year 1000, when his oldest son, Leif, was sixteen, ready to be sent to Norway to serve Olaf the King, Eric gave to the boy a small vessel, and the young, unskilled mariner started on his first sea voyage. North winds blew the ship to the Hebridean Islands, and summer was far advanced before fair winds carried it away. The delay must not all be blamed upon wind, for Leif, at sixteen, had the makings of a young Aeneas. "A woman of fine family, possessed of rare intelligence," caught the boy's attention, and held it. When, at length, he prepared to depart, she asked if she might come with him. Had she the approval of her kinsmen? queried Leif. The lady, named Thorgunna, replied that she did not care for it. "Then," said Leif the cautious, "it is not the part of wisdom to abduct so high-born a woman, in a strange country, and we so few in number."

"It is by no means certain that thou shalt find this to be the better decision," said Thorgunna.

"I shall put it to the proof, notwithstanding," answered Leif.

"Then I tell thee," declared Thorgunna, "that I am no longer a lone woman, for I am pregnant and upon thee I charge it. I foresee that I shall give birth to a male child; and though thou give this no heed, yet will I rear the boy and send him to thee in Greenland. And I foresee," continued Thorgunna cryptically, "that thou wilt get as much profit of this son as is thy due from this our parting. Moreover," she added, "before the end comes, I mean to come to Greenland myself."

Leif quieted her with worldly skill: he gave her a gold finger ring, a Greenland Wadmal mantle, and a belt of walrus tusk. Then, prudently, he sailed for Norway and put in at Nidaros to visit the Christian King. Olaf Tryggvason, monarch of Vikings, kept Leif with him during that winter, and converted the boy to Christianity; he converted his shipmates as well. In the spring Leif sailed to Greenland and in the summer he proclaimed Christianity there. His mother, his brothers, even his sister adopted the creed, but Eric the Red and Thorhall the Hunter would not forsake the old gods. The family tried drastic persuasion. Eric's wife refused to have intercourse with her husband unless he became a believer; whereupon the old Norseman lost his quick temper but kept a firm hold on his faith.

A man's religion was not casual in the eleventh century. The schism in the family may account for Leif's determination, at seventeen, to stake his fortune on a westward venture in the hope of finding the new lands that Biarni Herulfson had described. Leif visited Biarni, bought from him his ship, and collected a crew of thirty-five men. Then he returned to his father (veteran explorer and daredevil), and asked Eric the Red to head the expedition. The old man hesitated. He was stricken in years, not able to endure long exposure; but when Leif declared that Eric would bring good luck to the undertaking, the patriarch yielded and rode on horseback from his home toward Ericsfirth Harbor. On the way the horse stumbled and the old warrior-mariner was thrown. "It is not designed for me," he exclaimed, "to discover more lands than the one in which we are now living!" Sorrowfully he returned to Brattahlid, and would not be persuaded to depart. In his stead he sent Tyrker, the diminutive German tutor to his children, a likable man despite shifty eyes and bulging forehead, and one who was handy at odd jobs. Olaf the King contributed to the expedition two Gaelic runners, Haki, a man, and Haekia, a woman. The crew put the ship in order, and in the spring they set sail for the Westward Sea.

After persistent voyaging, they found a tableland of flat rock. Beyond it glittered a range of ice mountains, and Leif named the country Helluland. Next they came upon a level forested shore, and called it Markland. Then, for two "doegr," or half days, they sailed the high seas, fresh northeast winds nipping at their heels.

One dawn they sighted an island, northward, off a new coast. The sun rose in a clear sky, and they went ashore to look about them. Under the sea, beyond Nauset bluffs, in the long ocean stretch known as the "Backside" of Cape Cod, lies the island that Leif's men found. It was still above sea when Captain Gosnold, sailing past in 1602, named its reef Tucker's Terror and its outermost bluff Point Care.

The morning was warm, in August. Dew lay heavy on the grass. The men touched the dew, and lifted their hands to their mouths, and it seemed to them that they had never savored anything so sweet.

They were sampling "Honey Dew," a sugary moisture that tasted as though the Gods of Valhalla had tipped down their nectar cups on the wine-colored cliffs at night. With their backs to the rising sun, the Norsemen looked beyond the island, over Nauset Seas, blue as darkest iris, over long shoals, green as iris leaves. The island foliage lay crisp and fresh, lacquered with sea mist of dawn. To the west loomed a "Long Land" fringed by endless beaches diamonded in mica.

Leif and his men sailed southward along that sandy coast. At the peninsula's sharp elbow, they found harbor for their ship; and there the small knorr, or trading vessel, waited while the two Gaels were put ashore, with orders to investigate the country and return by the third "half day." Haki and Haekia disembarked, naked except for "kiafals," garments hooded at the top, open at the sides, sleeveless, and fastened between the legs with buttons and loops. Over dune and moor, through woodland they traveled, alert, wary of all living beings, two Gaelic serfs, a man and a woman, first white explorers of America, "runners faster than any deer."

When Haki and Haekia returned to the ship, they carried green sheaves in their arms, that the mariners might sample the produce of this new country. The two serfs were taken aboard, and Leif coasted alongshore till he came to a region indented with bays. Strong currents swirled around an island, and the ebbing tide left broad reaches of shallow water. The vessel grounded on a sandbar but the men were so eager to disembark that they abandoned ship and rowed to land. Later, when the tide rose beneath the ship's keel, they conveyed her up a river and into a lake, carried hammocks ashore, built themselves "booths," and decided to remain for the winter. The country possessed marsh fodder for cattle, also a good supply of fish in river and lake; and the warriors, settling in, completed a "large house and staunch."

One night they missed Tyrker, the German. Leif, who loved the grotesque little "Southerner," set forth in search of him and came upon the culprit returning to the house. Leif reproached him gently:

"Wherefore art thou so belated, foster-father mine, and astray from the others?" Tyrker, in hilarious spirits, rolled his eyes and grinned.

"I did not go much further than you, yet I have news from grapes and vines!"

"Is this indeed true, foster-father?"

"Of a certainty it is true, for I was born where there is no lack of either grapes or vines."

That night the mariners rejoiced, and the next day they began to gather grapes, cut vines, and fell trees to obtain a cargo for their ship. In early spring they sailed for Greenland, and even the afterboat was laden with dried grapes. Leif gave to the Long Land a name as he left it, calling it Vinland the Good.

They stood out to sea. Winds were fair until the watch sighted fells below the glaciers of Greenland; yet Leif did not head for shore.

"Why do you steer so much into the wind?" asked one of the crew.

"Do you see anything out of the common?" answered Leif.

The crew looked where he pointed, and discerned a dark mass on the water. The knorr approached cautiously, and the mariners discovered a company of Norse castaways who had taken refuge on a skerry. Leif offered to convey the unfortunates to Brattahlid in his ship. They accepted gratefully, and the crowded little vessel held away to Ericsfirth.

At the settlement the young master mariner discharged cargo and invited the leader of the castaways and his wife, Gudrid, to make their home at the Great Hall. So the fairest woman in all Iceland, first heroine of the Narrow Land, entered the Skali at Brattahlid, and grew to know the three sons of Eric and their weird sister, Freydis. Gudrid the Fair, the newcomer was called, and although she became a good Christian, she knew the old spell-songs of Iceland, and could sing them in a voice sweet and clear. A faithful, gentle wife she proved, yet all men who saw her longed for her. The "little Sybil of Heriolfness" spoke the truth when she prophesied that Gudrid's destiny would be great.

Through a winter of long shadows the Hall at Brattahlid echoed to tales of the peninsula called Vinland, to descriptions of long beaches on which the Great God Thor was known to walk, to accounts of visions over the silver dunes, to memories of green forests, gentle winters, honey dew, and sweet wild grapes.

THE LAND OF SKRELLING AND UNIPED

During the winter of Leif Ericsson's return, a serious illness attacked the settlement. Gudrid's husband and many of his party died. Eric the Red succumbed to the disease, and his oldest son, Leif, became master of the Skali. With the reluctance of one bound by new responsibilities, the young overlord listened to his brother's repeated protests that the new country had not been sufficiently explored, and in the spring consented to Thorwald's importunities. "Take my ship," said Leif wearily, "and go to Vinland thyself."

Thorwald asked, also, for the gift of his brother's house in Vinland, but the new master of the Skali, not so sure that he had done with voyaging, consented only to its loan.

Thorwald promptly engaged a crew of thirty men, put his brother's vessel in order, and stood out to sea. With him he took Thorhall the Hunter, anti-Christian, fat, old, devoted to the comforts of home; Thorhall, so pessimistic about the new lands that he could not miss a chance at seeing them.

Leif's younger brother, an able navigator, arrived with little difficulty at the booths set up by his predecessors; and where sands were white on the shores of little inlets, the mariners laid up ship. During the first months of their stay, the sea howled against sand cliffs; a cold, driving mist of spume swept steadily across the land. They caught no fish; game became scarce; they could not row to the adjacent islands to collect eggs. In that barren wilderness, the warriors knelt on a bleak shore, to beseech a Christian deity who was not prompt.

Then old Thorhall disappeared. For three "half days" men searched for him, and at last found the old man on a crag that projected over the sea. Flat on his back, he stared at the sky and mumbled; his mouth and nostrils gaped as though in a trance, and Thorwald spoke charily, asking him why he had disappeared. The Hunter roused himself. "It does not concern anyone," he replied in his taciturn way; yet without further comment or protest he followed the searchers to the house.

As the warriors were stacking their spears, a cry echoed from a seaward cliff where the watch had sighted a whale spouting off the outer bar. Starving men leaped into the afterboat and drove it with urgent oarstrokes over a rough sea; they killed the whale, towed it ashore, flensed it (probably the first recorded whale captured off Cape Cod); but no man could tell by the look of it of what variety it was. Yet the cooks prepared it and hungry men ate it, and when at last they were replete the old Hunter spoke: "Now," he boasted, "did not the Red-

beard prove more helpful than Christ? This is my reward for
verses that on yonder high crag I composed to Thor the Trustworthy;
seldom has he failed me."

When the good Christian mariners heard that Thor had been summoned by the spell-songs of Iceland to walk the Long Land, they cast
that pagan whale of his into a sullen ocean, and they that ate the
meat grew ill, and made anxious appeal to God. In response, the
weather improved; the mariners caught many small fish; game appeared in the green forests; eggs were found on the islands.

In the spring, Thorwald decided to sail south for an exploration
along the coast. Characteristically, Thorhall the contrary desired to
sail north. Thorwald was very young, and though he had exhibited
skill and courage as leader of the expedition, the bailiff's opinion held
weight. The young mariner decided to divide forces, give Thorhall
the afterboat and nine men for a northward exploration, while he,
with the rest of the ship's company, sailed south in the knorr.

As the two groups prepared for their separate journeys, Thorwald,
watching the Hunter, sensed in him an unnatural elation. Ever since
the departure from Brattahlid Eric's bailiff had been homesick, although he derived a certain consolation from his opportunity to
point out that reports of the first voyagers had been false. His companions seemed to agree with him; and young Thorwald followed
them to the water spring one day, where he heard the sound of merry
laughter. There, fat Thorhall, who found it difficult to stoop, filled
his pail with water, held it aloft, and sang to a delighted audience of
followers:

> "Trees of the metal-meeting, warriors,
> Trees of battle, look on me
> Who was promised wine and honey
> From the dew and from the bee.
> In my hands this water pail!
> At the spring my lips are wet!
> Of Vinland's wine that cannot fail
> I have never tasted yet!"

The men laughed, and their young leader turned away. The bailiff was always making verses, most of them bad ones. Thorwald was
no poet. If he sensed mutiny in such songs, he gave no sign of this

knowledge; and after the Cape mayflower had rusted into the pine slopes, and before the first wild rose fell from its prickly stem, Thorhall the Hunter, at the prow of his afterboat, sang a farewell chanty, while his seamen hoisted sail:

> "Now let the sailor who knows the blue canopy
> Over the sands, the sea,
> Explore that broad highway of ships.
> Let us return to our homeland, while he,
> The rest-hating warrior and maker of sword-storms,
> With praise on his lips,
> Remains, alone, in this desolate land
> Cooking whale steak on the Wonder Strand."

Before Thorhall and his small company had sailed the length of the long beaches (Furdustrandir — Wonder Strands) they encountered westerly gales, and for an unrecorded number of days were blown toward the rising sun. In "far Ireland" the afterboat reached harbor; and the Irish, ever a wild race, seized the bailiff and his warriors, maltreated them, and made slaves of them. Many years later, traders from Erin brought word to the Great Hall at Brattahlid of the death, in defiance, of Old Thorhall, America's first white poet, huntsman, eccentric, its only worshipper of Thor.

Meanwhile, Thorwald waited for word of the bailiff. He could not believe that any crew would consent to cross the open ocean in an undecked afterboat; so, when the gales subsided, he cruised to the north in search of his missing men. Rounding the heel of the Cape, he sailed the full length of the "mirage country," and near the tip of the peninsula, afterward to be called Province Lands, the knorr, encountering a high wind, damaged her keel on the bars. This injury took long to repair. When at last the ship was rekeeled, Thorwald erected the old timbers on the tip of the Cape, and named the place Keelness. Later expeditions, recognizing that upright wooden shaft, spoke of Keelness as a landmark from the sea.

Skirting treacherous reefs, the rebuilt knorr came about and sailed into Cape Cod Bay. A headland covered with woods projected into tranquil water; near it the mariners found anchorage and put out a gangway to land. "This is a fair region," said Thorwald, "here I should like to make my home." So the Norse adventurers examined the headland as a base for permanent settlement; and as the expedition reembarked, the men noticed three mounds on the sand. They approached these cautiously. Three skin canoes were lying overturned; three natives crouched under each canoe. Thorwald, planning a simultaneous attack on all three objectives, divided his party of warriors and succeeded in capturing all but one of the hidden men.

Only twenty-one mariners were left in that depleted Norse expedition. Eight prisoners would eat too much of their scanty rations, need too constant a guard. If the natives escaped, they might rally a thousand of their copper-bodied people. One savage already had gone to tell his tale; better that these be placed where they could speak no word of the invaders. Thorwald ordered his men to kill the prisoners. Eight copper-brown bodies fell on the bay shore, and lay like dark drops of amber in the curve of that silver bowl — like broken beads of the human necklace said to belong to a sea giantess, who lived, so Cape Indians believed, in a cave nearby.

Thorwald climbed the headland again, peered about, and descried small hillocks that looked like habitations. He called his men together, and as they watched, a sudden drowsiness beset them; a slumber magic overpowered their senses. Fear lulled itself into forgetfulness; bodies insupportably weary sank into tall grasses and the warriors closed sun-dazzled eyes. They slept on the hill that belonged, by native tradition, to Squant the square-eyed Sea-woman, who later became Granny Squannit of the ogre-eye and mismated feet; her greatest magic was a slumber trance, and she knew the spells that would drug her victims into unnatural dreams. No mention of her is made by the scalds who sang Icelandic sagas, and yet, nine hundred years ago, the Norse heroes, after they had killed her dark-skinned followers, fell asleep in magic, less than a stone's throw from her cave.

They were roused, suddenly, by a voice above them, that cried an urgent warning: "Awake, Thorwald, thou and all thy company, if thou wouldst save thy life. Board thy ship with all thy men. Sail with speed from this land." A fleet of skin canoes advanced from the inner part of the bay. The warriors hastily reembarked. "Put out the war boards," ordered Thorwald, "on both sides of the ship. Defend ourselves as best we may and offer no attack." The Skrellings, as the Norsemen named the inhabitants, shot at the invaders with arrows, but were defeated and fled. Thorwald first ascertained that all of his men were unhurt, then confessed to a mortal injury. "I am wounded in the armpit," he said. "An arrow flew between the gunwale and the shield, below my arm. Here is the shaft of it, and it will bring me to my end. I counsel you: retrace your steps with utmost speed. But me ye shall convey to yonder headland which seemed to offer so pleasant a dwelling place. Thus it is fulfilled, the truth sprang to my lips when I wished to abide there for a time. Bury me there; place a cross at my head, another at my feet; call it Crossness forevermore."

At Hockanum, near Yarmouth, a little hill dark with pine trees rises from the chrome yellow of the tidewater marshes. There, those who hold in their hearts friendliness for this boy sailor may stand upon his unmarked grave and look toward the quiet waters of the inlet where his ship sought harbor.

From Iceland, in the course of time, came a miraculous version of young Thorwald's death, not as a victim of slumber magic, nor of war, but as killed by a fabulous mortal who roamed the oak and pine forests of Vinland. One morning, according to this story, Thorwald and his men, looking landward, discovered in an open space in the woods a speck that seemed to "shine toward them." They shouted and saw the bright figure stir, advance; its body appeared to be supported by only one leg. A Uniped the warriors named it. To the shore nearest the ship it hopped, and fitted an arrow into a bow. Thorwald watched at the helm. The arrow, drawn swiftly, pierced the young leader's body, and the boy, drawing the weapon from his wound, exclaimed with prophetic implication: "There is fat around my paunch. We have come upon a fruitful country, and yet we are not like to get profit of it."

The Uniped, after it had shot Thorwald, fled to the North. Warriors gave furious chase; but that weird, hopping form outdistanced them. They caught glimpses of it, now here, now there, through the pines, and when at last it disappeared among the sun-fringed reeds by a river bank, the Norsemen abandoned pursuit.

THE SHIP OF DEATH

While Thorwald and Thorhall the Hunter were challenging death on the Wonder Strands, in Greenland the third son of Eric the Red married the widowed Gudrid, whom Leif had rescued from a skerry. Thorstein, this third son, refitted the masterless knorr that had put back to Brattahlid, and determined to make, in his turn, a voyage to Vinland the Good. A learned man, a tender-hearted, devout Christian, he longed to bring home from Crossness the body of his brother.

Twenty-five stalwart mariners were engaged for the expedition; and Thorstein decided to take his young wife, Gudrid. After her previous experience of shipwreck, she showed no fear in this new venture; but from the moment of her departure the sea seemed angry at her hardihood. All summer the Viking ship drove over a wild course. Once the sailors sighted Ireland; again they saw birds from the Irish coast. Thorstein lost all reckoning, and worn out by toil and exposure, in the autumn he made land in the Western Settlement of Greenland.

When sunless winter merged into the daylong dawns of spring, when salt ice groaned aloud and drifted slowly to the south, the knorr sailed back to Brattahlid. At the helm, Gudrid the Fair, loveliest woman in the Northland, stood watching sea patterns of gray over blue reflect sky patterns of blue over gray, as gull-colored clouds flew north. The little vessel moved slowly as became a funeral barge, for it bore, not the body of Thorwald for which it had set sail in the previous summer, but the body of Thorstein, third son of Eric, and the bodies of more than half of his crew. Twice widowed, twice shipwrecked, Gudrid reentered the Skali to narrate to Leif and his bowed warriors the story of Thorstein's death.

A plague resembling the Black Plague had come upon the Western Settlement. Many of Thorstein's followers died; and since he desired to give them Christian burial, he conveyed the corpses to his ship. Grimhild, mistress of the house in which Thorstein and Gudrid had made their home, was stricken with disease. Then Thorstein grew ill. The next day, Grimhild rose from her bed, went to the outer door, and uttered a loud cry. "The cold strikes thee. Let us go in," exclaimed Gudrid, who accompanied her, but Grimhild answered, "This may not be. All of the dead folk are drawn up before the door. Among them I see thy husband and I can see myself there." The vision passed and toward dawn she lay as though in death. Her husband went forth to get a deal upon which to place her corpse. During his absence Grimhild wakened, rose from her trance and stretched out her feet from the side of the bed. "Look!" exclaimed Thorstein excitedly, "The goodwife — she is groping after her shoes." Grimhild approached Thorstein who lay on an adjacent pallet, and tried to get under the covers beside him. Gudrid screamed and Grimhild's husband, rushing in, held a poleaxe to his wife's breast, for Icelanders believed that in such a way one could exorcise devils or ghosts. Grimhild returned to her pallet. As she sank slowly back, every timber in the house creaked, and she lay in death's ultimate quiet.

Then Thorstein Ericsson grew weaker. He, too, woke from a death trance, and called aloud for his wife. Grimhild's husband took Gudrid in his arms and carried her from the chair upon which she was seated to a bench beside Thorstein. Three times Thorstein called, "Where art thou, Gudrid?" Gudrid turned to her ghost. "Shall I give answer to his question or not?" she asked. Grimhild's husband, who was named Thorstein also, bade her make no reply; but he spoke, himself, to the dying warrior: "What dost thou wish, namesake?"

"I desire to tell Gudrid of the fate in store for her."

She drew nearer to her husband, and he addressed her solemnly. "Beware," he counseled, "of marrying any Greenlander. Thou art to marry an Icelander. Ye shall dwell together for a long time, and travel to the Southland. Thou shalt outlive him and go abroad, and return to Iceland to thy home. There a church shall be raised and thou shalt take the veil and give thy property to church and poor. There thou shalt die." Gudrid leaned over her husband. He seemed to her to be weeping and spoke a few words in a low tone that only she could hear. Afterward he commanded that his body be carried back to Brattahlid and buried in the shadow of the church. Breath forsook him a few hours later and he was placed beside those of his mariners who waited in an icebound knorr for the breaking seas of spring.

THE VOYAGE OF GUDRID

That summer a trading ship sailed from Norway to Greenland. Ericsfirth men rode down to the harbor and lively trade began. When the shipmaster, Thorfinn Karlsefne, saw the beauty of the widowed Gudrid, he requested her to take her choice of all his wares. Leif, in

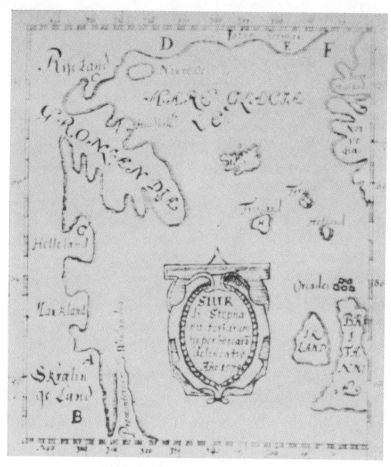

ONE OF THE FIRST MAPS OF THE NARROW LAND
A map of 1570 showing the peninsula of Vinland the Good

return, asked Karlsefne and his crew to spend the winter at Brattahlid, and the young trader accepted.

A lean winter emptied the grain bins, and as dark days drew toward Yule, Leif became despondent. To Karlsefne's questioning, he replied reluctantly: "I am troubled at the thought that men shall say ye have never passed a worse Yule than this, at Brattahlid, in Greenland."

"There shall be no cause for that. We have malt, and meal, and corn in our ships. Ye are welcome to take what ye will."

Leif gratefully augmented supplies, and after the warriors were well fed, Karlsefne broached the subject of a marriage with Gudrid the Fair. Leif gave a prompt consent, for he had a debt to pay to this Icelander; also he believed that in such a marriage Gudrid would fulfill her destiny. After Yule Feast, the wedding banns were celebrated. Gudrid, for the third time, became a bride.

In the quiet winter evenings, talk of Vinland was renewed. Men urged Karlsefne to make the venture, Gudrid joining with the others. Freydis also desired a voyage and she and her husband, a rich weakling, agreed to accompany Karlsefne, though not in the position of leaders.

Sixty men and five women assembled to embark in two ships. They decided to make a permanent settlement and took cattle with them. Karlsefne asked Leif for his Vinland house. Leif replied that he would lend it.

In the summer the two vessels made the sea passage to Leif's booths. Before the men had slung their hammocks on shore, a whale was driven into the shallows and secured. The cattle were turned out on the meadowlands and the adventurers decided to remain where they had landed, for they found grapes near at hand and captured fish and game. Karlsefne's men felled trees, hewed them into timbers, and piled the green wood upon a cliff to dry.

Natives discovered them in the summer succeeding their first winter in Vinland. Early one morning, skin canoes approached the settlement, paddling from the south; canoes so numerous that they appeared "as if coals had been scattered broadcast upon the waters." From each boat staves were waved, revolving in the direction of the sun, making a noise like flails. "What may this betoken?" exclaimed Karlsefne. A comrade suggested, "This is a signal of peace. Let us take a white shield and display it." The Skrellings, dark-bodied men, "the hair of their heads ugly," rowed toward the Norsemen, disembarked, and made signs to convey the desire for trade.

Restive cattle were feeding close by. As the strangers approached, a bull roared, and the terrified savages raced for Karlsefne's house. The Norse leader barred the door. After the Skrellings became more accustomed to the lowing of cattle, they put down their packs, offered peltries for barter, and tried to procure weapons in exchange. Karlsefne ordered the women to carry out buckets of milk, and the natives no sooner saw this white liquid than they desired it, and nothing else. So they carried their wares away in their stomachs and left their packs behind. They also bought red cloth, in exchange for skins, and bound strips of scarlet around their brows. As cloth became scarce, Karlsefne and his men divided it into pieces of not more than a finger's breadth, and the savages paid as much for these as they had for larger strips.

When green grapes swelled on the vines and beachplums turned the color of old Burgundy, Gudrid gave birth to a male child. A few months later the Skrellings came again. Karlsefne told the women to carry out milk, and in return the savages tossed their packs over the palisade. In the doorway Gudrid was seated beside the cradle of her infant son. Suddenly a shadow fell on the door, and a short woman dressed in a black namkirtle stood near the threshold. Her hair, light chestnut in color, was bound by a fillet to her head; her cheeks were pale, her eyes larger than "any ever seen in a human skull." She approached Gudrid and inquired, "What is thy name?" "Gudrid," replied the Icelander. "What is *thy* name?" "My name is also Gudrid," said the stranger, and she advanced toward the cradle. Before she had seated herself on the bench that Gudrid offered in courtesy, a heavy detonation startled Norsemen and Skrellings alike. The mysterious guest disappeared. A savage tried to seize a Viking weapon, and was instantly killed by Karlsefne's men, while the rest of the Skrellings fled to their boats, leaving garments and wares behind.

"Now we must take council," said Karlsefne. "They will visit us a third time, in great numbers, and attack us." He distributed his men at points of vantage, and in a short time a multitude of canoes approached from the south. The staves in the canoes were waved in a direction contrary to the sun, and the natives yelled in fury. Karlsefne displayed war shields, as the Skrellings sprang from their narrow boats. A fierce battle began.

The attackers, using war slings, sent before them a heavy shower of missiles. On a pole they raised a ball-shaped body, almost the size of a sheep's belly, and nearly black in color. This they hurled from the pole, and as the bag struck the earth it exploded with deafening detonation. Fear seized Karlsefne's mariners; they could think of nothing but flight. Troops of savages seemed to rush toward them from every direction, and the Norsemen ran for a jutting cliff at the foot of which they rallied and turned.

Meanwhile Freydis, daughter of Eric, emerged from the Viking house. She called to her countrymen: "Why do ye flee from these wretches? Ye might slaughter them like cattle. Had I a weapon I would fight better than any one of ye." No man gave ear to her. She had been ill, and when she tried to follow her kinsmen, the pace proved too fast. Natives caught up with her as she reached the edge of the forest not far from the house. A dead Norseman lay at her feet, his skull cleft by a flat stone, his naked sword at his side. Freydis stooped, took up the sword, and turned to confront the savages who raced across the clearing, shrieking as they came. The daughter of Eric stood alone at the edge of the forest, a tall, majestic figure outlined against the pines. As the natives drew near, she stripped down her shift and slapped her breast with the broadside of the sword. The Skrellings paused, stared. This tall woman was a giantess, her ominous gesture an evil portent. The gleaming weapon that beat her breast reflected sunlight into their eyes. They shrank back as from a goddess, or fury, and in panic ran to their boats.

Slowly, from their place of safety, the valiant warriors joined her. In words and ways sheepish, they gave praise to her courage, but Skrelling warfare had definitely shattered their morale. Dread of renewed hostility, shame at the quick defeat, fear of again succumbing to alien tactics preyed upon minds equipped with the Viking superiority complex, minds of daring raiders without the tenacity and stoicism necessary to colonists. Rapidly the expedition disintegrated from within; and men who were without wives, lawless in their desire for women, attempted seduction, "whence the greatest trouble arose."

Karlsefne realized that his dream of a kingdom was over; yet his son, born in Vinland, was three winters old before the father finally made the decision to return to Greenland. The ships were laden with fine furs, dried grapes and "mosur wood." Two little native boys, from a region north of Cape Cod, were captured by Karlsefne, taught the Icelandic tongue, and included in the cargo. Safely arriving at Brattahlid, Freydis returned to her husband's house at Garder, and Gudrid brought her little son into the Skali where Leif Ericsson gave him a home.

THE BROTHERS

Helgi and Finnbogi, brothers born in Iceland, purchased between them a trading vessel, shared command of her, and prospered in their trade. They put in at Greenland for the winter following Karlsefne's return. Young, steady, ambitious, in possession of one of the finest ships that sailed northern waters, the two brothers listened in growing excitement to tales of the narrow peninsula. Freydis came from Garder to join in the discussions, and was quick to see that Helgi and Finnbogi were eager to profit by Karlsefne's experiences, and to build for themselves a settlement where the other expeditions had failed. As spring approached, Freydis invited the two young Icelanders to sail with her to Vinland, they in command of their own vessel, and she, of the Ericsson knorr. The brothers quickly consented, promising to maintain an even division of the profits between the two ships. Then Freydis appealed to Leif, asking for the gift of his Vinland home. She received the loan of it.

That forces might be equal, each shipmaster contracted that his vessel should carry no more than thirty able-bodied men. The number of women to be taken on the voyage was left to the discretion of the individual master. Secretly, Freydis violated her compact. She concealed five additional men on her ship, a treachery that the brothers did not discover until the expedition arrived at the Furdustrandir.

On the sea the two trading vessels attempted to keep together. Although they were never far apart, toward the end of the passage the brothers outsailed Freydis and arrived in advance at Leif's house. They carried in their belongings, and were arranging them when Freydis appeared at the door. "Why did you carry your baggage in here?" she demanded truculently, and the startled brothers saw that there were five more men in her party than in theirs.

"Since we believed," they answered her, "that all promises made to us would be kept."

"It was to me that Leif loaned this house," said Freydis.

"We brothers cannot hope to rival thee in wrong-dealing," exclaimed Helgi, as the two Icelanders removed their possessions.

Freydis persisted in her claim to sole right in the house, so the brothers built a shelter on a strip of fair high land between the ocean and a lake. While they were busy preparing their house Freydis stocked her ship with wood, and made ready for the winter. Soon coldness closed around them; the seas were not good for sailing and the brothers proposed that the two groups amuse themselves with games. For a time they played in accord, then began to disagree. Gradually the dissension became serious; the games were abandoned, visits between the houses ceased, and a state of wordless hostility lasted far into the winter.

One morning, when a chill dew frosted the greening earth, Freydis rose from her bed, dressed herself with the exception of shoes and stockings, wrapped her husband's cloak around her and walked to the strip of land, between sea and lake, on which stood the brothers' house. She found the door ajar. Pushing it open, she stood silently on the threshold, and Finnbogi, who was awake, inquired, "What dost thou wish here, Freydis?"

"I wish thee to rise, and go out with me, for I would speak to thee."

Finnbogi assented; the two of them walked to a fallen tree and seated themselves side by side.

"How art thou pleased here?" asked the daughter of Eric.

"I am well pleased with the fruitfulness of the land," answered Finnbogi, "but I am ill-content with the breach which has come between us, for there has been no cause for it."

"It is even as thou sayest," responded Freydis, "but my errand to thee is that I wish to exchange ships, for ye have a larger ship than I, and I wish to depart from here."

"To this I must accede," said Finnbogi, "if it is thy pleasure."

After this brief agreement, Finnbogi went back to his shelter and Freydis returned home, climbed into bed, and awakened her husband by touching him with her cold feet. He asked her why she was chilled and wet. "I have been to the brothers," she answered, "to try to buy their ship, but they received my overtures so ill that they struck me and handled me roughly; what time thou, poor wretch, wilt neither avenge my shame nor thine own, and I find that I am no longer in Greenland; moreover I shall part from thee unless thou wreakest vengeance for this."

The harassed husband could stand her taunts no longer. He ordered his men to arm themselves, and the little band, accompanied by Freydis, crept to the house of the brothers where the warriors were heavy with slumber. Freydis' men entered silently. They seized and bound their victims and led them, one by one, out of the house. One by one, Freydis caused them to be slain. When only the women were left in the house of Helgi and Finnbogi, the men of the Ericsson expedition considered their work complete. But Freydis was not content. What her men were unwilling to perform she completed with her own hand. She asked for an axe, and when one was given to her, "fell upon the five women and left them dead."

The murderers turned from their carnage, and Freydis addressed her men: "If it be ordained for us to come again to Greenland," said she, "I shall contrive the death of any man who shall speak of these events. We must give it out that we left them living here when we came away."

Early in the spring they equipped the ship of the brothers, freighted it richly, and put out to sea. When they reached Ericsfirth, Freydis bestowed on all her companions liberal gifts in the nature of hush money. But after she had returned to her home at Garder, some of her men who remained at Brattahlid were not close-mouthed. Leif Ericsson heard the gossip. He took three of the men who accompanied Freydis and forced them, individually, to confessions of the affair. The three stories tallied.

"I have no heart," said Leif, "to punish my sister Freydis as she deserves." He was slow to anger, and had little heart for any deed of cruelty. Also he had his own troubles: a witch-woman from the Hebrides had arrived in Greenland, and at her coming miracles startled the inhabitants. Her name was said to be Thorgunna. She was old, too old, men thought, to have been the mistress of the boy, Leif Ericsson; yet a strange man-child, one not quite natural in his ways, appeared at the Great Hall. Leif acknowledged paternity, and the boy was given his will.

Of Freydis and her children, nothing more is reported. "No one thought them worthy of ought but evil," says the scribe contemptuously; and this mental ostracism seems to have been the only retribution that Freydis encountered in this world.

Far different is the story of Karlsefne and Gudrid the Fair. They stayed for a time in Norway, and eventually settled in Iceland. After Karlsefne's death, Gudrid and her American-born son took charge of the farmstead. When her son was married, Gudrid máde a pilgrimage to the south where she visited populous Christian lands. Her son built a church at Glaumboea in Iceland, and there, after her return, Gudrid took the veil. In quietude ended the life of the first white woman to dwell in the Narrow Land. Thrice married, she started on three perilous voyages — with each husband in turn. She knew plague and shipwreck, faced savages at war, gave birth to a child in the wilderness at the edge of a new continent. Always she is spoken of as wise, tactful, beautiful; and from her son, the first white, native-born Cape Codder, sprang a proud line of Icelanders including the greatest bishops of the realm.

No other Norsemen recorded voyages to Vinland. The peninsula slept in sunlight, forgotten by men of the white race. On a hill facing the baywater lay the body of Thorwald. On a strip of land between a blue-green glacial lake and a green-blue shoaling sea, the bones of unburied warriors and of fair-haired women bleached on bone-colored sand. No low-slung, black, marauding craft plundered the harbors of Vinland. A battered and forsaken knorr drifted, derelict, over the reefs; and the Skrellings, their brows bound with scarlet, told of a winged island that moved across the sea.

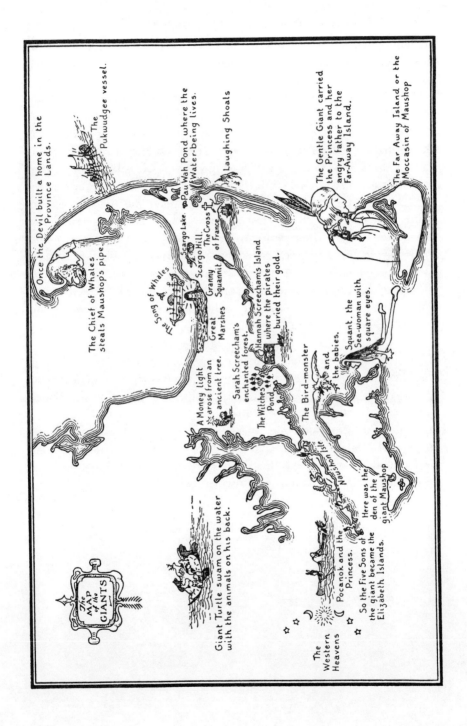

The
MAP
of the
GIANTS

Once the Devil built a home in the
Province Lands.

The
Pukwudgee vessel.

Pau Wah Pond where the
Water-being lives.

Laughing Shoals

The Gentle Giant carried
the Princess and her
angry father to the
Far-Away Island.

The Chief of Whales
steals Maushop's pipe.

Scargo Lake
Scargo Hill
The Cross
Granny Squannit of France
Great Squannit
Marshes

The Far Away Island or the
Moccasin of Maushop

The Song of Whales

Sarah Screecham's
enchanted forest.

Hannah Screecham's Island
where the pirates
buried their gold.

A Money light
arose from an
ancient tree.

The Witches'
Pond

The Bird-monster
and
the babies.

Squant. the
Sea-woman with
square eyes.

Giant Turtle swam on the water
with the animals on his back.

Naushon Isle

Here was the
den of the
giant Maushop

Pocanok and the
Princess.

So the Five Sons of
the giant became the
Elizabeth Islands.

The
Western
Heavens

THE DEATH OF THE GIANT

They beat on drums and sang in the night on the highlands of Nauset. They lifted their arms to the yellow dawn, and prayed for corn and strong sons; and they journeyed toward Death in the Western Heavens, over the Turkey Sea. They were protected by a Gentle Giant, and molested by a Pygmy People. Every hill and lake of the Long Land told them its story. They had copper-colored skins, and copper discs that hang from their ears and at their breasts; and their dark eyes, of a somber cast, held a flash more of lightning than sunshine. They bent saplings to make a framework, and wove mats to pad the walls of igloo-shaped houses. The mats turned to leaf-brown when the south wind blew its weathering breath on them. Inside the huts, braided reeds were painted in gay colors, a fire burned, and men and women were taught from youth the peace of controlled emotion. Unlike white men or black men, they did not know how to be conquered. They were the first lords of the Narrow Land, and no other owners of the seaward peninsula have experienced their intimacy of possession.

1.   THE ANCIENT TRADITIONS

THE INDIAN LEGENDS in this section were told to the author by Chief Red Shell, Historian of the Nauset Wampanoag Tribe, and by Chief Wild Horse, Wampanoag Champion of Mashpee, who have generously contributed them to this book. The stories, repeated orally from generation to generation, are only known to a few living Indians. These retain and treasure the legendary beliefs.

CREATION AND FLOOD

In the beginning there was nothing but seawater on top of the land. Much water, much fog. Also Kehtean, the Great Spirit, who made the water, the land under it, the air above it, the clouds, the heavens, the

sun, the moon, and the stars. Kehtean dwelt in the Spirit Land, in the
Western Heavens. He was called the Great Spirit, and under him
were lesser spirits, such as Geesukquand, the Sun Spirit, and Yotannit, Spirit of Fire.

Once Kehtean left the Western Heavens, came to the world, and
passed over the waters that covered it. He reached down to the bottom of the sea, took a grain of sand and of that made the earth. He
created four guiding spirits to guard the four corners of the earth;
and he made four winds. Then he made animals in the likeness of
spirits of earth and heaven, birds in the likeness of the four wind
spirits, fish in the likeness of the Water Spirit, Nibah-Nahbeezik; and
he gave life to them all.

After he returned to the Western Heavens, he realized that he had
not made anything in his own likeness, so he took the form of a great
hare, and went back to the earth. There he made Uskitom, the first
man-being, giving him the man spirit; and Netimigaho, the first
mother, giving her the Eshquaganit, or woman-guiding spirit. In
time an evil presence came among the man-beings, and brought others
of his kind. His name was Mahtahdou, and he created flies, gnats,
fevers, diseases and miseries. He spread these sorrowful ills among
the children and grandchildren of Uskitom. As a result, wars took
place and man-beings quarreled with one another.

Kehtean saw this and was angry. He caused the waters to flood
the earth. They washed away the flies and gnats and quarrelsome
man-beings, but they did not wash away Mahtahdou who hid in the
company of Maskanako, the Great Snake, in deep holes beneath the
sea.

While the Flood was over the land, Giant Turtle swam on the
water, carrying on his back Eagle, Owl, Crow, Deer, Fox, Turkey,
Muskrat and Beaver. Beholding this fine company, the Great Spirit,
Kehtean, came down on Turtle's back and again took the form of a
hare. He sent Crow to search the water, bidding him find brown
earth. Crow came back without any earth. So Kehtean sent others,
but they all returned to Giant Turtle without bringing any part of the
land's substance. Finally, Kehtean sent Muskrat who was gone a
long time and at last appeared on top of the waters, holding sand in
his paws. From this sand, Kehtean refashioned the world. New life
was brought forth; the land was covered with animals and birds; man-

beings roamed the forests; and from hiding places under the sea came the Evil Spirit, Mahtahdou, and the Great Snake, Maskanako. Kehean was a wise god; he made Maskanako into the medicine man of the tribes.

THE LEGEND OF WEETUCKS

In the long ago a son was born to an aged squaw in a Wampanoag village. When he was very young this boy disappeared from the tribe. Many braves hunted for him, but nothing was heard nor seen of him until a full moon had passed. Then, one day, he entered the village and fell, exhausted, on the water path. Kind hands carried him to his mother's hut, laid him upon a bed of bearskins, and there, for many days, he tossed. While he was recovering, he summoned the leading men of the tribe, to instruct them in the uses of roots, herbs, flowers, barks and berries. This knowledge was in turn given to the medicine men who told it to their successors. Some of the wisdom became well known, but other secrets of the boy named Weetucks have been closely guarded and are still sacred to the medicine men of the tribe.

Weetucks taught the Wampanoag to make shining fire. He taught the young boys to prepare for manhood, and the young girls to prepare for womanhood. He taught the Wampanoag to be kind to strangers. He initiated them into the Sweat Bath and Mud Bath Ceremonies, showed them how to paint pictures, make wampum, fashion canoes, spears, bows, arrows, shields, and other implements.

He who was believed to be the son of Kehtean returned, one evening, to his mother's wigwam, after a long day of hunting. As he lifted the mat at the door he saw two strange figures huddled before the fire. To these he offered a share of the household food, but when the evening meal was put before them, they snatched at the choicest portions of meat, devoured it, then slunk back into the hut shadows. Weetucks and his mother spoke no word. At the hour appointed for sleeping, Weetucks lay down. He had not slept long when a cold hand awakened him and, looking up, he saw the strangers' eyes gazing at him like four balls of fire.

"We are spirits of the departed," they said slowly, "sent by Kehtean, your father, to warn you that your mother will soon leave for the

Spirit Land. You may sorrow much, but be comforted, all the living will some day meet the departed in the Western Heavens."

In the morning Weetucks looked upon his mother and knew that she was dead. He buried her with the Death Ceremonies; stones were heaped on her burial place and, afterward, Weetucks lighted Spirit Fires over her grave.

The Turkey People, who lived to the westward, came during the next summer, and smoked the pipe of peace. The warriors of the Turkey People had long been at enmity with the Wampanoag, so there was great rejoicing at the conclusion of hostilities. Feasting lasted far into the night, and the next day brought to the earth the full beauty of summer. Then Weetucks, who had completed his teachings, bade his people farewell. In the dawn light he walked across the waves of Turkey Bay, and vanished toward the Western Heavens.

THE FORMATION OF THE ISLANDS

Years ago, in the days before the first white people came across the sea, a young giant named Maushop lived in the Narrow Land. He was so large that no wigwam or council house could hold him, so he slept under the stars. Sometimes he lay on one part of the Cape, sometimes on another. To him snowdrifts were like handfuls of beach sand and wrapped in his robe of many hundred bearskins, the heat from his body kept him warm in the cold winter weather. If he awakened on an icy night and found that the chill had crept under his robe, he warmed himself by jumping back and forth across-Cape.

In summer he could not sleep when the heat of the land grew oppressive. On such nights he made a bed of the lower Cape, of the cool lands that lie narrowly between ocean and bay. There his body twisted and turned, changing position, seeking repose, until he shifted the level sand into dunes and hollows.

Once, on a night when the wind ceased blowing and stars hung heavy with unshed lightning, Maushop became more than usually restless. He tossed, he flung himself about, till his moccasins unfastened themselves and burrowed into the ground. When Geesukquand, the Sun Spirit, lighted the tepee fires of dawn, Maushop awoke, missed his moccasins, and felt about for them. He found them and holding them tightly he raised his arm and flung the sand from them far to the south. This sand became the South Sea Islands, Nantucket and Martha's Vineyard.

THE BIRD-MONSTER AND THE BABIES

In the days of the Giants and Pygmies, scores of whales played in the waters off the east side of the Cape. Maushop often busied himself by catching these whales and throwing them upon the land, as a boy tosses pebbles out of a pool. Once, while the giant was amusing himself in this way, a Bird-monster, larger than twenty eagles, flew over the land. The bird swooped down on villages, seized babies in its strong talons, and carrying the stolen papooses flew away to the south. Skilled hunters tried to shoot the monster, but arrows scarcely scratched its hide. When the great bird landed, one thrust of its beak, one blow from claws or wings, meant instant death.

Maushop, returning from whale catching, came among the Nauset-Wampanoag, and at once the people of the Land between the Waters told him of this Bird-monster, and of the loss of their children. The giant thereupon determined to destroy the evil bird. Flat on his back among the tall trees, he lay and waited until he saw the bird flying over him, carrying tiny babies in its claws. Quickly as the plover rises, Maushop sprang from his hiding place and followed the monster across Martha's Vineyard Sound, which was no deeper than up to his knees. Peering ahead, he saw the bird settle on a tall tree in the center of an island that rose out of South Ocean. That tree was the only vegetation in sight; not a bush, not a spear of grass waved welcome to the stranger. Around the tree piles of small, dry, baby bones were stacked. As Maushop approached, the bird dropped its victims and flew at the invader.

Then waged one of the greatest battles ever fought between a giant and a Bird-monster. After several days of unceasing struggle, both combatants fell. But Maushop rallied for one final effort, and landed a blow that killed his adversary. Leaving the body of the evil bird under that tree on the lonely island, Maushop gathered into his fingers the Indian papooses who were the monster's last captives, and carrying these he waded the waters back to the Narrow Land. He gave the children to their mothers who were anxiously waiting in wigwams.

Thereafter, he seated himself on a high cliff overlooking the south shore, filled his pipe with poke-weed, and sat for a long time, smoking. Clouds from his pipe covered the marshlands, covered the highlands of Scargo and Nauset. Ever since then, when fogs are thick, rolling along from the Southern Sea, the Indians say to one another: "Look! Now Maushop is smoking his pipe!"

HOW MAUSHOP MADE SCARGO LAKE

Once the giant went visiting on the north side of the Narrow Land. The Indians there grew fond of him, and asked him to leave them something to remember him by, when he had gone away. Maushop, in his eagerness to please them, dug a deep hole and placed the earth from it in a large mound on the southern side of the hole. He dug fast and he dug deep, until at last the hole was so great that in it a giant could bury more than the largest Wampanoag village. When Maushop had finished this work, he lighted his pipe and puffed forth smoke that formed into dark clouds whence issued the drumbeats of the Thunder Spirit and the lightning of Yotannit. After he had completed his smoke, Maushop emptied his pipe. Ashes fell upon the high mound, and rain poured from above. Night extended upon the land without the coming of Nanipaushat, the Moon Spirit. For two days and two nights the waters descended from the heavens. On the morning of the third day the clouds rolled themselves together and drifted north. The sun shone upon the people. They came out of their huts and saw a great lake, where Maushop had dug a hole, and beside the lake towered a high hill covered with pine trees. The hill they named Scargo for the pine trees made from the ashes of Maushop's pipe, and the lake has been known ever since by the name of Scargo Lake.

THE PRINCESS AND THE GENTLE GIANT

Long ago a princess fell in love with a young warrior who was poor, the son of a common Indian. The father of the princess, a wealthy chief, told the brave that he could not wed the princess until he owned a whole island. The young brave, who owned less than an arrow's flight of land, not to mention an island, despaired of ever being able to bring the princess to his wigwam. Once when they met alone he told her of the demands of the chief, her father, and how he must abandon his wooing because he was without hope. The chief's daughter took him by the hand and led him to a high hill. There, at twilight, before the first star, Giant Maushop came striding along, stepping high to keep his feet clear of the soggy marshes. The princess and her lover told Maushop their story, and the Gentle Giant promised to help them, if they would return to their tribesmen.

The brave and the chief's daughter went their separate ways. Maushop filled his pipe with a mixture of tobacco and pokeweed, lighted it with a flash of lightning, and sat down to smoke. Fog covered the Long Land and the waters to the south of it. When he had done with the smoking, Maushop waded into the sea. He dumped out the ashes from his pipe. As the embers fell, thunder roared; a hissing noise like fire on water was heard in the Place of Bays. Fog cleared. Far to the south the people of the tribes beheld an island which they named Na-tocket, the "Far Away Land" (Nantucket).

Maushop returned to the shores of the Cape, lifted the young brave to his shoulder, placed the princess in the crook of his arm, and carried them both to Far Away Island. He left them there, went back to the tribes, picked up the princess's father who did not desire to be carried, and placed the old chief on the island, where the first man-beings that he encountered were his daughter and the young brave. But when he learned that the whole island belonged to that common warrior, he rejoiced, and willingly consented that the princess should become the warrior's wife. The young brave and his squaw lived all their lives on Na-tocket, and so did their children and their grandchildren who are still grateful to the Giant Maushop although he visits them no more.

THE BATTLE WITH THE PYGMIES

On an island in Poponesset Bay, below South Mashpee, Maushop kept his wife, a giantess born to a common-size brave and squaw at a place called Cummaquid. Since she did not stop growing when she reached the height of a man-being, she soon became so tall that the highest trees only reached to her shoulder. Even so, she was far shorter than her husband, who knocked trees over as if they were so many weeds, and thought nothing of eating a small whale at a meal.

Maushop's wife, named Quaunt, bore him five sons who were also giants and had good hearts. Quaunt was not so good-natured as these menfolk with whom she lived. Sometimes she nagged Maushop, or beat her sons; sometimes she tried to prevent them from doing good to the Indians of the Narrow Land. Often she repented of her periods of evil, and attempted to befriend man-beings, to make amends for her folly.

In the days when Maushop and his five sons and his quarrelsome wife used the Cape for their wigwam mat, a Little People lived in the swamps of maple and birch, and around the salt ponds and bays. They built their homes in high grasses or bulrushes, and divided their forces into seven bands, each with its own leader. These pygmies, or Little People, were called Pukwudgees. Only a handful of them were in each band, yet so potent was their magic (even a common Pukwudgee had charms greater than those of the tribal medicine men), so terrible were their miracles, that Maushop and his sons and his wife could not always prevail against them.

The chiefs among the Pukwudgees had more power than the pygmy warriors, but the chief of the chiefs, the leader over the seven bands, was the greatest magician of them all. In height he was the tallest Pukwudgee, and at that he scarcely reached the knee of an ordinary man. Around his neck hung a string of bright shells. His body was entirely covered with green leaves, and he carried a white oak bow equipped with arrows which were not a finger long. He and his band lived in the marshes near Poponesset Bay, where he could keep an eye on the doings of Maushop and trouble the Gentle Giant with small botherings.

The Pukwudgees were bad. Now and then they befriended a man-being, but that was only to show what they could do. They trained the Tei-Pai-Wankas (Will-o'-the-Wisps) to shine lights near the trails at night. Traveling Indians followed these lights and were lured into the marshes where Mahtahdou, the devil, trapped their feet in quicksand and sucked them into the earth. The Pukwudgees delighted in scaring women and girls. Sometimes the Little People appeared in the form of bears, and when the hunters shot at them, pulled the arrows out of their hides, broke the arrow shafts and ran away; or vanished into air as soon as arrows touched their bodies. They pushed Indians off high cliffs and killed their victims. In the form of wild-cats they jumped upon man-beings and fought to the death. Jealous of Maushop, and of the love that the Indians bore toward him, now and again the Pukwudgees performed good magic, solely to make Maushop aware that their medicine was more powerful than his.

The Gentle Giant was slow to anger, yet there came a day when he could endure the tricks of the Little People no longer. He took a large tree in either hand, waded all the way around the peninsula, stooping down to inspect the shores, bending low to look into the marshes and along the reeds of the baywater. The Pukwudgees kept rabbit-still. The giant could not see them, so he enlisted his sons in the search. The five sons, who were smaller than their father, lay down among the pine trees near Poponesset Marsh. The wind blew from the south. The reeds swayed back and forth and the giants saw this motion and did not realize that Pukwudgees, hidden among the salt grasses, were creeping nearer, nearer. Suddenly, the tiny war-riors threw bad magic in the giants' eyes, and the sons of old Maushop were cruelly blinded. With huge hands they struck at the grass and crushed a few Pukwudgees. But all the rest of the pygmy warriors escaped to a safe distance; and as the giants could no longer see them, they stood in the open and threw poisoned darts into the hides of the sons. The young giants became so weak that they could not rise. In great suffering they waited for the coming of Maushop who, when he saw his strong sons stricken by the Little People, worked all the magic that a giant knows, then summoned the medicine men; but neither he nor any Indian could save the five blind giants.

They died beside the marshes near Poponesset Bay. Maushop lifted their young bodies and carried them to Succonesset Waters. He heaped sand over their corpses, building it into huge mounds which became small islands. He planted trees and grasses to grow on the graves of his sons. These islands are called by white men the Elizabeth Islands, or the Town of Gosnold.

THE DEATH OF MAUSHOP

After his children had perished, Maushop became very sad. He had never known defeat before, and he spent all his time thinking what next he should do to rid the land of Pukwudgees. He could think of nothing except that he was old and brokenhearted.

One morning, as Geesukquand the Sun-being cast handfuls of mica pebbles over the Eastern Sea, Maushop saw a small white bird riding upon the waves. As it drew nearer, the giant perceived that it was not a bird but a canoe over which hung two white skins on sticks. He waded through the sea and stooped to pick up the magic boat. Before he could touch it, sharp darts, like flung pebbles or the arrows of Pukwudgees, stung against his legs. In fear that the vessel was an evil charm sent against him by the Little People, Maushop strode back to the Narrow Land, picked up his wife, threw her against Succonesset Point, and made his escape to the south. The magic of the Pukwudgees, or of that white-winged vessel, may have occasioned his death. He has never returned to the Place of Bays; and the Indians who love him, believe that he would come if he could.

THE LEGEND OF THE MASHPEE MAIDEN

In the long ago, there lived among the Wampanoag of the Mashpee Village a maiden called Ahsoo. Her legs were like pipestems; her chin was pointed and sharp as the beak of a loon; her nose was humped and crooked; and her eyes were as big as a frightened deer's. Day after day she sat on a log and watched those around her. No one cared for her; none of the men desired her friendship. She was an idle, lazy maiden who would not work in a wigwam or carry wood for a fire.

Although Ahsoo was ugly, no woman could equal her in singing. Birds paused on the bough to listen to her, and the river, running over rapids, almost ceased its flowing to hear the Mashpee Maiden. On a low hill near the river Ahsoo would sit and sing. Beasts of the forest, birds of the air, fish of the lakes came to hear. Maugua the Bear came, and even the great War Eagle; but Ahsoo was not afraid for she knew that they had only come to listen to her songs. The river at the foot of the hill became alive with fishes, journeying up from the South Sea to hear the voice of Ahsoo. Every animal, bird, and fish applauded in its own manner, since they all greatly desired that Ahsoo should continue.

There was a big trout, chief of all trout, almost as big as a man. Because of his size he could not swim up the river to hear Ahsoo sing. Every night he burrowed his nose further and further into the bank. At length he planed a long path inland and the sea water, following him closely, made Cotuit Brook. This chief of the trout loved Ahsoo and he could not see how ugly she was, for she always sang in the summer evenings after the sun went down. So he told her that she was pretty; and of course the Mashpee Maiden fell deeply in love with that trout. She told him how she loved him and invited him to visit her wigwam.

At this time, the Pukwudgee chief lived with his followers in the marshes near Poponesset Bay. He observed the Great Trout who was making a new brook for the use of the pygmy people, and one day the little chief overheard the trout lamenting because he could not have Ahsoo for a wife.

"The charming Mashpee Maiden and I love each other dearly," sighed the monster fish, "but, alas! neither of us can live without the other, and neither of us can live where the other lives."

The chief of the Pukwudgees was sorry for these lovers, so he changed the Maiden into a trout, and placed her in Santuit Pond. Then he told the monster fish to dig his way to the Pond, and have the Maiden for his wife. The trout dug so hard and so fast that, when he reached Santuit Pond, he died of too much exertion; and the Maiden who had become a trout died of a broken heart. Indians found the defeated lovers, and buried them side by side in a large mound, called Trout Grave, near the brook dug by the chief of trout.

GRANNY SQUANNIT AND THE WICKED BOY

Too-quah-mis-quan-nit, or Granny Squannit, was an old woman who lived, many years ago, at Cummaquid, in a cave among the sand dunes on Great Neck, a strip of land at the entrance to Barnstable Harbor. She was Ki-eh-pah-wesh-hok, or great medicine woman, who bore no respect to any chief, kept to herself and made her own trail. Nevertheless, if a child was bad, repeatedly bad, Granny Squannit was certain to appear in forest or wigwam, or among the dunes, and the child who saw her became so afraid that all wickedness departed from it.

Granny Squannit was short and stout, like other Indian women. Her long hair fell over her shoulders, and over the upper part of her face, so that only her mouth and chin could be seen. Every year she planted little seeds in the woods, from which grew a small bush. This she tended, and later in the season gathered the pods to use for magic.

In one of the villages near a marsh lived Bad Young Boy. His mother scolded him, his father punished him. He was very bad after that. His father took him to the chief of the tribe who talked to him. Three times he was taken to the chief, and on the fourth time the chief himself administered punishment. Bad Young Boy went home to his wigwam and broke up wampum belts, destroyed paint shells, burned war arrows, and when the father took him again before the chief, the great warrior gave him into the care of medicine men. They worked on him, using charms, chants, medicines, and powerful magic, but they could not drive the devil out of that Bad Young Boy.

The next day when he went with the other children to play near a brook that led into a river, he pushed the younger children into the water. Then up the river and into the brook silently glided a canoe. In it sat old Granny Squannit, her dark hair hanging over her face, and she seized Bad Young Boy. Into her canoe she pushed him, jumped in herself, and paddled away.

After a ride down the river they came to the sand dunes. Granny beached her boat and shoved the boy into a dark cave. There she made him drink a broth of green herbs, and, soon after, he fell into a heavy sleep in which he remained for many days. The old woman administered to him magic and medicine to drive out the devil. When at last she thought that she had cured the boy, she wakened him, told him to play in the sunshine, but on no account whatsoever to push her hair, or touch her head, while she took her sleep.

As soon as Granny Squannit slept, the boy moved the mat at the cave's entrance, that he might have more light. Then he crept over to her and pushed the hair from her forehead. And there, instead of the two eyes of an ordinary Indian, he saw, placed in the middle of her forehead, one great dark eye, wide open and glaring.

"Woee Nap-ee Nont!" he exclaimed. Slowly Granny Squannit

rose; her hair fell back into place. He had found her secret, and
that scared the devil out of him; and when Granny perceived what
had taken place inside the spirit of Bad Young Boy, she worked strong
magic and quick medicine, and kept the devil away. Then she took
roots and peas from her bush and wove them with grasses and barks.
In a pouch of skin she sewed the pods, roots, barks and grasses, decorated the pouch with small shells, passed a thong through it, and
handed it to Bad Young Boy. With it he returned to his home, where
he grew up to be a great chief among the Nauset-Wampanoag.

2.   TALES OF THE PRAYING INDIANS

On Sabbath mornings, standing in sunshine on the quiet hills of
Mashpee, John Eliot, or John Cotton, or Richard Bourne, told to the
people of the Place of Bays stories of a squaw who bit wisdom out of
an apple, of a Great Chief nailed to crossed wood, of a medicine man
named Jonah who worked canoe magic inside a whale, of Red Water
that divided into two sections like a clamshell, and of a Sagamore
named Samson whose strength secret lay in his hair. In turn, the medicine men and chiefs offered accounts of Kehtean, of Weetucks, of
Mahtahdou the Devil-bird; but the three white men, who spoke the
language of the Wampanoag, refused to hear. Old Maushop, they declared, was an instrument of the White Devil. That was difficult
news to a man who loved Maushop as a friend and knew him to be a
hero. Better keep the old tales within the tribe, not attempt to share
them with intruders. The Long Land bore witness, every lake, hill,
and river of it, to the truth of the stories. The contours of islands
and bays explained themselves, if a spirit-being looked on them with
wisdom.

Beside new, stone hearth fires, discussion centered on problems
of war, rum, windmills, and ministers. Converts, especially Indian
children, imbued with Christian tenets, looked over their shoulders
fearfully, for instead of a Gentle Giant one might now expect to encounter the White Lucifer in the forest, or alongshore. Stories of the
friendly Giant-being were transferred to Satan, who was obviously of
great stature, since he managed to perform mischief now in one part

of the land, now in another, and all while the eyelid of the tame cat moved across its moon-green eye.

HOW THE DEVIL THREW A RATTLESNAKE

Once the Devil put his head on one side, laid his finger along his nose, and sat down on Succonesset Hill to smoke. To him, there came Pocanok, an Indian of the South Sea.

"Mr. Devil," said he, "I have a favor to ask."

"What do you want?" asked the Wicked One, while thunder rumbled in his pipe.

"Mr. Devil," said Pocanok, "on Naushon Island lives a chief who will not trade with the tribes. He is puffed in pride and sits like a frog croaking over the waters."

The Devil listened politely, though his thoughts were not altogether with his ears.

"Mr. Devil," continued the South Seas Indian, "the chief of Naushon Island has a daughter who owns a lame crow that talks like a man. Moreover, her eyes, unlike those of other women, are the color of a leaf drowned in sea water. Her father has promised that any man, be he Giant or Pukwudgee, chief or warrior, may take her to his wigwam, who can make a beanpod swim the ocean, climb the shores of Naushon Island, come into the chief's wigwam and lie down there forevermore.

"Alas," continued Pocanok sadly, "I have told every beanpod in the fields of this. I have offered each one of them my bow, my arrows, my lean dog, and even my gun; but the beanpods only rattle their heads together and will not leave the stalk."

The Devil was thinking of faraway things, so he smoked his pipe and gave no answer. Pocanok made a last appeal:

"Mr. Devil," he pleaded, "I have asked the Lord's Minister at Mashpee; I have prayed to the White God, but the beanpod stays on its stalk."

Then the Devil roused himself, for he knew that the time had come when he should help Pocanok.

"If I do what you ask," said he, "you must bring me, from among the chief's daughters, the one who has a lame crow that speaks

like a man, the one who has eyes dark as a leaf under sea water."
Pocanok promised to bring the girl as soon as she should come to
his wigwam; but in his heart he planned treachery, for he thought
that he could fool the Devil and keep the Naushon princess for himself.

Now the Devil knew exactly what Pocanok was thinking, and he
was very angry. It is no small task to make a beanpod swim the
ocean, climb the shores of Naushon, enter the wigwam of a chief,
and lie down there forevermore. The Devil, however, said nothing
of his anger. He only scowled and the sky grew black with storms.
Pocanok was a brave Indian; he spoke no word, showed no fear,
staunchly stood his ground. The Devil reached over into Ordihon's
bean field, the finest field in the Long Land, and there he cut a pod.
With his other hand he reached into the bottom of Succonesset
Marsh and pulled up a brown snake. With a deer thong he fastened
the beanpod to the brown snake's tail, holding the snake very tightly
by the head so that it could not bite him. The Devil was stronger than
he realized. Almost before he knew it, he had flattened with his thumb
and forefinger the brown snake's head.

When the Devil had completed his work of tying the beanpod to
the end of the snake's tail, he lifted his arm and threw the snake
far out to sea in the direction of Naushon Island. The brown snake
sank beneath the waves. A few moments later, its head came up, it
looked around, and the nearest land was the shore of Naushon Isle.
So the snake swam straight for the island, came ashore there, and
tried to sun itself. Unfortunately, no sun was shining; the smoke
from the Devil's pipe lay heavily across the sky.

In the wigwam of the chieftain, a warm fire was burning, and on
mats beside the fire lay the chief's daughters. The snake crawled
close to the wigwam to get warm. After a while, when all was quiet,
the snake crept inside the wigwam and lay down on the bed. By and
by, the Princess, the one with green eyes, stirred, turned in her sleep,
and accidentally struck the brown snake. The snake was cold, tired;
its tail hurt badly; it stuck out fangs in anger. At the same time the
beanpod, who has always been friendly to man-beings and given its
life to keep them from starving, rattled a sharp warning to awaken
the chief's daughter. She sprang up; but the warning came too late.
Snake fangs pierced her arm, and with them entered a poison that

was made by the angry Devil when, with his two fingers he flattened the snake's head.

All the medicine men of the tribe were summoned; all the potent charms of the forest were used in vain. The Princess with eyes like a sea-green leaf perished by snake's poison, and the snake wriggled away, and in time brought forth young. They had the same flat heads with deadly poison and the same beanpods for tails. They were always angry and ready to fight; but the beanpod tails were still friendly to man-beings, ready to rattle a warning when the snakes were about to strike.

The old chief kept his word to Pocanok. He put the dead Princess in a canoe; with her he put a bow and arrows; over her he laid a blanket of leaves. Her lame crow kept watch at the prow while the canoe drifted slowly down-channel. The Pukwudgees followed along the marshes. The tallest of them were hidden by swaying salt grasses, but they called aloud to the lame crow, and inquired who rode by. "A chief's daughter going to her marriage bed," answered the crow; so the Pukwudgees laid down their bows and arrows and threw white beachplum blossoms in the wake of the canoe.

Meanwhile, Pocanok stood waiting by his wigwam door. When at last the canoe came in sight, he was so transported with joy that he took his paddle, stepped into his canoe and went to meet the Princess. As he first saw her, she lay so still, she was so lovely that he thought that she was sleeping, until he looked into her green eyes. Then Pocanok knew what had happened because he had tried to deceive the Devil, and his heart smote his breast with medicine drums of shame.

"I shall take her myself to the Western Heavens," he said, "and plead with the White God, that she may be made well." He fastened her canoe to his, and paddled into the darkness until he was lost to shore.

No Indian knows whether or not Pocanok and the Princess reached the Western Heavens. The old people of the tribes believe that they still ride over the waters. In the night, when fogs are thick, you can hear the hoarse call of her lame black crow. In daylight, when a certain green color passes along the sea, the Nauset-Wampanoag point to it and say, "There goes poor Pocanok, bearing the dead Princess who has eyes like a sea-drowned leaf." The canoes are always far away; no voice may hail them; but the Devil and the snake with the beanpod tail are here on the Narrow Land. The snake hates the Devil, because its tail still hurts, and it roams the mainland in the hope of getting even with its enemy, although it has taken for its home-place a cave on Naushon Island.

The chiefs of Naushon refuse to trade with the tribesmen. They blame the mainland people for the death of the green-eyed Princess, and for the coming of rattlesnakes to their island.

HOW THE DEVIL MET A CHICKADEE BIRD

Richard Bourne was the only man that the Devil could never defeat. He was pious good, and he prayed so hard that when the Devil came down from the north to wrestle with Richard Bourne at night, the Devil always got the worst of it. Now the Devil was six times the size of Bourne, and the Devil's muscles were as sinewy as a young pine tree. No one ever could understand why he always failed to win. Of course, Old Man Bourne had the Lord on his side, and that gave him the strength of an Angel-being. Yet, sometimes, he was hard put to it, for the Devil was crafty and quick.

Richard Bourne lived in Bourneland; and the Indians, who loved him, crept close to his room at night, when they saw the pine knots burning there, and heard him moan aloud. They knew that he was wrestling with the Evil One, and sometimes his cries were so piteous that the Indians fell on their knees and prayed for him, in the dark by his window light.

Every evening the Devil came, stepping high from hill to hill to keep his feet out of the bogwater. He had built himself a den in the wastelands of the Lower Province; and there, by day, he waited for the bones of wrecked ships, and tried to seize upon the souls of the departed. When dusk came, and he could no longer watch the destruction of fair vessels, he always bethought him of Richard Bourne, who was having things all his way, and that meant the Lord's way, down in Bourneland. So every twilight the Devil decided to walk up-Cape, and take a little of the godliness out of Old Man Bourne.

It took the Devil many years to realize that Richard Bourne was always going to defeat him, no matter how hard he tried. When at last the Evil One understood that his giant's strength was of no avail, he grew crafty, and one evening as he came from the tip of the Cape to Bourneland, he gathered the stones along the beaches, every stone that he could find, and put them all in his apron. He felt exultant as his load became heavy, for he thought that he had found a way to destroy Richard Bourne.

Just after sundown he reached the forest that lies to the east of Bourneland. There, on a tree, sat a chickadee bird watching the Devil who appeared against the sky like a great black eagle, hurrying over the hills. The chickadee waited until the laden Devil was close to the tree on which it perched. Then it opened its beak and sang a song:

> "Howdy, Giant,
> Howdy, Devil,
> You're gonna wressle
> With Richard Bourne.
> You're gonna git
> The worst of it.
> You're gonna git
> The worst of it."

The Devil was furious with that bird. He lost his temper entirely, and took a rock from his apron and threw it after the chickadee. But the chickadee flew straight up from the tree and was not hurt at all. As it flew it sang again, till the song echoed through the forest:

> "Howdy, Giant,
> Howdy, Devil,
> You're gonna wressle
> With Richard Bourne.
> You're gonna git
> The worst of it.
> You're gonna git
> The worst of it."

The Devil could not endure such contempt. He started to run after the chickadee bird, and stumbled on a root and fell. His apron string broke, and the stones rolled out. There they lie, in Bourneland, to this day. Look high, look low, there are no stones on the Nauset beaches, or in Truro, or in the Province Dunes. They were all brought to Bourneland in the Devil's apron and spilled there when the apron string broke. As for the Devil, he knew when he was thoroughly defeated, and after that never came back to wrestle with Richard Bourne. He went to the lonesome tip of the Cape, sat down there, waited for the bones of wrecked ships, and tried to seize upon the souls of sailors who washed up on the shore.

HOW THE DEVIL BUILT A BRIDGE

That Devil was a wise giant. He liked dry places, and hated to get his feet wet. One day he decided to build a bridge from the mainland to one of the Elizabeth Islands. He pulled up at least a thousand pine trees, and laid them one beside the other from the mainland into the sea. He did not like the feeling of the cold, slimy sea bottom, so he stood on the bridge, as far as it was made, and reached down and laid the logs in front of him, each log beside its brother.

All the fishes came to watch, and remained to admire. They had never seen anything like it before, and they swam around all sides of the bridge. Word passed along the sea bottom that there was something worth seeing. So the squid came, and the mackerel, and the horse-foot, and the starfish, and the lobster, and a hundred others, too. They all stood around and admired the way that the Devil was building his bridge.

Among the dwellers of the deep came the delicate, dancing crab. He was more excited than all the rest, danced on the very tips of his claws, and stared so hard and steadily that his eyes popped far out of his head — and they never have popped in since.

There were a great many logs to lay. The sun was hot, and after a time the Devil began to tire. He grew careless as he swung his heavy burdens, and by mistake he hit the crab with the root end of a tree trunk. You have no idea how that crab was hurt! Hurt in his pride, hurt in his back, and hurt in his legs; so badly that he never walked straight again. The way he walked was unnatural. All the other dwellers in the sea bottom laughed at him. So the crab grew sour in his mind, and determined to have revenge on the Devil. He lurked under the lee of the bridge till the Devil came walking down it, to lay another log. As the Devil placed the log close against its brother, the crab ran up, sidewise, and caught hold of the Devil's finger. The Devil

pulled his hand up from the sea, and the crab came up with it. The
Devil yelled, to stop the pain, and with his other hand he pulled one
of the crab's claws. But that crab would not let go. Then the Devil
exerted his giant's strength, and pulled one great claw completely
out of the crab's shoulder. The poor old crab had to release its hold,
and the Devil flung it as far as he could throw — to an island twenty
miles away, where the one-claw crabs breed.

The Devil gave up building his bridge. He went down-Cape, where
he lives in the dunes of the Province Lands. Accordingly, the South
Sea crabs are not afraid any more. They run, sidewise, over the
beaches, and chase the other dwellers of the ocean who laugh at the
way they walk. The ones that are descended from the Devil's enemy
have only one large claw (fiddler crabs); but all of them have eyes
popping out; and so have the lobsters and the horsefoots, and the
squid. So would you, if you had been there when the Devil was building his bridge!

SQUANT THE SEA-WOMAN

Every Indian knows the story of how Maushop fought the Bird-monster, challenged that man-eating eagle to come down from a tree and
fight, how the eagle flew at Maushop's eyes, tried to claw out the
giant's heart, how talons tore at living flesh and great beak ripped at
veins and muscles of neck and shoulders; and how, finally, Maushop
permitted the monster to come so close that it seemed as if the Bird-
demon were beating its black wings on his breast. At that moment a
storm arose over the sea; the islands shook with thunder of battle;
lightning flashed; waters howled; and Maushop reached out his two
hands, caught the eagle around the neck and wrung that neck as if it
were a deer's hide washed after the drying.

The Black Demon fell dead. His wings, falling over the white
shore, covered the bones of children that he had stolen and devoured.
Weary with battle, Maushop sat down in the eagle's den. There was
no tobacco on the island, so he filled his pipe with pokeweed, for he
needed to smoke and rest awhile with the great Bird-monster at his
feet. Wind raged over the sea; waves snarled and showed their
teeth. Suddenly, among them, a Sea-woman arose and approached the

THE SMOKE OF MAUSHOP'S PIPE DRIFTING OVER THE NARROW LAND

den. Her eyes were square, her head was covered with locks of sea-weed, her fingers were webbed as the tern's feet, and she sang a wild song, in which joined the Wolf-Waves who followed her, howling as they came.

Maushop continued to smoke his pipe, though he watched that Sea-woman well. She came close enough to make sure that the Black Eagle was dead; then tore her hair and whimpered, and turned away with the tide. When the tide came in again, she drifted along with it, and this time she smiled. The storm went away; the wind blew from the south; the sun came out; and Maushop saw that her hair was green, glistening, her body wide and flat like a ribbon of kelp. He knew then, that she was Squant, the sea giantess, so he waded into the ocean and reached for a hold on her braids. They slipped like green water through his fingers. Squant laughed, sang a song, and hid in an underseas cave not far from the cliffs at Gay Head. Maushop desired to follow her, and wrap her hair around him; but he feared lest he lose strength in that way, and be unable to rise to the surface. She, like a fish, could live under water, but he, a man-giant, needed to breathe the wind.

Every day Squant came with the incoming tide, smiled, and beckoned him to follow. Maushop sat in his den and thought about it. Sometimes he swam in the sea with her, but when she went down to the underseas cave he did not dare to follow. Back in Poponesset on the Narrow Land he had a wife and sons who were waiting for his return; and the Indian mothers also waited to know the fate of their eagle-born children. Maushop's wife was ugly, a terrible scold. There was no peace in their wigwam, so, occasionally, Maushop grew a little tired of her. It was pleasant to rest in the eagle's den, and watch the smoke from his pipe drift over the mainland. When Squant called to him and he did not come, she frowned. The wind veered to the north-east, the sea grew white, and Maushop knew that it would be no use to attempt to return to the Narrow Land. Squant could stir up such fearful weather that not even a giant might breast the waves, or fight the north wind that beat him steadily offshore.

Year by year Maushop rested. To have an excuse for his absence, he began to build a bridge from Gay Head to Cuttyhunk. He filled one of his moccasins with sand and waded out to empty it on the intended line. Along came a crab who was looking for something to do, and when he saw Maushop's uncovered foot, he took a hold of it. Crabs have no use for giants. Giants have no use for crabs. Maushop reached out his arm and broke off a portion of Gay Head Cliff. The crab let go of Maushop's foot in a hurry and scuttled out of the way. Maushop lifted that piece of cliff and heaved it after the crab. It fell directly on top of the offender and buried him deeply in the sea bottom. A part of the cliff stuck out of water, and is called No-Man's-Land.

Maushop gave up building his bridge, and that spring determined to return to the Cape, to visit his wife, and tell the Indian people the story of the eagle's den. Then he remembered that it was the season for planting corn, which should be put into the ground when the leaf of the white oak is as big as a mouse's ear. He knew that his wife would bother him about corn, and in the villages the men and women would stop their work to mourn for the eagle-borne children. So he waited a little longer, till he chanced to think of his wife's strawberry bread. Like other Indian women, she bruised strawberries in a mortar, mixed them with meal, and baked them into loaves. Maushop climbed from his den and started across the South Sea, to advise his children, discipline his wife, and eat strawberry bread. In the summer Squant never lost her temper as she did when the days were short. She sat in her cave and blew bubbles, and sang a song that made Maushop desire to cover himself with her green hair. He walked quickly away from her. Squant laughed, and sang another song that meant that he would return.

On the mainland, he came upon his wife in a wigwam with a bad Indian from the north. The Indian was like an ant crawling over her. Maushop picked him off and threw him into Great Marshes. There the land lapped over him, and he lies to this day in the mound known as Scorton's Neck. The giant spoke to his wife. He was very angry; for Indians, unlike white people, are loyal to one another and believe in keeping their wives. He ordered her to bake strawberry bread. She only covered her head with ashes and mourned for the man from the north. Maushop lost his temper. He picked her up and tossed her across-channel to Succonesset. He picked up his five children and threw them into the sea. They were transformed into fishes and swam away to the south. Sometimes, when storms are heavy, they come close to shore again. Hidden in waves, they wail aloud and suck at the sand as though they were still giant babies suckling at a squaw's breast.

Maushop sat down on a hill and bowed his head in his hands. He thought of the bed that he had made of eagle feathers and bear-hide in the den at Gay Head. He went back to the island before the sun was fallen, and sat on the edge of a rainbow cliff to smoke his pipe. The waters churned. Squant came up between the waves and shook her hair.

That night, as the tide went out, the Gentle Giant followed her to her underseas cave. The Sea-woman twined her green braids about him and so he fell asleep.

Maushop has never awakened from those long years of slumber. Squant sits in the cave, day and night, with the young giant's body laid across her knees. Sometimes she sings to make his sleep happy, or blows bubbles and smiles. When winter comes and the days grow shorter, she is in terror that he will never waken. Then the waters over the underseas cave seethe and circle like fighting eagles. Into that whirlpool white men's ships are sucked down as readily as Indian canoes. The Sea-woman takes them in the hope that Maushop will rouse himself when he feels in his hands these reminders of life on the Long Land.

Mariners, it is well to know where that whirlpool lies!

THE PRINCESS AND THE MAGIC BOWL

After Chief Sagam's young wife was carried to the Spirit Land, the chief grew so melancholy that the medicine men feared that he was possessed by the devils of Mahtahdou. They practiced sacred arts upon him and gave him rare potions from forest roots. He only sat with his head bowed and his body fronting to the west. After the medicine men had removed all possibility of devils from the heart of Chief Sagam they retired in discouragement to their wigwams. Then a young squaw, sister to the dead favorite, took the chief's infant daughter (for whom the mother had laid down her life), and placed the tiny papoose at the feet of its father. Sagam contemplated the ground. His youngest child opened her eyes and looked into the eyes of the chief. Immediately his heart left his breast and found lodging in the body of the papoose. He named the child Scargo, and grew to care for her more than for wampum, or corn lands, or carven pipe.

To please Sagam, the people of the Place of Bays and runners from distant sachems brought presents to the little princess. They knew where the father's pleasure lay, and, also, as time went on, they loved the princess for her gentleness toward forest dwellers. She was the child who took for friends a lame deer, and a turkey with a broken wing, and a fallen gull, and a treacherous fox who had twisted its back, and a blind, stupid mole. Gradually the people of the tribe came to know that she had the healing power of the Pnieses and had brought secrets with her from beyond the Turkey Sea. Squaws suffering from pains of childbirth, warriors wounded in battle, learned that the little Princess Scargo could drive out pain devils, and heal sour wounds. One sad gift came to her from her dead mother: the gift of the fear of death. Scargo could not bear to see the animals of the forest die. Her father, who was aged, humored her in this caprice. He hid the passing of the tribesmen from her knowledge, and kept from her sight the perishing of forest-beings.

Once, in the early springtime, a runner from a distant chief brought to the little princess a pumpkin that had been dried and carved by a scribe. On the outside was wizardry in Indian totem. The inside of the pumpkin had been removed, and the shell made into a bowl. In the bowl water glistened, and tiny perch and trout swam. Scargo loved the bowl of fish more than she loved all her other presents. She fed her pets and watched them grow. Soon they became too big for the pumpkin bowl, so Scargo made a little fishpond near her wigwam and deposited the perch and trout in their new home.

That spring a terrible drought came to the land of the Nauset-Wampanoag. Niba-nahbeezik, the Water Spirit, was angry with man-beings, and withdrew the water from springs, rivers, and lakes. A dance was made to appease Niba-Nahbeezik. In vain. The skies remained clear of cloud droppings and the water already upon the earth disappeared into the interior where the cruel Water Spirit kept it beside him. Indians dug far down to reach the waters of Niba-nahbeezik, and in some places no water could be procured. The little fishpond of Princess Scargo fared badly. Dug by her tiny hands, it proved a shallow affair and in almost no time the fish that she loved became ill. Scargo, when she realized that her pets were dying, performed the rites of grief. She cut off her hair, daubed her forehead with white clay, and stuck a leaf in each ear and nostril. Her father, when he saw these tokens of protest, called together his squaws and ordered them to make a punkwood smoke. The squaws threw green pine needles on a large bonfire, and twirled fire sticks as they danced.

Sagam's warriors, answering the signal, assembled in council. The old chief, dressed in a deerskin robe and skunkskin cap, sat at the head of the council table, and Princess Scargo was brought before the warriors that she might plead for her "Brothers of the Tail and Fin." The princess spoke with such wisdom and feeling that the warriors, in an unwise moment, promised to make for her a fishpond that would never go dry.

The young men went to the seashore and brought back large clamshells. The older men, who knew the pathways of safety, entered swamps and brought back cattail flags which the squaws wove into hundreds of shoulder baskets. Then the braves stood forth, and from them Scargo chose the strongest warrior. He placed an arrow in his bow. While the wind was blowing from the north, the warrior pointed his arrow south, and drew the bowstring taut. The arrow flew high and far. Young braves of the hawk eye marked the place of its descent. By tribal promise, the breadth of Scargo's fishpond was to be that arrow's flight.

After the ceremony of the arrow, the men made dances, while the squaws, using clamshells, dug within the area of the arrow's journey. They piled the sandy soil in cattail shoulder baskets, and dumped it on the southern side of the declivity near the spot where the arrow fell. Spring ripened into murmurous summer, but no puttering sounded in streams, no flip-flap on the shores of lakes, no purling at the river's edge. The squaws dug ceaselessly and sighed among themselves. As they grew work weary, they whispered Scargo's name.

At first the little princess did not hear them. She replaced her perch and trout in the carven bowl that was too small for them, and waited in strange fear for the coming of death. Her new fishpond grew wide and long, and very deep. Where the sand from it was piled, a high hill rose toward the clouds. Niba-nahbeezik, the Water Spirit, watched with an unfriendly eye. He kept the springs in the center of the earth, and did not reveal himself to men. On the new-made hill the braves danced. In the great earth bowl the squaws dug steadily, although their backs were breaking and their ears full of thunder. "Scargo," they sobbed in protest, "help us, we are weary, tired of the dry earth! If we are not soon released we shall go away to death in the Western Heavens."

Scargo heard them and her young heart misgave her. She looked upon the fishpond and knew that it was deep and wide and long, and would keep a thousand speckled trout from perishing and be the home-place of a thousand silver perch. "Work no more," she said to the squaws; so they ceased their labors and in discouragement turned their backs on the dry hole that they had made.

Night came over the Narrow Land. On the hill, the braves danced around the flaming fire of Yotannit. In the wigwams tired squaws rested, grieving that they had failed to fashion a lake of unfailing waters. Nanipaushat, the Moon Spirit, climbed the sky to look upon the deep hole and the high hill. Scargo, in her father's wigwam, saw that her fish were gasping. With the pumpkin bowl in her two hands she crept out of the wigwam door, and by the rays of Nanipaushat found her way to the bottom of the deep hole. There she was close to Niba-Nahbeezik, the cruel Water Spirit. From his home-place under the earth, he could hear her speak and she, in turn, could understand his answers.

"Give me water, Niba-nahbeezik," she begged. "My fish are perishing; my people are too weary to labor any longer."

"Come below and serve me, Princess Scargo," said the Water Spirit, "and I will give to your people, and to all Wampanoag of the Narrow Land, unfailing waters forevermore."

"It shall be as you wish," said little Scargo.

She knelt beside the pumpkin bowl, and spoke gently to her fish. "Be of good cheer, little brothers," she said, "soon you shall swim in so fine a lake that the stars will drop down to visit you, and the sun with yellow fingers will stroke your shining fins. In time of famine you shall give food to my people who have labored faithfully to save you."

As she spoke, the few drops of water remaining in the pumpkin bowl mounted upward, filled the bowl, and welled outward from it so fast that the princess was caught in their swirling eddies. At the same moment, Niba-nahbeezik, who had returned the waters from the inner earth, released the droppings that he had concealed in clouds.

Rain put out the sacred fire on the hilltop where the braves were dancing. Rain and wind almost drowned the cries of the little princess who called to her tribesmen for help. Old Sagam heard her voice above the wailing storm. He and the bravest of his warriors ran down the hill. When they reached the foot of it a lake spread before them, and they heard, far away, the voice of Princess Scargo calling a last farewell.

In the gray morning, the body of the princess drifted to the door of her father's wigwam. Some of the old people, who are credulous, say that she was carried on the backs of the trout and perch that she had saved. Chief Sagam buried his favorite child on the hill that the squaws had made for her, beside the lake that she gave to the Nauset-Wampanoag.

All this happened before the moon unfolded itself into so many autumns. Scargo still serves Niba-nahbeezik, and the Indians of the Narrow Land need never fear a drought. The pumpkin bowl with magic on it lies at the bottom of Scargo Lake, and if you go to the place beside the lake, where old Chief Sagam's wigwam stood, and call, "Scargo, Scargo!" you will hear, from far under the waters, or perhaps from the great mound called Scargo Hill, a clear voice which answers you, almost in your own words. In the dry season of summer go at night, when Nanipaushat, the Moon Spirit, touches the water. Among the dry reeds a sighing echoes, and sobbing voices murmur, "Scargo, Scargo!"

The squaws are still grumbling at the making of so deep a hole!

THE CORN COB DOLL

When Mercy Lowe's husband died, she was left with four little children to feed. She lived in Mashpee where the corn grows tall, but she had not enough food to keep her children from starving. A short distance from her house lived Ordihon, a kindhearted Indian who was sorry for her, and ready to give extra supplies from his broad fields. There came a day when no corn was left in the little hut where Mercy lived, and her children were crying for food. Mercy gave them a corn cob doll and told them to play with it. Then she strapped her basket over her back, and went down the road to get help from Ordihon.

The corn cob doll had a wooden head, and a bit of cloth wrapped around it for a shawl. The four children took their treasure with them when they went out of the hut to watch their mother depart. After she had disappeared around a bend in the road, they played for a while with the corn cob doll, but they were too hungry to forget their hunger, and in almost no time they were crying bitterly.

Up the road came a little noise, tap, tap, tap, the pounding of a pointed stick on the ground. An old woman, tiny and bent, hobbled toward them. "Why are you crying, children?" she asked.

"Because we are hungry," the children replied.

"Where is your mother?"

"She has gone down the road to get from Ordihon some corn."

At that the old woman muttered, and tapped her stick sharply against a stone. The children did not know whether she was angry at them for being hungry, or angry at Ordihon for giving them corn. They said nothing, dried their eyes, and the oldest held tightly to the doll.

The old woman was Abisha Pockmonet. She glanced up and down the road and made a circle in the dust with her stick. "Come into the house, children," she said. "I'll wait with you till your mother comes home." They followed her into the tiny hut where she seated herself by the stone hearth and looked into the fire. The children drew close. She turned to speak to them again, saw the corn cob doll, and gave the cry of the swamp owl before a killing at night. The doll fell upon the hearth. The children, frightened, backed away to the corner of the room beside a window that looked upon the road.

Abisha Pockmonet never took her eyes from that image wrapped in a rag. She did not stoop and pick it up. Instead she gave it a poke with her stick, putting the point of the stick well under the cob so that the little doll flipped into the air and seemed to jump toward the fire. As she poked at it, the old woman called aloud, "Look, my pretties, look out of the window. Your mother is coming down the road." The Indian children were frightened. They needed their mother, and they needed food. They forgot about the corn cob doll, and did as Abisha said. The old witch gave the wooden head another poke with her cane, and once more the doll seemed to jump toward the fire. "Keep watch, my children," Abisha called, "your mother is coming now." Even as she spoke, the doll leaped toward the hearth; and every time that the children turned from the window, Abisha told them to keep watch for their mother, and every time that they looked out of the window, she managed to flip the wooden image nearer to the flames. At last she poked her stick directly under its grinning head and the corn cob doll jumped high. "Hark, children, your mother is calling, your mother is calling you now." The children turned to the window to listen, and with one final cast of her stick, old Abisha Pockmonet sent the doll into the flames.

A blinding flash of light shot from the hearthfire, a wild light that banded itself into the colors of the rainbow. Old Abisha disappeared in it, and the frightened children heard their mother gasping. They ran out of the hut, and saw her, breathless, frightened, running up the road, without any basket of corn. "What is the matter?" she sobbed as she came, "Oh, what is the matter at home?" They told her about the corn cob doll and of old Abisha Pockmonet; and then they asked for food. "We must return for it," she said. "I left it near a tree by the road." She spoke with hope, but in her heart Mercy Lowe knew that when they went back to the trailcrossing, where she had set down her basket, there would not be any corn.

Ordihon had given her a full load. She had started home with a thank prayer singing in her heart, but she had not gone far when fear came upon her, as though a hundred swamp devils were swarming over her basket, putting their dry fingers down her throat, whimpering, "Hurry! Hurry! Sorrow at home! Sorrow at home!" She ran as fast as the weight on her back would permit. Weak from lack of food, to her it seemed as if the basket grew heavier at every step. All the fear devils sat in it and laughed. To get rid of them, she hid the basket by a tree and ran swiftly to the hut.

The weary, hungry family crept back to the crossroads. No basket of corn was there, though they searched at the foot of every tree. Then Mercy knew that a spell had been put upon her. Abisha Pockmonet, the cruel witch, had taken Ordihon's corn for herself, and hated Mercy Lowe.

This is the first story of Abisha and Mercy. After the burning of the corn cob doll there were many sufferings in that little house. Hunger lived with them, sorrow followed them. All dwellers in Mashpee saw that Abisha Pockmonet brought evil to Mercy; and at last Ordihon, who was a good Indian, took the little family into his house and gave them protection and food. Then Abisha stopped her torments, for she knew that Ordihon would punish her, and since she could get no more of his corn, her jealous rage was done.

THE SCREECHAM SISTERS

Off Cotuit lies Screecham's Island, now called Grand Island. For years no one could settle there, for the ghost of Hannah Screecham frightened men away. She and her sister, Sarah, lived alone on the island; but one day they quarreled, and Sarah moved to South Mashpee and built herself a hut in the forest by the place called the Witches Pond. Both sisters were evil, and while Sarah became a witch, Hannah befriended the pirates who sailed along the coast.

Captain Kidd, Black Bellamy, Paul Williams, Baxter, all of them knew her, feared her, yet trusted her with their gold. While a pirate sloop lay offshore, the captain flew signals to Hannah. Then a boat put out from the pirate ship, a boat with the captain and one sailor and a treasure of Spanish pieces of eight (such as are found on the beaches today), or perhaps bars of bullion, or caskets of jewels from Spain. Hannah went down to the sea beach, kissed the captain, and nodded to the sailor. The captain gave her a shawl, or a locket of hair, or a finger ring. At her direction, the sailor carried the treasure into the interior of the island where a deep pit had been dug. When the last bar was laid in place, and the last coin safe in its box, Hannah pushed the sailor into the yawning pit. Quick-running sands seeped over him, and he was buried alive. Then she screamed like the gull in storm, a cry that mingled with the wind in stunted trees, or the waves shrilling on the outer beach. At that signal, the captain put back to his ship; and even the Black Bellamy, cruelest of buccaneers, shivered as he heard her wail. Yet he knew that his treasure was safe, its whereabouts known to only two, Hannah Screecham and himself.

She was never able to dig for gold. The moment that earth-buried metal touched her, the sandpits on the Island opened and the ghosts of the men that she had murdered put their blue hands to her throat. She has been dead this long time, but at evening, when you hear her calling over the waters from Grand Island, you will know that she warns the pirates that someone approaches their gold.

While Hannah lived on Screecham's Island, Sarah, her sister, built a house in South Mashpee by the Witches Pond. The forest there was without moon. The shooting looked good and when deer were scarce the hunters were often tempted to track in her forest, although they never succeeded in bringing game to ground. Whenever they appeared, Sarah Screecham grew angry, and threatened evil luck. She appeared, now here, now there in the forest, and always, just after she went from sight, a young deer leaped through the brush, or occasionally, after dusk, the hunters saw a great black mare. Whether they shot with bows and arrows, or with the white man's thunder, it made no difference — they could not kill the deer in her forest, not catch the great black horse.

Once Sarah fell in love with a Mashpee man. He was afraid and would have none of her. She grew angry and brought him bad luck. He became tired of her threats and that he might discover the secret of her magic he invited her to spend the night at his house. She came, and after dusk, turned into a horse. She was still sufficiently friendly to the man so that she let him catch her. He shod her with three iron shoes, and a silver shoe on her left front hoof, and tied her to a tree in his yard. The next morning when he looked out of the window, the black mare had disappeared. He went to a neighbor's, told his story, and they started for Sarah Screecham's house. They found her moaning in pain. She tried to hide her hand in the folds of her skirt, and when they seized her by the arm they saw that a silver horseshoe was nailed to her left palm.

She was so cruel a witch that the tribe longed for her death. Game grew very scarce in the land, and hunters went often to Sarah's forest in the hope of breaking the charm. Always the wind blew their arrows aside, their guns missed fire, or for some other reason the bullets took no effect. Always Sarah appeared in the forest and taunted them for lack of skill.

One day a man who remembered the story of the horseshoe fashioned a silver bullet and put it into his gun. He went at dusk to the forest beside the Witches Pond. Old Sarah laughed her witch cackle, but he paid no attention. Just after the sun went down, Sarah disappeared, and a few minutes later a young doe leaped through the brush. The man raised his gun to his shoulder and took careful aim. He had only the one silver bullet with which to shoot but that flew straight to its mark and lodged near the heart of the deer. The ani-

mal jerked into a high leap, keeping stiff in the mid-body. Then it
sped away. Swiftly the hunter followed, he who was swiftest tracker
in Mashpee, for he knew that the deer was mortally wounded and
could not travel far. Yet almost immediately he lost its trail, while,
in the forest, night shadows thickened until, like black furry cats,
they slunk around his knees. Tei Pai Wankas called from the swamps,
making voices like maidens. The marsh owl woke in the cedar tree
and cried "Gone, gone," in the Monomoyick tongue, his favorite
night speech. The Indian tracker spoke no word to shadow or swamp
or wild marsh owl. He searched steadily for the wounded animal
until Geesukquand's sun canaries nested in the tops of pine trees.
Then he returned to Sarah Screecham's house. No smoke issued from
the stone chimney; and when he entered the dwelling room he found
a very old woman lying dead by the hearthside, with a silver bullet
in her breast.

GEESUKQUAND, THE SUN SPIRIT

Matilda Simons lived in a little house, about a mile from Ordihon's
cornfield. Her husband was tall, young, and strong; he worked well,
but he could not always agree with the whipping master. In the old
days, the Indians were lashed cruelly, tied hand and foot to the whipping post at Marston's Mills. John Simons was whipped until his chest
hurt and he died. He left his young wife, Matilda, with three little girls
to raise. The land was poor on John Simons' cornfield. Many of the
stalks never came to ear. Matilda labored day and night, her children
working at her side; still there was not enough to eat. Those were
the days when Indian preachers stood in the pulpit of Mashpee
church and spoke in the quiet way of tribesmen, without the childish
turbulence and excitement of white ministers. Matilda Simons went
to church, and taught her children to worship the White God. When
they were in dire necessity, she knelt down and invited the angels to
save them from death.

The White God and all his council overlooked that prayer. Matilda received no manna from heaven, and a scant supply of corn
from her field. She rationed her food among the three little girls, giving them so little to eat that they ceased to care about play. They
sat, listless and frightened, watching their mother.

As the days drifted by, Matilda Simons saw that she was coming to the end of supplies. She took her father's bow and arrows and went into the forest. She shot at the deer that leaped in the brush, but the deer went unharmed away. She hunted the rabbit that ate of the grass, but the rabbit heard her footfall and hid in an underground hole. She made a snare for the wild turkey, but he was a wise old bird and flew over the trap. The crow jeered in the swamp cedar tree, and Matilda returned to her home. Into her thoughts obtruded a memory of the past, a way of praying that belonged to Geesukquand, the Sun Spirit, giver of food and light. She tried to remember that Geesukquand was an evil demon, that only the Great Spirit should be approached for help. Yet she could not rid herself of the feeling that if she asked Geesukquand, he would bring food to her door.

When the last kernel of grain was gone, Matilda put her starving children to bed, and went into the forest to ask for forest aid. Nothing stirred in the darkness. The deer slept in his bedded lair; the brown rabbit slept in his burrow; the wild turkey slept in the mockernut tree; and the crow, who was the first giver of grain, teetered on a bough of the swamp cedar and jeered softly in his dream.

All night Matilda spoke to the forest dwellers, but no one of them was ready to aid her, and toward dawn she returned to her hut. The children were sleeping in their beds by the fire. They could not do much but sleep by day or night, for they were too weak to walk. Nevertheless, Matilda wakened them, shortly before dawn, carried them out of the house and stood them in front of the door of the hut. The door faced east. The children tried to obey their mother but they staggered and leaned against the wall. "Geesukquand, Sun Spirit, help thy Sisters of Earth," chanted Matilda, raising her arms in greeting to the east. She repeated the whole of that ancient prayer, while the three little girls, who knew no word of it, reached their wavering arms toward dawn and vaguely hoped for food.

Geesukquand, the Sun Spirit, was always ready of will; but all the grain that he had raised that year belonged to good Indians. A lean year in Mashpee produces few extra supplies. Geesukquand knew that if he waited for another season to bring forth more corn in Matilda's field, the children and their mother would die. When he heard Matilda speaking the old prayer he went at once to his friend, Paum-pa-gusnit, the Sea Spirit, and asked for the loan of fish.

With the warmth of rum and the yellowness of ripe corn, the tepee fires of Geesukquand signaled their promise from the east. Sunlight streamed on the upturned faces of the children, on the moving lips of the mother. Suddenly, in front of the hut, between two trees to the east of it, four giants appeared with four giant codfish at their backs. The children, frightened, crouched behind their mother. Matilda Simons rubbed her eyes, and stood, swaying, in the light. One of the giants spoke in the guttural voice of the sea: "Two of these fishes are the gift of Paum-pa-gusnit, the Sea Spirit. The other two we would trade for corn, if you will tell us where corn may be had. Paum-pa-gusnit is pleased to know that his friend the Sun-being receives Indian prayer."

Matilda took the two giant codfish into the house. They were of sufficient size to feed her children for many a long day. She directed the four giants to Ordihon's wigwam, for Ordihon was wealthy and would exchange corn for fish. Before Matilda had prepared cod-muddle for the excited children, the giants returned with enough corn to feed Matilda and her family for the rest of that year. In courtesy for their kindness, Matilda invited the sea giants to eat of the food that they had given. They only shook their green heads and went away in the direction of the sun.

THE WATER-BEING OF PAU WAH POND

Pau Wah, chief of the Potonamequoits, erected his wigwam at Namequoit, near the house of John Kenrick (at South Orleans). On the neck of land that stretches seaward, to the east of Namequoit, lived Quansett, the old chief of another tribe. Quansett had a daughter whose gentle ways were like the wild dove for which she was named. Young chief Pau Wah decided that she would make a good wife. He went to her father with offerings of wampum and furs. Old Quansett weighed the wampum, closely examined the peltry; then shook his head in grim refusal. His daughter was worth more than any amount that Pau Wah could offer, he proclaimed.

In gloom and anger Pau Wah returned to his wigwam. The more he thought about it, the angrier he grew. It seemed to him that Quansett had refused much wampum, and fine peltry, so Pau Wah summoned his braves, and told them of the insult that he had received.

After a long council the followers of Pau Wah determined to raid Quansett's wigwam and carry away the princess. One night in midwinter the braves assembled at Pau Wah's home-place. Armed with tomahawks and heavy battle axes, they crept eastward through the forest toward the camping grounds of Quansett's tribe. All was silent in wigwams that loomed darkly in winter starlight. Pau Wah's braves crept around the tent where the princess was known to sleep. Not a dog barked, not a twig cracked. At a signal from Pau Wah, the braves let forth their war cries, and rushed upon the tent. The Wild Dove had flown! At the same moment, from the other wigwams came the braves of Quansett's tribe, armed for a fight and led by their old chief in the red mask of war. A sanguine battle ensued, fought at close quarters and in darkness. Warriors fell on the snow-grained earth, like bleeding wild cranberries crushed into the white dunes at harvest. From this encounter, the small peninsula received its name of "Bloody Neck."

Pau Wah, who was young and brave, managed to hack his way clear of the ambush. His men had fallen never to rise and he knew that he had lost his chance ever again to encounter Quansett with any hope of success.

A tribesman has a right to the disposal of his daughters. Pau Wah, in the pride of youth, had attempted an unjustified vengeance. In his extremity, no other tribes were ready to help him. He crept back to his wigwam and grieved and brooded alone.

Winter moved its stiff finger over the Narrow Land. Game was scarce and ponds were thickly coated for many weeks at a time. The Indians, after the fashion of their ancestors, the Mohig, erected tents upon the ice, cut holes in the ice flooring and fished in comfort. Pau Wah, after his defeat, avoided the hunters' trails lest he encounter other tribesmen who would deride him for his failure to capture the Wild Dove. Instead he took his tent of skins, his dog, his bow, his quiver of arrows, and his fishing tackle, and went to the pond near Namequoit, where he knew there was abundance of fish. He erected his tent on the ice, cut a hole and prepared his lines.

Now the most important thing to remember, whenever one goes fishing, is that Niba-nahbeezik, the Water Spirit, owns all the fish. Niba-nahbeezik must be propitiated with an oration of courtesy or preferably with an offering. Pau Wah, immersed in his troubles, forgot Niba-nahbeezik. Without asking the permission of the Water-being, he put down his fish lines and drew up a fish. The Water Sachem, as every man knows, is short of temper, and quick to act. He wasted no time on Pau Wah, but withdrew his Spirit-shoulder from the ice under Pau Wah's wigwam. Indian chief, dog, tent, bow, arrows, and fishing tackle went to the bottom of that ice-coated pond.

Pau Wah has never again been seen in the land of the Nausets. Nevertheless, he fares better than many another tribesman. He has his tent, his dog, his bow, and all the fish that he wants to eat. He has set up housekeeping down there, and the only desires that he cannot fulfill are his love for the daughter of Quansett and his longing for tobacco in his pipe. No day, no night occur, to vary one's existence at the bottom of a pond, so Pau Wah grows no older and does not realize that many moons ago the Wild Dove journeyed over the Turkey Sea. Customs have changed in the sea-girt land. Old Man Treat put a Christian Indian Church less than an arrow's flight from the place where Pau Wah used to live. The bravest of the Namequoits have disappeared from the forests, and the people who have taken their places are neither brave nor strong.

The pond is named after Pau Wah. If you want fish from its waters, carry with you a supply of tobacco and follow the directions of John Kenrick who first recorded this tale. "When I was a lad," he writes, "an aged white man who, if living in the year of grace, 1890, would be over one hundred and forty-five years old, repeatedly gave me the facts of this Indian tradition, he having received it from his father, living at the time. Said the narrator to me: 'When I wish to take fish from that pond, I go upon it with a supply of tobacco and with my head near the water I three times repeat, *Pau Wah, Pau Wah, Pau Wah, give me fish and I give you tabac.* I throw down a piece of tobacco and always get plenty of fish.' He earnestly believed that Pau Wah was at the bottom of that pond, ready to trade fish for tobacco; his son believed it; his grandson believed it; and his great-grandson cannot eliminate it from his nature."

THE SONG OF WHALES

In the Great Marshes, at Barnstable, First Cranberry was born; also First Frog, First Toad and First Little Black Snake. All this happened in the days of Maushop, the Giant, who was careless, once, as he walked down-Cape and tore his cap on a star. Maushop was proud of his cap made of skunkskin of good quality, so he journeyed to the edge of Great Marshes and called to Granny Squannit:

"What will you take, Devil-sister, to mend my skunkskin cap?"

"I'll take a puff of your pipe," said Granny, who had seen Maushop make thunder and fog, and desired to make some too.

"You may have a puff, Devil-sister, but first you must mend my cap."

Granny Squannit took the cap on her knees and threaded a shell with fiber root. The skunkskin was heavy and thick and the needle would not go through. Granny Squannit pricked her finger, and a storm raged in the Marsh.

"What are you doing, Devil-sister?" called Maushop from the edge of the swamp.

"I am throwing your cap to sea," screamed Granny. "I am laid open in the finger by it and the water is pouring out of me. Soon I shall be no more."

Maushop was sorry for he knew that Granny had no blood with which to stop a wound.

"Give me back my cap, quickly!" he called. "The water runs fast out of you. You will trickle away in the marsh."

"First, give me a drop of your blood to cover the hole in my finger," she wailed.

Maushop took a black stick in his hand and with it he pricked his finger. A round drop of blood oozed out, of which the black stick tasted. Immediately it became alive and hid in the bottom of the Marsh. Maushop reached his arm across the swamp, but the wind beat that drop of blood into the cattails before Granny Squannit could catch it. She howled and tore her hair. Green Frog jumped from her head and hid in the bottom of the swamp.

"Give me another drop of your blood!" screamed Granny, "and I will give you your skunkskin cap and your wife's copper breastplate that I plucked from the breast of Indian-from-the-North who sleeps at Scorton's Neck."

Maushop took the breastplate and pressed out another drop of blood.

"Come close, Devil-sister," he called. Granny Squannit limped to the edge of the bogwater. Toad, who always had wanted to visit dry land, jumped out of her hair. Maushop reached his arm into the swamp where the storm was raging fiercely. The drop of his blood fell upon Granny's finger and covered its open place. Granny hissed and flung back his cap with the tear still in it. Maushop put it on. The skunkskin hung down behind as he strode away to the north.

The First Drop of Blood and the Little Black Stick lay very still in the Marsh. In time they took the names of Cranberry and Little Black Snake.

The drop of blood on Granny's finger burned her like a flame. She bore ill will to Maushop because he had brought this suffering by the tear in his skunkskin cap. He shall never have another of good quality, she vowed, and spit upon the animal from which had come the fur. Shortly after that Maushop met Skunk. "Give me your skin to mend my cap," he said, but Skunk only spat and Maushop decided to wear his torn cap for the remainder of his life.

Granny, to forget her troubles, decided to borrow Maushop's pipe and make a little thunder and fog. That evening, when the Giant came down-Cape, she followed along the swamps, and when he sat down to rest and smoke, she crept close. Now it happened that Maushop was singing the magic Song of Whales. All the whales came into the baywater and played and sang at Maushop's feet. The whales sang bass; Maushop sang giant voice; and the clams also sang a little, very high and clear.

Granny Squannit listened carefully and learned the Song of Whales. Then she asked Maushop for the loan of his pipe. He took it out of his lips and passed it on to her. Granny Squannit took one puff and knew what it was that she needed to make her forget her troubles. After Maushop had gone to sleep with his head on the dunes, Granny Squannit crept to the edge of the bay and sang the Song of Whales. The whales heard, were surprised, and came to shore to play and sing at her feet. They sang bass. She sang woman voice. The clams also sang a little, very high and clear.

"What do you desire, Sea-woman?" inquired the chief of whales.

"I'll give you a thousand silver trout, very good eating," said Granny Squannit, "if you will take from between his teeth my Devil-brother's pipe."

"Done," said the chief of whales, for he was very fond of trout. He paddled down-Cape till he came to the Province Lands where the giant laid his head. Very gently the chief of whales removed Maushop's pipe. The chief of whales started back to the Marshes. The pipe looked dead, so he took a puff to keep the pipe alive. Then he took another puff. Then he did not swim so fast. "This," said he, "is better than a thousand silver trout. I will catch my own supper, and keep this magic myself." Blowing that pipe, he stood out to sea, but before he had disappeared Maushop woke and saw him. Maushop sang the Song of Whales. The chief of whales covered his ears with foam and did not return for fear that he might lose the pipe. Maushop leaned on his bow and watched. He caught a glimpse of the chief of whales, offshore, puffing like a sachem. "Be of good cheer, brother," said the giant, "I will fashion me another pipe."

Meanwhile Granny Squannit howled and seethed in the Marshes. In her turmoil she forgot the magic Song of Whales. But sometimes, on a clear night, she remembers a snatch of it; and when the whales come close to the land to sing, the angry Sea-woman sucks away the tidewater, and the great fish die on the shore.

THE LAST OF GRANNY SQUANNIT

Man-stories journey to the Fourcorners of the Moon where, in the presence of Nanipaushat, they sit on weary haunches and wait, hour by hour, for a traveler to pass. Child-stories grow out of themselves into something else again. But neither moons nor years destroy the gossipy tales of women, that Squonanit whispers in their ears. Over and over her tales are told, backward and forward like ocean combers. Medicine men of the Upper Cape say that Squonanit drew her knowledge of the underness of women from her even deeper knowledge of the underness of the sea. She, as a kelp-squaw, dragged ships down and held them below till their hulls crumbled. She, as the water witch, square-eyed, mischievous, knew how to haunt the Gentle Giant till he lost remembrance of wife and children, and followed to her cave. As a mer-woman with a sea-green tail, she drifted in the wake of ships, and slowed their sailing by hanging to the keel. The captain put out topgallants and cursed the barnacles on the hull, but the Cape sailors knew that Squant would abide unless, by chance, the mate sang the Doxology, or the moon's path cut across her trail, or star spikes, sharp in the water, pricked her and drove her below. As a bog-witch she scolded the owl and the marsh owl scolded her. She planted quicksand on ancient trails; gathered to her breast young swamp devils with reedy voices, and while they floated on her long, black hair, she wallowed in the mud.

Only the very old Indians talk of Squant the Sea-woman; but many who live in Mashpee remember Granny Squannit as the bogey of their youth. A bad boy was certain to see her, and she was no sight for even a grown man: better keep her off by obedience and by going to sleep when told!

On a special morning in spring, within the lifetime of living Indians, cannikins were packed before dawn, and families set out on foot or in oxcarts, to celebrate Granny Squannit's Day. Trained "Swamp-flitters" led the procession over quicksand and bogwater, on a secret, intricate, dangerous trail that led to Granny's den. Arrived there, breakfast was served in the darkness before daylight, the choicest morsels set aside on a stone altar, as bids for Granny's favor. When the sun rose over swamp grasses, ceremonial dances began in honor of the witch. Braves, with brightly painted faces, formed in two rows and swung turkey feathers in the wind. The feathers made a cattail rustling; the wind across them made a rippling. Gradually medicine drums beat faster. The dance grew quick and, one by one, as the braves wearied, they stood aside. He who danced last and had foam at his mouth was called Granny Squannit's Son, and received presents from the rest. Later, wrestlers sat on their heels, in "Sacred Circles," put their hands on their opponents' shoulders, and tried to overbalance one another. Squaws did not join in the dances, played no games, sang no chants, for Granny Squannit was partial to men and hated a woman's song.

Sailors who feared unfavorable voyages, Indian harpooners who desired that Granny guide their weapons, made other visits than annual ones to her lonely fen. There they left food and carven offerings, whales' teeth, models of ships; then quickly went away risking never a glance where Granny lurked, lest she be angered by curiosity and send them evil fortune. When she made trail outside of the bogwater, trackers could follow her by the imprint of her feet, one male and one female foot, their path always curving like a waterline on the sand. If, before the stars paled, a sailor traveled across-marsh, he was likely to perceive, low in the bog, her ogre eye staring, lighted, yellow-green. As soon as she knew that she was observed, she pulled her black hair over her eye and with webbed fingers combed and braided tresses that made a sighing as they floated in the marsh.

Granny considered that all gold buried under the earth was hers, and resented any Indian who dug to discover treasure. Over the places where gold was hidden, she put glimmering balls of fire, Money Lights, that started at the ground and spiraled upward, widening as they rose. Some of these balls, said to survive her, have been seen by full-blooded Indians who are aware of earth secrets denied to other men.

Once when the moon was black as thunder darkness after lightning, an Indian riding Poponesset Road saw a Money Light rise upward from an ancient, forked tree. He marked well the location, in Sarah Screecham's forest, not far from her pond; turned into the witch trail, and when he came to the forked tree, about the base of it he saw yellow luminous air. The Mashpee man stepped boldly into that golden circle. Immediately a very old woman with an eye of purple like stormy water, one eye only, set in her forehead, appeared within the Light. Crouched by the tree trunk, she sang the song of a brook that goes to a summer ocean. She wove a basket as she sang, and the Indian saw that her fingers were webbed; then looked downward and beheld her foot, large as a man's, and the mate to it no bigger than a child's. He made swallowing in his throat. Granny looked up, and he heard her laughter — the hissing of a spent breaker that draws away from land. That Indian was no coward! Yet he fled her presence as a saint the devil, and never would say what happened there, save that he refused, as long as he lived, to walk abroad at sunset when the Narrow Land was circled with clear and golden light.

3. TALES OF THE HISTORIANS

During the first two decades of the seventeenth century, in London and Plymouth, in La Rochelle and Paris, in Genoa and Malaga, ship-masters, noblemen and speculative merchants met to "sign articles" and plan New World voyages. Tongues wagged with gossip of pearl-strewn beaches, gold-lined rivers and red-skinned "Salvages"; while on the cliffs of Nauset, and around the fires of Turkey Bay, and on the sloping hillsides that overlook Granny's Marsh, bright knives, shining kettles, cloth and beads were exhibited in wonder tinged with a first faint fear. Winged islands came over the water with ever-increasing frequency, laden with men in search of whales, goldmines, mermaids or sassafras; men who gave to the Narrow Land half a dozen different names, who came ashore to trade, quarrel, and sometimes to make merry. One brought his "gitterne" and played tunes to tribesmen who danced about him "twenty in a Ring . . . singing lo la lo la lo."

Back again in London's waterfront taverns, or in courtyards and garrets of the "Inns of Seine," or in the castles of rich, noble patrons, scribes of these voyages took quill and logbook and wrote accounts to appease investors with unreplenished pockets, or to loosen pursestrings for the financing of new exploits.

THE UNINHABITED ISLAND

One Friday in March, 1602, the bark *Concord* set sail from Falmouth with thirty-two persons on board, twelve to return to England with the ship, the rest to remain in the new country "for population." "Our barke being weak," wrote John Brereton, "we were loth to presse her with much saile; also our sailors being few, and they none of the best." The weather was "foggie" off the "North part of Virginia," and the voyagers not "overbolde to stand in with the shore." After a brief landing somewhere on the Maine coast, they bore away "southerly off into sea" and the following morning, a fresh gale blowing, found themselves "embayed with a mightie headland."

Captain Bartholomew Gosnold, John Brereton and three others disembarked on a "white sandie and very bolde shore"; marched all afternoon with their muskets "on their necks," and, standing on the highest hills, soon perceived that the headland was part of a long peninsula. For five or six hours they explored dunes, cliffs and seaward valleys. Then, as the sun lowered over the bay and the spars of the *Concord* darkened against the sky, they retraced their course. Near the shallop they met a young Indian "of proper stature, and of a pleasing countenance," and after "som familiaritie" they left him, to re-embark upon a ship seething with activity. During their absence the waiting mariners, commanded by Sir Humphrey Gilbert's son, "Bartholowmew," had whiled away six hours of leisure by fishing in "seven faddome" water, within a league of shore. The catch came up so fast and merrily that enthusiasts filled the decks from bow to stern, "pestered the ship with cod," and proclaimed the fishing "woonderfull."

That night, in the beamed cabin, Gosnold and young Bartholomew Gilbert, and perhaps John Brereton, gave a name to the "mightie headland": Cape Cod they called it; and the bay where the fish were so abundant became Cape Cod Bay.

Some four weeks later, John Brereton sat on a shiny "Minerall Rock" on the shore of an uninhabited island off the south coast of the peninsula. Beside him ranged some twenty "Gentlemen Adventurers." John planned to return to England; yet as he looked from the stony beach toward the interior of the island, he was tempted to remain. On that June day it seemed an earthly paradise; sixteen miles of shoreline indented with miniature bays and inlets, and on fire with mica. Inland from the pebbled coast, "plaine places of grasse" twinkled with the wet scarlet of strawberries; and at the core of the land stood high timbered oaks, their leaves "thrise so broad" as broad oak leaves at home. The voyagers had assembled on the beach to meet a band of "Salvages" who were paddling in nine canoes from the mainland. Fifty "Salvages" there were at a guess, and John studied them in wonder. They were dressed in "deere skins," had "furres" hanging about their necks, and wore chains, earrings and "bandolieres" of copper.

The natives landed, beached their canoes, and seated themselves at a distance from the adventurers. A period of inspection followed while each group took careful measure of the other. John admired the newcomers: "for shape of bodie and lovelie favour, I think they excell all the people of America; of stature much higher than we; of complexion or colour, much like a darke Olive: their eie-brows and haire blacke, which they weare long, tied up behind in knots, whereon they pricke feathers of fowles, in fashion of a crownet."

After an interval, Gosnold suggested that Brereton "go unto them, to see what countenance they would make." John approached cautiously, then with more assurance as the Indians made "signes of joy." The native leader offered him the present of a large beaver skin; and when the Gentlemen Adventurers beheld it, they came on the run to get presents also. In no time the two contingents were "very great friends." Gosnold sent to the shallop for meat "readie dressed." From a purse of "tewed leather" a savage took a "Minerall Stone" and struck spark for a beachwood fire. Indians and whites dined together, and the English captain passed pieces of dressed meat, seasoned with mustard, to the chief, who sampled them, made a "sowre face" and passed them on to members of his tribe. All the braves made "sowre faces," for mustard proved an unacquired taste!

When the meal was over, the adventurers bargained for furs. Beads, knives, and trinkets were exchanged for peltry, although a few of the tribesmen coveted novelties. John overheard one brave offer a "beard of their making to one of our sailors, for his that grew on his face, which because it was of a red colour, they judged to be none of his owne."

With the coming of dusk the English retreated to a fort which they had constructed on the banks of an inland lake, and the "Salvages" established camp on "the furthermost part of the Island." For four days the visitors remained while acquaintance ripened into affection. John found the men "wittie" and possessed of linguistic facility. "How now (sirha) are you so saucie with my Tobacco?" he exclaimed smilingly, and was not a little astonished to hear his words echo back from the lips of a young warrior. Copper-skinned natives aided in the freighting of the *Concord* with sassafras, and a few of the more daring underwent the experience of sleeping on board. On the fourth day, all trading completed, the Indians signaled their intention of returning to the "maine." In their canoes, a short distance from shore, they lifted paddles in gestured farewell, uttering "huge cries and shouts of joy." On the beach the Gentlemen Adventurers cast their "cappes into the aire," brought out trumpet and cornet, and played the tunes of Old England, to which the "Salvages" plied their paddles until only a white trail on the water (the mark of the tame sea snail of Maushop) pointed toward the Narrow Land.

July, 1602, found Captain Gosnold and John Brereton safely back in London, but the adventurers were in sore trouble: Sir Walter Raleigh was irate. A shipload of sassafras, cure for plague and "plant of Sovereigne vertue," had been dumped on the London market, and, according to Sir Walter, that act infringed his rights as patentee.

The Earl of Southampton, patron of the expedition, listened to John Brereton's tales of the parklike forests on the island, of the cherry trees whose "stalke beareth the blossomes or fruit at the end thereof, like a cluster of grapes, forty or fifty in a bunch," of other fruit trees with orange bark "in feeling soft and smoothe like Velvet," of "ground nuts, fortie . . . on a string . . . as big as hennes egges . . . as good as Potatoes"; and of "Scallops, Muscles, Cockles, Lobsters, Crabs, Oisters and Whilks." Then he heard about cod! *Lie about horses, boast about dogs, but send for the Marbury Fish Stuffer if you will talk about fish!* A friendly playwright seated at the earl's table may well have listened with faint mockery to John's fish stories and to John's descriptions of courteous natives, "gentle of disposition."

The Earl of Southampton promised to appease "mightie Ralegh," and thought it not altogether amiss if Brereton write an account of the voyage. Despite Sir Walter's absorption in colonial schemes, he suffered from author's vanity, liked his name on a title page, and might be inclined to forgive a drop in the price of sassafras if he was supplied, to offset his unsuccessful voyages, with a "happie" expedition undertaken, according to title, "by the permission of the honourable knight, Sir Walter Ralegh." John complied and wrote an account that, of all early "Travailes," is, perhaps, sunniest. They had a good time and they all came home "improved in health" and much fatter than when they left England. In the taverns and on the streets, a sailor with a red beard, and others less resplendent, told of an island, "Elisabeth's Isle," where magical visions rode the sky, and fruit such as no man has seen clustered on orange branches: a paradise that they had left behind "with as many true sorrowful eies, as were before desirous to see it."

On such an island in a Brave New World, enchantments filled the air! So, one evening betwee 1603 and 1610, the players at the Globe Theatre in London found themselves strutting the boards in a comedy that poked fun at fish stories; the scene of their histrionic adventures an uninhabited island "of subtle, tender and delicate temperance," the grass lush, "lustie" and green, the ground tawny, like, as John Brereton would say, "our hempe lands in England." On the island a native appeared: "a man or a fish? dead or alive?" Trinculo, who saw it, exclaimed, "Were I in England now, as once I was, and had but this fish painted, not a holiday fool there but would give a piece

of silver: there would this monster make a man: when they will not
give a doit to relieve a lame beggar, they will lay out ten to see a dead
Indian . . . this is no fish but an islander."

Islander, fish-monster, Caliban — the native was agreeable to service, and, following the reputation of thieving "Salvages," traitorous
at heart:

> "I'll show thee the best springs: I'll pluck thee berries:
> I'll fish for thee and get thee wood enough . . .
> I prithee, let me bring thee where crabs grow;
> And I with my long nails will dig thee pig-nuts:
> Show thee a jay's nest and instruct thee how
> To snare the nimble marmoset; I'll bring thee
> To clustering filberts and sometimes I'll get thee
> Young scamels from the rock."

The courtier Gonzalo exclaimed:

> "For, certes, these are people of the island
> Who, though they are of monstrous shape, yet, note,
> Their manners are more gentle-kind than of
> Our generation you shall find
> Many, nay, almost any . . ."

Had a playwright his tongue in his cheek? Was the necromancing
of Prospero a jibe at such visionaries and optimists as John, who saw
Utopias in every grove, and peopled earth's uninhabited islands with
natives of "lovelie favour"? If John Brereton went to the stalls, in
1610, and heard Miranda say:

> "How many goodly creatures are there here!
> How beauteous mankind is! . . ."

would he have smiled, and smiling sighed for the land in which "in
mid May we did sowe . . . Wheat, Barley, Oats, and Pease, which in
fourteene daies were sprung up nine inches and more"?

BAKED BREAD AND ARROWS

"Yo, Yo, Yo," sang an Indian, dancing on the wet sand to attract the
attention of French sailors in a shallop that nosed its path toward

shore. Among outer shoals drifted an eighteen-ton bark, her rudder mended precariously with ropes. The Sieur de Poutrincourt, in command, cautiously maneuvred his vessel into a safe anchorage at the elbow of Cape Cod, perhaps passing through the very channels in which, six hundred years earlier, Leif Ericsson waited while a Gaelic man and woman ran over the wooded hills.

In 1606, Indian houses covered with thatch of woven grass were grouped among fields where corn waved, the yellowing stalks interlaced with a fringe of climbing beans. Cimnel and pompion glowed on the ground like fallen moons of harvest. Tobacco and furs hung high for drying. Grapes sagged under canopies of green, three-fingered leaves. "An excellent place," thought Samuel de Champlain, "to erect buildings and lay the foundations of a State, if the harbor were somewhat deeper and the entrance safer."

To mend the rudder a forge was necessary, so the Frenchmen set one up on land and also constructed a baking oven. In the departure from Port Royal fishing tackle had been forgotten. Fortunately the natives were ready to trade fish for almost any sort of trinket, and the beaches swarmed with oysters and clams. The shooting, too, was excellent. The Sieur de Poutrincourt killed twenty-eight sea larks with one shot — very remarkable — yet not to be contradicted when the master marksman was Ship's Captain and Gentleman of France. Samuel de Champlain busied himself sketching the harbor and lands adjacent. The maker of maps for Henry of Navarre was searching for a suitable place for the new "State" of which the Sieur de Monts would be patron and he, Champlain, provincial governor.

During the stay of the French vessel, five or six hundred savages assembled on the mainland. Eager to trade chains, collars, corn, beans, bows, raisins, and fish; naked save for loincloths made of "doe or seal skin," they danced and sang for the strangers; and when de Poutrincourt desired to find a safer way between the reefs, a friendly Indian piloted the boat, then leaped from it and swam to shore, fearing, as he maintained, to be taken by hostile tribes who camped along the southern coast.

Nearly a fortnight was required for the mending of the rudder. At the same time the cooks made bread that would last some fifteen days. The natives appeared in groups of ever-increasing size, warriors from more distant tribes — Cummaquids, Pamets, Nausets from the

region north by east that the French called Mallebarre. To overawe
gathering multitudes the Sieur de Poutrincourt sent ashore his ablest
swordsman who "brandished and flourished" two blades of tempered
steel. "Olive" warriors watched politely. They knew the tang of
sharp-edged weapons; but at sight of a bullet that passed through
wood on which their arrows made scant impression, they expressed
astonishment and fear.

On the tenth day of the visit, an Indian crept away from camp, a
stolen axe in his hand. The French fired after the miscreant, and the
Nauset Wampanoags withdrew in panic and fury. In a few hours all
wigwams within musket shot of the forge were taken down and carted
away. Into the woods went laden squaws, carrying on their backs
household wares and babies. Braves repainted their faces, fires burned
till dawn whitened the dunes of Mallebarre.

To quiet the native turmoil the Sieur de Poutrincourt, who saw life
in a French way, made an armed expedition to the place where the
Indian women were kept, and presented them with bracelets and rings.
He also gave hatchets and knives to the "old and distinguished men."
Braves repaid this generosity with "dances, gambols and harangues"
of which the Frenchmen understood neither word nor symbol.
Through it all medicine drums shook a faraway warning. The Sieur
de Poutrincourt, de Champdoré, his lieutenant, and Samuel de
Champlain, who had a knack for sensing the crux of a situation, believed that the feud was not terminated, and suspected the Indians
of a plan to attack the men who were working on shore and who stayed
at night "to guard that which could not be embarked . . . except
with much trouble."

On October 14, 1606, the rudder was staunch, and the bread baked.
The Sieur de Poutrincourt mounted a wooden cross upon the mainland, and at the same time ordered that the forge and its utensils be reembarked upon the ship. The baker and two men with him were engaged in baking hot cakes. They pleaded for time to finish their work,
and de Poutrincourt offered to send the shallop for them in the evening. No one, by his order, might spend the night on land.

As stars came over the many-cornered harbor, the shallop headed
for shore. Cakes were not cooked, though they smelled very sweet,
and the bakers not ready to go. For ten nights the French had slept
on land in safety. Why fear the eleventh? The beat of Indian medi-

cine drums and the weird and windy howling were only "Heathen Ceremonies." If two men from the shallop remained, that would make five, and a thousand savage "rabble" would never attack after one shot from a well-aimed gun. Two of the men who had come from the ship, overwhelmed by taunts of fear, and by the odor of hot, sweet bread, consented to remain.

Slowly the shallop regained the shadow of its vessel. The Sieur de Poutrincourt slept in his bed and no one fancied waking him, to report that his orders were unfulfilled and five men left at the ovens. Night continued cool and peaceful; but as the sun climbed Laughing Shoals, four hundred warriors crept toward the baking tent, and sent before them such a volley of arrows that "to rise up was death." Four of the sailors were asleep, the fifth sitting guard by the fire. The five swayed to their feet and, shouting for aid, raced toward the shore. The Sieur de Poutrincourt waked in a hurry; the whole ship waked with the pounding of feet on wooden decks and the cry of the watch: "Aux armes l'on tue nos gens."

De Champdoré took command of the vessel. De Poutrincourt, Champlain, Hay, Gravé, Loys Hebert the apothecary, and some eight or nine sailors crowded into the shallop and pulled swiftly for land. A sand bank lay between the vessel and the beach by which stood the baking tent. At ebb tide the shallop could not climb this bar, so the men, their muskets high over their heads, leaped into the water and waded to the waves' edge. There already, two French sailors drifted, face down, arrows in their backs, and foam about them reddening. A third, grievously wounded, struggled to keep his feet.

The men from the shallop fired their muskets and waited for powder mist to rise. When once again they could see clearly, all the natives had disappeared in the long, dawn shadows of the forest. Swifter than Wish-oh-wun-nan, the hawk, clever in ambush, at home in every bog and moor, pursuit of them was fruitless. The sun rose brightly behind harbor islands that lay to the east and took to themselves the underdarkness of the sea. The Frenchmen carried their dead to the foot of the cross that stood upon rising ground, and a wounded sailor, breathing his last, was laid beside the two who had been killed.

Against the low rhythm of orisons beat medicine drums. Over Latin funeral prayers, high derisive howling echoed through the motley of October's scarlet trees. Later, the French manned their shallop, rowed back to the ship, cared for their wounds, and looked from the rail to the Cross of France that guarded her first New England dead.

In less than three hours the savages, exultant with triumph, reappeared, beat down the cross, disinterred the bodies, stripped them of shrouds and built a fire preparatory to their burning. Once again de Champdoré took charge of the vessel while de Poutrincourt with an armed guard attempted a land attack before which the natives fled. The French reraised their cross. Mutilated bodies that had been flung "here, and there amid the heath," were brought together and buried. Prayers were intermingled with vows that "when it pleased God" the French would take a stern revenge.

It pleased God to send contrary winds. Twice from the harbor, named Port Fortuné (Stage Harbor, Chatham), the bark set forth and was driven back; and at the time of the second return, the natives approached in friendly mood, ready for trade. An armed contingent landed, but whenever the tribesmen saw weapons, they rapidly withdrew. Therefore the Sieur de Poutrincourt decided upon an "artifice." The most "robust and strong" of his men, supplied, each one, with a chain of beads and a fathom of match (hemp rope that burned slowly and was often used for the lighting of pipes or fires), were ordered to smoke with the Indians, and to "coax them with pleasing words so as to draw them into the shallop." If they proved unwilling to enter, "each one approaching should choose his man, and, putting the beads about his neck, should, at the same time, put the rope on him to draw him by force." If the natives proved too "boisterous . . . they should be stabbed, the rope being held firmly; and if by chance any of them should get away, there should be men on land to charge upon them with swords." During the "artifice," the cannon on the bark was kept in readiness to fire, to cover the retreat of the shallop if the victims attempted an attack.

"Through too great haste," the kidnapping failed. With swords the Frenchmen butchered some six or seven unsuspecting, unarmed Indians. Heads, cut off, were carried away to be exhibited at Port Royal. Nobody knows whether or not the murdered men were of the tribe that attacked the French ovens. Monomoyicks or Nausets, they laid themselves open to capture with a friendly innocence that would belie memory of previous treacheries. Their betrayers, uneasy by virtue of harsh success, beset by increasing misfortunes, had neither heart nor strength for continued exploration. Of the twenty-five mariners who set forth in June from Port Royal, by October three were dead, one dying, several wounded and several ill. Robert Gravé, son of Pont Gravé, had shot off his hand with a musket. Baffled, discouraged, with provisions short and men suffering from lack of medicines and salves, the Sieur de Poutrincourt ordered the ship's course north. Lovely Port Fortuné was no place for the immediate formation of a state. On its hills seven Indian bodies lay not far from the graves of three foreign sailors who rested in the shadow of a Cross of France left vigilant and solitary.

THE DEATH OF TISQUANTUM

Tisquantum, with blood at his lips, the "blood of death" Wampanoags call it, lay on a hill near Mallebarre and stared at the long sea. He had sailed across it as chained captive in the hold of Captain Hunt's vessel, crowded in with a cargo of dried fish and kidnapped Indians. He had been put up for purchase as a slave in the market at Malaga, redeemed by the Spanish Inquisition, and transported to London to the home of the Worshipful John Slaney where he learned to speak the English tongue in the lanes and markets of Cheapside. Sent to Newfoundland under Mason, Governor of the Plantation, he had been rediscovered there by Captain Dermor sailing under Sir Ferdinando Gorges. Dermor listened to nostalgic tales of the home of Pokanokets, of the "sickell Baye" and the Long Land cloaked with "verdurante soile." In 1619 Tisquantum sailed with Dermor, in an open five-ton pinnace, southward from Monhegan to the home of his childhood, future site of Plymouth Colony. The bones of the dead lay unburied among the ruins of his deserted native village; and of a "grate Pepol" who once mustered so many warriors that "God could not kill them," only a plague-stricken remnant survived, their courage "much abated" and they "as a people affrighted." Heartsick, in terror that the fever would smite him also, Tisquantum turned from the home of his fathers to follow his "Englisshe Captain."

Within three hunter's moons, a mortal fever racked the body of the faithful Indian guide. Lying on Monomoyick cliff, his thoughts returned to the time when he had rescued Dermor from detention by hostile Monomoyicks. Diplomat, loyal advocate, he "entreated hard"

for his captain and saved him, only to undergo with him a surprise
attack at Martha's Vineyard Island where an ambush was laid by
Epanow, like Tisquantum a kidnapped Indian, but one who proved
after escape from captivity a sullen, unforgiving foe. With fourteen
arrow wounds in his body, Captain Dermor escaped to his pinnace.
Tisquantum nursed him, followed him. In Virginia his English captain died.

Through sorrow, memory revived of "goodly fields . . . without
men to dress" them, where "sculs and bones" were still lying above
ground, "sad spectackle to behould." The young interpreter journeyed
north to help his tribesmen resow their acres and bury their plague-
marked dead. Among other unsolved mysteries he inquired concerning the fate of five Frenchmen who had been shipwrecked on Cape
Cod, two of whom were rescued by Dermor from cruel servitude as
slaves to sachems. Of the other three, one, he learned, was hewer of
wood and drawer of water for a vengeful Nauset chief. One had fallen
into the hands of a kindly master who gave him lands and an Indian
wife by whom he had issue. One carried a Bible, mastered the Wampanoag tongue, and translated bits of the Good Book to incredulous
listeners to whom he prophesied God's displeasure and the coming
of a destroying race. All five of the castaways had suffered and
"weept much."

In March, 1621, Tisquantum joined the English Plantation at Plymouth. After a life among hardy, resourceful adventurers, these settlers with their blank reliance upon prayers and God seemed to him
the veriest children, "not any amongst them that ever saw a beaver
skin!" The day after his arrival he realized that they were hungry;
went at noon to fish for eels and at dusk returned with as many as he
could lift in one hand. He taught the goodmen "how to set their corne,
wher to take fish," and explained that maize would not ear "excepte
they gott fish and set with it." He watched Massasoit, ruler of Wampanoags, don a "Horse-man's coat of Red Cotton . . . laced with a
slight lace"; and one day in August was informed by a perturbed settlement that John Billington, young nuisance, had wandered away
from the colony.

Procuring word of the youngster, he guided Bradford and ten companions in a shallop across the Bay to Barnstable Harbor. There a
squaw "judged to be no lesse than an hundred yeeres old" came to

look at the white invaders and made lament for her three sons carried off by Captain Hunt to servitude in Spain. Tisquantum heard her "great passion." It put him into sorrowful remembrance that no member of his own family survived to mourn for him, a thought that troubled him deeply as the shallop moved alongshore to Eastham where the boy, John, was said to be held in the custody of Aspinet, chief of the Pamet tribe.

The shallop eased into harbor. After sundown Aspinet came with a "great traine"; fifty unarmed warriors waded over bars to the shallop; fifty "stood aloofe with their bow and arrowes" in their hands. John Billington, "behung with beades," was delivered to Governor Bradford, and Tisquantum, serving as interpreter, took the chance to make covenant of peace between the Pamet chief and Plymouth men.

From the time of that expedition to Cape Cod to rescue John Billington until the second voyage that was to prove the undoing of the "White Man's Indian," Bradford remained unfailingly Tisquantum's friend. Another Wampanoag joined Plymouth settlement, one close to Massasoit's ear. Tisquantum thoroughly hated this Indian, named Hobamack, a fawning sycophant who made his way into the good graces of peppery Captain Standish, undermined Tisquantum among his white friends, and claimed that his words were no longer good and his influence among the tribesmen gone. No match for his rival in craft, hurt, jealous, the White Man's Indian invented a clumsy ruse, a pretended Wampanoag attack. This he designed to alienate the colonists from Hobamack and Massasoit. The ruse failed and an angry Massasoit demanded Tisquantum's head.

Governor Bradford did not rebuke his Wampanoag interpreter, nor did he give him up at once to the waiting emissaries of Massasoit who had come equipped with the sagamore's own knife with which to dispatch the offender. Known as he was in Monhegan and among northward tribes, Tisquantum might easily have found sanctuary. Instead, he walked into council, before the assembled community, faced the embassy of his chief and made fiery declaration of the ways in which Hobamack had been worker of his overthrow. Then he yielded himself to the magistrates and showed no sign of weakness, nor resentment, when they decided by treaty law that he must be given over to his tribe. He bowed his head in earnest prayer to the wise White God. As if in answer, around the Gurnet a wide-winged

vessel appeared, a ship that startled colony and embassy alike. Bradford permitted the suggestion that this craft might convey French
and Narragansets come to make war. Apprehensive, "mad with rage,
and impatient at delay," the embassy of Massasoit "departed in great
heat."

The ship heralded new colonists who later settled at Wessagussett;
and in the autumn (1622), the Governor of Plymouth foresaw that
supplies for the coming winter would be inadequate, especially as the
undisciplined newcomers were hungry and likely to remain so. He
planned a joint expedition using the *Swan,* Wessagusset pinnace,
for the collection of winter supplies. With Standish in command the
small vessel weighed anchor in the first days of November, encountered easterly wind, and was forced to put back. The expedition embarked again, again to return, and the Captain contracted a fever.
Bradford then took command. The pinnace passed successfully over
the "dangerous shoulds and roaring breakers" off Race Point, edged
along the coast of Nauset and into Chatham harbor.

There Tisquantum sickened of fever. The governor found for
him a native house, and from a bed of mats by the doorway the Wampanoag guide and interpreter looked toward the sea. He was forced
to keep the doormat open for he could not breathe in the stifling
smoke of the hut fire. Beyond his vision the Laughing Shoals bared
their teeth along the Rip. Further eastward over Lost Island shone the
sea trail of the last of Giants, who long since had forsaken the Nauset-
Wampanoag. Tisquantum thought of him, friend of the fallen race
whose power and courage, forever "abated," had been conquered, not
by avenging war, but by plague, most terrible of destroyers. The White
Man's Indian perceived neither victory nor defeat in the White Man's
possession of lands that rimmed the Bay. He looked long at grained
beaches, pale barriers to a slate-dark ocean. So the "sculs and bones"
of his tribesmen, assailed by the waters of Niba-nahbeezik, had been
sucked away into darkness, into the oceans of death. Pnieses, wizards,
medicine sages, sagamores, warriors. brown-bodied children: for them
no chanters wailed the death rites, no Christian God, no Kehtean,
cleaved the mists to save them. Too many they had been for burying.
No hand strong to bear them.

Governor Bradford entered the hut and sat down by his friend.
Tisquantum asked the Governor to pray that he might "goe to the

Englishman's God in Heaven"; then bequeathed "sundrie of his things to sundry of his English freinds, as remembrances of his love." He tried to tell his kindly master of what he had been thinking, but his throat burned and English words would not come to his tongue. On the sea night descended, cold, green, and gray with winter. Tisquantum buried his face in a deerskin cape and made no moan as the "blood of death" seeped into the woven mat.

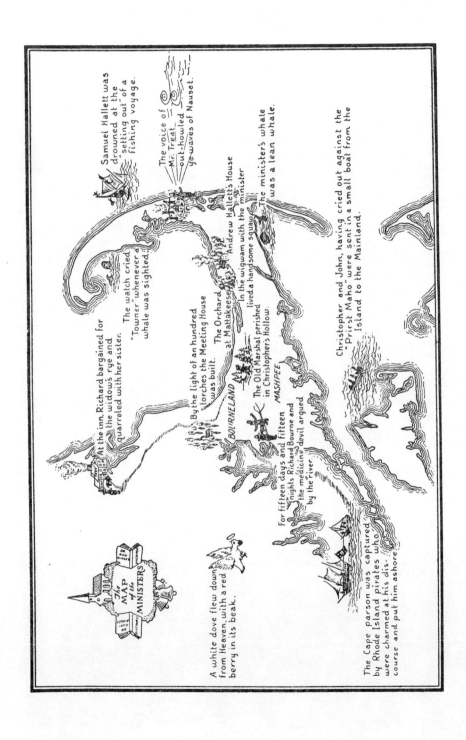

The Map of the MINISTERS

Samuel Hallett was drowned at the "setting out" of a fishing voyage.

The voice of Mr. Treat out-howled ye waves of Nauset.

At the inn, Richard bargained for the widows' rye and quarreled with her sister.

The watch cried "Towner" whenever a whale was sighted.

Andrew Hallett's House

In the wigwam with the minister lived a handsome squaw.

The minister's whale was a lean whale.

By the light of an hundred torches the Meeting House was built.

The Orchard at Mattakeese

Christopher and John, having cried out against the "Priest Maho" were sent in a small boat from the Island to the Mainland.

BOURNELAND

The Old Marshal perished in Christopher's Hollow.

MASHPEE

For fifteen days and fifteen nights Richard Bourne and the medicine devil argued by the river.

A white dove flew down from Heaven, with a red berry in its beak.

The Cape parson was captured by Rhode Island pirates who were charmed at his discourse and put him ashore.

CHAPTER III

MEN OF GOD
AND THE PRIMITIVE EARTH

On opposite shores of a turbulent ocean, two peninsulas stretched toward each other their mist-blown, beckoning arms. On the one, mirages flashed, signal fires burned, shining arrows leaped through forest lanes. On the other, rock cliffs glinted in an armor of rain, knights of Arthur rode the valleys, and Mark's castle crumbled into an encroaching sea. When Camelot became less than a dream and Queen Elizabeth who understood seamen lay stiff in her jewels under the Abbey arches, these two peninsulas bespoke one another. The great mariners of Devon and Cornwall freighted their ships for a westward venture, and interested the hearts and pockets of Englishmen in the founding of a colonial base for supplies.

Settlements struggled for existence at New Plymouth and Massachusetts Bay. Less than a decade after their founding, a few bold and ambitious landowners ventured southward to the narrow peninsula where they first had landed, where mariners found pleasant harbors in which to dispose of their cargoes of cattle, wormed grain, Bibles, and men who were hard to get along with at home. Serious, opinionated goodmen plowed the round hills and swamp-furrowed valleys, and pastured their sheep on barren upland moors. Unskilled in husbandry, girt in the doubtful armor of a wordy faith, they subdued and Calvinized that sea-rimmed arm of a continent; their Round Table a meeting house pulpit, their Knights of the Holy Grail ministers of a holy faith.

Men of the old stock of Devon and Cornwall, they wore fog for their coats and felt at ease in it; and when they heard "Wilde Lucifer," or the old Cornish Giants, moaning in a sea swell, wailing over the moors, they nodded comprehendingly for they felt that so it should be in the "New Peninsula, blood brother to the Old." Wooden houses, facing south, served as dials to the sun. When night salted the sky with stars, in wide hearths the children sat, looking up to these "ingle lights," listening to the howl of Indians — "Devil's Spue" to be fed with doctrines and rum.

Hearts ached for little towns of England, where fairs were held, where cottages crouched in the lee of red cliffs clustered beside Channel water. Lonely English expatriates sent back for a cloak or a wife, or a pair of silver buckles; perhaps for a forgotten recipe, or a remembered chair. At first their Colony newssheets and broadsides were devoted to the doings of King and Court, as though they were a stone's throw from Whitehall, or from Exeter where the royal messengers brought tidings express. Fash-

ions changed in England. On the "New Peninsula" posts were slow and life moved fast. Old clothes were remodeled to fit the new climate; old songs reechoed from new tavern rafters; old ghosts were remet on the sandy ruts of the King's Highway.

THE MISSIONIZING ZEALOTS

In the spring of 1637, oxen bearing cruel loads plodded along the ancient Indian trail that followed the curve of Cape Cod Bay, through the finest of arable land. The burdens consisted of beds, boxes, looms, linen, farm tools, trade tools, iron kettles "century strong," books, kegs, a marriage chest of English oak, women and children (though these took turns at walking). The load was heavy, the procession slow; and at its head, inscrutable as the Indian guides that led the way, marched "Ten Men of Saugus," their rifles in their hands. Despite impassivity, tumult throbbed at the pulse. These ten seasoned pioneers had endured already the rigors of the new continent, and after wise deliberation, had chosen for the site of their grants the inner curve of Cape Cod Bay. They were determined, *Deo volente,* to possess the silver peninsula, reap its meadows, plunder its timber, sleep on its hills till the "Trompe of the Judgement Day."

The Narrow Land wore a young green-yellow as though branch and blade had been dipped in frosted sunshine. Foredunes glittered in sudden mica, bay waves trilled like chickadee birds, far hills took color of violet, and so did the dunes where shadows deepened. Fresh pine tips enmeshed the light, while inward branches of tall trees held undeciphered blue. Over the earth drowsed opaline air that was mist of the soil, not fog; and no man could doubt the serenity of so indolent a countryside, save, perhaps, when he passed bogwater and heard a steady, hollow sighing at which the oxen shied and the dogs barked; and Edmund Freeman remarked to his wife that the marsh sobbed like a woman.

The Ten Men of Saugus unloaded their beds and kettles, not far from the hill where Thorwald Ericsson lay buried in his alien "home." Fair-haired invaders of the "Second Coming," they, also, erected booths while more permanent homes were in process of construction. But before autumn reddened the knee-high whortleberry bushes, a tiny cluster of "daubed dwellings" took shape around a narrow clearing, and the settlement known as Sandwich gave promise of success.

Curious natives stared from the hills, watched from the shadow of giant oaks, lurked in the near bog islands, safe from white man's thunder. Courage, a few rifles, a stockaded meeting house were all that the settlers could summon for protection; but peace and strength came neither from stores of powder, nor stockades, nor from the cross-Cape wall designed to keep out "ye hongrie ravening wolvs." Peace came from the "workes" of two men who rode unarmed through "Salvage Forrestes" to recruit new warriors of God from the "dark Spawn of Cain."

The White Sachem   Drums beat a rolling summons. Townsmen
of Mashpee   doffed their deerskin coats, buttoned themselves
into "Northumberland Cloth" and assembled in Sandwich Meeting House where, for the "Appetising of God" and the "Prompt Confution of the Devil," Richard Bourne of Devonshire expounded "faire doctrine." Lawyer trained at the Inns of Court, thickset, with iron-gray hair, he stood humbly, as became a secular, on the stair below the top step of the pulpit. His courage, his oratory controlled that dissenting flock who had been "rent with sore divisions" from the day when the Ten Pioneers "dug in" until in 1653 their "settled minister" abandoned them, leaving the benches in the meeting house ranged in two well separated rows, lest the opposing factions there "doe Violents to ech other."

Richard Bourne came to Sandwich in the autumn of 1637. He married young Bathsheba Hallett (daughter of Andrew Hallett, Gentleman), took up a large grant of land, built a house, acquired livestock, and was promptly fined eighteenpence for the keeping of three pigs "unringed."

Fourteen years of service he devoted to the welfare of the township, as one of two deputies to the General Court in Plymouth. But stimulated by his experience as speaker in the meeting house, gradually the destiny of the human spirit became more important to this clear-headed lawyer than the control of civil affairs. For twenty years, while new men were tried and found wanting, Bourne and his friend, Thomas Tupper, preached in a quaint alternation. When the congregation was assembled, noses were counted, and that one of the two amateur preachers who had the more numerous adherents delivered the sermon of the day.

Land disputes arose in the colony and involved Indian sachems. Richard learned to speak their language, and he, alone of all Cape goodmen, foresaw that a time was coming, even into that paradise of undeveloped farmsteads, when natives who thought a bead or a kettle more valuable than a score of acres would be without hunting lands or homes. Bearing this problem in mind, he appealed to the General Court for new land grants until his domain extended from the "South Seas to the Baywater"; a strip, across-Cape, that separated the lower part of the peninsula from the main body of the coast.

Dominance in land tenure assured him strategic supremacy. After he had acquired this control, he petitioned the court to set aside a grant, adjoining his own, in the finest agricultural region of the upper Cape, for the permanent use of Christian Indians. Incredulous outcry greeted this folly. Half the populace loved Richard Bourne; the other half whispered that he intended to make himself monarch of a heathen empire. John Cotton of Plymouth made a special expedition to Sandwich to "reason with the missionising zealot"; conversed with Indian preachers whom Bourne was training to lead their people and became convinced of the Cape lawyer's wisdom. As a result of his advocacy, a deed was signed, December 11, 1665, for a region of blue lakes and round, green hills to be called the "Mashpee Kingdome." In this way Richard Bourne gave to his followers sixteen square miles of territory, purchased from the Indians for the Indians; and in the year of Richard's death, his son, Shearjashub, succeeded in entailing this land "to the South Sea Indians and their children forever."

Slowly Richard acquired an army of Wampanoag converts, "Praying Braves" permitted to retain war dances and powwows, skilled bowmen ready to die for their Little Father. In the night on the hills of Mashpee a hundred pine torches were struck into the ground to form a fiery circle within which dark bodies moved ceaselessly, directed by a square-shouldered white sachem of bodily energy and gentle disposition. In the center of this circle, a little rectangular building gradually took form; for there, after the work of the day was done, the first Indian meeting house was constructed. In the darkness, squaws brought to Richard their ill or backward babies. He prayed over the papooses, held them quietly in his arms, prescribed cures for their ailments. Doctor, nurse, architect, legal adviser, judge, teacher and minister in one, he became, in the estimation of his converts, a super-being, capable of such miracles as the revival of a native baby who had been dead for hours.

In 1649 famine desolated the Narrow Land. Chilren died of the "chin-cough"; adults and children alike were "swept away by pox." Through the entire winter Richard fed his Praying Braves with corn purchased at his own expense and in the following autumn, when they repaid him, he gave the supplies to the poor. European diseases devastated Mashpee. The white sachem administered continually to victims of plague, smallpox, pneumonia, tuberculosis and cholera. With uncanny understanding of contagion, he tried to isolate the ill. The resultant separation of papooses from their mothers caused him enemies. His refusal to admit the medicine men of the tribe to the bedsides of the suffering brought upon him the hatred of a group of older braves. His rugged constitution withstood the unnatural strain upon it and the credulous whispered that he dabbled in medicine magic and bore a charmed life.

Mutterings never dared to come far from cover; too many warriors sharpened their spears to defend the Little Father. The faithful who gathered on the Mashpee hills, in mid-August, 1670, to see Richard Bourne ordained, were as ready to battle for him as to worship beside him; a host of dark faces that seemed to John Cotton and John Eliot "such an multitude as would make a swaying sea." All the distinguished Puritans were present at the ordination. Governor Prince attended; Josiah Winslow came from Marshfield with his charming wife, Ruth, daughter of William Sargent; gentle Thomas Walley rode over from Barnstable; and Thomas Hinckley of Yarmouth traveled the "Indian Trail."

They stared at ranks of Praying Braves who eyed them impassively, until English curiosity was tinged with a chill of fear. In less than five years these colonists were destined to face Wampanoag hostility, yet as they watched the "Ceremonies" they had only an imperfect realization of the significance of Bourne's work. Eliot and Cotton "laid on hands." Richard bowed his head in solemn acceptance of a ministry for which no high-tiered pulpit waited in New Boston or Plymouth, from which no pamphlets would "smite the Soule," nor cross the seas to England. Yet he held a key to the closed understanding between two races, knew the solution of the interracial problem of how to live and let live. When he set aside his own money to endow, forever, a Christian Indian settlement, he did not grasp the complexities of adjustment that might undermine the physical resistance of a dominated race. If the "Kingdome" that he formed came to sore pass, it was not for want of effort on the part of the white sachem who became a hero of legend.

Not long after the ordination, Richard's wife, Bathsheba Bourne, fell ill of a fever. The doctor administered "dosage and pills," the Indians brought forest herbs. Neither treatment cured her, and she died at a time when the colony was about to enter the critical period of King Philip's War. Richard, unaided, held to their new loyalties the Praying Braves of the Cape. Tired, footsore, discouraged, he labored through this period unceasingly, and at length turned for comfort to another staunch spirit, one also recently bereaved. Ruth Winslow of Marshfield had lost her husband, Josiah. The widow Ruth, no longer young, was "a little, lively smart Gentlewoman of very good sense and knowledge of ye strictest Piety, an excellent Spirit of Family Govt, very good skill in ye Diseases of Women and Children, very helpful to her neighbors." Richard wooed her with ardor and some fear of rivalry, although she had cancer of the lip. Older than the average suitor, he was not without opportunity to marry "in other quarters." "I have had divers motions since I received yours," he wrote to Ruth, in December, 1676, "but none suits me but yourself, if God soe incline your mynde to marry me . . . I doe not find in myselfe any flexableness to any other but an utter loatheness."

As the winter of 1675-76 passed, the Cape goodmen died in the war against Philip; the Cape Indians grew more bitter and restless; the widow remained coy. Disillusionment, almost despair, crept into the courting letters. Richard "rode upp to Plimouth," then on to Marshfield, to plead his suit. On the return from Plymouth, he bargained for the sale of the widow's rye, and quarreled with her sister. On a clear April morning, the horse stood saddled at the inn door; Richard was about to leave for Sandwich, when Ruth's sister, "above in the chamber," sent for him to come up. He felt inclined to dodge argument, to ride, instead, into the untroubled sunshine. He replied that he was on the point of departure, and asked her to "step down." She "would not." The "Missionizing Zealot" had a genuine

THE ORDINATION OF RICHARD BOURNE BY JOHN ELIOT AND
JOHN COTTON, MASHPEE, 1670

dislike of appearing "proud or uncourteous"; he went at once to the upper room and "cald for one quart of wine to make the drink." The lady and the minister drank in ominous silence, then she let fall the "tydings" that as soon as the couple were married she intended to sue for land. Richard wrote to Ruth about it. After an ironic description of the quarrel and of the threat of legal process, he offered his "beloved" that terrifying consolation of the protective mind: "I give you but a hint of things . . . I would not have you disquited."

When spring deepened toward summer, the widow, in a letter to her parents, bemoaned her "sad and solitary condicon." The Sargents recognized the symptom and offered to their daughter "full liberty of chois." Ruth then sent word to Richard that she was coming to Barnstable, via Sandwich, and would be married from the home of relatives there. The busy minister received her letter, recovered spirits, and sent her a "paire of shoes by William." "I pray you make use of them, you have them freely," he wrote; then added, as a final appeal, "come to our house as you goe to Barnstable. Doe not break my heart quite as to go by and not see me."

The two were married a few weeks later, while Elder John Chipman of Barnstable, destined to be Ruth's third husband, shook his head in disapproval of the match. The widow was too "worldly" to be the wife of a man of God about whom a halo shone as he preached at night in the forest, and because of whom the Devil, in despair, slit his Satanic tongue.

Elder John Chipman believed much of the gossip; of the tales that sleep, long since, in ancient Burying Acres. All men agree that strange stories of Richard existed, but only fragmentary memories, recollected phrases, remain. At one time an angel appeared before him in the forest and touched his brow with a golden sword of which he always bore the scar. He frequently wrestled with Lucifer and always defeated his adversary, though his arms became twisted, his shoulders thick with the weary strain of the fight. He met a witch doctor by a river, and solicited Christian conversion. The angry magician chanted a bog rhyme and Richard's feet became rooted in quicksand. With all his strength he could not stir. "Let us have a contest of wits," said he. "If I lose I agree to serve you. If I win, you shall release me and trouble me no more." The medicine devil agreed to this, so for fifteen days and fifteen nights they discoursed by the river.

The tide swam up; the tide swam down; the sun climbed over Nauset Sea, and paused for a while on the top of the sky to hearken to their wisdom. Still Richard Bourne and the witch devil argued by the river. The medicine man began to feel empty, like an air-full reed. He swayed where he stood; but Richard Bourne was as firm on his feet as when the contest began. Every now and then, while the witch doctor spoke, taking his turn at showing what he knew, a white dove flew down from heaven and laid a round, red berry on the lips of Richard Bourne. Once the dove let go his burden "one sand-dropping" of the hourglass too soon. The berry rolled to the edge of the bank and caught in the river mud. Then the witch doctor saw what the dove was doing and tried to lay his spells on it. But the bird flew past, merry as a song, and came and went, giving sustenance to the white sachem and none to the heathen witch.

By and by the medicine devil could stand upon his legs no longer, so he laid him down on the ground. The minute that he stepped off his feet, Richard Bourne could walk again, and went at once to his house to fetch a bowl of wild turkey soup. Before he took one taste off the ladle, he offered the bowl to the fainting witch who put his lips to the rim and drank till all the soup was gone. Now that bowl, made of pure silver, shone inside as bright as a mirror, and in the bottom of it, when the last drop of soup was drained away, the medicine devil saw reflected all damnation and the Judgment of sinners. He fell on his knees, and the good white sachem blessed him and taught him how to become a loyal Christian brave.

Meanwhile the berry that the dove let fall grew and fattened by the river. Finding it there, the Cape men knew there was truth in the story that the cranberry came down from heaven in the beak of a winging dove.

No man knows how the white sachem died, or where his bones lie buried. Some of his disciples maintained that he walked across Turkey Bay and like Weetucks, Giver of Knowledge, vanished in the west. Others believed he was murdered by a band of hostile Wampanoags who objected to his method of isolating the ill. His followers are reputed to have come upon his mutilated body, carried it into the Indian church, and by torchlight secretly buried it under the altar floor. Because of this, the Indian meeting house became a site of pilgrimage. A light was seen on the packed sod of the flooring, over the spot where the body lay. Ailing children, brought in the night and placed in the glow of this incandescence, recovered their lost strength. When the church was torn down and another built in its stead, no bones were found in the sod, which is proof, according to some tribesmen, that he was never buried there; but according to others, it is only an indication of great sanctity, since, without having to wait for the blaring trumpets of Judgment, *all* of Richard rose to heaven when he grew tired of listening to evil, and when no more babies were brought to him to cure.

After his death, his sons and his grandsons served the "Mashpee Kingdome," and so did Indian preachers, equipped to rule as well as teach; such men as Simon Popmonnet and Solomon Briant who loved the Bournes and the Bournes loved them, and who would have made a great race of the Wampanoag from the territory of Mashpee, if disease had not taken such heavy toll, and if the cupidity of lesser white men had not wrested power from the Bournes and placed it in the hands of politically appointed "Superintendents."

In time the broad acres of Bourneland were sold and divided; the strip across-Cape was tethered by thick ribbons of road; and of late years a great canal cuts a gash through the slopes of the "Kingdome," bringing to mind the prophetic qualities of an ancient rhyme:

> Richard is walking the Hills of Bourne
> Crying for his Lost People;
> So he will walk till the waters churn
> Over the topmost steeple.

The Arc of   Governor Robert Treat of Connecticut had twenty-one
Crystal   children of whom Samuel was the eldest. Early in life
Samuel learned to dominate. Fate gifted him with a voice whose harsh resonance penetrated to vast distances, and Samuel cultivated the quality of being heard. He was graduated from Harvard in 1669 and settled at Eastham as minister in 1672, with a house and land and a good supply of firewood cut and brought to the door. He received £50 annually as stipend, no mean salary for a young minister when one considers that Thomas Prince, as Governor of the Colony, drew £58.

Samuel looked about for a wife, selected Eliza Mayo, and they were married in the second year of his pastorate. In the following twenty-two years she bore him eleven children and continued in all ways a model of "piety and acquiescence." Samuel was not easy to live with. He shouted when he was offended and he shouted when he wanted a glass of water. He indulged in unnatural peals of laughter sudden as thunderclaps and completely devastating to the nerves. He was intense about hell and intense about the way that Eliza cut his hair in "ye thrid weake of ye moone." Eliza was a strong woman, but in time even she wore away, and died twenty-two years after her marriage, leaving a houseful of frightened, tempestuous children, and a husband who genuinely grieved for her and endeavored to be prompt and wise in the finding of someone who could fill her place. The widow Easterbrook, daughter of Mr. Willard, minister of the "Old South" in Boston, consented to marry Samuel and take charge of his household. Three more children were added to the family and Samuel continued to shout.

Mr. Willard, a man of importance and distinction in the colony, sometime President of Harvard, invited his son-in-law to preach at the Old South Church in Boston. Samuel produced his best sermon, burning with sulphuric oratory. "Impenitent sinners will writhe in Hell with a thousand devils rending and tearing and mascerating them throughout all Eternity," he yelled, in a voice that could be heard "at a great distance from ye meeting house where he was preaching, even in the midst of ye winds that howl over ye plains of Nauset." The congregation of the Old South suggested to Mr. Willard that he should refrain from inviting that strange Mr. Treat, of Cape Cod, to discourse in their pulpit again. The Cape minister was no doubt pious and worthy, but "horrid preaching" made his doctrine difficult to attend. Mr. Willard smiled politely — not without reason was he to prove a diplomatic college president. He borrowed his son-in-law's sermon, waited a few weeks, and then delivered it verbatim from the same pulpit. The Old South was delighted — such grace, such wisdom! Never had Mr. Willard preached a more interesting sermon; so excellent that they requested that printed copies of it be made.

No record tells us whether or not Samuel heard his father-in-law repeat his unwelcome words. He had not much time to observe the manner in which other men preached, for Samuel Treat was an eccentric, dominated by a "great worke." His voice, his erratic laughter, his rhetorical flights of brimstone were more or less understandable to his people, but they could not follow his determination to speak the Indian languages, to mingle with Indians at their festivals. Powwows were unquestionably ceremonials of the devil. Good Mr. Treat had no business to caper around in them, taking his turn at smoking a magic pipe, and jibbering heathen words.

Samuel paid scant attention to the protests of his deacons. The Doanes were always deacons, and the Doanes were always protesting. Samuel recognized that he, and he alone, had supervision over all the souls on the lower Cape; *all* the souls from Pamet Lands (in Truro) to Monomoyicks (in Chatham). The woods were full of red men who were established in more or less settled villages. Would the guidance of a handful of Christians be anything in the sight of the Lord, when Samuel stood before the ultimate tribunal and reported on his entire district? Missionary work was at hand and a born missionary to do it. The louder he yelled the more the Indians admired him. He preached "good medicine"; he preached action; and he understood the necessity for developing in the natives their own powers of thought.

"I have from time to time imparted the gospel of our Lord Jesus Christ to these Indians in their own language," he wrote to Increase Mather, "and I truly hope not without success. I continue in the same service, earnestly imploring a more plentiful outpouring of the Spirit upon them . . . They have four distinct assemblies in as many villages belonging to our township; with four teachers of their own choice, who repair once a week to my house to be themselves further instructed, *pro modulo meo,* in the concernments proper for their service and station. . . . There are besides four schoolmasters, who teach their youth to read and write in their own language. They have six magistrates, and three stated courts."

All this, so modestly recounted, was the work of Samuel himself, with little aid from the church members who regarded his mission as a waste of time. In storm and sunshine, in illness and health, he rode over his wide domain, sometimes a four-day ride from end to end of it, teaching, supervising, judging and, despite the deacons, risking his immortal soul by partaking in Indian ceremonials of whose meaning he was not always sure. At Potanumaquut, Thomas Coshannag,

Indian preacher and schoolmaster, was always needing help in teaching, in economic problems, in land controversies, as well as in the saving of souls. Samuel rode from Coshannag to Meeshawn and Punonakanet where Munsha was trying to teach Indian trappers and fishermen the words of the White God. Then, without rest, to Sakatucket where dark-skinned Manasseth had set himself the difficult task of instructing without books in the reading and writing of two languages: his own and that of Samuel Treat. Finally off to Monomoyick where John Cosens was waiting for him, anxious to refer a bit of unclear doctrine requiring the aid of a scholar in the "writing down" of Monomoyick dialect that differed in small but important ways from the Nauset tongue. Laughing men in the taverns up-Cape remarked that Sam Treat's Indians could write the King's English, which Sam Treat's deacons could not.

A queer torch, this, that flickered on the edge of an angry ocean; a single torch that soon went out leaving no dedicate fire. One of the few white men on the American continent who saw that the way to help Indians was to give them the tools of knowledge and then let them manipulate those tools in their own fashion!

Samuel's constitution of iron could not withstand the relentless requirements of his "domayne." Yet he lived to a good age and was spoken of as the "little father." Never a Bourne of Bourneland; no romance, no magnetism; the heroic aspect was alien to all thought of him. Indians would never canonize him, nor build about him legends of bouts with devils, or martyrdoms of the flesh. Yet at his death, a "manifestation of the heavens" occurred, as though singling him out for that greatness which never had been his upon earth.

The "Great Snow," a storm famous for generations, came in the winter of 1717, while Samuel Treat lay dying of palsy. The Indians, with their queer clairvoyance, had prophesied that he was dying several weeks before his illness became serious. They brought their wigwams and gathered in great numbers in the vicinity of his house. Now and again they sent their preachers, men whom he had known and loved, to inquire at the door. Hearing that his hour drew near, they withdrew silently, and the snow that had been falling steadily for a long time became suddenly so dense that the watchers could not see a hand held out in front of them. They settled down in their wigwams and waited for the storm to pass. The little house of the minister would be knee-high, window-high, finally ceiling-high in snow, if the white birds of the devil god, Mahtahdou, persisted in fighting among the heavens and scattering their plumes upon earth. Driven by fierce winds from Nauset Sea the flakes continued to fall and to be swept, now here, now there, in drifts as high as dunes. Then, as suddenly as the storm had come, it ceased. The wind dropped to a whisper, the sun shone upon newly contoured hills and valleys glittering in white. "Our little father has gone," said the Indians to one another. They strapped their snowshoes over their moccasins and hurried through the forest to the clearing around the minister's house.

When they reached the edge of the brush they stared for a moment in shocked bewilderment. A huge drift had piled up in the clearing and the little house was nowhere to be seen. For a moment they waited, horror-stricken, then saw smoke rising from the center of the expanse. Swiftly they climbed the slope, only to pause again in a be-wilderment greater than the first. From the top of the snowhill they looked down on a little brown house with the "curtins" of the great-room lowered, a little house completely untouched by snow, in the basin of an enormous, circular drift. Before the coming of the great storm, the winter had been mild. Around the dwelling place where Samuel Treat gave up his soul to God, the grass was still as green as though he lay in an eternal springtime. Outside that area of immunity, drifts eddied into a ring of white higher than the rooftree. The Indians circled around that ring, voicing their wild, monotonous cries of mourning and staring in reverence at the house of one so powerful in Christian magic that even the white birds of Mahtahdou could not touch it with their wings.

Deacons, goodmen, Indians worked all that night and all the next day tunneling drifts that had melted in a sudden thaw, then frozen into silver ice. Deacon John Doane was not there to direct the work and grumble at its accomplishment. Ten years before, at the ripe old age of one hundred and ten, he had gone to his own reckoning, rocked in the cradle in which he insisted upon sleeping during the last years of his life. But John Doane, Jr., dug for him, and protested for him when the Indians sought the right to bear their "little father's" body to the grave. Five hundred praying warriors, at least a thousand Indian men, women and children stood outside the minister's house, and every one of them had been taught by Samuel with the aid of only eight native teachers.

Fifteen years after Samuel Treat's death, the Indian inhabitants of Eastham numbered one hundred and six souls.

In well-populated Boston and Cambridge, the "Great Snow" so blockaded the streets that the magistrates of the city were not able to return to their homes from Parson Brattle's funeral. But the desolate road to the Burying Acre in Eastham was smoothed and cleared long before the body of Samuel Treat was ready to take its last journey. John Doane, Jr., was overruled. Relays of Indian converts bore Samuel to his resting place. He passed, for the last time, over the grass by the doorstone, then through a triumphal archway that no hero knew before him and no hero has known since; under an arc of crystal, shining in the sun like a fallen rainbow.

Something of the awe of that passing crept into the epitaph on his tombstone. In an age when puns and sordid verse stripped dignity from every grave, chiseled in stone at Eastham are the words:

> Here lies the body of the late
> learned and reverend Samuel Treat,
> the pious and faithful pastor of
> this church, who, after a very zealous
> discharge of his ministry for the
> space of forty five years, and
> laborious travail for the soules
> of the Indian natives, fell asleep in Christ.

"AMOROUS MR. BACHILER"

June 5, 1632, was a fair morning in New Boston. The good ship *William and Francis,* Captain Thomas in command, eased into harbor after a voyage of eighty-eight days. On the deck stood Mr. Stephen Bachiler surrounded by his little group of "followers," six in number, "mostly daughters and sons-in-law." Stephen, nonconformist, seventy-one years of age, looked about him with the ardor and excitement of seventeen. His youthful temperament, his great physical and mental strength, his power over human souls, had caused the Bishops of England to argue against his heresies in a struggle to prevent his secession from the Established Church. When at last they realized that he was irretrievably lost to them, they "ejected" him with a bitterness that put the king's guards on his trail. He fled to Holland for sanctuary, but found there no opportunities for the construction of that "Holy House without Ceremonies" toward which his heart yearned.

In the winter of 1632 he embarked for the colonies, planning to sojourn for a time with friends, then lead his flock into some bountiful wilderness where he might fashion a church proud in its separation from state, unique in its simple service, with a congregation beloved of one another, and possessed of that rare tenderness of which at moments Stephen Bachiler himself exhibited no inconsiderable share.

The women were busy with the last-minute packing of their possessions for "landing hour"; the men, gathered in small groups, peered at the new shoreline, green and promising. Almost every man of them expected to plow a living from the soil. As Stephen walked around the deck, observing the "landskip" from all angles, he caught a glimpse of a solitary figure behind a drying sailcloth. He hesitated a moment, then turned, and circling the sailcloth faced a young girl, her dark eyes red with tears, her white cap awry.

"My poor daughter," said Stephen figuratively, since at the moment he could not remember her name. He took her cold hands into his, and reminded her gently of the comfort that lay in submitting to the Lord's will. She nodded disconsolately; and having done his duty as minister, Stephen descended from the general to the particular and inquired what was wrong. The girl hesitated for a minute, then lifted streaming eyes.

"I cannot bear to leave thee," she sobbed. The white-haired nonconformist was amazed. This particular phenomenon in women always startled him, although in his seventy-one years he had encountered it many times. He tried hastily to recall when he had talked with the pretty child. She might have been one of half a dozen, for during the long eighty-eight days, battling with rough seas, sickness and fear, Stephen found it necessary to have "spiritual understandings" with almost every woman on board. To his rescue came a technique acquired through long experience. He comforted her tenderly, told her about the settlement that he intended to make in the wilderness, where, God willing, she could join him — she and her family, he added hastily. He was ashamed, after eighty-eight days spent in that

small company, that he was hazy about the girl's name. He wondered
whether or not he was growing old; seventy-one, yet the sensations
of youth surged through him like an influx of the Divine Will.

Suddenly the girl stood on tiptoe, and kissed him upon the lips.
Stephen glanced around anxiously. The drying sail hid them from
passengers, and from shore they could not be identified. He breathed
a sigh of relief; for that had been a wicked kiss, worldly, conveying
the thrill of devils' brew. He must correct the error at once. Eyes
kindling, he leaned down from his commanding height. His white
hair, the look of ministerial sovereignty about him, created the impression of a halo. He kissed the maid on her red lips, a stately, ceremonial kiss, full of the quiet benignity and harmony of the church.

Nineteen years later, in the autumn of 1651, Stephen Bachiler
stood on the deck of a little vessel that was awaiting fair winds to clear
Boston Harbor for a return to England. Stephen was ninety years of
age and his work in the colony was done. He had founded a thriving
plantation that meant nothing to his spirit. He had lost a plantation
that had embodied his soul. The "Holy House without Ceremonies"
had been started at Mattakeese, an Indian place on the peninsula of
Cape Cod, and the settlement had failed of permanence. He tried to
relive the passionate strivings of that winter, as he had relived them
a thousand times; tried to see wherein he might have labored harder,
endured more, or so have governed the spiritual lives of his little
colony that their enterprise should have merited success. Winthrop
and his "proud-mouthed hierarchy," insisting on the interdependence
of church and state, had wrecked the settlement; Winthrop and a host
of gossipy enemies who read into Christian gentleness a score of evil
things. Stephen tried to shut the failure from his memory. Remembering it too bitterly was like reproaching the Lord. Yet whenever
he stopped thinking of the "Holy House," his mind reverted to his
third wife, young Mary Bachiler, who was to undergo torture — hard
to believe in relation to her young, silken body.

Before the ship sailed for England, word reached him of the verdict
of the court:

We do present George Rogers and Mary Bachelleer the wife of Mr.
Stephen Bacheleer minister for adultry. It is ordered that Mrs. Bacheller

for her adultery, shall receive forty stripes save one, at the first town meeting held at Kittery, 6 weeks after her delivery and be branded with the letter A.

What had Stephen done, that this dark affliction was placed upon him? His young bride an adulteress, lovely Mary Bachiler with full red lips and smiling eyes! After the death of his second wife he had chosen Mary among many "eligibles" because she gave promise in all things of warm, household joy. He shuddered as he remembered the iniquity of her mind. All the chance peccadilloes, the trivial, spontaneous demonstrations that his enemies twisted into evil intent, with all these she had charged him, comporting herself as no wife should, telling him that he was too old for love! She did not seem to realize that his youth (at ninety!) was a thing to rejoice in, a miracle, a gift of God.

Twenty years before, when for the first time he stood upon the deck of a vessel in Boston Harbor, with the New World before him, the colony that was to be his own had been a living project in his brain. He journeyed first to Saugus (Lynn it was called, later), where friends were waiting to welcome him. Immediately upon arrival he formed a little church, six relatives and a few friends constituting his "flock." The church was devoid of the usual ceremonies, but into it he tried to infuse a sense of the Lord's presence and mercy. Almost immediately trouble began. Women came to hear him. Women stayed to pray with him. The strange power that he never understood made him able to convey the word of God lucidly to goodwives and turgidly to men. His opposition to the proposed union between church and state alienated him from Winthrop and the civil powers in Boston. He was persecuted in New England as he had been in "Ould England," except that the bishops condemned him on "churchly grounds" whereas the colonists failed to understand his magnetic power over the weaker sex, and condemned him for moral frailty.

Four months after he reached Lynn he was arraigned before the court at Boston: "Mr. Bachiler is required to forbeare exercising his gifts as a pastor . . . until some *scandles* be removed." "Scandles"! The word haunted him. Ever since those first few months in Saugus he had been watched with suspicion, his kindliness attributed to false motives, his attraction for women regarded as a crime against the Lord. He petitioned to leave Saugus, with his family of sons and daughters.

The petition was accepted, and then, before removal could be accomplished, he indulged in public prayer. The magistrates sent for him, alleging the formation of a new church. He refused to have speech with them, so they summoned a marshal and he was led, like any common criminal, into their presence. He promised to leave town in three months, and to fulfill that promise went to Ipswich in February, 1636. Almost immediately difficulties arose. All the women of the parish turned from the church which their husbands had formed and elected to worship under the guidance of Mr. Bachiler. A few of the husbands followed the wishes of their wives, and Stephen saw at last his wilderness community in process of formation.

He was too impetuous to be discreet. Early spring was the time for "setting up a plantation," for planting, and building of houses; but if he waited until spring, he feared that the smoldering anger of goodmen, whose wives worshiped with him in defiance of their husbands' wishes, would reach the magistrates, and that he would again be forbidden the right to preach. The few families who cleaved to him might lose interest, without the inspiration of his spoken faith, and the chance for his "settlement" would die. Better starvation in the wilderness than that, reasoned Stephen Bachiler, who believed in himself and in a Lord that provides for wilderness sparrows.

The little group of "Worshippers" decided upon a grant of land on the peninsula of Cape Cod. Already a thriving community had taken root in Sandwich and one was projected farther down-Cape at Eastham. Between those two settlements lay a region of tall trees, pure springs, and fertile meadowland. The men of Saugus who had settled Sandwich wrote, describing this new land and promising to the prospective plantation their hospitality and aid.

Stephen Bachiler's followers were men of the type that inclines to quarrel with those in authority, and such men have a habit of losing their worldly goods. No money was forthcoming to purchase horses to bear them over the hundred miles of forest that they must traverse to reach their plantation. So Stephen prepared to walk. He was seventy-six; and he and his companions started in the late autumn when wind squalls swept the gaudy leaves downward, to make a "Turkey Carpet." A hundred miles the colonists walked, with Indians watching in the forests, and poorly paid native guides to show the travelers their way. The autumn air felt tensely cold and an offsea storm was mixing. The last part of the journey they battled against surging wind. When the "Worshippers" stood at last on their grant at Mattakeese, salt mist pricked like nails against their haggard faces, wind sucked through soggy coats, and drifts of spicy fog billowed over the hills.

Stephen Bachiler found temporary homes for his people at Sandwich, and in adjacent Indian wigwams. He hewed trees, carried timber on his old back, dug with frantic strength at the frozen ground. His small personal possessions he bartered with the Indians in return for food and labor. He lived, himself, in the meanest Indian wigwam, an example to his people. A very beautiful Indian woman lived in the same wigwam. She was not very clean, but she was pleasant, and anxious to learn Christian ways. So the "scandles" continued. Before Easter, even his sons-in-law looked at him with smiles, or averted eyes.

When spring came, the settlement died at the heart. Men were too weary to attempt the early planting, too much of the land required difficult clearing, and the women were at each other's throats. One day, when the scent of the mayflower mingled with the smell, like salted violets, that the sea gives out in April, the little company disclosed to Stephen their intention to disband. He showed no emotion. To those who were still faithful to him, he promised a new settlement in a region less exposed. His body was paying for the cruel tax that he had put upon it, and for the first and only time in his life, Stephen felt old.

Thirteen years later, as he paced the deck of the vessel that was to convey him back to England, he thought of spring in Mattakeese, and knew, as he had not known at the time, that the vision of a wilderness Zion had shattered in his mind. Even his immediate family, who upheld him stalwartly, sensed this change, and no longer felt it necessary to remain with him, as a religious group. Deborah, his daughter, had always been one to love the sea, and John Wing, her husband, decided to settle in Sandwich. Stephen gave them his blessing, though his pride cried out against their desertion.

Once he walked to the edge of a bog in Great Marshes where an Indian she-devil was said to suck men down. He looked at the marsh for a long time, then walked away. His second wife, Helena, kind-hearted, motherly, saved him from desolation. He ate her good cooking and knelt under the speaking trees to pray for heavenly guidance. Then, once more on foot, a tall old man with white hair, he led his little group of heartsick, weary followers to Newbury where someone was needed to preach.

In Newbury, Stephen received a grant of land and two houses; but when he started to make known the word of God, he met with instant opposition. Men did not want an old minister about whom there were "scandles," who had failed in his "settlement," who had strange ideas about the simplicity of the service, the unimportance of preaching, and the importance of gentleness and love. What had gentleness to do with the expounding of sound doctrine, or the strong exhortations needed to avert hell?

Stephen petitioned for the right to found a plantation at Hampton. The Massachusetts legislature, desiring to have him isolated among his kind, promptly granted this request. At Hampton the freemen appreciated good acreage and wanted a minister not too strict, not too young and zealous, not too expensive. They understood the ways of worldly success, and Hampton thrived with an almost unnatural rapidity. At first Stephen could not believe his good fortune; yet a curious stagnation of spirit beset him almost at the outset of his occupancy. The irony of this easy dominance obsessed him. His soul had gone into the making of Mattakeese, to no avail. Mattakeese was the "Holy City without Ceremonies." What travesty was this? Stephen, too simpleminded, too unanalytical to know the roots of his trouble, laughed a great deal, drank too much wine, and when Helena was not looking, chucked the "maides of Hampton" under their pretty chins.

His success as leader of the community resulted in offers from other towns. Newbury promised him more land if he would return to them. Ipswich proffered him a large grant if he would reside there for three years. He declined, and later came into the possession of three hundred acres in Hampton, and gradually acquired a reputation as an authority on problems of land tenure. As a token of his happiness, he gave to the meeting house a bell made in England. Bells were rare in those early days when townsfolk were drummed to service. He delighted to walk across the green fields, to preach in his little square church in answer to a summons from "ye merrie English bell."

Despite this worldly success, Stephen was not wise. Out of him

had gone the only true wisdom that he had ever possessed, the inspiration that perished in the frozen forests of the Cape. The Reverend Timothy Dalton established a rival parish at Hampton. Stephen
tried to care, meant to fight, for the community that was his; but
instead of the conquering of men's souls he contented himself with
the conquering of their wives. By women he was ruined, and by
women exalted; and in 1641 he was excommunicated for un-
chastity. Governor Winthrop records the case with obvious distaste:

> Mr. Bachiler, the pastor of the church at Hampton, who had suffered
> much at the hands of the bishops in England, being about eighty years
> of age and having a lusty, comely woman to his wife, did sollicit the
> chastity of his neighbour's wife, who acquainted her husband therewith;
> Whereupon he was dealt with, but denied it, as he had told the woman
> he would do, and complained to the magistrate against the woman and
> her husband for slandering him.

Stephen's complaint against the slanders was accepted, and in the
sweetness of revenge, he tried to find content. Instead, the irony of
this second victory brought not stagnation of soul but reawakening.
As always with Stephen Bachiler, the woman tempted him with
adoration. In response, he found her desirable, and "sollicited her
chastity." Believing that confession meant death to his career as a
minister, believing that it entailed the loss of his lands and home,
nevertheless when the "merrie English bell" called him to the church
that he had built, he walked across the green fields and as "the
Lord's supper was to be administered, he voluntarily confessed the
attempt."

Leaving a shocked congregation, he hurried home and awaited
the deacons who would come to dispossess him. They appeared
promptly, but by some strange process of mind, men who had been
foul in their suspicions were charitable in their triumph. He was to
keep his land, they said; his parishioners would before long endeavor
to reinstate him; in the late autumn his beloved flock would petition
that he be restored.

This mild refusal to accept his renunciation would have been the
making of many a man. For Stephen Bachiler, it was the beginning
of the end If he had been permitted to carry through his battle
against the wilderness, if he had been permitted to walk in the shadow

of his sin, paying full penalty for transgression, the world might have heard a different story of the minister of the "Holy House." In an age of stern punishment, Stephen went free, a belittling experience for a man with the makings of a martyr, but no daily saint. He lived on at Hampton and Helena fed him well. He chucked the pretty girls under the chin, and smiled his fascinating smile at a weak and pleasant world.

When his house at Hampton burned down and he lost his household possessions, Stephen did not care. Exeter invited him to "settle," but the court forbade his acceptance on the grounds of his evil reputation. He tried a dozen different churches, wandering always further to the north. When he was almost ninety years old, Helena died and his daughter suggested that he retire from active life. She offered him a refuge with her in Sandwich. Stephen shuddered at the summons. The memory of that winter at Mattakeese lay like ice in his heart. He could endure the sneers of men and the garrulous tongues of women, he could face the gossips who called him adulterer and false prophet, but he could not bear the mute witness of a few felled trees, of a few half-built houses, of unplowed land dedicated to the making of that earthly paradise of which he had been given custody but no enduring possession. Also, he was eighty-nine, and felt eighteen! He could not imagine an inactive life.

A few weeks after his daughter left him to return to Sandwich, he took a third wife. Beautiful as dawn she was; and, preoccupied by his new happiness, he failed to publish, according to law, his intention of marriage. In consequence he was fined ten pounds, half of which was afterward rescinded. For a few days he felt indescribably happy. Then he made a discovery that set the world askew. His young wife, Mary, was an adulteress. Shocked beyond mortal expression, revolted, stung with jealousy and shame, he appealed immediately for divorce. Mary also was ready for divorce. She called her husband a hypocrite, and said things about a pot that called a kettle black. Stephen felt vulgar, longed for escape. To his horror the court refused to grant a separation:

> It is ordered by this Court that Mr. Bachiler and his wife shall lyve together as man and wife as in this Court they have publicly professed to doe; and if either desert one another then hereby the court doth order

that the marshall shall apprehend both the said Mr. B. and Mary, his
wife, and bring them forthwith to Boston.

The old nonconformist could not believe his ears — he, a minister of God, ordered to live with a confessed adulteress, while men
smiled maliciously and Mary laughed in his face! With his white head
bowed, the shoulders that were once broad and straight stooped with
misery, Mr. Stephen Bachiler, aged ninety, enforced bridegroom, set
out alone and on foot for Boston Harbor, and there boarded ship
for England. Once safely offshore, he peered disconsolately at the
new land that was not large enough to contain himself and his third
wife. After his departure from Portsmouth, and while his ship
waited in Boston Harbor for a fair wind, he received word from Kittery that on the fifteenth of October Mary Bachiler was presented for
committing adultery with George Rogers and sentenced to "receive
forty stripes save one, at the first town meeting held at Kittery, 6
weeks after her delivery, and be branded with the letter A."

For a few minutes Stephen contemplated remaining in America,
to help Mary when she underwent that cruel penalty. Then he remembered that he would have to live with her afterward. He squared
his shoulders and held firmly to the ship's rail. A pretty woman, her
dark eyes red with tears, brushed past him. Something familiar about
her, there on shipboard, puzzled Stephen, yet he was sure that he had
never seen her face before.

"What can I do for thee, my daughter?" he said in his voice like
a warm caress. To the frightened girl, half child, half woman, about
to embark upon an angry ocean, this man of tall, commanding figure, a halo of white hair about his benign face, seemed the very em-
bodiment of comfort, understanding, peace. "Wilt thou stay near
me on the voyage?" she queried.

An offshore wind whistled over the roofs of "Boston Cittie," and
the ship sailed east. Stephen disembarked in England, and though
he had never been divorced from Mary, he married again in the
Old Country, and died at the age of a hundred and one, his young
wife by his side. His last words were of the "Holy City without
Ceremonies." He had forgotten how it had failed, and so, at the end,
he set out to refound it in some celestial wilderness. Meanwhile, at
the site of his lost settlement in Mattakeese, men with less lofty vi-

sion, less conspicuous defects, were finishing his forsaken houses, planting new trees in his orchards whose blossoms dropped their benediction over the acres on which he had toiled under the more relentless blossoming of snow.

ANDREW HALLETT

Andrew Hallett waked in the dark, before sunrise. Dressed in his short clothes and a long vest with lappets covering his hips, he climbed down the ladder that led from the "lodging chamber" into the front entry, and tiptoed to the door of the "up-step Bedroom" where Mehitabel slept. He never knew why he wanted to see the first light of dawn touch Mehitabel's eyelids. She seldom wakened when he paused at the threshold of the low-walled room, but she often stirred in her sleep. Andrew feared for her future. He closed his eyes with a sort of physical shrinking when he thought of hellfire for Mehitabel, yet he honestly could not feel that Mehitabel would escape.

Something of the worship that he had once given his brother, Samuel, went into his love for his youngest daughter. She, like Samuel, was endowed with gay inconsequent laughter, love of sea, star and sky, and of new ideas, and of old England. When she was a baby she ran away, and now that she was older, danced like a witch on the wet sands, and could sail a boat like any mariner. She was not good at counting pennies. Andrew sighed about that as he went into the "Great Room" where banked coals were red in the eight-foot fireplace. He laid in a new backlog, then a large forestick, placed two or three smaller sticks at right angles to the backlog, forming a square bed into which he raked hot coals. He wondered, as he laid dry wood on the coals, why he thought about Mehitabel so much more than he thought about his other children. She was mocking, disobedient; yet when she fell and bumped her knee, his heart contracted as it had not when Ruhama lay ill of fever, or when Abigail broke her arm. Mehitabel was so ready to expose herself to danger, and Andrew was a man of caution. It seemed a miracle that anyone quite like Mehitabel should be his child.

The dry sticks blazed brightly. While he went out and tended stock, they would sparkle and glow, then smolder into red embers, suitable for the cooking of the morning meal. Ann was always up before he returned from the barns, and so were Ruhama and Abigail, and his two young sons. Breakfast would be well under way when he reached the door; the smell of tea brew and "break-broth" would assail him a good three feet from the doorstone. Curiously, Andrew treasured the few minutes in the morning when he was alone in the Great Room, of which he was exceedingly proud, alone with firelight and suncoming, and with his love for Mehitabel who always slept soundly through dawn.

Andrew opened the front door, stepped over the threshold, and looked toward the east. Night skies, purple and thick as the Cape's own huckleberry wine, were yielding to marsh amber. Andrew loved suncoming. In the middle of the seventeenth century, there were no clocks in the Hallett household. Time was reckoned as "suncoming, sun-an-hour, sun-two-hours"; then, "midday, sun-four-hours-up, three-hours-up"; later, "sunset, sober-light, first-hour-night, second-hour-night." Andrew, a solemn man, orderly, puritan in his ways, deeply loved suncoming. Mehitabel, a child of joy, a little wild, a little gay, loved sober-light.

Andrew washed at the spring east of the house. Years before, he had sliced through a mammoth tree trunk, hollowed the center of the slice, and sunk the hollow circle of wood around a cold spring that bubbled unceasingly in his East Field. The wood made a circular curbing around the spring, and Andrew deepened the hole. When the droughts were on, settlers came from miles around to get supplied from that "fountain." Andrew believed that the clear, icy waters had medicinal power. Perhaps, if he had had this spring when little Dorcas, his "lost" daughter, lay dying, its coldness might have allayed her burning fever and spared her for a while. Andrew doubted if anything could have held Dorcas long, Dorcas for whom the Gates of Heaven opened, who conversed with angels while she was yet alive upon earth. She also conversed with devils; Andrew shuddered at thought of it. At least a score of the imps of Satan found refuge under her trundle bed. She begged them to leave her, cried aloud in pain when they pinched her delicate body. Andrew had wanted to wrestle in person with Lucifer, as good Mr. Bourne, his brother-in-law, was known to do; wrestle and defeat Lucifer, and order him to call off his fiends. Dorcas was only a baby; her haggard, haunting little face turned toward him for protection. She had been baptized in good order. She had led a godly life. Where could Satan have found crevice of sin in which to secrete imps?

Sometimes the taverners joked about the imps. His wife, Ann, had been too talkative. All the Besse women were talkative but Andrew had married Ann when she was so young that he hoped she would learn a few of his ways. Ann had been with little Dorcas on the night when the devils were at their worst. She had not seen the devils but she had seeen the bed lifted nearly a foot into the air while the dying baby screamed in an agony of fear. George Barlow, later to become Ann's stepfather, had been there too. He had seen the devils, and prayed, and prevailed against them. Slowly the bed sank downward and stood again upon the floor.

Andrew hated George Barlow; hated the things that the townsmen of Yarmouth and Barnstable and Sandwich said about him. They attributed Andrew's prosperity to the fact that George Barlow had taken cows, food, and utensils, as fines from the Quakers, and sold them to Andrew for a song. When Andrew obtained new livestock, farm implements, or finery for his daughters, the townsfolk nodded and smiled. They thought he took it from Quakers! In the peace and glory of that spring morning, he grew blind with fury. As if his wife's stepfather would give him anything cheap! As if he would take it as a gift! The one thing that made him believe that Dorcas was not one of the sainted children of earth, destined from the first for heaven, was that George Barlow, and only George, had seen the devils under the bed when the bed rose upward without aid of mortal hand. Barlow was a drunkard, and influenced Ann who was excitable. Barlow had put ideas into Dorcas' little head. Andrew clenched his fists, then unclenched them. What was the use of all this misery over a tragedy long past? Dorcas had been gone these many years and now his problem was Mehitabel. Taverners, who remembered the story of the imps, smiled about Mehitabel, and hinted that Dorcas, when she exorcised the devils, had not been able to make a good job of it. She had left one imp under her trundle bed.

Certainly, Mehitabel was no saint; neither was she a devil. Andrew could not imagine that she would ever confer with angels, but, in her red cloak and cape, with the warm spring wind ruffling her hair, as she went for a Sunday visit, "cooging" it was called, Andrew knew that she was very far from "one of Satan's throng."

He carried two pails of fresh water from the spring to the house. Then he turned toward the orchard. Cherry blossoms reflected the color of the flushed dawn sky, and from Orchard Hill Andrew caught a glimpse of far dunes blossoming into the color of tea roses. The sun steamed upward from the unseen cauldron of Nauset Sea. The Kentish cherry trees stood erect in a sweet, warm wind that blew ceaselessly from the south — from the island where the devil lived, according to Andrew's Indian servant, who also talked about a great bird whose flapping wings made the wind to blow.

Petals drifted down on his coat sleeve. Even the fallen flowers were dear, for these trees had enabled him to make a better orchard than any other on the Cape. He had planted them as sentinels, a border around delicate seedlings. They had brought sweet fruit from which Ann and Ruhama made cherry wine and "consarve." Furthermore, they had faced the winds gallantly and protected the delicate French Sugar and Black Worcester pears. Andrew held a fallen blossom in his hand. The petals were as delicate as baby Mehitabel's cheek; petals half curled and fragile as a flake of snow. Suddenly, he became conscious of the callused fingers that held them, the hand of a yeoman; a "yokel" his father would say. Mr. Andrew Hallett — Andrew Hallett, Gentleman — and now only Goodman Hallett, even in the church records.

Of the pioneers in that region, thirty had the right to the title of Goodman, four were called Mister, and only one was styled Gentleman on the first records. His father had been that aristocrat. His younger brother Samuel had been an aristocrat also, and he, Andrew, was only a husbandman; yet the richest man in Yarmouth. Samuel had been reckless in all things, reckless of debts, reckless of money. Andrew remembered the shame that he had felt when he came upon his father's name in a notice posted on the church door:

It is ordered by the court, that Mr. Andrew Hallett shall pay Massa Tampaim one fadome of beads (wampam) within two moones, beside the nett he alleadgeth the sd Massa Tampaim sold him, for the deare that Mr. Hellot's sonn bought of him about two years since.

The shame of this had been twofold. First, his brother was posted on the church door for a bad debt brought to court by an Indian. Secondly, as everyone in the little settlement knew, Samuel had started out to shoot his first deer. He had gone forth at dawn confidently; he had returned at night triumphantly, with a magnificent animal over his shoulder. In the taverns he had been toasted as marksman and sailor. How Andrew Junior admired him, above what was godly. And Samuel had not shot that deer; he had purchased it of Massatampaim, and failed to pay his debt. Yet Samuel continued to be the aristocrat, Andrew the goodman. From the very first this had been true. Andrew accepted the fact, just as he accepted the fact that Ann had a sharp tongue, and that Mehitabel was strange. He was born to husbandry, Samuel to inherit the sea. With characteristic impetuosity, Samuel put all his money into a vessel, and against the advice of wiser mariners stood forth from the Backside on just such a day in April, when the warm south winds were blowing up a squall. April, 1650, Samuel in his early twenties. Andrew could see Mr. Lothrop, the minister, when the news came. Andrew watched Mr. Lothrop write in the church book, in a hand less steady than usual: "Samuel Hollet drowned at the Harbour of Nocett att the first setting out from thence aboute a fishing voyage." At the time Andrew could not even write his own name but he knew the words that Mr. Lothrop was forming. He knew, too, that the minister faced death calmly. If it had been he, Andrew the husbandman, whose young body drifted along the Nauset shoals, Mr. Lothrop's hand would not have trembled at the "writing of it downe." Yet Andrew felt no resentment. The thought passed as quietly as thoughts of Samuel had passed in every April when the wind blew from the south. At the time of the drowning, Andrew had been married eight years, and as he watched Mr. Lothrop form mystical letters, he resolved that some day he would learn to write.

The orchard was like foam of sea in springtime. He seldom walked under blossoming trees without thinking of Samuel, whose life had been as gay, as inconsequent as cherry flowers. Froth of the seed — froth of the sea. God would be merciful to Samuel Hallett, Gentleman, who died at twenty leaving a score of debts. God would expect a very exact reckoning from Andrew Hallett, Goodman, owner of orchards and livestock, and a fine house, and cribs of grain. Would

God be merciful to little Mehitabel Hallett who did not care about pennies, who was as reckless as Samuel, who did not even seem to care about God?

When Andrew reached his barns he found all tidy there. His Indian servants had been up before him. He inspected their work carefully, did a few special chores of his own, and then turned to his cribs. Whatever Andrew neglected in his busy mornings, he never neglected these. In the seventeenth century, corn was the measure of value. With it men paid their taxes, their debts, bought houses and land, and negotiated for the necessities and luxuries of life. To have corn in the crib was like having stocks, or money, in the bank today. Andrew delighted to exhibit his extensive granaries, his herds and flocks, the breadth of his cultivated land. With the exception of hominy or samp, he consumed very little of his corn until it was a year old. He loved to point to one crib and say, "there is my last year's crop," to another, "there is my crop of the year before," and to a third, "in that crib are the remains of the former year's crop." He tried to stint himself on showing his granaries too frequently, fearing worldly enjoyment and the "luste for praise."

When he looked at his house in the liquid morning sunlight he felt again the sin of pride. He wished that little Dorcas could have seen that house. She had been such a round-eyed, solemn, admiring baby. She would have loved the Great Room. Ruhama and Abigail also felt pride of it; but his sons, Jonathan and little John, had never known the first house and, of course, to Mehitabel the baby, privation was only a hearthfire tale. Already the little one could suggest a dozen necessary changes in the new home.

In 1642, when Andrew and Ann decided to settle in Yarmouth, the country was spoken of as "outpost wilderness." Land was cheap, and in the region deserted by the colony of Stephen Bachiler, large grants could be procured. Andrew and Ann purchased of Gyles Hopkins his house, built in 1638. An excavation had been made into the easterly side of a hill; a stone and cobwork chimney built against this bank, outside the frame of a one-room structure. The roof was thatched, the seams in the boarding "daubed" with clay. Oiled paper, not glass, covered the tiny windows. The sills, hewn from large logs, projected into the room forming low seats on three sides. A cleat door with a wooden latch and spring completed the built-in fixtures. Yet he and

Ann had been happy there. They had not considered themselves miserly. Governor Hinckley lived for years in just such a house.

Ann was fourteen when Andrew married her, and fifteen when the twins, Ruhama and Abigail, were born in the one Great Room. Ann took the pains of childbirth with no outcry, a bravery that wrung from Andrew, whenever he thought about it, a recurrent pang of passionate admiration and terror. The Besse women were strong in body and mind. They had ideas of their own and understood one another, although nobody quite understood them. The "Quarrelsome Besse Women" they were called. Ann's mother, who was thirty years old, helped Ann to give birth to the twins. On the day following the arrival of her children, Ann requested her mother to take care of the babies while she went out in search of birds' eggs. This act of folly, or bravery — Andrew never could be sure which it was — became the talk of the colony. Ann had been proud of it; but Andrew still felt doubtful, as he thought of the way that the men in the tavern had laughed as they toasted the young mother.

When Dorcas was born, Ann became very ill, and Dorcas was frail from the first, needing constant attention. Andrew secretly believed that Ann's indiscretions with the twins had brought about Dorcas' fragility, but Ann hotly denied that there could be any connection between the two events. She attributed Dorcas' "sickliness" to the discomforts of their humble home, and demanded a wooden floor, glass windows, and an ingle oven. There was not much time for the making of elaborate dwellings in the first years of Yarmouth colony. Andrew had to live on the produce of his farm. Corn was his principal crop, but rye and wheat for home consumption were essential. Beans, pumpkins, peas, must be attended. He had no potatoes. Cattle were scarce and high in price, so Andrew bought goats and used their milk for the babies. He was a good shot, and the little house was well supplied with deer, wild turkey, geese, ducks and plover. Not a fisherman, he found it cheaper to dispense with a boat, and trade his produce for fish. There were no Indian servants to help him at first. The land was stubborn; and the work of clearing, for one man, however determined, proved a long, weary process. Season by season, Andrew delayed in the building of the new house; and meanwhile Dorcas lived on, precariously. Then, in one hot summer she faded, devils appeared under her bed, and angels took her away. If Andrew had only built the house a little sooner, if there had been a wooden floor, or glass in the windows would Dorcas have lived?

Andrew heard a sputtering noise, and then an attempt at a spurious Indian war whoop. Over by the spring, east of the house, he caught a glimpse of his son Jonathan's bright hair. He hoped that Jonathan was washing the back of his neck. The sounds suggested tremendous applications of cold water, but Andrew had been disillusioned about sounds. When Jonathan made the most noise he was generally doing the least washing.

Nevertheless, Andrew approached the house with a lighter step. At least Jonathan had never known the difficulties of the little one-room building. After Dorcas' death, Andrew worked as though the Lord directly guided him. The next baby should be born in the finest house that he could build. Andrew prayed that he might have a son. Perhaps even more than he wanted a son, he wanted to hold Dorcas, as his "daughter-baby," in the center of his thoughts a little longer. A new daughter, healthy and happy in a new house that Dorcas had needed; he would be jealous that little Dorcas never had her share.

Jonathan came into existence before the house was ready for him. Jonathan always would do the unexpected. But long before Jonathan learned to speak, the Hallett family were safely installed in their "farm," set high on a sunny knoll, facing due south. Andrew looked critically at the new house that was no longer new. Through the vista of orchard trees, it seemed a place of peace and friendliness. There were larger houses in Yarmouth, now that the settlement had grown about him, but the women in those larger houses worked harder than his. Some of the homes had newfangled staircases. Mehitabel seemed to crave a staircase above all other earthly possessions. Andrew did not "hold with" staircases. They were dangerous contraptions, "dizzafying to ye braine." Instead of going down them backward, you went down forward clinging to the wall or to a rail. If you stumbled you pitched headlong. Staircases were well enough in public places where dignity was essential; but for home comfort, safety, and economy of space, a trusty oaken ladder was worth a dozen of them.

When Andrew reached the doorstone, Mehitabel greeted him with the radiant announcement that at "ye sayinge of ye prayers" she was to "sette ye hym." Andrew looked doubtful. What Mehitabel lacked in tonal veracity she made up in velocity. Her delight was to set the pace so fast that the "hym" sounded like a dance tune. The result was generally a reprimand, sulks, and ultimate reprisals. Andrew said nothing. He hoped for the best.

When the family were assembled in the Great Room, Ruhama read a chapter from the Bible. Mehitabel was quiet with the look of a cat stalking a bird. Andrew knew that look, tried to catch her eye and administer silent reproof. But Mehitabel remained gathered unto herself, and her eye was not to be "caught." After Ruhama had finished the chapter, Andrew turned toward his youngest daughter, as a signal that Mehitabel "obleege":

> "I as a stranger am become
>   unto my bretherren;
> And am an aliant unto
>   my mothers childerren.
> For of thy house the zeale me hath
>   up eaten: every one
> Who thee reproach, their reproaches
>   are fallen mee upon."

As she sang, the words of the good *Bay Psalm Book* sounded somehow dreadful and grotesque. Andrew shivered. The other children did not "jine in." They watched their mother expectantly. Andrew also looked toward Ann who nodded quickly. "Mehitabel," thundered Andrew, "cease thy ribaldry."

"Yes, sir," said Mehitabel, coming to a sudden stop. There was a moment of complete silence. Andrew floundered in thought between two possible expedients. Should he invite little Jonathan to take his turn next, or should he omit the hymn and proceed directly to prayer? Would God forgive the slur of passing over the hymn? Would God consider a reckoning with Mehitabel in the middle of a service in His honor an unseemly interruption? Andrew decided that the way of peace would be less painful to God.

He knelt by the hearth. He sought the blessing of heaven on his country, his church, his household, his dear friends in England. As he prayed, the liquid April sunlight disappeared, and rain spattered suddenly against the window. In such a spring squall, Samuel —

sternly he forced his thoughts into the channels of duty. He was praying for his dear friends in England. How far away they seemed! His heart kept saying, "Lord, Lord, forgive Mehitabel, she is so young."

Breakfast was set on a well-scoured table without covering. Ann brought from hearth to table the great wooden bowl filled with "break-broth," a savory broth used only at "break-fast," hence its name. With pewter spoons the entire family dipped from the dish. Hulled corn supplied the place of bread. After the bowl was emptied, Abigail removed it, and she and Ruhama brought on samp, milk, butter, honey, a slice or two of meat, and a plate of fish. Ann brewed home-grown tea culled from garden herbs.

The silence of the meal was impressive. The children were waiting to know what was going to happen to Mehitabel. Whatever it was, Mehitabel would "speak Jesuit," and try to justify her conduct. Andrew ignored her. He knew that this indicated a weakness in his character but he excused it on the grounds of household serenity. The food was the Lord's and should be eaten in an appreciative and tranquil silence. Andrew directed the thoughts of the children to that unfailing source of delight, "ould England." All his life he had called it "Home"; but sometimes, when he looked on his broad fields, and on the little house on the hillock, he wondered if the new land might, in truth, be the real homeland for himself and Ann, and Jonathan and John. To the children, England bore a dangerous resemblance to heaven. Mehitabel was without shame in the matter. She preferred England to all celestial felicities, and volunteered to relinquish her chances of eternal salvation for a chance to visit the King. The children never tired of listening to tales of misty Devon, of the giants of Cornwall, of the towers of London, of the fabulous court, and of the King in his coach with scarlet outriders. They were even interested in stories of the uncivilized Scotchmen from the north, whom they recognized as the same sort of problem to England that Indians were to America. After the meal was ended, Andrew gave brief thanks for the food.

The rain beat sharply upon roof and window. Ann helped Jonathan and John into their greatcoats. Mehitabel came over to her father to have her bonnet tied under her chin. She said nothing as Andrew fastened a clumsy knot. Andrew said nothing, but they smiled at one another. Andrew felt vaguely guilty about that smile, for he was deferring Mehitabel's punishment for the morning's iniquity. He did not want to send her to school with her eyes red. After school he would reason with her in good earnest.

The annual expenses of a schoolmaster were too heavy for the little settlement of Yarmouth, so an itinerant teacher divided his attention between several communities. Usually only a few winter weeks were devoted to school and in the spring the children, as well as their parents, helped with the farm. But in this particular year, the schoolmaster had been ill, so Yarmouth children were delayed in their "larning." School was kept by Mr. John Miller at his house, a good mile distant from Andrew Hallett's farm, and the children, their dinners put up, before half-past eight were on their way. An older brother held firmly to either hand of Mehitabel. Unless she was earnestly propelled forward, she found the path so devious, the distractions so numerous that she sometimes failed to arrive at the house of Mr. John Miller at all. She never failed to arrive home, however, at approximately the returning time.

During the morning, ordinarily, Andrew, assisted by his Indians, watered and fed his livestock and attended to the planting and agricultural problems of his farm. Ann was as systematic as he. She followed the normal routine of the Cape housewife: Monday, wash day; Tuesday, ironing day; Wednesday, summer bake day, winter scouring day; Thursday, spinning day; Friday, weaving day; Saturday, bake day again. No meat was ever served on Saturday. The Sunday dinner was cooked in advance, and Mehitabel, who called it "sniff day," always wanted to eat her Sunday meal on Saturday while the victuals were hot. All servile labor stopped at four o'clock on Saturdays, and in the evening the children were drilled in their Sabbath lessons, and instructed concerning deportment. Sometimes their mother taught them, sometimes their older sister, sometimes Andrew. Most of the instructions concerning deportment had to be addressed to Mehitabel. Mr. John Miller said that she was "exceeding smarte in larning." If that was so, Andrew wondered why she was so exceeding muddleheaded about religion. Her attention centered upon Biblical problems that would disconcert even the great Mr. Mather who, if he encountered her, would no doubt condemn her as a witch.

Andrew watched the little cavalcade, three sturdy figures soon lost to sight in the rain. Mehitabel was trying to jump puddles, Jonathan yanking her away from them, while little John, functioning more or less as the tail of a kite, was jerked from side to side. The picture failed to stir Andrew sentimentally. They were difficult children, "stiff-necked Halletts," but they were his. He wanted them to escape the snares of Satan. When he thought of the accusations of witchcraft that were so prevalent, and of Mehitabel's sharp tongue and laughing eyes, he vowed constant vigilance for her sake. He reprimanded Abigail furiously when she called the child a little witch. It would not be long before outsiders said the same words.

The squall showed no signs of abating. Andrew decided to trust his stock, for the morning, to the care of his faithful Indians. He took his awl, leather, thread, wax and knife, and retired to the chimney corner. To him Abigail brought the shoes of the family that required a tap or a patch, the leather coats and breeches that needed a seam stitched, or a tear mended. Andrew made the repairs as neatly as any leather worker of the present day. A thorough knowledge of hides was part of the necessary training of a Cape husbandman. Clothwork belonged to women, leather to men. Ann, Ruhama and Abigail brought in their looms from the kitchen (that was not used for cooking but for storage in the early days). Ann wove five yards that morning, her "rainy day stint"; Ruhama spun six skeins of woolen yarn, and Abigail completed four of flax. While the women were busy with their "looming," Andrew paused occasionally in his work to turn the venison sirloin that was spitted on the andirons beside him. Now and again he basted the meat from the contents of the dripping pan. Later, vegetables, prepared before breakfast, were hung over the fire; and at midday, while the children were still in school, the older members of the family ate their dinner in a dignified silence. After Andrew had completed the blessing, he cut the venison on a wooden trencher, and served it on pewter plates. Vegetables, samp, and "spoon victuals" completed the meal. Beer, brewed regularly every week, was served at midday. Andrew was fond of beer, and proud of his wife's brew.

The rain ceased its sharp tattoo upon the windows. Clouds fled rapidly across the wide Cape skies, and a pale sunlight, that partook of the translucence of moonlight, filtered through blue apertures in the mist. In such a ghostly sunlight Samuel had perished — so brave — so gay.

The knocker on the front door resounded heavily and Andrew rose quickly from the table. No one called at such an hour. No one ever came to the front door, except on formal visits made after three o'clock (modern reckoning), when the tasks of the day were finished, the wheels put away, the parlor swept and dusted, clean sand "lumped" on the floor, or the old sand "herren boned." In response to this summons Andrew went to the door himself, signaling Abigail to wait. To his astonishment he found there little Rebecca Barlow, his wife's half-sister. She wore no cloak, and was wet to the skin with rain. Beside her in the pathway stood George Barlow's fat red mare. Andrew hitched the red horse to the block, and drew the child inside the house. Immediately she was surrounded by the three women. Ann went up-ladder to the lodging chamber to get dry clothes of Mehitabel's. Ruhama, who had a way with children, took the shaking child on her knee. Tears poured down thin, dirty cheeks. To all inquiries Rebecca spoke no word.

Ruhama signaled her father to draw away. Obviously, the eight-year-old was tongue-tied before a too large and overattentive audience. In a few moments she relaxed and whispered to Ruhama, who grew suddenly grave and stern. Ann came hurrying down from the lodging chamber with dry clothes, and carried Rebecca into Mehitabel's little up-step bedroom, to change. Meanwhile Andrew questioned Ruhama. Barlow had been drinking again, had beaten his wife, taken his terrified child, Rebecca, with him, and ridden away from the house at dawn. Ever since dawn Rebecca and her father had traveled down-Cape. At first Barlow sang loudly, and spurred his horse, and Rebecca had clung in terror to the saddle. Later, her father stopped singing and dozed, rousing himself at intervals when he lurched and threatened to fall from the saddle. The rain poured down on them. Rebecca pleaded that they turn toward home, but Barlow threatened her with his whip, and vowed that neither he nor she should pass across the threshold of his second wife's house again. Not very far from the Hallett farm, Barlow fell off the horse and Rebecca fell with him. Instead of getting up, the ex-marshal rolled to the side of the wheel tracks, and fell into a heavy sleep. Rebecca tried to rouse him, failed, and then, alone in the forest, climbed onto the red mare's back and rode for "Sister Ann."

Andrew groaned. He cautioned Ruhama to say nothing to his wife about the beating of Dame Barlow. Ann loved her mother dearly, and would resent her stepfather's cruelty. Andrew went quickly to the barn, and with the help of his Indian saddled his black horse. He rode back to the house, seized the bridle of the red mare, and started down the path through the orchard. Ann hurried out and called to him. She had extracted the truth from little Rebecca, and wanted Andrew to kill Barlow. Andrew rode rapidly westward. He had no intention of killing George Barlow, ex-marshal of Sandwich, Barnstable and Yarmouth, ex-"constable in all things," who once wielded a tyrannical authority extending to all parts of Plymouth Colony. If Barlow wandered far from home and fell by the roadside, it might be Andrew's duty to bring him to his senses with a few lashes of the whip. Andrew felt that he need not be reluctant in the performance of this duty.

On either side of the King's Highway, budding leaf and pine-cluster burned with the white fire of raindrops. So the world would all shine in the white fire of the millennium, thought Andrew. That would be a sight to see, a world consumed in shining flame, then crumbling into ashes scattered across eternity. Mehitabel was terrified of millennium. When Andrew read of it in the sermons of good Mr. Cotton, or wise Mr. Mather, she fled into the up-step bedroom and hid under feather pillabers. Only Ruhama could coax her out again, with promises of sweetmeats. No fit conclusion for a millennium, thought Andrew dryly, as he kept an eye out for the stout, drunken marshal. He hated George Barlow, and every year rode at least twice to his rescue. There was something ironic in these compromises of life, compromises with hate, with youth, with sin, with the devil. The older generation had lived to the letter and in the spirit of their religion. They had enforced principles. What was the matter with his generation? Could it have anything to do with that baffling difference between Andrew Hallett, Gentleman, of Hallett's Hall, Devonshire, and Goodman Hallett, farmer, of Cape Cod?

The horse shied sharply. A snake or a fox, perhaps a wolf, though not likely. Andrew heard a resonant snore. He dismounted, and approached a heap of caked mud to one end of which clung a cocked hat. Under the cocked hat protruded a red nose.

"Hie thee up, Barlow," said Andrew. "Get thee gone to Sandwich, and on thy knees to Mother Jane." Barlow opened a bleary eye. From his mouth came a stream of borrowed sanctimony, pilfered from other men's sermons:

"Andrew, thy mind is a nest of foul opinions, of heresies, thy heart is a sink of atheism, sodomy, blasphemy, murder, whoredom, adultery, witchcraft, buggery. If thou hast any good in thee, it is but as a drop of rose water in a bowl of poison. Thou feelest not these things stirring in thee at one time, but they are in thee, like a nest of snakes in an old hedge."

"Thou art the snake in the hedge, Barlow. Get thee up."

Andrew approached and let Barlow's eye fall upon a whip that stirred ominously. Barlow made as if to rise, then sank back complaining of pains in his "joinderies."

"Rise up!" Andrew snapped out the order as though the ex-marshal of Plymouth Colony were an Indian slave. He was a little astonished at himself, when he spoke with a voice that had the ring of Samuel's. The townspeople used to say "Lucifer himself would obey Sam Hallett." Barlow lumbered to his feet. He had completed his sodden sleep and was not as drunk as he looked.

Andrew helped him to mount again upon the red mare. "Tell Mother Jane that Rebecca stays with us," he said. Barlow nodded dully. Andrew gave the red mare a quick lash with his whip. She broke into a lope down the Sandwich road, the comic figure of the marshal clinging for his life. Ann would rebuke Andrew, first that he had not killed Barlow, and, later, that he had not brought Barlow safely home with him. "Women," said Andrew aloud, "have weathercocks in their heads." He did not care. The man leered at Abigail, and was no fit sight for Mehitabel to see.

Andrew peered at the sun that winked between lashes of clouds. If he took the back road and hurried he might pass the children trudging home from school. He quickened his horse to the ambling pace in which Cape "steeds" were trained. The road was lonely, and at Sabbath lecture meeting there had passed reports of a bad Indian. He was not seriously alarmed at this. Reports of bad Indians were too frequent. Andrew was known to be a man of justice and power. Indians respected him, and, whatever their failings, they rarely molested children. It occurred to Andrew that his fellow townsmen were not fair to Indians, who should not be expected to understand the customs of Englishmen any more readily than the men of Plymouth Colony understood the rites of savages. Men criticized Andrew for his friendliness toward Indians in a way that made him realize that it was better to keep opinions to himself. The Indians sensed his tolerance, and respected his fair dealing. They came to him frequently with a confidence that Andrew valued more than he cared to let the world know. With Indians, he shared to some extent the popularity of his brother-in-law, Richard Bourne, from whom Andrew learned something of the loyalty, the strange beliefs, and the profound lore of forest, swamp, and moor that the Nauset-Wampanoag possessed.

When Andrew caught sight of his three youngest children, they were walking single file, like three small braves on the warpath. Their feet were always clad in moccasins, but, to Andrew's astonishment, he perceived that Jonathan held a collection of dyed feathers in his hand, while little John bore a stone hammer decorated with "gewgaw cloth." Mehitabel — Andrew strained his eyes in an attempt to decipher the wild maelstrom of colors glittering around her neck! He spurred his horse and came swiftly abreast of the children. Jonathan held his hands behind his back. John, whom Andrew had always believed to have no worldly guile, sat down abruptly in the wet road, on top of his stone mallet, and from under him a few wisps of bedraggled scarlet protruded. Mehitabel put up her small hand and held tightly to her beads.

"What outlandish heathenism is upon ye?" demanded Andrew, his tolerance of a few moments before thrown to the winds, as he viewed, with mounting horror, the pagan implements of Satan with which his children were adorned. "Daughter, fling off thy vile trumpery!" Mehitabel made one frightened, appealing gesture of protest; then, seeming to realize that Andrew was genuinely scandalized, she took off three bright bead chains and let them fall slowly into the muddy silt of the road. Jonathan dropped his feathers, one by one, cautiously, behind him. Small John, usually the most tractable of children, made no effort to relinquish his hammer. He continued to sit on top of it, and stared at his father with a smoldering light in his blue eyes.

"John, rise from thy heathen toy." John came to his feet. As he turned to pick up the hammer, Andrew noticed that it had left a deep outline on his leathern breeches that elsewhere were caked with wet sand. John, his feet spaced wide apart, stood, without words, braced against attack, the Indian hammer hugged against his breast.

Seated on his black horse, facing these three small, defiant mortals, Andrew felt suddenly grotesque. They looked so little from the height at which he viewed them, and so unsubmissive. He glanced up and down the road nervously. More than anything else, he was desirous of having no audience view this episode. He particularly wanted to get the children away from the damning evidence of those bright beads. He stooped down and picked Jonathan up, putting him to the rear of the saddle. Jonathan, with the assurance of habit, put his arms around his father and held tight. Next John was hoisted up. He clung to the decorated mallet, and perched precariously in back of Jonathan, holding to his older brother with only one hand. Mehitabel protested. If John kept his hammer, Jonathan should have his feathers and she her colored beads. Andrew ordered her to be silent, and swung her to the pommel, where she sat, very erect, refusing to lean back against her father.

On the road homeward, Andrew tried to make his children understand why the adornments of heathens, worn on the bodies of Christians, were a deep affront to God. His auditors were unresponsive. Andrew felt that in some queer way they were chiding him at heart. He and their Uncle Richard had more traffic with Indians than other men, and always tried to uphold Indian justice. Yet he condemned his children for accepting the gifts that grateful Indians bestowed on them in appreciation of that difference in attitude between Andrew and other men. If their father could traffic with Indians more than other Christians did, why could not they? Besides, the gifts came from Praying Indians, who were good Christians and disciples of Uncle Richard.

Andrew tried to formulate arguments, while the black horse plodded homeward, carrying its component load without protest save for a switching of the tail as though Jonathan and John were flies that needed to be brushed from its broad back. Mehitabel remained consistently silent. She loved to ride in front of the saddle with her father, and gradually she began to peer right, left, and ahead, as though she were exploring a new country. Andrew had no proof that she was not listening to him, but his experience of her told him that she had ceased to pay rigorous attention. In the evening he would speak again, under the vigilant authority of Ann.

They rode through the orchard and up to the farmhouse block. Andrew lifted the children from the horse, and then hurried to the barns without waiting to explain his errand to Ann. The evening chores demanded immediate attention, and only after the milking was finished, and the horses and cattle bedded down for the night, could Andrew return to the house. When he reached the Great Room, the children had completed their "jonakin and mush." He sat down with Ann. She talked steadily of Barlow and of her mother who had not found life easy with her first husband, Anthony Besse, but who had found life so impossible with her second husband that the harassed, quarrelsome household had been forced to air its difficulties before the magistrates on more than one occasion.

Andrew expressed sympathy guardedly; not that he failed to feel sorry for Mother Jane. He commiserated her hard future, but he feared, if he gave Ann sufficient opening, that she might propose that his mother-in-law live with them for a while. Mother Jane talked so fast that Andrew could not follow her, and she talked so hard that Mehitabel said, "It speakes inside ye stomache."

After supper, Andrew administered punishment to his daughter-baby. She held out a hand small, silken as a cherry blossom. For lack of respect at the singing of the hymn, for wearing of beads in unseemly vanity, Andrew brought the rule four times across her pink fingers. She flushed at the fourth blow, but there were no tears in her eyes. When the punishment was over, Mehitabel drew away, withholding herself in offended dignity and with an air of exaggerated injustice born of false humility. Andrew never had any satisfaction from punishing her; he was never sure that she experienced genuine contrition.

He sighed as he took out his Bible preparatory to the reading of the evening psalm. Bedtime was shortly after candle-time, and when the psalm was said, the children repeated their short prayers, kneeling before the hearth. Then Ruhama and Abigail and the two little boys climbed the ladder to the lodging chamber. Ruhama would hear the bed prayers of the two boys. Practical Abigail would ascertain that their clothes were neatly folded, that their bedcovers were of a wise thickness, and that their nightcaps were buttoned neatly over their tousled hair. Ann took Mehitabel into the up-step bedroom, while Andrew lighted his pipe and sat smoking by the hearth. In winter when the roads were hard, or snow was on the ground, Goodmen and their wives "rode over," the men for a pipe and chat with Andrew, the women for a "chatterfest" with Ann. Visitors also came in the warm nights of summer, but in springtime the roads were soggy and evening guests were rare.

Ann came out of the up-step bedroom, that curious little room whose floor was raised at least two feet to give cellar space below. An adult could not stand upright; fortunately, Mehitabel's curly head was still a long way from the ceiling. The bed occupied almost the entire floor space. Mehitabel kept a terrible assortment of treasures concealed under the bed. Once in every week or so Ann cleared out this treasure, while Mehitabel wept angry tears. Ann paused at the ladder, waiting for Andrew.

"Thee go up," said Andrew, unconsciously using the Quaker phraseology so common in the district. "After a biding time I follow."

"Look well to the fire, Andrew. I have dreamt twice of a burning." Andrew nodded. Ann climbed to the lodging chamber, and after she was gone, he lighted the one remaining candle that stood on the table, and placed the candle on the wide window ledge.

"Samuel," he said, gently, then: "Samuel, I need thee. Thou wert ever a light in the darkness. Thy home is waiting here."

The wind had fallen, and the April night was dark, cloudless and starry. Andrew was roused from his reverie by a small, wistful voice.

"Father, I should like a new quilted petticoat, with roses on it like Mercy Gorham's."

"Hush, Mehitabel. Thou art of a worldly nature. Think upon thy Heavenly Father, and go to sleep."

"Sir, I could go to sleep faster if I might have promise of ye petticoat."

"Mehitabel, be silent."

"Yes, sir. Father — I am sorry anent ye colored beads."

"We speak no more of them."

"Good night, father."

"Good night, daughter."

Andrew reseated himself beside the fire. The candle flickered in the draft from the clumsily set window. The hearth flame quivered over logs in which the dead ash crept and stirred like worms.

"The canker worm is ever at the heart of the rose of virtue, yea, it shall destroy the virtue that is in youth." Andrew was convinced that the younger generation was leaguing itself with Satan. He knelt by the hearth to pray for his worldly sons and daughters; and though he struggled to believe that the spirit of the Lord was in them, his heart was heavy with a bleak certainty of sin. He looked into the embers and tried to foretell the future. Suddenly the flames died, leaving the ash dark with foreboding. Andrew prayed silently for his young sons who would, perhaps, sail the seas and grow wild and prodigal of youth like Samuel; and he prayed for his daughter-baby who could go to sleep faster with the promise of a quilted petticoat than with the assurance of an ever-present God. If Andrew had known that from these children would derive such men as Benjamin Hallett, who like Samuel followed the sea, who became owner of the *Ten Sisters,* the prettiest packet that ever sailed past the tip of the Cape, yet who raised the first Bethel flag for seamen's worship in New York and Boston, the pious goodman would have been comforted, and his hope strengthened.

The candle by the window died in a flower of sparks. Andrew rose, dusted his knees, and banked the dying fire. Then tiptoed to the threshold of the up-step bedroom, where starlight illumined the curve of Mehitabel's round cheek. Perhaps she needed a quilted petticoat. In the morning he would consult with Ann. He listened closely for the short, childish breathing. Mehitabel lay in quiet slumber, and Andrew felt a lump of thankfulness rise in his throat; for the memory of Samuel, for the presence of Ann, Mehitabel, and two staunch, brave little boys asleep aloft in the lodging chamber. And Ruhama and Abigail to care for them all until such time as the two sisters were called upon to rear families of their own. But of all the love bonds, the strongest, the deepest, lay between him and his daughter-baby, for whom he feared the most. This strange link between father and youngest daughter was recognized in Cape family life, and gradually the goodmen came to give it a name. The daughter-baby was the father's *tortience*. Andrew probably never used it; he may not even have known what it meant; but Mehitabel was his *tortient,* of that there is no doubt.

"By grace are ye saved, through faith, and that not of yourselves," said a minister over the body of Benjamin Hallett, a hundred years later. "It is the gift of God."

Andrew moved the candlestick from the window to the table. Then, quietly, he climbed the oaken ladder to the lodging chamber above. "By Grace, Thou wilt save them, through faith, and that not of themselves," whispered Andrew. "It is the gift of God."

THE "ARRAIGNMENT OF BLOOD"

Snow had fallen for two days, thick, clinging flakes like ghostly moss. No wind blew it from the pines where it hung in heavy silence. On the second night, the snowfall ceased, clouds scuttled across the Sound and a moon came up over flying scuds. Every diamond windowpane in the village of Sandwich wore a festoon of white, like a small muslin curtain drawn back at the corners. Sloping roofs, coated thickly, lent to the houses the look of sugar cookies baked in a German oven, and in the forests around the village, trees cloaked in snow and moonlight resembled Quakers in gray garments and broad, peaked hats.

A tallow dip burned late in the taproom of Will Newcomb's tavern. By this light an old man slept, his head on the oak table, his battered cocked hat clutched in his unkempt hand. He breathed heavily, wheezing, and when someone shook him by the shoulder, his body responded limply and he opened one eye. For two nights and days he had slept by the table in the taproom. Now and again, amused taverners roused him, to hear him rant, or sing, or pray; for once, many years before, he had been a minister "full of pious words," and these he was still ready to repeat if anyone paid for enough liquor to keep him in his cups.

On the second night of the "Long Snow" he was turned out of the tavern. Either drunk or delirious, he shook his cane and talked aloud as he wavered forward, leaving an uncertain pattern in the snow. He indulged in argument with himself concerning his destination: was he headed for home? where was home? His good-wife, Jane, was a long time dead; his drunken son gone off to sea; no welcome awaited him at the hearth of his daughter-in-law who had sat in the stocks a whole day as penalty for "chopping him in the back." His little daughter, Rebecca, to get away from a house "desecrated by impiety and drunken revelries," at thirteen had married William Hunt who, a dozen times, kicked his father-in-law out of the house. Old George Barlow was sufficiently conscious of his own condition not to attempt a return.

The night grew increasingly cold. The outcast, as if by habit, turned his footsteps toward the Quaker settlement at Spring Hill. On the road his memory became more than usually warped. He forgot that a score of years had passed since King Charles sent Samuel Shattuck to Boston with orders to "send imprisoned Quakers to England for trial"; a ruling that meant no more fat fines paid to local magistrates, and that brought to an end Barlow's power in the colony.

A house loomed against shrouded ground, and the aimless wanderer groped, instinctively, for the door. John Jenkins' house it was. The words of Bishop's *New England Judged* rang in the old man's ears: "He (Barlow) took the Pot wherein he (Jenkins) boyled his victuals," and after that the Jenkins family could not procure another kettle for a year and a half. John's wife offered "Cloath double the Sum" instead of the kettle, but Barlow refused. The drunkard chuckled to himself as he recalled the incident; then, abandoning his quest, he fled before the inmates could unbar the door. Floundering from house to house, like a moth attracted to any light in the blur of that mothlike storm, he knocked at the doors of more than a dozen homes and always, before his summons was answered, turned hurriedly away. After a while he began to run, obsessed by the belief that the men whom he had ruined were after him, their uncreaking footsteps muffled by the snow. He headed for Christopher's Hollow, the old Quaker Meeting Place in the forest where, in 1659, and '60, and '61, he had sought his townsmen for persecution. Forgetting that his power as colony marshal was gone, he planned, once more to seek out Quaker Meeting, "Tracking them by the Print of their Feet up and down in the woods . . . halling and pulling them . . . treading on their Feet . . . turning up their Hats . . . Threatening them with the Stocks . . . Smoaking Tobacco among them . . . Searching of their Houses by Day and Night . . . to see what they had there; and stealing away that which he should not."

He laughed in the darkness, then sprang aside in panic at his own voice. A clump of young pine trees closed around him and he bowed toward them, mockingly, mistaking these woodland inhabitants for a gathering of the people called "Friends." He lifted his cane and flicked a hat brim. The headdress slid to the ground. So, in true Quaker wont, the recipient of an insult offered no retaliation. Convinced of the validity of his obsession, he identified a tall tree as Mr. Edward Perry, whose cattle he had confiscated, driving them past their distressed owner whom he pretended not to recognize. He recalled how, with Caldwel, his deputy marshal, he had seized, in the winter of 1659, Perry's "Box and Writing and money and Plate therein," and "raised a report" that the papers disclosed a plot against marshal and magistrates. The townspeople accepted this pretense despite the affirmation of Thomas Clark in open court that Barlow "stood convicted and recorded of a lye att Newbury." Caldwel and Barlow destroyed Perry's papers and when a friend of the Quaker's exclaimed, "George, thou mayst wash thy Hands, but thou canst not wash thy Heart," the marshal was quick to retort: "One dram of the Bottle will do it."

Conscious of a long sigh behind him, he turned and peered at two shadowy forms, the shorter with broad skirts sweeping the ground. That would be William Allen and Priscilla, from whom he had taken all their earthly possessions, and when Priscilla and the children were living on bread and water, while William starved in a Boston prison, he had appeared, "sanctimonious drunk," entered the house, produced a warrant for additional fines, taken the last cow remaining to the family, the small amount of corn left in the bin, the bag of meal that a kindly neighbor had brought as a gift. He also seized a copper kettle and mockingly addressed the young wife: "Now, Priscilla, how will thee cook for thy family and friends, thee has no kettle?" To which Priscilla replied: "George, that God who hears the young ravens when they cry, will provide for them. I trust in that God, and I verily believe the time will come when thy necessity will be greater than mine."

When poverty and shame were on him, the old sinner lurched,

one day, against the door of Priscilla's house. She took him in, fed him, cleaned and mended his filthy clothes, and sent him out, half mocking, half worshipful, until, within an hour or so, he told a false story, and drank six bumpers of ale, two to her eyes, two to her legs, two to her white breasts. Hearing of that, William Allen lashed him with a horsewhip — all of which passed through the old man's memory and was quickly lost in a renewed conviction that he was again "Marshall in all Things." With his stick he struck off the hat of young William Allen. A blue gray shower fell softly to the ground. Beyond it the white kerchief of Priscilla seemed folded against the dark. Barlow put an unsteady hand toward the kerchief, drew the hand away wet. He turned then to the others: Thomas Greenfield, Robert Harper, Matthew Allin, whose corn and oxen he had taken, whose fence he had broken, whose house he had claimed, explaining, in the words of his deputy: "We must suppress you or you will go to hell alive."

In that midnight forest, all sixteen of the men whom he had haled before the assembled magistrates in the house of Richard Bourne, assailed his maudlin conscience. At the time of the persecutions, Bourne had refused to sit with his confrères, so only Governor Prince, Captain Willet, Thomas Hinckley, and Josiah Winslow determined the punishment of the "Friends." Three were cast into prison and kept there in icy weather. The rest were ordered whipped or fined, and Major Winslow, irritated by their answers, exhibited "Vehemency and Fierceness of Spirit"; whanged the table with his stick, then hammered it with his hand, and stamped his feet "like a Madman, saying, *He could not bear it.*" Whereat the Quaker, Thomas Ewer, reproached the Governor. Ewer was a man from whom Barlow had taken £20, 10s, a money chest, a "suit of Clothes even as good as New, a new Bed and Bolster Tick, Ten Yards of Canvas, a new Blanket, about £18 of sugar, Four Yards of Kersey, a pair of Stuff Breeches." The marshal cut out the "new Cloath and put [it] upon his own Back." Seeing it there, Ewer cried out to the court, asking, "Whether they owned George Barloe *in wearing of his Cloth?*" The Governor, in defense of his marshal, answered coldly that Ewer might "seek his satisfaction" if he could prove that Barlow had wronged him; and giving the Quaker no chance to present further proof, Prince sentenced him "To be laid Neck and Heels together."

George Barlow, wearing the "new Stuff Breeches" and the newly cut coat, executed sentence; and, some twenty years later, still clad in the Quaker's tattered greatcoat, striking at a tree robed in snow and moonlight, he believed that Thomas Ewer dropped his cloak and sighed.

A few minutes later, Barlow put his hands to his ears to drive out the reiterant prophecies of the "noisy Quakers," Christopher Holder and John Copeland, who were "moved of God" to cry out in congregational churches, and who had their right ears cut off by the hangman in Boston. Their famous words of threat and forgiveness, at the execution of this cruelty, echoed through both colonies and frequently recurred to Barlow's guilty thoughts: "They that do it Ignorantly, we desire the Lord, from our hearts to forgive them; but they that do it Maliciously, Let our Blood be on their Heads; and such shall know, in the Day of Account, that every one of these Drops of our Blood shall be as heavy upon them as a Millstone." After imprisonment in Boston, the two were "moved" to go to the island of "Martin's Vineyard," to cry out against the "Priest Maho." There, they were promptly placed in a small boat, manned by one Indian, and by him conducted to the mainland. Richard Bourne's native converts, good to all men afflicted, cared for the two fugitives; but as the Quakers approached Sandwich, Barlow seized them and carried them before the selectmen of the village who had been appointed by the court, in the absence of a magistrate, to witness the execution of the law. These "venirabel" townsmen, dominated by the tolerance of Bourne and Freeman, "declined to act in the case." Barlow, disappointed, removed the prisoners to his own house where he locked them up for six days and would have starved them if his wife, Jane, with the aid of little Rebecca, had not smuggled them so much of her good cooking that they fattened in captivity. On the sixth day of their imprisonment, June 19, 1658, he marched them to Yarmouth. There Thomas Hinckley resided, an "Anti-quaker" who had been appointed, that month, assistant to Governor Prince. After a brief interrogation of John and Christopher, Hinckley ordered the "Strapado." So Christopher Holder and John Copeland were tied to an old post, and had thirty-three stripes laid upon their backs by "a new tormenting whip, with three cords, and knots at the ends, made by the Marshal, and brought with him. At the sight of which cruel and bloody execution, one of the spectators . . . cried out in the grief and anguish of her spirit . . . 'How long, Lord, shall it be ere thou avenge the blood of thine elect?' "

In the forest where pines were sighing, George Barlow heard that cry, and kept his hands over his ears. Only liquor could drown the reverberation of such words; but the tavern would no longer keep him, and everywhere he turned, trees that were not trees rebuked him with accusing silence. Among them he thought that he perceived an Indian woman whom he had wronged and "on whom the terrors of God fell, but he got off them . . . hardened to the Purpose." "Lyar," "False-swearer," "Man of a Seared Conscience without Remorse" — over and over, epithets used against him rang through his bewildered brain. He alternately cowered and strutted in an evil pride.

Toward morning a delicate snow began to fall, and just before dawn the flakes took a tinge of rose. The broken-spirited marshal lurched, fell to his knees, then pulled himself abruptly upward, tore his cocked hat from his head, waved the hat in powdery air, and ordered the "Meeting" to disperse. Nothing stirred in the forest; the snow seemed slowly reddening; weight intolerable fell on his shoulders, weight that he could not hope to support. Again he heard Copeland and Holder: "Such shall know, in the Day of Account, that every one of these Drops of our Blood shall be as heavy . . . as a Millstone."

Sobbing, the old man tumbled down at the skirts of the burdened trees, and lay quietly as first-hour light struck the upward branches. The circle around him seemed to turn from a group of gray-cloaked, accusing Quakers to a white tribunal. The drifting clouds thickened. A new deluge of flakes veiled the ground in merciful obscurity; for that was the third day of the "Long Snow" in Sandwich. Four such days were to come.

Marshal George Barlow was never seen alive again. A long time passed before men knew what had happened in Christopher's Hollow; and for generations after that, when, in a snowfall heavy and still, weight suddenly dislodged from the woodpile a stick of wood that thudded as it fell; or when the wind put finger to latch; or when a drift slid from the eaves and thumped on padded ground — the housefolk nodded to one another, and whispered in the wintry darkness: "Old Marshal Barlow is knockin' at the door."

"PERFIDIOUS COWS"

Mary Walley, the minister's daughter, was eyable and knowful and yonderly of heart. Man, woman and child in Barnstable, they all loved Mary. Unlike other ministers' daughters, unlike anyone else in the world, thought Job Crocker, as he wooed her and suffered "trepitations" that she was not of "mortal mold." Everyone in the town knew how uncertain Job's temper was. When Mary gave ear to his courting talk, he felt it his duty to warn her against "cholerick naters." She smiled. He smiled. Somehow tempestuous hours seemed remote, unreal.

Her father agreed to the union, after Job, experiencing throat trouble, declared himself before the amused gaze of the Rev. Mr. Walley, who had been a great minister in London before he turned nonconformist and defied Archbishop Laud. Receiving a call to Boston in the "heathen Americas," the minister of William and Mary's Church, Whitechapel, preferred a settlement in Barnstable; a decision so incomprehensible to "Bostonites" that they demanded verification. His choice proved spontaneous. He had lost his heart to blown-grass marshes, apple-bloom farms, and brown young sailormen; and the townspeople of Barnstable were so proud of their "London preacher" that they even accepted his benighted tolerance toward Indians, accepted his tolerance in all matters save one. Not a word should mortal breathe against the Reverend Thomas Walley. Angry freemen stripped the shirt from the back of Robert Harper, and lashed his body with a knotted thong for "censuring" parson. They ruthlessly fined any man who disputed the minister's will.

When Mr. Walley consented to a marriage between his favorite daughter and Job Crocker, the young suitor speeded the wedding, fearful lest his prospective father-in-law undergo a change of heart. Mary, "dilligently educated," knew far more than her young husband, of which he was aware. Determined to remedy this defect, he made a clean breast of his ignorance to Mr. Walley who questioned him on a few points of doctrine, admitted that the answers were more than doubtful, and suggested a course of reading. Notebook in hand, heavy brows drawn together, Job haunted the Walley study, doggedly pursuing theology, Latin, and civil law. Mary casually accepted his application to problems intellectual. All her family read, studied, expounded doctrine. She had long companioned a father far from strong and in need of daily aid in secretarial and parish work. Subsequently she companioned Job and found his earnestness, his determination, his honest definite thinking a refreshing experience after the more conventional mental concentration of her brothers and sisters.

Under Mr. Walley's tutelage, Job blossomed into a deacon, very young, earnest, a little proud of his new wisdom, careful about his temper, his orthography and his wife.

When Mary was six months with child, he relaxed into dreams of the future, into a belief that Mary and he had been destined for each other. It had not occurred to him that he was like the rest of the irascible and impetuous Crockers, astonishingly lovable. Nevertheless, in the quiet ways that a woman has of making a man aware of her contentment, Mary made Job happy, and because he was a Crocker, it soon became necessary to him to give expression to his gratitude. Consequently he elected to fight the battles, real or imaginary, of his frail, gentle father-in-law who was, in Job's estimation, too other-worldly to know how to look out for himself.

Take the problem of Quakers. Job could not see why Mr. Walley allowed them to say cruel things about Sabbath Meeting; nor could he understand why his father-in-law was so careless in collecting the ministerial tax. When Quakers were poor, or had been persecuted by Marshal Barlow, Job recognized a reason for the minister's forbearance. But the Reverend Mr. Walley's family were obviously in need of clothes and the kindly parson was pretending that he no longer required his expensive medicine, nor new spectacles from London; and all this while Ralph Jones, Quaker, inveighed against him, disturbed worship, waxed rich in cattle and grain, yet refused to pay the ministerial tax to which, by the oath of freeman, he was legally bound. Ralph openly boasted that he would pay no tithes to "Priest Walley," although he well knew that the tax was a lien upon the land. Job could not see why Jones should not be forced to pay.

The fellow could neither read nor write, yet had the presumption to stand up in meeting and cry out against the wisdom of one who had preached before kings.

The position of deacon carried with it civil authority. Determining to take advantage of this prerogative, one morning Job cut a cow-thorn branch, and without revealing his destination, set out alone down the King's Highway. From West Barnstable he traveled to the boundary line between that township and Sandwich, where, on the Barnstable side of the line, he turned into the pathway that led to Ralph Jones' farm. Ralph was gone from home, no doubt in Christopher's Hollow where Quakers resorted for "Vile practises" that sounded more like witch gatherings than religious services. Job entered the large stable, unhitched four cows from their stalls, and took with them their calves. These he led away without notice to anyone; for Job was determined that Mr. Walley, and Mary, who seemed not to thrive as she should, were to have milk, calf meat and calf broth to strengthen them. Two of the cows belonged to the colony for failure to pay tax; but the other two were, Job believed, the legal property of his father-in-law.

He plodded slowly up the Highroad, drove his trophies through the parish house gateway and toward the Walley barn. The good minister heard a commotion, went to the study window, and stared in amazement at the arrival of Job and a herd. Hurrying out of the house, he accosted his son-in-law whose face was shining with the virtue of one protecting the innocent, succoring the oppressed.

Thomas Walley wanted the cows almost as much as Job did, wanted them for Mary, and understood Job's ardor; but he was a proud man trying to set an example of Christian zeal in a hotheaded colony. Also he was humble toward men who did not need him. If Quakers refused his guidance, he regarded it as evidence of his own failure to dominate and harmonize all souls within his charge. He looked at Job's triumphant face, and had not the heart to order this new, ardent, likable son-in-law immediately to retrace his steps. He thanked Job, admitted that the tax due the colony should be collected, but expressed his desire that word be sent to Ralph Jones that the cows due the ministry would not be required. Job refused to be party to any such message. With a rebellious glance at his father-in-law, he drove *all* the cows into the barn.

Another deacon took word to Jones that Mr. Walley would not stand upon his rights and that he, Jones, might retrieve his stock whenever he so desired. Ralph, with a Quaker's affection for martyrdom, sent word to the minister: "Your son-in-law drove them away. Now let him drive them back." Anxiously Mr. Walley suggested that the cows be returned. Job refused. Then the parson sounded out his son, John, and all his deacons, and every man of them met his request with avoidance or denial. The cows rightfully belonged to him. Ralph Jones needed a lesson; let Jones come for them if he chose.

This controversy lasted for weeks. It upset Mr. Walley's constitution, a result that Job refused to recognize, too young to understand ecclesiastical nerves. Also, Mary was approaching her time. Never had she seemed so beautiful, her skin clear, her eyes shining, her ways absurdly young. Job's whole heart was with her. It seemed to him that she was growing frail, so he killed one of the calves in the barn and a fresh serving of veal was prepared. Mr. Walley gave Job a thorough reprimand and decided to bestow the meat on the poor. Job pointed out that in the matter of household supplies, there were no families poorer than the minister's. Watching his son-in-law's face, realizing that Mary could eat little and longed for a taste of such meat, Thomas Walley weakened and permitted his daughter to "be refreshed with a Serving."

Almost immediately "Came the Angel of Death." Mary "no sooner did eat a little of the Calf, but fell into great Trouble and cryed, *Return home the Man's Cows, I hear a great noise of them,* and so died in that Trouble."

Mr. Walley, overcome by the shock of his daughter's death, was forced to keep to his bed. Excited townspeople gathered in groups to talk of the Quaker league with the devil, of the mysterious meetings in Christopher's Hollow, of the admitted hatred of the sect toward the ministry, and of "perfidious cows." Job Crocker listened, lost his head, and threatened to kill Ralph Jones; whereupon Mr. Walley summoned him to the bedside and reasoned with him quietly. Job found relief in sobs.

When Sabbath came Mr. Walley was too ill to preach the sermon; Mary's fair young body still lay unburied; and Job, his face haggard, his eyes blazing, went to a meeting that was not a service but a gathering of angry men and women who had chalked clay crosses on their barns to prevent fiends of the sect called "Friends" from bewitching supplies. "Quaker dogges, rone them out ye Towne!" Let Sandwich care for them, whose magistrates were reputed to be "tarnished with a lust for Quakery!" And then, suddenly, into the meeting house, walked the "London Minister," visibly aged, his hair white, his footsteps uncertain. Job Crocker saw him, saw the people give way before him, watched them gaze on the white, bowed head, and suffered a pang of jealousy. Thomas Walley's hair had turned white, a sign of overwhelming grief for Mary; whereas Job, who knew that no man had ever endured a loss that remotely paralleled his, had not a gray hair, nor a tear; only, inside him, burned a fiery need for action.

Mr. Walley ascended the pulpit stairs. The townsmen stood up in their pews. Making no mention of his loss, he expressed sorrow that the Lord did not give him strength in that hour to preach as he desired. He asked that his loving brethren conduct their meeting without him, but desired, before he left them, to utter for their sakes one prayer. The "loving brethren" bowed their heads. They were in need of protection: parents afraid for their children, young people who had played with Mary, frightened to think of her as dead. They listened, Job Crocker listened, hoping for some new formula for the destruction of Quaker magic.

They heard the Lord's Prayer. Slowly, with quietude, the minister spoke words that Job had repeated all his life and that he had never fully heard until that desolate hour. Every word, every implication of the prayer was as a covenant upon him, upon that startled assembly. The minister finished, descended the pulpit, walked quietly away. The townspeople stood still. Their bodies leaned against the walls of the high box pews on which their heads were bowed.

The afternoon after Mary was buried, Job went to the barn. He looked long at the perfidious cows. One of the beasts gazed back at him in a way that troubled Job. He watched the stock for the rest of the day, and at nightfall struck a bargain with the gravedigger's son, to come over and keep night vigil: emolument, fourpence per week. The gravedigger's son, aged eighteen, still had difficulty in distinguishing between the letters A and B; but he understood thoroughly the possibilities of "bewitchery," put a gray cross on the barn, wore witch hemp on his arm.

Time passed, and the gossip died; even the wild suspicions faded. Jones never came for his cows nor did Mr. Walley return them. The London minister, unable to rally from the blow of Mary's death, sat by her grave all day, forgot the hours, and had to be "fetched" home. Job invariably came for him, for he and his father-in-law had grown close to one another. He neglected his farm, even his position as deacon, and stood for hours whittling, near the stalls of the "tithe-money cows." Once he went to the barn at night and found the gravedigger's son snoring. He abandoned then the payment for a nocturnal vigil and asked his father-in-law's permission to return the herd or to slaughter them. The Barnstable parson advised against it and urged upon Job the necessity for intelligent men to beware of spiritual panic.

The winter passed and the summer came; the summer passed, while Thomas Walley perceptibly failed and Job Crocker made nothing of life. The cows behaved with bovine complacency. At last Mr. Walley decided that there was only one way to save Job from himself. The boy must feel exonerated from responsibility for Mary's death. It must be proved to him that the meat that she had eaten bore no infernal poison, that her passing was a dispensation from Heaven.

One morning in autumn Mr. Walley walked out to the barn. He saw the wild birds flying south over the marshes, he heard the leaves of oak trees crack against the painted cold. Job was standing by a stall. With a pang the minister saw that the boy's shoulders were stooped. He laid a hand on his son-in-law's arm, and ordered him to "kill a Quaker calf." With a heart straining in excitement, with terror for his idol, with also a wild hope that his morbid fears might forever be stilled, Job slaughtered one of the perfidious cows and prepared the meat. He intended to eat of it, himself only; but this intention Thomas Walley guessed and sternly forbade. They should partake together, said he, they two who loved Mary; and if no evil befell them, then they should know that her going was not the work of a Quaker curse made potent by Job's persistence, but the will of God. Thomas Walley, who was an old man and loved his son-in-law, deceived him. Secretly he ordered one "serving" to be cooked, without word of the meat's origin. He alone ate of it and that night he died.

Barnstable parish was terrified. The plague from France was not so dire as this curse visited upon them. They filed past the preacher's body, and saw Job Crocker standing at the foot of the bed. They cursed Ralph Jones. Sabbath service hour came with no minister to guide them. Men appeared with guns in their hands; women with gray crosses embroidered on their sleeves. The group was potentially what in later years would have been called a lynching party, waiting for such a leader as young Deacon Crocker of fiery temper, swift, impetuous. "Quaker Dogges!" Run them out of town! Tar them, feather them, hang them to trees! Every cow and heifer that they owned should be burned on a great funeral pyre!

Into the meeting house Job Crocker came, and the people cried out at sight of him, then grew silent in perplexity. Not ordained or blessed with a "calling," he had no right to mount the pulpit. Yet, to the amazement of his friends and sympathizers, he staggered up the stairs. Before he reached the top step he fell against the pulpit wall, buried his face in his arms, and from muffled lips a voice came chokingly. Fighting for utterance, slowly, fervently, he repeated the Lord's Prayer.

After it he fainted, though a breath of cold sea air revived him; and that same Sunday with a cowthorn branch in his hand he marched down the King's Highway to Ralph Jones' farm, driving before him the remainder of Jones' cows. Ralph was gone from home, probably gone to Christopher's Hollow where Quakers met of a Sunday. So Job hitched the cows in their stalls, and at night, with the large stars close at his elbow, he returned to Barnstable parsonage, to the children of Thomas Walley, who were needing his strength.

A sequel to this story pertains to the family of Jones. Ralph's son, and a cousin from Sandwich, grown affable over their liquor, agreed one night to exchange farms. Ralph's son went to Sandwich, and Simeon Jones became a townsman of Barnstable, and though he was no ardent Quaker, refused to enter Barnstable Church. He desired, however, to establish proof of personal integrity, so when Thanksgiving came, he dressed a fat young turkey and sent it to the minister, the Reverend Lemuel Shaw. Would parson decline it? Would parson be afraid to eat of it? Simeon instructed the boy who carried the gift to inquire carefully whether or not Mr. Shaw desired the turkey. Conforming to directions, the boy questioned the minister who, having been previously supplied, thanked him and declined the offering. Then Mr. Shaw took the precaution of asking whence the turkey came. "From Quaker Jones of the pisen cow-meat," said the boy expectantly. Lemuel Shaw smiled. "If that is so, I'll take it," said he; and he ate the turkey and thrived and fattened, although certain townspeople say that his escape was due to precaution, in that he repeated the Lord's Prayer over and over as he ate.

THE ASSEMBLY OF SAINTS

Summer and winter on Abner Hersey's bed reposed a dozen all-wool fulled blankets. In hot weather he turned down one or two, using the rest as an upper layer of mattress. In cool autumn he turned down three or four; and when the winter wind howled around the eaves, he buried himself under the whole twelve. By day he wore a greatcoat made from seven calfskins tanned and prepared by Mr. Joseph Davis, and also an inner coat and waistcoat always lined with baize. He wore a shirt of the same cloth, and a pair of broad, homemade breeches. Huge cowhide boots came to his knees. His sparse brown hair was covered with a white wool wig topped by a red buff cap. A strange apparition, the townsmen said; a madman, strangers declared if they chanced to meet him riding the roads in all sorts of weather, sometimes astride a sleek black mare, sometimes driving a carriage as oddly constructed as his dress. Built like a sulky, the carriage was closed on every side, with two small openings in front, one for the reins and the other for Abner to see to guide his horse. From this equipage a hollow voice groaned aloud directions to the mare, epithets against the cold, or the sea wind, or the rain. Children hid when the carriage passed; strangers gave it a wide berth. In just such a fashion the devil himself might ride!

No physician in Massachusetts ever had a more extensive practice than Dr. Abner Hersey; no man ever secured more completely the confidence of his patients. Individual towns of the colony, in the mid-eighteenth century, had their local physicians, but only one "Cape Doctor" made rounds of the entire peninsula. Knowing his route, anxious friends of patients, and those suffering from minor ailments, waited by village green or lonely crossroad for the appearance of a black horse, a red buff cap or, when the weather was

inclement, for a carriage that looked like a giant octopus holding to a mare's flanks by long tentacle arms.

In 1743 Dr. Hersey married Hannah Allen, and their wedding was
celebrated in the old Allen house where sixteenth-century armor stood
in a greathall. The Allens were aristocrats, and the doctor's bride
was not only "fashionable" but "gently nurtured" as well. She
found the transition to Abner's house a frightening experience; his
whims and sudden passions "productive of no domestic felicity." At
the end of a year a daughter was born to Abner and Hannah, a frail
child, who took by storm the father's heart and brought to the troubled young mother comfort and serenity. Abner set the clock of his
days by this daughter, grudging every minute of absence; and Hannah, grown tolerant of his eccentricities, found herself happy again.

When little Mary Hersey "sickened" of the "dreaded Pox" not all
the doctor's skill could save her; and after her death his eccentricities
became more extreme. He developed an insane fear of smallpox;
at one time would not approach a house where it occurred. Once
he visited a patient who revealed symptoms of the disease. Terrified,
the neurotic physician fled from the door, rode his mare into a
lather, then secreted himself in his bedroom and refused to come
forth for more than a week, believing his last hours had come.

Edward Childs mixed all of Dr. Hersey's medicines, under careful
supervision, and also kept meticulous accounts. The doctor never
demanded money yet recorded to a farthing what each man paid or
owed him. Jonathan Davis, upon receiving his annual bill, found on
it to his credit: "for chasing a calf and not catching it, fourpence."

Edward Childs was often sorry for the doctor's young wife, who
spent all her days soothing Abner's irritable temper. Every evening
she went to the Burying Acre, carrying in winter a sprig of evergreen,
in summer the garden flowers. No other child came to unite the couple; no guests were ever made welcome for any but the briefest of
calls. Once Abner's sister-in-law proposed making him a visit. "Ma-
dame," said he, "I cannot have you here; I am sick and my wife is sick.
I have no hay nor corn for your horses; and I have no servants in my
family, and I had rather be chained to a galley oar than wait on you
myself."

With the exception of Edward Childs, no servant consented to remain to help Hannah fulfill her difficult days; but Edward, who went

home at night, did what he could to give her the town news and the light gossip that a woman needs to cover a heavy heart. One day Dr. Hersey, in appreciation of his assistant's services, declared, "Edward, I have given you one hundred pounds in my will. What do you intend to do with it?" "Dress up," said honest Edward, "and marry off my girls." The doctor was disgusted and changed his will at once.

A great part of Abner's earnings he put into arable land, extensive, well cleared acres, surrounded by a five-rail fence, its posts driven two and a half feet into the ground. Throughout the Cape, "Land fenced as well as Abner's" came to be the measure of good fencing, and as he always put back into the ground more than he took from it (an almost unheard-of custom in the days when goodmen bled their farms) the townspeople came to estimate their acreage by the quality of Dr. Hersey's. Despite the wealth accruing to him from this wise and unusual knowledge of the soil, Abner suffered severe losses from the depreciation of Continental currency during the Revolutionary War. He refused to take sides with the "Whipsnapper Whigs," and solemnly attended three Tory meetings. Unfortunately, at each of these he rose from his seat and addressed the assemblage as "fish"; a platform method ill calculated to endear him to his party. They flung him a cabbage and told him to go home and with it make a poultice for his hot tongue. Incensed, he betook himself out of the Tory ranks, and professed neutrality; a relief to both sides, for a curious, passionate confidence in his medical skill persisted. More thoroughly trained doctors practiced in all of the larger towns of the peninsula. Yet when a child lay ill, be it of Tory or Whig family, the father rode, posthaste, for Dr. Hersey, who fought the normality of death as fiercely as he fought the normality of life.

During the revolution he lost his famous black mare, a horse "pernickety" as her master. Fearful that she would be "commandeered," he spent unnecessary energy in explaining to the militia how unsuitable such a mount would be for a cavalryman whose first requirement should be a dependable horse. The mare was as stubborn as she was sleek and yet, in some strange way, she responded to Abner's melancholy adjurations, or to his irritable temper, whereas Edward Childs' affability invariably sent her ears back and made her eyes white with scorn. Neither coaxing nor the whip put her forward, but if someone lay dying and Abner shouted from the depths of the octopus carriage and told her about it, she ran her legs off as if there existed a knowledgeable communion between master and horse.

Edward Childs killed her. Angry at her stubborn ways, he struck her on the head; she fell heavily, in the stable, and died almost immediately. Edward ran to the house to tell Hannah, who also disliked the mare. Neither of them had the courage to break the news to Abner. Hannah secluded herself in the attic while Edward hid in the woods, and at noon Abner found his mare dead on the stable floor. He did not return to the house for dinner, but at dusk he came in, climbed wearily to his room, and called to Hannah on the way. She hurried down-ladder from the attic, and met him in the hallway; but before she could comfort or reassure him, the knocker clamored, and the reiterant cry that echoed through all their nights, their meals, their very hours of prayer, recurred — the eternal appeal, "Doctor! Doctor! Come! Ye are wanted."

Hannah went with him to the barn and the two of them dragged the body of the black mare to one side. Then Hannah, with her own hands, hitched her beloved saddle horse to the octopus carriage. She watched her husband as he drove away, dinnerless, supperless, steadying a panicky animal that found itself suddenly, ruthlessly, attached to the strangest obstacle that ever a horse drew.

As she went out of the barn where the mare that she hated lay covered with a blanket, she was suddenly aware that Abner and she had made of their disjointed union something better than either of them might have made of life alone.

The possibility of separation from her husband had never entered Hannah's head. Cape women "married" their men. Many of them lived difficult lives; most of them knew the wearing strain and blessed reward of children. But all that was normal to their days had been denied to Hannah, who placed her whole heart with an evergreen twig, or a spray of lilies, on a small grave. Yet if ever woman gave proof that quietude, confidence, union of spirit, could be maintained between two bitterly opposite characters, Hannah was such a one. She lived out her days with a man who refused to eat, sleep, dress, spend his waking hours as other men of his time, or of any time for that matter; a man with whom all men quarreled, and to whom in their need they came. He hated people, and saved them; he hated

life, and maintained it; was piteously afraid of death, and fought it
again and again without tremor, and with a power that embued essential confidence. He was always on the point of catching cold, or
some disease, or a "humer"; he was always suffering from symptoms
of spleen, and rheumatism, always prophesying imminent digestive
disaster. His house, his food, his clothes, were never completely to his
satisfaction. Yet he and Hannah made a life together, a lonely life,
lived as he devised it; and in the end her rebellion turned to a deep
tolerance, and every irritable word that came from a tongue that always seemed to be in need of a "cool poultice" became an admission
of the childish dependence of one oversensitive to life, overpercep-
tive, overintuitive. Upon the very qualities in him that made him a
difficult companion depended his peculiar diagnostic genius. He who
suffered every known disease, knew how to assuage the suffering of
others. Hannah never put such thoughts into words, but she administered to neurotic sensitivities that many another woman would
have ruthlessly brushed aside.

In 1787 Dr. Hersey died, aged sixty-six, and it was inevitable that
such a man should make a bargain with death. Hannah had money
from the Allens and was not interested in farming. So the doctor left
her more money, and then, because he loved his farm, he thought
to defy death by holding these lands as his forever. He left at his decease a scheme for the "Immortality of his Fields."

He divided his estate among the thirteen Congregational Churches
of the Cape, in the proportion in which each parish had employed
him as physician. Annually, three deacons from each of the thirteen
churches were to assemble at the Crocker Tavern in Barnstable, there
to direct the business of the farm, and to receive their due shares of
income from the land. Thirty-nine deacons were appointed to abide
for three days in the tavern, and this annual gathering came to be
known as the "Assembly of Saints."

At Abner's death the Hersey estate was under high cultivation,
but its management devolved upon men more pious than practical,
more greedy than wise. The "Saints" reinaugurated the old system
of cropping without manure. They cut the forests and sold the wood,
glutting their market and lowering prices. Yet despite this mortal
blow to the project, enough income was derived to fulfill Abner's
bequest:

$\frac{1}{3}$ of the rents to be used in the purchase of Dr. Doddrige's Rise and Progress of Religion.

$\frac{1}{3}$ to be expended on Dr. Evans' sermons on the Christian temper.

$\frac{12}{63}$ in the purchase of Reverend Henry Grove's discourse on the Lord's Supper.

$\frac{18}{63}$ in Dr. Doddridge on Regeneration; and on his Salvation by Faith.

$\frac{9}{63}$ in Dr. Doddridge's Discourse to young people.

$\frac{12}{63}$ in Dr. Doddridge's Education of children.

$\frac{13}{63}$ in Dr. Doddridge on the Power and Grace of Christ.

For one hundred years the ministers of each of the thirteen churches were ordered to distribute these books "for the interests of religion and virtue." Furthermore, Dr. Hersey gave notice that he would return at the end of one hundred years to inspect the "immortality of his fields," and to demand from the deacons an accounting.

On Saturday night in the old Crocker Tavern, then owned by Lydia Sturgis, the Cape deacons assembled; their nags were bedded in the stable, for they came by saddle, and the down-Cape men made a two day ride of it (all charges paid by the fund). Three days followed of conference, of conviviality, of religious discourse, interspersed with troubled estimate of distribution by sixty-thirds. At the end of the three-day conference, the "Assembly of Saints" disbanded. The deacons were hoisted upon their horses, the numerous discourses of Dr. Doddridge were strapped at the back of their saddles, and three by three, through the sandy highways, these good men rode away.

At the end of ten years no books were strapped behind the saddles of the "Saints." They had so mishandled their earthly estate that the Hersey fund paid only for reunions; no money was left for the purchase of books designed to enhance the virtue of the young. The deacons shook their heads in despair and took refuge in an old comfort: the young were clearly gone to the devil, beyond Dr. Doddridge's aid.

At the end of twenty-nine years, Abner Hersey's forests were a bare brown stubble, his rich fields were arid, and there was no longer money even to pay for the "Assembly of Saints." No money for horses to carry them. No money for taverns to house them. No money for ale. For some years the deacons had begun to absent themselves from the annual meeting, and, February 12, 1816, the General Court authorized the thirteen churches to sell the Hersey property. It was auctioned off in October. Very little was paid for lands long abused, and when that little was divided, the majority of the churches regarded it as income to be promptly expended. Long before the one hundred years had passed, at the expiration of which Abner had threatened to return for an accounting, nothing was left of his estate.

The old Crocker Tavern still stands by the highroad. Those who visit it are shown the common room where the deacons held their meetings. They are also shown "Hagar's Bedroom" in which a group of jolly taverners met to smoke, gamble, drink, and make love to pretty women; a room that was a focal point for what has been called "tavern life." Here, if we may believe tradition, a few "Saints" went astray.

In the old Cape houses, brown-covered books lie unread on the shelves. Every secondhand bookshop in the land is stocked with the same commodity. But the people who finger the discourses of Dr. Doddridge today are not perceptibly in search of virtue; nor do they say a prayer for Abner Hersey, that baize-covered bundle of mortal frailties who fought for a lifetime the dire battles of mortality, and whose white-wigged ghost, in a seven-skin coat and a red buff cap, drives over the long Cape roads in search of someone who can give him an accounting of the "Immortality of his Fields."

EXILES FROM BOURNELAND

Benjamin   Benjamin Bourne, with his feet in the brush and his
Bourne   head and shoulders coated with snow, explained for the
one hundredth time to old Parosilver, Chief of Patagonian Giants, how he, Benjamin, was "Duke of Mashpee, Earl of Sandwich, Emperor of Naushon Island and Royal Ruler of the Kingdom of Cape Cod." Parosilver listened with a romantic credulity unhampered by intellect. For three long months and a long week, Benjamin Bourne, onetime mate of the schooner *John Allyn*, had been held captive for ransom by the seven foot "cannabils" of Patagonia, ever since he made the grave mistake of rowing ashore to trade for supplies while his

ship lay off the Straits of Magellan. A storm forced the vessel away before the mate could be rescued, so the natives were left with an embarrassing prisoner who, by the look of his portrait, was not edible. They decided to keep Benjamin as man of all work in the chief's household, assistant to the five wives, nurse to the naked children, and royal entertainer when tribesmen or their visitors were in need of a marvelous tale.

Benjamin soon discovered that his only road to escape lay in spinning yarns of his fabulous importance. The Patagonians had recently murdered a white man, Captain Eaton, whose name woefully suggests his destiny, and they were loath to approach a white settlement lest they be held to account. Benjamin promised immunity, wherever they chanced to take him. All the white race, he declared, paid tribute to the Bournes. Mashpee bowmen, their arrows tipped with poisons, stood, as many as trees in a forest, waiting for word of their king. Benjamin advised Parosilver to act at once, while there was yet time, and deliver his captive to the nearest white village, there to receive rum, tobacco, rice, bread, beads and brass.

Now and again the Patagonian chief, at the advice of his councillors, was inclined to make way with Benjamin, who seemed to bring no luck at hunting, or caused unnatural droughts. Then the promises and boasts of the captive, expressed in pidgin Spanish, filled Parosilver with a mixture of anticipation and dread — fear of the Bourne armies, hope of a royal reward. He decided to risk an attempt at ransom, packed up his household, and with a thousand tattered tribesmen, started on a long trek down the Gallegos River, at the mouth of which was situated a white settlement too small and isolated to have received word of the consuming of Captain Eaton, yet possessed of sufficient rum to offer pleasant prospect.

Benjamin slept in the chief's tent, in the place farthest from the fire, ate the vilest portions of dog meat or guanaco; and when the chief's wives were hungry, often he starved. At one time he came close to death from dysentery. Believing that his hour was come, he crawled out of the greasy tent, thinking to die where the ground was green and the wind sweet. As he lay quietly, at the end of his strength, a dock weed fell under his hand; this he took as a message from God, crawled back into the tent, roasted the dock root in hot ashes, and by eating it, and abstaining from meat, he cured the dysentery and was able to push forward with the tribe.

He learned to ride without a saddle, and proved so useful on guanaco and ostrich hunts that he was permitted to accompany the huntsmen, though always equipped with the poorest horse to prevent his attempting an escape. When an ostrich was "started up" the chief drew out his "bolas," spurred his mount and set forth in pursuit. "His mantel fell from his shoulders; his long, straight black hair, so coarse that each particular hair stood out independently on end, streamed in the wind; his hideously painted face and body loomed up with grotesque stateliness and the deadly missile whirled frantically over his head." When the bolas hit its mark, the chief reined his horse abruptly, dismounted, wrung the neck of the captured ostrich, and deposited its carcass across the saddlebow of Benjamin's horse, or rather across the place where the saddlebow should be. Then Parosilver remounted and the hunt continued until the sailor and his nag looked like "a kind of store-ship."

Before the tribe left the region of the Straits, Benjamin had been permitted to signal passing vessels. In this way his undergarments were "desperately expended." Cravat and pocket handkerchief were appropriated by the chief's wives; and by the time that he reached the Gallegos River, his "sole article of linen" was in shreds. His coat and trousers, glazed with dirt and grease from the tent floor, shone like a glass bottle." All the contents of his pockets had been confiscated; his pistol taken to pieces and the brass mountings hung about the necks of the five wives. His watch, wrapped in a rag, then enveloped in coltskin, hung suspended among other valuables from the tent stake nearest Parosilver's bed. Whenever visitors appeared, runners from distant tribes, or councillors, or senior tribesmen, Benjamin was required to demonstrate the wizardry of the watch. At least forty times a day he was summoned to hold the "little machine" to the ears of distinguished guests while the Giants stood "in every attitude of silent amazement, their eyes dilated, their countenances lighted up in every feature with . . . wonder."

When the tribal migration neared the mouth of the Gallegos, and the island settlement of Holland was within a day's journey, the chief ordered a more permanent encampment, and selected a "deputation" as escort for the captive and to negotiate a ransom. In the darkness of night, Parosilver, five warriors, their wives, an old hag who desired to go, and Benjamin made a start for the bay from whose shores Holland might be signaled. They crossed a frozen marsh, forded a shallow river, traveled a few miles, and then took shelter for the remainder of the night, thrusting their feet into a thicket, while their heads were "lodged out of doors." During the journey Benjamin was permitted to carry his precious watch and in the rest hours of evening was forced to repeat his extravagant boasts of greatness, over and over, until the Giants fell asleep with the music of promises in their ears. In the morning Benjamin helped gather fuel, cook meat, lasso horses, and about midday the company reached the mouth of the Santa Cruz River. The Patagonians pointed downstream. Far, far away, several small huts were huddled on a little island. "Esta Holland Sarvey!" exclaimed the warriors, "plenty of houses, abundance of men, plenty of rum, tobacco, bread, tea, flour and rice!"

They made a fire that afternoon and talked late into the night, discussing plans for attracting the attention of the islanders. Snow, sleet and rain fell, and Benjamin, shaking with cold, "every tooth chattering," lay on the frosty ground, his feet sheltered by a bush. The next morning he displayed the colors of the English brig, *Avon,* a flag salvaged from the wreck of the vessel and brought at his request. The weather continued squally and no boat came from Holland. So Benjamin built a signal fire from bushes that had an oily leaf; yet twilight came with no response from the white settlement. Again the warriors, their wives and their captive slept with feet thrust into a thicket and heads exposed to the snow. Benjamin suggested that they try putting their heads into the thicket and leaving their feet exposed to the weather. The Patagonians rejected this as foolhardy advice. They discussed the failure of their plans and advocated an immediate return to the tribe; but Benjamin pleaded so earnestly for one more chance to signal, that they gave him another day.

That afternoon, when he had almost abandoned himself to despair, and while he was pacing the beach beside his signal fire and his flag, Parosilver, seated by a bush, reported a boat moving outward from the island. Benjamin hardly dared to look. At last he turned; the boat was there, drew steadily nearer, and stopped alongshore, within an eighth of a mile of the signal, the rowers resting on their oars. The

Cape sailor knew from the tragedy of his first experiences as captive that the natives would seize any ransom offered, and fail to release their prisoner; so he made no sign either to the Giants or to the white men, but ran, headlong, over the beach. The Patagonians yelled and started in pursuit. Their prisoner had the advantage of them in that his tattered shoes protected his feet from the sharp shells and beach stones. "Stop! Stop!" bawled the Giants. "Now, my legs," said Benjamin Bourne, "if ever you want to serve me, this is the time!" When he reached the shore opposite the dory, the natives were within ten or fifteen feet of him, and their hands had gone to their knives. Benjamin drew out his watch and flung it into the bushes. For a moment his pursuers hesitated; the "little machine" was a far more coveted possession than the body of a dead sailor, and while they salvaged it, Benjamin plunged into the surf and swam toward the boat. The white men from Holland, judging accurately of the situation, kept their guns leveled on Parosilver and his tribesmen. The swell was heavy, thick with spume, and Benjamin was scarcely able to keep afloat. As he neared the boat's stern, one of the boatmen thrust the end of a musket into the water. "Pull the dear man in," cried the boatman, and Benjamin seized the musket and managed to hold while his rescuers reached down and helped him to clamber over the side. He lay for some time, breathless, unable to explain himself; but the oarsmen pulled for Holland while the Giants howled on shore.

For some days after his escape the Patagonians lurked on the edges of Santa Cruz Bay, though they fled inland whenever an expedition of armed whites landed. Perhaps they believed Benjamin's promises; and they who seldom kept a trust expected a return, laden with rum and tobacco, of the "Duke of Mashpee, Earl of Sandwich, Emperor of Naushon Island, and Royal Ruler of the Kingdom of Cape Cod."

Sylvanus   Sylvanus Bourne, aged nineteen, set out alone for Chilli-
Bourne   cothe, Ohio, determined to make a fortune in the west where his brother had gone before him. He found traveling by stage extravagant — eight cents per mile — but he enjoyed the company "though they be very rude and profane." When he had covered the considerable distance from Bourneland to Pittsburgh, he "tock the opportunity of communicating" to his parents that, since his departure from his "native land for a foreign soil" he continued in perfect

health. Although he claimed to "have an eye that took much delight in viewing different scenery," observation of the "curiosities of the state of Pennsylvania" proved a "tegius" task. From Pittsburgh to Chillicothe pioneer conditions prevailed, in sharp contrast to the lazy staging of the first half of his journey. He wrote home that for seven days his "accomadations . . . were on a board in the open: $\frac{1}{2}$ of each night I stood centery."

He arrived in Chillicothe, June 24, 1816, "6 days from Pittsburgh, in perfect health, about dark." "Trembling for fear of non-reception," he inquired for the house of Mr. Hough where his older brother, Alexander, lived. His brother, he learned, was gone to Sandusky to "lay out a town there and another at Fort Meiggs." Anxiously young Sylvanus asked of Alexander's employer if there might be work for him. "O yes, a-plenty," answered kindly Mr. Hough, and invited the young Cape Codder into his house. At once Sylvanus "took to making towns," aided by the experience of his brother; and soon he wrote home that he could enjoy himself in Chillicothe "as well as any place in the nether world." But when it came to describing the country on which he was placing the first imprint of civilization, he referred his family to "Geographys"; and since he had not reached a score of winters, found it necessary to exercise the sense of longevity: "Remember me to all my friends," he begged. "Tell them in all my changing scenes I have never forgotten youth's friendly smiles."

Meanwhile, in Wareham, part of old Bourneland, Sylvanus' brother, Ebenezer, turned himself into a schoolmaster, and received the "ample stipend" of fifteen dollars a month. Ebenezer had been left in charge of Sylvanus' Sailor's Snugbox, a wooden chest in which all Cape families kept their best possessions. "I have your chest nailed up," wrote Ebenezer, "as Mercy Savery and Bathsheba was so anxious to get the key, to get a book. I asked them what book and they smiled. I told them I would get the book for them if they would tell me what book, and they would not, but laughed. I then nailed it up . . . They found the key and broke the key trying to get it open." Sylvanus, when he left Wareham, had been courting Mercy Savery, but now, engrossed in the role of young surveyor, he found, to his own surprise, that he was no longer interested in either the girls or the chest. He was earning a thousand dollars and enjoying an adventurous life. When Mercy Savery, in the following winter, married "Hatch the painter," Sylvanus languished for a long half day then cocked his hat and smiled.

Two years later, while Ebenezer was entrapped by "a powerful reffermation in Wareham," and like all young reformers planning to take a "female pardoner," Sylvanus came of age. He had acquired his thousand dollars "capatul" and was on the road to wealth. With something of the air of a man of the world, he celebrated his birthday by a letter declaring to his parents his ambitions, his assets, his success:

> . . . the world is a mirey road and without perseverance all would get stuck in the mud, and with it some do. This day the law liberates your last child — *one,* poor soul was never liberated; but think not your fate hard, for few parents see a greater proportion of their children at adult age than you have; one sixth only having gone to the regions where all living have but an imperfect knowledge of. . . . Time and distance wears away neighborly friendships, but natural affection endures for ever. Had I been a child of fortune no foreign land could have been my home, though many I would have journied through . . . All appointments are uncertain, yet I flatter myself that once again I shall see my native land, where all my boyish tricks were played and many a useful idea hatched. But greatness as yet I have never known and honour only by its name; my views were small but little would have satisfied both body and mind. As I saw splendour I craved, and knowing I could not obtain that portion I wished for, I set bounds to my views and enhanced my mind and made myself content whither it was natural or not.
>
> My friend Mr. Wallace has taken a female partner . . . he gives me thirty dollars a month of which I save about one half. . . . I have taken no side in politicks or priesticks unless questioned when I have kept nothing back. . . . I have braved storms — swam creeks — carried my provisions on my back — slept in a swamp with nothing but a beechen tree to shelter me from the midnights torrents and rains amidst the howling of many wolves; and I think I never enjoyed myself so well as I have in these excursions . . . the more fateigue I have . . . the more fleshy I get.

In 1819, he cleared one thousand five hundred dollars, and had acquired five hundred acres of land worth two dollars an acre. That was good property in 1819. He continued to take no side "in politicks or priesticks," and announced that he "would not put crape on his hat if the members of both houses should kill each other." He was young, upright, a little impudent, happy and ambitious; the stars "seemed to smile." He began making preparations for a wife, "predetermined to marry one raised in the state of Mass." In the spring of

1819 he started on his most ambitious expedition, five months "in the woods inhabited only by Indians and wild beasts"; and young Sylvanus alone in charge of a crew of seasoned men. Fever caught them before the job was half over. One entire crew perished, but the men were replaced as they "droped off one by one." An older leader would have returned to the settlements; but Sylvanus had never admitted failure. Although he, too, caught fever, and shook and burned, he worked unremittingly on his assignment. At the Rocky Fort of the Little Scioto, he suffered with such "shakes of the ague" that he thought his body would tear apart. Again his men died or deserted. Sylvanus "downed three large potions of Phine," and did the work himself. At the end of five months he returned to Chillicothe; one thousand three hundred dollars cleared, six hundred and forty miles surveyed. He did not realize, till he stood before a doctor, that he had forfeited his chance, ever again, to explore the malarial West. Since no expedition could be put in charge of a fever-bird, Sylvanus was no longer wanted as captain of a surveying crew.

At first he could not believe this, and planned a visit to Wareham. The Cape air would mend any ailment, and he might soon return. Fifteen days it took, from Chillicothe to Bourneland, and Sylvanus "shoke seven days without ceasing," received counterfeit money on the road, and arrived in Wareham in time to act as Ebenezer's brideman and be introduced to the bride's sister whom he describes as "a chois peice picked out for me." Ebenezer's position as schoolmaster, at fifteen dollars a month, looked poor to Sylvanus who could already count his wealth in thousands. But the Cape air failed to perform its miracle, and Sylvanus burned with a dull fever that lasted from six to twelve every evening. Slowly, inevitably, he realized that his life as a surveyor was done.

He decided to "read for Amusement & so live that his neighbors would feel small regret for the loss when gone." He made no outcry, asked no sympathy, invested his small capital well, and settled into the quiet life of a goodman. In time he married and went to housekeeping in the house built by that archadventurer Captain John Kenrick, who explored the Columbus River and ended his life mysteriously in the Polynesian Isles. Sylvanus, equipped to model the outpost towns of a young nation but tied to a Cape doorstone, looked for hours at the voyaging sea, walked in the night to watch the stars, and speculated on their motion. It occurred to him that these walks were "journeys more than terrestrial," were, in fact, "explorations of the solar system." So he made a model of "solar workings," a "contraption" that the townspeople marveled to see. He also journeyed outside of time and "took to reading books of 15th. and 16th. century."

Three small babies, aged respectively three months, one month, and six days, were carried from the darkened Kenrick house to the Bourne lot in the Burying Acre. Sylvanus' alert face grew lined and at times like a mask. Hannah, his wife, suffered and prayed, and refused to give up hope of children. By a sort of miracle, the fourth baby lived.

When he was fifty, Sylvanus, aided by his daughter, "mastered the French language." He read avidly, and at long last learned to spell almost correctly. He delighted to throw verbal spice into town meetings, a sense of humor that never diminished nor hardened into irony. "My health portends a premature old age," he wrote, and added, "it might have been worse." Unembittered, unafraid, he went on life's last adventure, having, as he said to his brother, "surveyed this world."

Ansel   Ansel Bourne, born in Sandwich, was seven years old when
Bourne   his father died. His mother, Betsy Green Bourne, gathered together her few possessions after the death of her young husband and with her three small sons returned to the state of Rhode Island where she had been born and bred. In Providence Ansel grew up, working at odd jobs, studying intermittently, attending Sunday school and church. Occasionally in summer he was sent to Sandwich on a visit to his cousins, the Bournes of Bourneland. Before he left Providence, his mother always mended and pressed his threadbare suit.

He was ashamed of patches, hated shiny seams. When he looked at his cousin Meletiah who wore a flowered waistcoat, when Betty Bourne tied under her chin a bonnet decorated with "howdy flowers," he rebelled at thought of walking to church beside these young aristocrats; preferred to follow like a servant and sit in a rear pew.

When Ansel was sixteen years old, "Uncle Henry Bourne" offered him a job in Sandwich and he went to live in the "hithermost" Cape town at a time when it was undergoing religious awakening. All the young men signed temperance pledges, fell from grace, suffered con-

trition and resigned, usually once a month. The pledges were taken
in the vestry on Sunday after meeting, and there, one morning, the
minister reasoned with Ansel before the congregation. The boy had
never tasted liquor, but had made himself unpopular by refusing to
pledge abstinence. Shy at first in his responses, heckling roused his
temper. Recipient of a long harangue, he grew hot under the collar,
announced that drinking was no sin, and shocked the minister by
ideas so unorthodox that the parson inquired ironically whether or
not Ansel believed in God. Too excited to care what he answered,
the boy thundered: *"No!"* A fraught silence eddied around him like
wind in grass; and for the first time in his young life Ansel felt important. He raised his head and added, as if to confirm his discovery: "No!
There is no God!"

Uncle Henry walked home with him and did not seem to notice that
the young heretic's knees shook. Uncle Henry made no comment as
Ansel went upstairs. The boy packed his carpetbag, putting into it
his "other" shirt, his two red flannel nightgowns, his two go-to-meet-
ing collars. As he worked, doctrinal heresies whirled around in his
head.

Downstairs, he came upon his uncle smoking a pipe by the fire.
"Uncle," said Ansel, "I have become an atheist."

"Struck sorta fast," answered Uncle Henry, without looking him
in the eye.

"Shall I leave Sandwich? Leave Bourneland?" Ansel tried to keep
out of the query a hollow croak that sounded like a bullfrog in the
marsh.

"Ye might return in a month or so, when ye git a little less cocky.
Until ye explain away life, son, ye better not explain away God."

Ansel picked up his carpetbag and left the house in a hurry. He
spent five long days walking from Sandwich to Providence, and arrived
home while Mother Betsy was brewing the evening tea. He had slept
the last night in a haymow, and forgotten to comb his unruly hair. She
took one look at him, and groaned. "Ansel," she said, "you've been
drinking."

"Yes," said Ansel, "for I have concluded that there is no God."

In Providence he worked in a grain shop, and soon discovered an
aptitude for adding figures in rows. He attended church regularly
and neither he nor his mother alluded to that Sabbath in Bourneland

when he had alienated his kin. In Providence the temperance pledge was not so omnipresent; also, there were two doors to the church. When the minister exhorted the young in the vestry, Ansel made a hasty exit by the little door at the far end of the meeting house.

Fifteen years of uneventful routine ensued. Mother Betsy seemed scarcely to note the passing of the days, and Ansel found that his thwarted passion for the ancient "kingdome of Bourneland" could be better satisfied by daydreams than by frustrate visits to the Cape.

He was thirty-one when Uncle Henry came to Providence and brought with him Betty and Meletiah. On the twenty-seventh of October, 1857, they arrived at the Crown Hotel, and the next morning, a Sabbath, they walked over to Ansel's house. Only Mother Betsy and her third son were there to receive the visitors (the two older brothers had wives and homes of their own). Betty Bourne, grown to be a lady, wore black mitts on her white hands and a fichu of foreign lace was draped about her throat. On her bonnet howdy flowers nodded briskly, pansies, verbenas, even more of them than on the day of the temperance pledge. Ansel could almost smell them, and wondered if Betty had taken to sin and was using "Paris Scent." Mother Betsy always hoped that Ansel would marry his cousin. He smiled, though his heart contracted in fear lest she reveal this hope and be wounded by Betty's scorn.

Young Meletiah, man of the world, possessed a waxed mustache, a cane and a watch fob. On the end of the fob there was no watch. He had, he declared, an introduction to the Bucks' Club; would Ansel care to join him in the evening for a round of poker or a cockfight? Ansel accepted doubtfully, wondering whether he could get a chance to run over to his brother's house and borrow an evening suit. He knew that Uncle Henry's children expected entertainment, and there was nothing to offer in the humble home, not even a good dinner. Into the midst of his anxieties penetrated his mother's voice; she was offering an invitation to church, to sit in their forward pew. Betty primly accepted, Meletiah less cheerfully. Uncle Henry pleaded an engagement, and to Ansel's consternation, he and Mother Betsy were left to conduct his two cousins.

During the sermon he was conscious of envious glances at Betty, of respectful ones at Meletiah; but jealous pride made it difficult for him to accept homage for their magnificence. He was *not* proud of his Cape cousins; he was only conscious that his own clothes were cheap and badly cut.

The congregation filed into the vestry, and the minister's sonorous voice petitioned that those who had failed to sign, or failed to maintain, the temperance pledge step forward and raise their hands. The scene was an echo of an earlier one, long ago in Sandwich. Ansel glanced at Betty and saw by her slanting, little smile that she, too, remembered. Perhaps she thought that he lacked the courage to uphold his early views. In front of him his mother walked, her back bent, her black Sunday silk rustling like trees in storm. Could such a girl as Betty realize what the church meant to his mother? No man's convictions were worth the taking of peace from the old.

"Hold up your hand, Ansel." Mother Betsy smiled as she spoke for she was sometimes pleased, sometimes vexed, that he was not a "tee-tot'ler."

The minister repeated his request. Half a dozen young men sheepishly lifted their arms and were asked to step forward. Ansel walked among them and the minister addressed him: "Mr. Bourne, no worshipper should stain his lips with the vile sin of intoxicants. Will not years of discretion soften your stubborn heart?" To this Ansel replied: "I believe that the fruit of the vine is no more injurious than the fruit of the tree. There was an apple in Eden that proved more dangerous than wine."

"There was a judgment in Eden —— "

"But not for ferment of grapes —— "

Ansel's mother touched his arm: "Do not be disrespectful, son."

The minister addressed Mother Betsy: "Ansel is the only young man among the Brethren who has never sought Light in perplexity, nor come to the Elders for guidance. See that he prays God, humbly, to forgive his stiff-necked pride."

He turned suddenly to Ansel: "Young man, will you not pray with me for the salvation of your soul?"

"I cannot pray in public," said Ansel, "nor do I like to think of a God eavesdropping with a thousand ears."

"Sir, you approach blasphemy! The All-Powerful King of Heaven who sees each sparrow fall, who hears each whispering voice, made man in His image. Do you disbelieve in Him?"

"No God in man's image could count the sparrows falling, nor listen to all the public prayers preached betwixt here and Boston."

"Do I understand, Sir, that you deny the Omnipotence of God?"

"There is no such God," said Ansel with sudden dull hostility, "as you people pray to. He could not be that mean."

Ignoring the startled, muttering auditors, Ansel turned to his mother and was shocked by her drawn face. Betty Bourne giggled; Meletiah twisted his mustache and looked mildly bored. The Elders crowded forward to the support of their minister, and Ansel was left in a widening circle, alone except for his mother who clung tightly to his arm.

For a moment the minister paused, weighing words, gathering forces. "There is no God but God," he thundered, "and He is the One God worshipped in this House."

Ansel felt a sense of futility, a weariness weighting him down. As if in antiphony, he echoed: "There is no God —— "

The room swayed into darkness. He reached toward Mother Betsy. Noonday of October Sabbath: where was the light of the sun? If this were Millennium, he must reassure his mother who would be frightened in such blackness, in such unearthly silence.

The congregation stared in perplexity. Something had happened to Ansel Bourne; his eyes stared, his hands groped and he fell forward heavily.

"Behold the Judgment of Heaven!" boomed the minister. "Let unbelievers take warning from this miracle of Our Lord."

Ansel's mother dropped on her knees beside her son's body. His fingers moved feebly though his trembling lips formed no coherent word. When he found her hand he fondled it and raised it to his cheek.

Meletiah, with the aid of two young men of the parish, carried Ansel home. Betty comforted his mother. The girl's eyes were wide, without tears; and Mother Betsy leaned on her heavily. The hat with pansies and verbenas fell back on drooping shoulders.

It took Ansel three days to understand that he was deaf, dumb, and blind. Just as he had never known happiness so he seemed not to know sorrow. He tried to walk about as usual, motion supplying the only relief that penetrated a sensory vacuum. He forgot about

food and after a week began to absent himself from home for long
hours at a time. He felt his way along country roads, lay in sheltered
woodlands, in the warm sun of November's Indian summer.

On the eighteenth day of his affliction he went as far as Westerley.
For two days he had seemed to hear voices but, when he wrote on his
slate of these, his mother tapped back answers assuring him that no
one had spoken. Betty, he knew, was staying to help in the first hard
weeks of his affliction. Although she never touched him a sixth sense
told him of her presence in and out of the rooms. He thought about
her gently as he groped his way to Westerley, thought of her inconsequent youth, her delight at incongruities. Thinking of her, he found
that he was oddly happy and content. He had always been aloof. The
new bars of sensory paralysis only proclaimed to the outer world a
long-enduring reality. As for the Judgment of God: Ansel exulted in
it! Had he not received special proof of the vigilance of deity, of the
fact that man and sparrow were watched, in actual surveillance? What
was this bodily punishment of his, when the darkness and the silence
were direct signals from God?

Trudging along with a cautious vigor he put his hands in his pockets
and pursed his lips for a whistle. The idea of whistling pleased him
although he did not know whether or not his lips made sounds. All life
was pleasant. Future worlds lay ahead, and someday he might wake
to possess new capacities, since the Lord controlled and guided him for
service yet to come.

He stumbled against an obstacle that struck him below the knee.
Leaning forward he felt with his hands, found that he confronted a
flight of steps, and edged along to pass. They seemed to go on for
many paces, like the portico of a church, or a town hall, or perhaps
the county jail. He mounted upward cautiously, his stick held before
him. At the top of the stairs he came upon a large, closed door. Paper
flapped at the touch of his fingers, notices posted; not a jail, but a
church. For a moment Ansel forgot that he was deaf as well as blind.
No sounds issued from within so he assumed the building deserted,
and was about to descend the stairs when a clear voice called, a voice
like Betty's or possibly his mother's. He fumbled for the latch and
pulled open the heavily hinged door. His stick tapping and thump-
ing, he stepped into an aisle. A hand was immediately placed upon his
arm and he was guided to a seat.

Ansel had already begun to understand the sensory messages conveyed by vibrations; communications only recognized by the deaf and blind. He knew that the church was thronged with people; could feel the peculiar impact of their presence. He took out his slate, wrote upon it an apology for his entrance, and held the slate before him until it was taken away. The reader evidently had no idea how to formulate answers. The slate was replaced in Ansel's hand, and an arm was laid, briefly, along his shoulder. He took out his slate cloth, wiped the slate, then sat still and hoped that he was making no disturbance. When the congregation departed he would return to the woods.

Waiting, when one can neither hear nor see, is without period. All life was a waiting to Ansel, who had no idea how long an interval ensued until he heard the voice again. This time it came full and clear like a child singing. He wanted to join in the song, opened his lips, then closed them hurriedly. Deaf mutes, he remembered, made only weird, strangling sounds which might frighten a child.

He wrote on his slate: "Who is the child singing like an angel?," realized that no one knew how to tap out an answer, and tried again: "I can hear singing like angel songs. If you hear it please touch my arm." The slate was taken away from him, then returned, without a touch.

Into the darkness of his days colors and lights sometimes flashed, patternless and without external stimulus, but they brought with them a peculiar mental excitement. Now as he listened to the voice, a whiteness seemed to grow before him, a calm whiteness totally alien to the eccentric flashes of the last eighteen days. He had a sudden conviction that death was close, and that he must tell these worshipers the purport of his affliction. "Take this slate to the pulpit," he wrote, "and let the minister read it aloud." In as few words as possible he told the story of his denial of God and of the judgment upon him. The slate was removed. Not many minutes afterward his hands were taken in a steady grasp and he was drawn forward down the aisle. He knew that his confession of faith had been read and that he was being asked to testify to it from the pulpit. Up carpeted stairs he stumbled, steps narrow and curving, and before he had thought out the conduct that would be required of him, he was guided a pace or two on level ground. His hands were placed gently upon the open pages of a book.

He smiled deprecatingly. Mother Betsy when she heard about this would sorrow that his clothes were torn, his hair unkempt. He thought of her gravely, and the whiteness seemed to widen. She was in it, part of its radiance; so were Betty and vain Meletiah and wizened Uncle Henry.

Then, as from a great height, suddenly he saw the hills of Bourne and beyond them, the peninsula like a silver anchor suspended over the sea. The land was crowded with men and women, young men, old men, sailors, landsmen, girls with bonnets, women with shawls. Children were waving "daffrodilles," laylocks, plumberry bloom! Indians, tall, silent, lifted their arms in the old Wampanoag salute. Across the pages of the book he reached his arms toward them; and the whiteness, increasing, grew as sharp as summer lightning. The one child-voice became a thousand, chanting celestial hymns.

"Glory to God and the Lamb forever!" Ansel could hear himself shouting the words! He fell on his knees, while the heavens flamed, and the earth blossomed around him. Then he spoke words that men could hear and looked with earthly vision into the eyes of a congregation seated in rows before him.

Later, they crowded around the pulpit and wept and laughed and shook hands with him. They were young, glad, and a little incredulous, like Betty; they were tired, doubtful, yet sustained by faith, like Mother Betsy. One of the Elders set a hymn. Ansel, the minister's hand on his shoulder, sang aloud, and then, without self-consciousness, prayed openly in public. Afterward he walked home through the brown woods of November. Every twig and branch glittered with the white radiance of the sun.

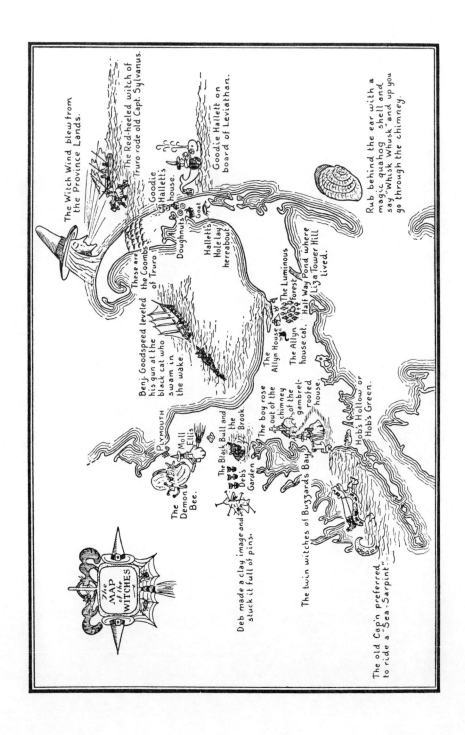

The Map of the Witches

CHAPTER IV

WITCHES, GOODWIVES,
WIDOWS FOR SALE

They hid their faces under masks to prevent "cheek forrowing" on a frosty day, also to protect complexions from the noxious evening air. No bold wayfarer, lifting his lantern, discovered them too clearly. Scarlet cloaks with gathered hoods were swung over dresses white, checked, or colored. Quilted petticoats glinted with "stuff and stitch embroidery." "Friskie ruvvles" half concealed a dimpled elbow "jint."

They cooked, baked, scoured, wove, rode long hours in the saddle. Many performed "midwifferie." They closely followed the Sacred Word, sang Baye Psalmes (one knows not how!), and were "pillars of Non-conformacie."

Some of them sinned delightfully; some of them regrettably. From suncoming to sober-light, women sat in the stocks to repent; others bared their backs to the last. A few said what they wanted to say about parson or squire's daughter. Gagged for it, often recalcitrant, they were "set up" on their doorstones "for all comers and goers to gaze at . . . an Effectual remedy to cure the Noise that is in many Women's heads."

Few complaints left behind them suggest that life was not as it should be. They fished, farmed, even cleared land while their men were conquering the sea roads; and sent their sons (ten years old was the "right" age for the first voyage) to Mother Carey for "larnin' o' water tricks," and the making of the greatest master mariners that this continent has known.

Women died young; or they toughened as they aged, some of them becoming unpleasantly sure of the Lord's precise design. Others, suspected of intimacy with Lucifer, the Lord's Defyer, were accused of suckling "Satanes impes," riding the Night's Mare, churning milk to sour butter and the sea to "soure fome."

1. RIDERS OF THE BROOM

LOW, FERTILE meadows, small in area, roughly circular in shape, surrounded by brush and scrub pines, retain their green flooring through the mild winter weather. A sunken green near a Burying Acre, or a meeting house, or a village tavern became known, in the seventeenth century, as a "Wiche holloa," a platform for devil dancing and the return of the iniquitous dead.

In Hob's Hollow, or Hob's Green, a rendezvous near Buzzards Bay, two old maids, called "Jenkin's Hens," supervised the revelry. At Carver's Green, close to Carver's Corners, on the ancient road from Buzzards Bay to Plymouth, Ould Betty partnered Lucifer in the "Sailor's Minuet." In the heart of the Ghost Forest glistened Half Way Pond (now Mary Dunn Pond) "lit up by witch-fire," with waters of enchanted silver rimmed by invisible quicksands that sucked men swiftly down. In Apple-tree Hole, near the cemetery in Eastham, Goodie Hallett capered in the moonlight until the scandalized towns-folk drove her to the wilderness of Nauset Dunes. Across a valley in Truro a woman rode with a man for her steed, silver spurs at her an-klebone, red lacquer heels on her shoes. Truro said that she was the minister's wife from Eastham. Eastham maintained that she was the "furrin" wife of a Truro sea captain.

To escape the black enchantment that draws unwary mortals into such revel rings, goodwives were invoked to gather wakerobin root, or "witchwood," on a moonless night and keep it always by them. Maidens were warned to cut their hair at the young of the moon and singe the ends to burn away sin, else witch women, clinging to the "splits," might drag away their victims by the second- or "devil-hairs" at the termination of the Christian curls.

A death in the family was told to the bees and the hives trimmed with crepe. No loom might be touched on All Saints' Eve; no book, paper or cloth placed on top of the Bible. If a black cat walked before an unwed maid, precaution suggested that she gather a handful of grass and scatter it as she followed. Neither goodman nor good-wife considered it safe to ride an all-black horse on the eve of the new moon. If a bogwalker desired to bespell a snake, he recited, over and over again, as fast as his lips could form the words: "The seed of the woman shall bruise the serpent's head." If a toad was killed, a shower of rain was almost sure to follow, since storms attended the death of witches and "Satanes wifes" took the forms of their familiars.

At the Beldames' Sabbath, in Cape hollows, the fiddle was played by an "old black man," by a "black-eyed sailor," by the Devil dressed in scarlet cloth. Assemblies danced, signed the Black Book, ate Red Bread, drank Blood Brew. Old hags, leaders of the "Pack," rode on sleek horses. When steed and rider reached the Hollow, the lady, mysteriously rejuvenated, dismounted, and for the first round, she and the Night's Mare danced together to the throbbing of a violin.

OULD BETTY

Ould Betty, who partnered Lucifer, grew young and beautiful as soon as she put shoe upon the turf of Carver's Green. Always she tried to lure Goodman Pease to the revels; always he escaped in time. She lived in a house in the Haunted Wood, not very far from the Green; and he lived alone on the edge of the forest. Some men declared them lovers. Certainly Goodman Pease gave her food, and firewood, and one summer she visited him each day. But when her attentions grew "steady as a hen settin'," he wearied of her and ordered her from his door. Thereafter she came for food while he was at work in the fields. Even when he barred the door, climbed out of a window and hid the ladder, Ould Betty managed to get inside his hut. When he was not there to give her presents, she took whatever she pleased; and since no lock can hold a witch she walked in and out at will. Riders passing the hut at night often saw a candle burning in the window, and heard the voice of Ould Betty raised in entreaty or imprecation. When the goodman accused her of theft, and threatened to have her burned or hung, she laughed. A bee flew from her lips into his glass of cider. Immediately, his heart grew soft toward her and he thought her a fine woman and fair. But, despite all her tricks, her "devil-blandishments," she never could persuade him to enter the Haunted Wood by night or to visit Lucifer at Carver's Green.

One day Goodman Pease caught her in "red-handed" theft, a leg of a roast wild turkey in her hand and the juice running down her chin. To end disputes, he put her in a bag, tied the mouth of the bag, dragged it into a closet, locked the closet door, put the key in his pocket, and went back to his work in the fields. As soon as the sound of his footsteps died away, Ould Betty muttered a charm. The bag quivered, then untied itself, and Betty stepped out. The locked closet door was no trouble to her. Shaking with fury she emerged into the hut's one room, and peered out of the window. Goodman Pease was far down the hill, hoeing Indian corn. Ould Betty pursed her lips and whistled a strange tune. The goodman's dog answered the tune and came in at the door. He walked stiffly; his eyes were glazed, and he stood motionless before Ould Betty. "Come, my pet," said the old witch and she picked him up by the hair of his neck and threw him into the bag. Again she looked out of the window. Goodman Pease was far down the hill, hoeing Indian corn. So the witch pursed her lips and whistled a tune. The goodman's cat came over the doorstone. Her back was arched, her eyes were green, and her tail was as big as a "crooked squish." "Ah, my little love," said the witch and she took the cat into her arms, kissed its two ears and the tip of its tail, and thrust it into the bag. Again she looked from the window. Goodman Pease was far down the hill, hoeing Indian corn. She pursed her lips and whistled a tune and slowly over the doorstone came the goodman's red-feathered cock. The cock's eyes were as shiny as whortleberries and his plumes were as bright as a "frost-bit pison-ivy leaf." "Come, my pretty," said the old witch and she picked up the cock by his scarlet comb and thrust him into the bag. For the last time she looked out of the window. Far down the hill, Goodman Pease was hoeing Indian corn. There were no more animals in the yard, for the goodman was poor. Then Ould Betty bethought her of the pig tied by a rope to a tree on the edge of the Haunted Forest, behind the little house. So she pursed her lips and whistled a tune, but there was no reply. "Whish," said Ould Betty crossly, and she took her quahog shell out of her pocket and with it she scratched her chin. Again she whistled a tune, and sure enough, in at the door walked the goodman's pig. "Ho, ho, ye are late, my pretty!" exclaimed the witch, and she picked up the pig by its crooked tail and thrust it into the bag. Then she tied the mouth of the bag, dragged the bag into the closet, and by repeating a simple charm relocked the closet door. She hid herself in a corner of the inglenook and waited for night to fall.

When it was too dark to work anymore, Goodman Pease came home. The animals inside the bag were making a fearful din. "Ah, ha! Ould Betty, are ye there?" said the goodman merrily. "Keep still, for I'm wore out, tonight." The noise in the bag redoubled. "If ye haint quiet, Ould Betty, I'll dash ye down kerplunk on the doorstone," warned Goodman Pease; but the noise only grew worse until it sounded as if the bag rocked from side to side of the closet, leaped up to the ceiling, and thundered against the door. The goodman was exasperated. He unlocked the closet door and seized the turbulent bag. He dashed it on the doorstone, again and yet again. A laugh echoed from the ingle. "Ho, ho," said a cackling voice, "Ye haint killed Ould Betty yet." Goodman Pease dropped the bag and rushed toward the hearth. The stars were out and the moon was high over the Baywater. Ould Betty rubbed her chin with a quahog shell. "Whisk, whusk," she called, and was up the chimney and off to dance with the Devil at Carver's Green.

THE WITCH SISTERS OF BUZZARDS BAY

On the edge of the forest, near Buzzards Bay, lived two very small old maids. The crow's foot was on their eyes and the black ox had trodden on their toes, and they never walked out by the light of the sun. But they could put a strong murrain on cattle; and if, during the year, they received no gifts of grain from a farmer, they cast a spell on his next crop and then his rye refused to head, and his corn refused to ear. Always together, always muttering, nodding, smiling, they never failed to walk at dusk down to the edge of the sea. The story goes that they were not sisters, but twin wives of a "sea-farin' man" who had sufficient sense, after his old women discovered one another, never to make the home port. Each night they came to the shore to look for him, "neither one a sol'tary step ahead of tother, nor tother a sol'tary step behind of each"; "both on 'em" ready with potent spells to turn the delinquent into a "sea-sarpint" and ride him from dusk till dawn.

One day the "twin witches" cast a spell upon a small boy. Dazed and in total bewitchment, he followed them back to the gambrel-roofed house on the edge of the forest, overlooking the sea. They put him to sleep in a trundle bed in a lower room, and then disappeared up a ladder into the loft. Despite his "bewitchery," the boy was unhappy and could not sleep. At midnight he heard a noise, and peering from under his "crook-stitched quilt," saw the two witches come down the ladder. They were dressed in red-heeled shoes, satin dresses, peaked stomachers, and "modesty bits." They went to the oven, and from it took a quahog shell. Each witch rubbed the shell behind her ears and said, "Whisk!" Quick as a flame, each flew up the chimney. As soon as they were gone, the little boy rose to attempt an escape, but he found the door and windows barred. Then he thought of the quahog shell, went to the oven, found the shell, and rubbed it behind his ear. "Whisk," he said, and quick as a flame he shot up the chimney flue.

In the yard, the witches were sitting astride black horses whose manes and tails were edged with moonlight, glittery, like the rim of a cloud laid against the moon. When the witch women saw the boy, one of the sisters dismounted. "He shall ride with us," she said, and the other sister nodded in the moonlight and muttered, "O-aye." The witch who had dismounted went into the house and returned with a witch bridle and a thin bundle of straw. She laid the straw upon the ground and over the straw she flung the bridle. Out of it stepped a black pony, as pretty a piece of horseflesh as ever a boy has seen.

"Now we shall ride," said the witches, as they put the boy on the pony's back. "Sail away, sail," sang the three, and off they cantered across Great Meadow, and into the forest in the direction of Hob's Green. After a time they came to a brook. When the witch horses leaped over the water, the little boy saw that their hooves were shod with a thin white flame. "Jump, my little moon-calf," he cried. The witches had cleared the brook at a leap, but the black pony soared too high and as he landed on the opposite bank, one silver hoof splashed into the stream. The pony vanished. The boy stood alone. In one hand he was holding a "witch bridle," in the other a bundle of straw.

Night shrouded the forest. The boy ran helter-skelter after the black riders. Soon he came to a deserted house, and heard the singing of a violin. He crept close to the window. A black man was playing a fiddle, and around him danced the two sisters and other old women and men. Owls hooted in the treetops. Will-o'-the-wisps were waving sea lanterns on the Green. The boy dropped the straw and the witch bridle, ran swiftly down the road, and when he came to a farm house, knocked, and crouched against the door. The farmer took him in, cared for him, and returned him to his home.

CAPTAIN SYLVANUS AND THE WITCH OF TRURO

One of the strangest enchantments that ever befell the master of a sailing vessel overtook Captain Sylvanus Rich while his ship lay off the backside waiting for favorable weather in which to round Race Point and deliver a load of North Carolina corn to the Boston trade. The captain, who was an elderly man and had a son already master of a vessel, lacked youth's appetite for "etarnel cod muddle." So he went ashore near Truro, purchased a bucket of milk, and brought it back to the ship. The milk was sold by a shabby old woman who, beneath her linsey-woolsey skirt, exhibited to the captain's gaze a pair of scarlet heels.

As soon as the shipmaster boarded his vessel the bad weather abated and he put out to sea. No sooner had he reached open water than a great gale began to blow. The ship wallowed; the sails tore. Shortly, all sails were blown away and the vessel was little more than a wreck. Yet what happened to the sails was as nothing to what happened to Captain Sylvanus! The milk, he maintained, was bewitched. For every night at moonrise an old woman with scarlet heels on her slippers came into his cabin. She put a bit in the captain's teeth. She saddled him and bridled him, and all night long she rode him over the Truro hills. Along the Coombs and through the woods, up the dunes and down the dunes, across the inlets, through the town, even around Bound Brook Island! Like Treageagle with the devil for rider, Captain Sylvanus had to carry the witch wherever her fancy drove.

When she released him, just before dawn, he was too weary, too ill to be a sane shipmaster. He grew thin and "of a strange complexion." He gave no orders, made no effort to direct his wrecked vessel. The condition of the crew was desperate. No one of them understood navigation. They pleaded with Captain Sylvanus to cast aside this hallucination; but the very plague that he dreaded seemed to have a gruesome fascination. Before moonrise he went to his cabin, locked himself in, and waited for the "scarlet lady" to come. Meanwhile the ship drifted toward the Grand Banks, with a crew unskilled to direct her, and a captain immersed in a tragic delusion.

One morning they sighted sail! Frantic distress signals were raised. Young prosperous Sylvanus Rich, Jr., brought his ship alongside, and hailed his father's men.

The son's coming broke the enchantment, restored the old captain's sanity, and supplied the wrecked ship's needs. But one cannot refrain from speculation concerning this coincidence. If it had been other than his son, in whom the captain's pride was great, would the old seadog have shaken off his witch mania, accepted aid, put his vessel in order, and brought his men in safety into Boston port? How did that young shipmaster exorcise the witch of Truro? That he exorcised her, that both father and son took her visits seriously, may be inferred from the captain's report to authorities in Boston, ascribing his losses to "sweet milke of Satan."

Possibly Captain Sylvanus took other fluids than milk into his cabin, and young Sylvanus knew enough to remove stimulating motifs. At all events he averted tragedy, and no other tales are recorded of Captain Sylvanus and the witch.

GOODIE HALLETT WHO LIVED IN A WHALE

In a ramshackle hut in the heart of the dunes lived the "little old woman of Nauset Sea." By night she danced in Hallett's Green, a hollow near the old Eastham cemetery, and a stone's throw from the site of Higgins' Tavern. Seated in front of the greatroom fire, the tavern gatherers, when they heard a shriek mingling with the high sea wind, drew their cloaks about them and murmured, "Thar be pore Goodie, dancin' with the lost souls." Post riders, on the King's Highway that bordered Hallett's Hole, spurred their mounts after dusk, and risked no unwary glance into the hollow. Even the horses sensed danger, for they pushed on, with a rush of speed, past the Burying Acre to the lights of the tavern beyond.

After dusk Goodie Hallett returned to Eastham town, whence she had been stoned away in the second decade of the seventeenth century. She built herself a little hut, far from village or farm, in a region that has since become part of Wellfleet; and at times her pranks have been confused with those of the red-heeled witch of Truro, whose broomstick put out the seamen's light that burned in the Old Meeting House on the Hill of Storms. Six vessels were wrecked in the darkness, twenty lives lost; and Goodie Hallett, known to hate sailors, was accused of the crime.

Her familiars, a black cat and a black goat, were said to ride on porpoises' backs, following in the wake of ships. Seamen of Wellfleet, Truro, Eastham, "Bankers" setting out for the Grand Banks, whenever they saw two green eyes staring from the spume, exclaimed: "Thar be Goodie Hallett's familiar waitin' to pick up souls. Reef sail, a squall's to wind'ard!" A few moments later, low in the sky would hang a cloud as black and "portentous" as the witch cat's tail.

GOODIE HALLETT'S MEADOW, EASTHAM
This area of sand-stubble was called 'Satan's Harvest' or 'Lucifer Land,' and
brought ill luck to those who walked across it without uttering a prayer

Goodie could hold a ship in port, beyond all weather reckoning, by putting that cat of hers under a "berry-bushel." A "dead calm" or contrary winds were the result. "The Old Woman has got the cat under the half-bushel" was a proverb among the seagoing men when contrary winds held.

She became a legend, and like Jonah inhabited a whale. Through the courtesy of Lucifer, she "possessed" the body of the "Whistlin' Whale." Cozy inside this fabulous mammal she lived for a century, and deflected the thrusts of harpooners, upset whaleboats, and stove in the ribs of ships. While ice coated the rigging and sailors froze in the crow's nest, Goodie and the devil sat night after night, comfortable and warm, drinking hot rum and dicing for souls in the "front parlor" of the "Whistlin' Whale." She hung a ship's lantern on the tail of her leviathan, and drove him among dangerous reefs. Vessels, seeing another ship safely in course, followed these lights and were wrecked, or marooned on the bars.

She was reputed to have been the mistress of the pirate Samuel Bellamy; though some reports have it that she was a yellow-haired girl with eyes like the sea and that Sam Bellamy ruined her. If so, she made her pact with the devil in a spirit of vengeance and with the determination to ruin Bellamy. In return for her immortal soul, Lucifer agreed to drown the pirate captain at the door of her hut, and in due course he fulfilled his contract. The Black Bellamy was buried in Goodie Hallett's "Meadow," that strange stubble of poverty grass and sand (unlike any other area on the Cape) that still stretches between the ruins of her hut and the sea. The house long since has tumbled down, but even the foundations that remain are reputed to be haunted.

Game after game, Goodie defeated the devil at "salt water dice," and so, one night, he choked her to death, and deserted the "Whistlin' Whale." Many years later the famous gang known as the Seed-Corners killed the "Whistlin' Whale"; and when they came to open her up, they found in the belly a pair of red lacquer shoes.

Landsmen say that Goodie the witch married an Indian from Mashpee, a praying fool who did not know that she was in league with the devil. One night, when he came home late, he found Satan in the form of a baby imp, suckling at a witch teat on her breast. He tried to fling the Evil One away, but the devil clung, and Goodie cried out against her husband. What could the Indian do? He wanted to save his wife and he knew that imps could not stand water. He picked up his wife, devil baby and all, and flung her into the sea. She swam eastward, in the shape of a whale, with the devil astride her back. The Indian, crazed with horror, wandered away from the hut in the dunes, and no man has seen him since.

THE SAILOR AND THE DOUGHNUTS

In the spring of 1780, when the fishing fleets were preparing for their trip to the Grand Banks, a young sailor hurried down-Cape to join his ship at Provincetown. In the old days, the King's Highway lay nearer Nauset dunes than the present state road. The trails were deeply rutted in sand, and it took a man's strength to walk them. Also, in any century, April days are hungry days when the sea wind is blowing; and a sailor taking a long land voyage needs frequent refreshment to ward off shore fever. When the young "Banksman" saw a little house, somewhat off the road in a barren stretch of moorland, he decided to ask for a "bite and snuck," and waded through the sand to the door. No one answered his knock, but the door yielded to his touch, so he stepped inside and found the house solitary, except for a black goat lying by the hearth. "Good-day to ye," said the sailor to the goat, and doffed his seaman's cap. "Good-day to ye," answered the goat and stared into the embers.

The sailor had no desire to pursue such a conversation. On the table a pan of crisp doughnuts, fresh from the oven, assailed his senses. The goat stared at the sailor; the sailor at the doughnuts. He reached out his hand and took a few. With his other hand he felt in his pockets, but drew the hand out empty. There is nothing to lay hold on, in a seaman's pocket, at the end of shore leave. "Good-day to ye," said the sailor, as he put on his cap and went out of the door. The black goat lying by the hearth made no reply.

On the following morning, Captain Ridley, late pilot of Boston Harbor, with all hands aboard sailed from Provincetown in the vanguard of the fishing fleet. "There's a man knocked out, Sir," reported the mate, before the schooner was clear of the Point.

"Have ye doused him?" inquired the captain.

"Aye, Sir. He don't smell — nohow — of nothin'; he ain't hurt, neither."

"I'll take a look at him, Mr. Mate." The captain went down to the fo'c'sle where a young boy was lying insensible on his berth. In the eighteenth century, masters of schooners that sailed to the Banks for fishing knew how to amputate a leg, mend a broken bone, or stitch a long wound. They knew, also, something of the symptoms of plagues, fevers and cholera. During the first days of a voyage they were on the lookout for contagious diseases; in the "fo'c'sle," a whole crew could become contaminated unless prompt action was taken.

The captain examined the young sailor carefully. The boy was not drunk, and he had no fever. The shipmaster administered a dose of grog and the sailor opened his eyes. "What ails ye?" demanded Captain Ridley. The boy shook his head. The captain, a kindly, intelligent man, put his hand on the boy's shoulder. "What ye bin eatin'?" he inquired mildly. "Doughnuts," said the young sailor. "Lay off," said the captain firmly, and the boy promised to obey.

The next morning the mate approached the captain. "The boy's knocked out, again, Sir."

"Have ye tried dousin' him, Mister?"

"Aye, Captain."

"Has he et his vittles?"

"Same as the rest, Sir."

The captain sighed, "I'll be down presently." The prospect of a mysteriously ailing sailor, at the outset of a voyage, is not a pleasant one. This time the captain was more thorough. He saw to it that the boy received a complete purging.

The next day the mate reported, again: "He ain't naturel, Sir. He's more like asleep than fainted. Except ye can't wake him. The crew think he's bewitched."

The captain snorted. He summoned the sailor to his cabin, and accused him of shamming sleep to avoid duty. The boy was indignant. "Then what ails ye?" thundered the captain in righteous exasperation.

"Doughnuts, Sir. I stole them, and the witch that owns them comes after me. As soon as ever I lie down, she turns me into a horse, and rides me over Sable Island. As God is my witness, Sir, this is the truth." The sailor bared his arms, black and blue to the forearm. "That's where she kicked me, Sir, when I tried to bite her. She twits me, all night, for stealin' the doughnuts."

Captain Ridley scowled. Such nonsense could not be permitted to circulate before the mast. He sent the young sailor below, and ordered him not to repeat his story.

A few days later the mate came to the captain. "The boy, Sir, poisons our water."

"What do ye mean, Mister?"

"Captain, I wish that ye would come and see for yerself."

The captain followed the mate to the water casks where a group of the crew were gathered. The young sailor stood beside a cask, an empty pail in his hand. "Pump," ordered the mate. The boy, who looked more like a ghost than a man, filled the water bucket and passed it over to the mate. The mate held it up for the inspection of the captain. "Taste it, Sir." The captain took a draft, and found the water salt and "Rough." His heart misgave him. Foul water meant a prompt return to port. The mate flung the water away and handed the bucket to the "bosun." "Pump," ordered the mate, while the sailors watched with unrevealing eyes. The "bosun" filled the water bucket from the same cask and passed it to the captain who took a long draft. The water was sweet and pure.

"What is the meaning of this?" the captain inquired sternly.

"It has no meanin', Sir." The mate spoke hesitantly. "Every time the boy draws water, it comes salt. We feel somethin' ought to be done."

"Send him to the galley, where he belongs. He's been trickin' ye long enough. Let him salt vittles for a change. That'll cure him."

There is no more ignominious job on board a "Banker" than that of cook's boy — at least for an able-bodied young seaman who plans to study navigation. The boy flinched, but he took his orders without protest.

The next day the cook knocked at the captain's door, and announced that the flour in the dough basket was bewitched. The captain indulged in the prerogative of seamen, and then followed to cook's quarters. The young sailor was stirring dough. His bent shoulders and bowed head spoke despair.

"Watch the spoon, Sir," whispered the cook, and even as he spoke the bowl of the spoon with which the boy was stirring severed itself from the handle, and dropped into the dough. At the same moment a new bowl formed on the end of the spoon handle; seemed to grow out of the handle in the way that a leaf unfurls. The boy continued to stir the dough, and the process repeated itself at intervals, until the dough was full of spoons.

Suddenly, the young sailor dropped the bucket, and hid his face in his hands. "I can't stand it, Sir," he blubbered. "She's got me. I'm wore out."

The captain, who was a good man, ordered the sailor to his berth. Then he went back to his cabin, took a stiff dose of grog, and sat down to think. The men were gathering into groups that dropped into a silence more than respectful, whenever he approached. Some of the sailors were singing hymns. Others wore bits of hemp tied into "witch-knots" on their sleeves.

The captain's glance strayed to his "Go-to-Meetin' coat," hung over a chair to keep its "figger set." His eye caught the gleam of silver coat buttons. He had bought them against his wife's wishes, and she sewed them on with a look of Thou-art-worshipping-Mammon in her eye. He loved their clear, metallic luster. He avoided her glance. They were the first silver buttons that he had ever owned, and destined to be the last. As he looked at them, a plan came to him! Witches could not withstand silver; silver went to their hearts.

Captain Ridley sighed as he took down his "Go-to-Meetin' coat," drew out his bowie knife and severed the silver buttons from the cloth. He went to his sea chest, and brought forth a gun. Carefully unloading this, he put the silver buttons in place of bullets. Then he sent for the young sailor.

"Lie down in your berth," he ordered, "and if ever the witch comes again, shoot before she touches you — shoot straight through the heart."

The young sailor went away with a look of hope in his eyes. The captain took out his old bone buttons, laid his "Go-to-Meetin' coat" on his knee, and started to sew. Before the last button was in place, a shot echoed from the galley. The captain rose, then sank back in his chair. Hurrying feet, a sharp knock, and the mate's head was stuck in at the door. "The boy, Sir, is lyin' like one dead on the galley-deck. There's a gun beside him, has gone off. His shins is covered

with warm blood, though he ain't bleedin' none. It looks like murder, Sir, but the crew's all accounted for, and there's no dead body
and no wounds." The mate shook his head in perplexity.

"Give the sailor a dose of grog," said Captain Ridley without excitement. "He'll be on his feet directly."

"Aye, aye, Sir," said the mate, though disbelief gleamed in his
eye.

"And bring that gun here," ordered the captain, "there might be
some bullets left."

The captain's prophecy proved correct; the boy recovered
promptly. Was it Goodie Hallett, or the witch of Truro — that seagoing lady who owned a goat? Nobody knows her identity. After
she was shot through the heart by the captain's silver coat buttons,
she never again troubled the sailor who stole her doughnuts in the
spring of 1780.

DEBORAH BURDEN, WEAVER OF SPELLS

Deborah Borden, or Deb Burden, cast spells over Wareham and Roch-
ester, and also flew down-Cape to visit Sandwich and Barnstable where
she took contracts for weaving. She wove skillfully and slowly, and
delivered her carpet when it was ready, or more often when she was
ready. Once an impatient housewife, who had a web of cloth on Deb's
loom, sent her daughter and a child named Phoebe to the witch
weaver's house. When the two children appeared and asked for the
cloth, Deb was angry. She left them standing outside the door, near a
tree full of ripe, red apples. Phoebe looked at the apples. "Won't
you please give me an apple?" she asked politely of Old Deb. "Drat
you. No, I won't," said the witch.

Phoebe's friend, the child who had been sent for the cloth, was un-
daunted. She picked two apples from the tree, one for herself, and
one for little Phoebe. "I ain't afraid of ye, ye old witch," she announced. "Ye ain't!" screamed Old Deb, "then I'll make ye afraid afore
ye git home!"

The two children returned through the woods. In the middle of
the forested area stood a fence with bars. Beyond the fence ran a
brook. Suddenly the children heard a roaring behind them and
saw a charging black bull. "Oh," cried Phoebe, "Captain Besse's bull

. . . he will get us!" They ran for the bars of the fence, climbed through and jumped across the small brook. The bull had gathered his bulk for a leap, and as they glanced back, his great body crashed over the fence. But when he came to the little stream, try as he might he could not cross it. Unseen magic stopped him on the edge, and the children knew, since the "Witchbane Water" stopped his furious charge, that Deb Burden was inside the bull.

Terrified, the girls raced home and told their story to the goodman and his wife who had sent them for the cloth. "Never mind," said the goodman, comforting them, "I'll fix Debby."

When Old Deb brought to the house the work of her loom, she was invited to come in and sit by the fire. When she was seated, the goodman crept up behind her and thrust a darning needle through her dress, pinioning her to the chair. Old Deb felt nothing, for witches do not suffer at the prickings of steel. "Well, she sot," says the story; and every time that she said "I must go," and started to rise, she found that she could not stir. Perplexed, unwilling to admit that a spell was upon her, she remained quiet for a time and then remembered the things that needed doing at home. "I must go tend my fire!" she declared; but could stir "no more'n a milestone." The goodman kept her in that chair all day, in front of the hot flames. At nightfall, he pulled out the needle. "Scare my gal, again, ye old witch!" he said. But Deb was gone, quick as a cat when the field-mouse crosses corn.

Once Deb sat by the fire at Thankful Haskell's house. Thankful's daughter was sweeping the room. She was only fourteen, and did not know about the handling of witch women. In the course of the sweeping, the child thrust the broom underneath Deb's chair. "Ye can't insult a witch more'n that!" Deb was furious. She cursed the child and wished her trouble. The next day Thankful's daughter grew very ill. The doctor was summoned but could do nothing for her. More doctors were summoned, but all of them "gin her up." Finally her father, Tom Haskell, sent for Old Doc Bemis of Middleborough. Old Doc Bemis put on his spectacles and leaned over the girl. "This child is bewitched," said he. "Go, somebody, and see what Deb is up to."

Mr. Haskell saddled his horse and rode to Deborah Burden's house. When he arrived no one was at home but the devil, in the form of a cat. Searching for Old Deb, he found her at the bottom of the garden beside a pool of water. She was molding images out of clay, sticking the clay with pins. Tom held his horsewhip in his hand. When he saw what the old witch was doing, he drew back the whip and brought it curling around her shoulders. "Stop that, Deb, or you shall be burnt alive!" he threatened. Deborah Burden cringed at the lash but Mr. Haskell "laid on" fiercely. The black cat came out of the house and bristled its ebony tail. When Old Deb could stand no more, she screamed, "Your young one shall git well!" The earth opened suddenly. Into it the black cat disappeared.

Tom Haskell wheeled his horse and rode at a gallop toward home. Long before he reached the door, his daughter began to mend. So promptly was she restored that she ran to meet her father as he came over the doorstone.

LIZA TOWER HILL OF THE LUMINOUS FOREST

In the early part of the eighteenth century, the lonely lands around Crooked Pond and Half Way Pond were almost uninhabited. Forested areas were dense; boughs, interwoven, hid the sun. Wolves and other wild animals menaced the traveler on the Great Indian Trail from Hyannis to Barnstable, through the region of Half Way Pond. "Wild" Indians lurked in the forest, hunting game, watching opportunities for petty thievery. Watch fires and signal fires burned, at intervals, on the hills.

Benjamin Lewis built a house near Crooked Pond; and there, away from settlements, companions, educational opportunities, his daughter, Elizabeth Lewis, was born. A bright child, with a quick tongue, a shrewd, mischievous humor, a sturdy, valiant little body, she wandered, solitary, in a region beset with dangers; played fearlessly in the forest, accompanied "bad Indians" on their hunting forays, seemed unafraid of night, or the dark, or wolves.

Apparently, nothing harmed her. The townsfolk of Sandwich and Barnstable, and the "South Seas Colony" began to feel that she was connected with the Evil One. She had none of the airs, foibles, delicacies of a girl child. She worked in the fields, was unlettered, though, being of quick mind, she absorbed much general knowledge, especially of farm and forest. If a cow was ill she could give sound advice about a cure. If the corn had rot in it, she vouchsafed a reason, and the reason was generally accurate. She had a merry, mocking laugh that made one think of a bird in a tree. Undoubtedly she had charm.

William Blatchford thought so, for he wooed her when she was not quite sixteen, and wed her when she was a scant sixteen and a half. He built a home for her, in the wilderness, a mile west of her father's house, and on the borders of Half Way Pond. She lived, a young bride, as she had lived, a young child, away from the colonial world. Her baby, Peter, was born in that lonely little house in the forest, when she was just eighteen. She laughed at the people who pitied her, bargained with them shrewdly for farm tools and produce; but men muttered, when she got the best of them, that one so young and beautiful, yet so unnatural, must be allied to Satan. She laughed at Pilgrim ideas of decorum, and at Old World superstitions. Unlike many reputed witches, she had no laughter for religion. Somewhere in her life of sky, pond, river and farm she found a God who was not quite the deity of the other Nonconformists. In her simplicity, the church of the East Parish in Barnstable symbolized His rule.

When she journeyed there to hear the minister, strange glances followed her. Women drew their skirts aside lest they touch her. Greetings were offered less in friendship than in propitiation and fear. She gave no sign that she was conscious of this ostracism. Witty, caustic in criticism, she nevertheless possessed a dignity, an aloof strength that was the natural heritage of years of solitude serenely sustained. When her second child was born, a girl who died in early youth, she was admitted into full communion, and until her death remained an exemplary church member, with only one complaint lodged against her. Thankful, the wife of Samuel Gilbert, charged her with abuse. A nimble and witty tongue brought her into this trouble, and she readily confessed fault. Her confession, read aloud, was publicly accepted in the church.

Her husband's family, the Blatchfords, came from the Tower Hill section of London; and so, for her witch name, Elizabeth Lewis Blatchford received the title of Liza Tower Hill. Her husband seems never to have made any decisive move in her defense. He was not a religious man, never accompanied her on her expeditions to "meeting," and only joined the church, probably under compulsion, the day before he died.

Half Way Pond (Mary Dunn Pond) was, in the minds of the credulous, "Liza's Revel Ring." In mid-darkness, when the trees in the
enchanted forest flared like shredded granular moons, Liza Tower
Hill danced over the surface of the pond as though it were a floor of
glass. White flame edged her naked feet, her skirts were scarlet, her
bare breasts and shoulders gave forth white fire. Under her, luminous fish circled, with glittery eyes and waving horns, and sharp, split
tails. Around the edges of the pond crept abortions of the forest;
pigs with heads of cows, cocks with heads of pigs, bodies of wolves
with faces of women, beasts that whined and howled and danced in
the blue water grass. A cloven-footed rabbit came, his ears, like
horns, laid flat on his head. Swamp devils waved their sea lanterns
and flung high their shaggy legs, like shaggy legs of goats.

As soon as traveler set foot on the Indian trail from Hyannis to
Barnstable Harbor, he exposed himself to the enchantments of Liza
Tower Hill. G. L. Kittredge tells a story of one night traveler on that
road. "I obtained it about forty years ago," he writes, "from a lady
of eighty-four, who had heard the story from 'Old Mr. David Loring's
wife, the victim of the spell.' " Mrs. Loring was riding on horseback
along the enchanted trail. As she neared Half Way Pond, Liza Tower
Hill cast a spell on horse and rider. The animal ceased to obey
whip or rein, and started to circle Half Way Pond. Mrs. Loring was in-
capable of stopping, or directing the horse, so steed and lady rode
around and around the pond for a long time. If old Mrs. Loring had
only known it, she was pixie-led in the Devonshire way. Had she
turned her cloak inside out, she might have reversed the spell.

Mr. Wood of West Barnstable charged Liza with putting a bridle
and saddle on him and riding him many times to Plum Pudding
Pond in Plymouth where the witches were holding an attractive series
of night orgies.

Benjamin Goodspeed of East Sandwich maintained that Tower
Hill, in the night, compelled him to act as horse for her. He became
exhausted, determined to go to sea to escape the enchantment, and
shipped before the mast. Outward bound from Barnstable, he
watched the pointed pines of the Haunted Forest disappear from
view. Scarcely were they out of sight, when he saw in the white foam
of the wake a black cat's head. All day that black cat swam behind
the vessel, and when night came, it boarded ship, took the shape

of Liza Tower Hill, and rode Benjamin Goodspeed till dawn whitened the sails. Then Liza turned again into the form of her familiar, and with tufted ears folded back and whiskers beaded with salt spume she swam after the ship.

In despair the sailor told a shipmate who advised him to shoot her with a double-barreled gun and use Bible leaves for wads. Benjamin tore pages out of the Bible, wadded his gun and clambered aft. The black cat bobbed in the wake, and regarded him with narrow eyes as he crouched by the taffrail. The combers rose and the combers fell, and the cat swam nose to the ship's keel. The sun dropped in the evening sky. Foam turned scarlet. The cat's eyes grew large and green; she gained on the ship, and swung alongside as if to climb aboard. Benjamin aimed the shotgun primed with Holy Scripture, and fired at the cat's head. Swiftly the red light died from the foam; green eyes, black ears disappeared. The body of the animal churned beneath the waters and the ship heeled gracefully over a tidal wave. Into the quiet of sober-light, the stars came slowly, while Benjamin took paper, made note of hour and day, then went to his bunk and slept at last in peace.

As the shot struck the sea, Liza Tower Hill stood spinning in her house by Half Way Pond. Back and forth she moved at the wheel, singing a sorrow tune. From the spindle dripped a yarn as white and flaky as foam. The sun crept below pointed pines, throwing into sudden blackness the area of the Haunted Forest. On the pond the sky lay down to sleep in quilted scarlet. Suddenly the song died on the witch's lips and she dropped beside her spindle. Her young daughter ran to her, raised her body, looked into her eyes. They were green as the sea, shining and beautiful, but in them there was no life.

Despite this story of her death, many townsfolk recall the belief that Tower Hill sold her soul to Satan for continued survival upon this earth. As evidence of her charmed existence, Amos Otis tells of a small boy who went with his father to assist Liza in breaking up a new piece of ground. She was over seventy-five but she took the difficult part of the work, the task of holding down the plow. Suddenly the plow brought up against a stump. The concussion was so violent that it threw her over the shafts. She arose, gave no evidence of discomfort, and continued her work until it was complete.

Mrs. Chloe Blish, who lived in Governor Hinckley's house, and was an octogenarian in 1880, has perpetuated Liza Tower Hill's name in association with the "Allyn House Mystery." The old Allyn House, that stood originally across the road from Governor Hinckley's home, for many years had the reputation of being haunted. Strange lights, black cats, rappings, the swish of skirts, breaths of fresh air, terrified its inmates.

The Allyn family allied themselves with some of the most interesting families on the Cape. Elizabeth married Colonel John Gorham in 1732. In 1735 Suzanna married Captain Jonathan Davis, Jr., shipmaster. Hannah, in 1743, married the eccentric Dr. Abner Hersey. In 1751 Mary married Nymphas Marston, and in 1752 there were two marriages in the family: Thomas married Elizabeth Sturgis and James, Jr., married Lydia Marston. In this family almost every profession was represented: one son was a saddler and one a cabinetmaker; two sons-in-law were military, two were in the legal profession, one was a minister, and one a doctor. All of these varied individuals were puzzled and alarmed by the evidences of what a later age calls psychic phenomena.

James Allyn, Sr., died in 1741 and left to his son his "armour, valued at £16.10.0. and all his warlike weapons and appurtenances." Sixteen pounds was no small sum of money in 1741, and collections of armor were seldom mentioned in wills or inventories of the eighteenth century. The presence of this armor may well have been a cause for rumors concerning ghosts; but the fact that gatherings of the Allyn family were called to investigate these mysteries suggests that some outward and visible signs of abnormality must have occurred.

Into the Allyn household came Lydia, daughter of Liza Tower Hill. She was badly treated as a servant, or so Liza thought, and the witch woman threatened vengeance. A night or two thereafter, a strange cat appeared in Mr. Allyn's house, "mewing and caterwauling." Unseen hands upset or turned "bottom upwards" everything in the house. Six new chairs brought in the day before were smashed into small pieces. All night the Allyns were kept awake, and ever after, strange noises were heard at intervals, as though a cat were mewing or pattering down the stairs, as though unseen skirts were swishing, as though chairs or tables were suddenly overturned. The peace of the family was gone, rent by fears, discussions, finally by a desire to allay the increasing and unpleasant curiosity of the townsmen. Was Liza Tower Hill guilty of these disturbances? Some of the Allyns blamed her bitterly; others took her part.

She died in July, 1790, old, worn-out, weary of contumely and cruel bickering. Almost to the end, her eyes were as bright, her tongue as quick, as when she was a "wilderness child."

The tradition of oddity and magic followed her family. William, her youngest son, married a girl named Monica. She lived at one time in a house built over a large flat rock on the west side of "Monica's Swamp" in Barnstable. Will-o'-the-wisp lights gleamed over the swampland after Monica's departure, and the townsmen said "thar be Monica, dancin' with swamp-devils." After her marriage she lived in the witch house of Liza Tower Hill at Half Way Pond. Tales of magic were on the wane, but stories of the luminous trees in the forest adjacent to Half Way Pond continued. Gradually Monica's name began to be associated with these stories. Her husband was a soldier in the revolutionary army. After an illness, he found that he could not stand straight, and became a deserter. Colonel Otis, whose duty it was to report him to the military authorities, mercifully looked the other way as William Blatchford, Jr., shuffled down the street. The townsmen joked at the expense of his crookedness. As he was returning from camp, he met a group of Barnstable men. "Where do you come from?" they inquired. "Straight from camp," said he. "Then you've got badly twisted on the way," said one of the group; and this reply was recounted as wit for upward of an hundred years. It is included in Mr. Otis' genealogy of the Lewis family; a wit that could only be applied, without censure, to a deserter, the son of a witch.

Sally, the granddaughter of Liza Tower Hill, married Nathaniel Bacon, a poor man not prone to overwork. At first the couple lived near Ebenezer Sturgis. When winter days were cold, they would watch the Sturgis family caring for their cattle, trudging their farm in hail, sleet and snow. "I am thankful that I do not own that stock of cattle," Nathaniel said to the witch's granddaughter, and he pointed out to her the advantages of sitting at ease by a blazing fire, while other men toiled in the storm. Sally shared his sentiments. She also shared his poverty. In the course of time they acquired a large number of offspring. While the townsmen of Barnstable were chuckling over Nathaniel's statement that "Squire Bacon and I keep more cows than any two men in Barnstable" (Nathaniel had one, the squire twenty), while the men in the blacksmith's shop were recounting his clever trick of biting a bar of iron, Nathaniel was finding it impossible to retain his house in town. He and Sally were forced to move to a tiny hut far from all neighbors, and so the granddaughter of Liza Tower Hill returned to a forest home. She, also, worked in the fields. She, also, was "queer." Townspeople continued to discover luminous trees in the woods at midnight. Some of the narrators attributed these phenomena to the ghost of Liza; others ascribed them to Monica, the daughter-in-law. A few claimed that Sally, the granddaughter of the witch, had been seen dancing around a burning tree, her partner the squire's black cow.

Sally lacked her grandmother's courage and initiative. The Bacon family had no comforts, few necessities. There came at last a stormy winter morning when, in the little house in the forest, there was no wood to kindle a fire, no provisions, no food of any kind. Six small children were clamoring for breakfast. Sally rose, scraped the crystal patterns of frost from the windowpane, and looking out "exclaimed in piteous tones: 'Oh, what would I give for one pipe of tobacco.' "

Stories of the Luminous Forest usually terminate with the spicy adventure that befell Dr. Richard Bourne in 1810, an incident that occurred exactly twenty years after Liza Tower Hill's death.

Dr. Bourne "was never intoxicated at his own expense." Nevertheless, there were few tavern gatherings from which the jolly doctor was absent. He lifted his glass, he sang "Old King Cole," he narrated the astounding experiences of his youthful visit to the far country of Maine. He always sang the same song; he always told the same story. Among his cronies, few stories were really new, and this repetition was not censured. As one waits in knowing expectation for the recurrence of a ballad refrain, so they waited for the rollicking notes of his one aria. Apparently they were never disappointed. As the evening wore on, it became increasingly difficult to restrain Dr. Bourne from singing encores of "Old King Cole" continuously. When at last he was helped on his horse, he caroled to the sky and pines, while his gray mare carried him home.

Every night he laid saddlebags and spurs on the table, ready for a prompt response to a medical summons. He had received a good education, and had a sound knowledge of the theory and practice of medicine; nevertheless, the calls upon his medical skill were infrequent, so he applied for and received the position of first postmaster of Barnstable. His house became the post office, a place of constant resort. At first the mail arrived once a week. There was not much of it, but before its arrival a large group of citizens assembled in the doctor's parlor. They sat in a semicircle around the fire, the boys sprawled on the floor, their feet pushed between the rundles of the chairs to obtain fire warmth. Night after night, while the company waited for the arrival of the post horses, Dr. Bourne would describe his experiences in the north. He became, more or less, a public character, and that accounts for the widespread remembrance of his delusion on a Christmas night.

Invited to attend a holiday celebration at Hyannis, he arrived soon after sunset, dismounted, and hitched the gray mare that had carried him safely home from parties for more than twenty years. Cups were plenteously refilled; the liquor was good. Dr. Bourne sang "Old King Cole" and recited his adventures in Maine. The party broke up at midnight, the ripe hour when taverners ambled homeward in those days of early rising. Christmas evening; the moon was clear, the ground covered with a light snow, a northwest wind was blowing, and the air bitterly cold. To cross the Cape from Hyannis to Barnstable, Dr. Bourne had to ride through four miles of almost unbroken forest. The road was narrow, the trees high, no friendly houses edged the trail. The horse knew the way better than her master, who sat back in the saddle, cocked a friendly eye at the moon, and sang his favorite song.

If you will recall accounts of New England witches, you will remember that Old King Cole, in person, was reputed to be present at those "festive gatherings of the iniquitous" called by Cotton Mather "rendezvouses." Dr. Bourne, on Christmas night, rode his old gray mare through the heart of the forest haunted by Liza Tower Hill, and as he rode he caroled aloud the tune to which devils dance. It is hard to conceive of a more thorough challenge to Old Nick than such conduct on the night of Christ's nativity.

No one knows when the mare left the main road. Contrary to custom, she carried the doctor along a path that led to Half Way Pond. Soon Dr. Bourne caught sight of a stump aglow with phosphorescent light. Witch gossip says that he danced with the ghost of Liza Tower Hill around that stump, and shook hands cordially with the devil, not quite recognizing the latter in the moonlight. He spent the remainder of the night in the forest, cozily, with Liza; and when at dawn the ghost witch ceased to warm him, he awoke to see a little old man presenting him with a black book to sign. Doctor Richard's mind was clearing from the effects of alcohol. Suddenly he realized with whom he had been carousing. His gray mare stood waiting in the pathway. He leaped upon her back and spurred her toward the main road. In his haste to escape from the devil he failed to put on his boots.

More rational accounts of this midnight adventure maintain that the doctor saw a phosphorescent stump and imagined it to be a fire. His feet were very cold. Here was an opportunity for gratuitous warmth. The good doctor dismounted from his horse and placed his feet on the stump. When sufficiently warm, he remounted, but unfortunately forgot to put on his boots. In a pitiable condition he wandered about the woods until morning. Then, as dawn came, he found his way to the main road. Still befuddled, instead of turning toward his own house, he started toward Hyannis and forced his horse into a gallop.

The morning after Christmas, Abner Davis and a group of friends, journeying through the mid-Cape wilderness, met Dr. Bourne riding without footwear, galloping away from home, looking "wild and excited," but quite unfrozen after his long hours of exposure to increasing cold. The doctor reined up his horse. "Gentlemen," he asked, "can you tell me whether I am in this town or the next?"

The men realized that he was in need of assistance. He was invited into one of the nearest houses, given breakfast and a pair of great boots. After a rest of several hours he rode home; and for many days after his Christmas party, Doctor Richard remained "lack-a-daisy." And thereafter, in truth, he seemed to be haunted by the bad luck supposed to follow men who have slept with witches. He became the butt for practical jokes. Boys knocked at his door to inquire whether or not he had found his boots. "Am I in this town or the next?" they yelled, and made a dash for safety, dodging the long whip that the doctor now kept hanging by his front door. Troubles multiplied. He ceased to go to the taverns. He ceased to sing "Old King

Cole." When Matthew Cobb succeeded him as postmaster, his heart was broken. When his accounts were settled and he was accused of defaulting, the shame and sorrow hastened his death. The amount for which he was supposed to have defaulted, nearly a thousand dollars, was levied upon his estate. His small property was set off by execution and sold, and the proceeds paid over to the Post Office Department. There were no more parties in the taverns. Men looked at him askance. There was no one to whom to tell his adventures in Maine; no need to place upon the table his saddlebags and spurs. His skill in medicine was as useless to him as his years of faithful service to the post office. Yet he was a Bourne of Bourneland, descendant of reputed saint and martyr, one of a family who held their heads high. He died before the federal government discovered its error. Too late to bring comfort to the heart of the old doctor, the government made restitution. It discovered that federal accounts were in error and that Dr. Bourne had owed the post office exactly thirty dollars. By that time the man who sang "Old King Cole" in a haunted forest one Christmas midnight, and who was reputed to have slept with a witch on the banks of an enchanted pond, lay buried in a haunted churchyard. Abigail Bourne, his only daughter, received approximately a thousand dollars on her wedding day.

THE WITCHCRAFT CASES

Ladies with red lacquer shoes, black steeds that obey no rein, magic quahog shells, haunted forests — all these are more or less in the tradition of hearthfire tales. When we turn to the more serious memories, to the legal accusations and suits for slander, we find that the guardians of civic responsibility on the Cape were unmoved by the witchcraft hysteria of Salem and Massachusetts Bay. Cape men relished good "yarns" of witches. They accepted and discussed the superstitions of their day. Sailors shuddered when they saw St. Elmo's fire glitter along mainmast or spars, and cursed the "little old woman of Nauset," who was perched aloft "whistlin' up a storm" or "broodin' for a calm." But when God guided the ship to port, animosities faded and no old crone was forced to pay for the dangers that seamen face.

Tales as dramatic as those in Salem were whispered at twilight, when looms were quiet; but magistrates refused to condemn legally any man or woman as a witch. Gossip rose and fell, like long Cape waves that gather, shatter, and dwindle with slow intake of breath.

Two trials are remembered that once were anxiously discussed. In 1677, little Mehitable Woodworth developed violent fits. The neighbors watched in wonder; and Walter Woodworth, her father, summoned medical aid. Mehitable, "almost bereaved of her senses . . . struggled as against demons," and "greatly languished" between virulent attacks. There seemed to be no doubt — Mehitable was bewitched. Old Mary Ingham, wife of Thomas Ingham of Scituate, bore a grudge against the Woodworths. With the haste and fury of a distraught parent, Goodman Woodworth sought alleviation of his child's unwarranted suffering, and brought sudden action against Mary Ingham who "by the help of the Devil, in a way of witchcraft or sorcery" was destroying the health and sanity of Mehitable.

Mary Ingham pleaded not guilty and put herself "on trial of God and the country." Governor Josiah Winslow presided at the hearing. Mr. Thomas Huckins, John Howland II, and John Woodworth were among the jurors. Ruth Winslow, the daughter-in-law of the judge, later to become the wife of Richard Bourne, was strongly in favor of Goodwife Ingham's innocence; and although the trial caused much talk, Deity and country stood by the old dame, and the verdict came in: not guilty. So far as we know Mehitable Woodworth recovered from her fits.

In the second trial, Dinah, the wife of Joseph Sylvester, claimed that her neighbor, Goody Holmes, conversed with the devil, who appeared in the form of a bear. The story spread, and the people of the colony looked upon Goody Holmes askance. Her husband, William, determined to put an end to such nonsense, brought suit for slander against Dinah Sylvester; and while Governor Prence presided, Dinah was tried by the General Court.

"What evidence have you of the fact that William Holmes' wife is a witch?" Dinah was asked. "She appeared to me as such," was the reply.

"In what shape did she appear?"

"In the shape of a bear."

"How far off was the bear?"

"About a stone's throw from the highway."

"What manner of tail had the bear?"

"I cannot tell as his head was towards me."

The devil, it seems, was also masquerading as bruin, and took an undue pleasure in the metamorphosis of William Holmes' wife. The story, told by Dinah, was presumably a coarse one. Morton fills up the "proper number of lines" with rows of stars like a modern author, and we are left to conjecture on the doings of Dame Holmes as a bear.

The court had no use for farce. Governed by legal evidence they "ordered that the examination be recorded for the clearing of the accused, and that the accuser be publicly whipped or else pay the sum of five pounds; but in case she made a public acknowledgment of her crime, she shall only pay William Holmes the charge he has been at."

Whatever Dinah Sylvester's private beliefs may have been, she was in no position to pay five pounds, a small fortune in those days when a house cost two-pound-ten. Also, a whipping was no nominal performance, and Dinah was not a young woman. She made public acknowledgment that the "accusation was false and malicious." That meant that the people who had shaken their heads over Goodwife Holmes now shook them over Dinah. Yet the termination of the trial brought with it a sense of relief. Secure in the knowledge that legal measures were dependable, strange tales of "witchery" continued to circulate unabated, unabated — but *intime*.

In the seclusion of inglenooks, while the spice of burning red pine mingled with the down-glancing "pin-fire" of stars, one heard that a dozen black crows from John Doane's cornfield had flown to the barren waste of Goody Hallett's Meadow where they were pecking sand as though it were kernels of corn. In the Hollow by Eastham churchyard, Meletiah, the post boy, reported a flash of scarlet, too late for the flight of the red-winged blackbird, a flash that resembled a dancing beldame's shoe. Such wonders were recounted without fear or sadness, for the Cape has a clear conscience and remembers its witches pleasantly. Also, since the days of Maushop, the Cape has felt a certain tolerance for the devil and his affairs. Lucifer is something of a Cape man. He built his house in the Province Lands;

and if, on moonlight nights, he chances to swing a halyard, or dances
a few measures over the dewy grass with giddy old ladies, so long as
he minds his business, Cape folk will attend to theirs.

2. GOODWIVES AND WIDOWS

To the Narrow Land came sunny days when the stir of the earth
and the whirl of the sea made music in men's minds. Even the most
neurasthenic of puritanical ministers felt in himself an awakening to
blithe New England spring: "I see all Creatures everywhere full of
their Delights. The Birds are singing; the Fish are sporting; the Four-
footed are glad of what they meet withal; the very insects have their
Satisfactions." How could the primmest of country maids refuse
the boy that "went wooing with her," or be "Transported with this
Zeal of Voluntary Virginity as knowing there's few Practise it?" Banns
were published; settlements concluded; all too soon maids became
goodwives, subject to stern discipline and the bearing of many children.

THE THREE HINCKLEY ROSES

In Barnstable, long ago, lived the Three Hinckley Roses, Hannah,
Samuel, and Elisabeth who was the Smallest Rose. They had blue
eyes and the two girls wore a "french fringe" of brown hair cut across
their foreheads. Sammy, their brother, was capped with shining
curls. The three, not far separated in age, were like "three steps of
a gradual stairway," and they were seldom separated, from the time
when they rocked as "cradle-mites" until Hannah, the eldest, outgrew
her trundle, in the year when the Boston plague came along the
Bay to Barnstable.

Hannah, the first to be smitten with disease, was put to bed in the
west front room. The two younger children were sent in to "comfort Sister." A few mornings later, Samuel awoke with his small back
aching, his eyes blinded and dizzy, his throat "wondrous soar." Then
Elisabeth, the Smallest Rose, began to be frightened. Hannah and
Samuel were having the plague and she was left out. This "tor-
tience-baby," the youngest, some folk said the plainest, since her

hair was a little more lank than Hannah's, her eyes a little less blue, was always struggling to share every adventure of her older sister and brother to whom she was Cape-loyal and sometimes much of a nuisance.

She was the last one over the fence and never would be helped. She secretly ate Sammy's porridge for him when he could not have plum cake until his porridge was consumed. She also ate his plum cake as well as her own whenever he became lost in daydreams from which he bitterly awakened to the discovery of his loss. She borrowed sister Hannah's sampler and stitched it to "supprize Sister." Mistress Hinckley, mother of the three, pulled the false stitches out, while Hannah looked on in superior wisdom and Elisabeth loudly wept.

When she developed the plague and was not very ill of it, she accepted the suffering as part of life with brother Sam and sister Hannah. Then one wintry day, the two older children took a turn for the worse, and good Mr. Walley, the minister, came to prepare Hannah and Sammy for heavenly judgment. He told them exactly what to say, how to talk to the angels, why they must not be afraid. Elisabeth listened with eyes wide; later she put her hands on the great man's knee and asked what should she do. He pinched her cheek and answered that such problems were not for those who must live in a "World of Sorrows."

After the minister had gone, Hannah and Samuel grew excited about going to heaven. Hannah's eyes became shiny. She did not see her younger sister. Instead she beheld angels to whom she gave good welcome, and beseeched them for kind mercy. Sammy shook his small fists and started a battle with "Satane's impes," big ones, under his bed. Elisabeth, to reassure him, removed the trundle and crawled under the poster, but found only a lost white button and linsey lint from his plague jacket.

The grown people knelt in prayer. Mrs. Ruth Bourne who knew about plague rode over from Sandwich and sat with Hannah's hand in hers. She kept stroking the child's forehead, then held her by the wrist and listened, with her head on one side like a bright-eyed robin. Mistress Hinckley told Elisabeth that soon she must say goodbye to sister Hannah, and perhaps to brother Sam.

In the afternoon a weathergall (rainbow) shone over the ocean, like a handle to a great blue basket. The weathergall was taken as a "sign." Later, sunsucker clouds turned a shadowy crimson. Elisabeth was sent into the east front bedroom to sleep in the big bed usually occupied by her father and mother. Neither of them seemed to remember that sober-light was descending. They kept candles brightly burning and stayed with Samuel and Hannah.

Elisabeth crept into the bed in the east front room. No one came to tuck her in, nor heated the sheets with a warming pan. In the west room, Hannah breathed queerly. The minister remained there with Elder Chipman and others. Samuel shifted and moaned. Suddenly, in the darkness, Elisabeth began to shake. They could not go to heaven without her, sister Hannah and brother Samuel, she to stay in a world of sorrows while Hannah talked with death-watch angels and Sammy fought like a warrior. She had no angels to "speake her faire"; she had no devils to fight. The Good Lord would reward Hannah with soft wings and a halo; Sammy would get him a crown and a golden sword for his service; and she would not be there to see, left in a world of sorrows. Her heart thumped a queer summons, like the meeting house drum.

She crawled out of bed. In her white nightdress she ran into the lighted west room where Hannah and Samuel were lying on the goose-feather mattress of the pineapple poster. Grown folk knelt beside them. Radiant, smiling, she swayed for a moment, then lifted her arms and delivered to the watchers a swift exhortation:

> "Behold! Hannah talketh with Angels!
> Behold! Sammy battleth with Devils!
> But Elisabeth walketh with God!"

She toppled forward on her face, this Smallest Rose who had no care at all, no ministerial guidance, yet who was the first to walk with God of the Three Hinckley Roses.

THE DOUBLE TRIAL OF ABIGAIL

Mistress Abigail Muxom entered Old Wareham church. She paused, once inside the building, and looked toward the high pulpit. Over it towered a dome-shaped sounding board, behind it shone a great window. Lost in the pulpit's cavernous depths stood Rowland

Thacher, the minister. He could not see out, and she could not see him, for the pulpit was built on a heroic scale and Rowland Thacher was not.

The deacons, ready to condemn Mistress Abigail, sat forward on the deacon seats at the foot of the pulpit, facing the congregation. Near them, the pew of the minister's wife gaped, so lately empty, so soon to be occupied by pretty Hannah Fearing, widow of the squire's son. As goodmen and their goodwives rose to peer over the tops of pews, seats snapped upward in the square stall pews around the walls; noisily, if the hand of caution failed to ease their progress; squeakily where hinges were stiff or wood had warped in fog. Alone, on the narrow pulpit stairs, sat the son of the gravedigger, waiting to turn the minister's hourglass, watching to give the deacons word of improprieties.

In the center of this church stood two sections of benches, the forward bench reserved for sinners, behind them the deaf and the old; on the rear benches children, carefully guarded from slumber or activity by the vigilance of tidy men (tithing men) who bore rods with a rabbit's foot on one end and a copper ship's nail on the other. For a first offense one was touched with the rabbit's foot; for a second one encountered the nail.

Abigail Muxom seated herself on the forward bench. Her head was high, her cheeks flushed, and she "wore no garment of humility." When the time came for her condemnation, Rowland Thacher, from his impenetrable stronghold, read three depositions against her:

> Elisha Benson Saith That he was at Edmund Muxom's house sometime since & saw sd Muxoms wife very familiar with Joseph Benson by talking of balderdash stuff & kissing and hugging one another in the absence of her husband. At another time I saw them coming out of the house together & discovered none but they two. Middleborough, Octr. 1750.

Abigail rose from the forward bench. So far as we know she had come alone, had no friend, no attorney to represent her, and her husband was not present to defend her though he had not put her by. The man who might have demanded justice for the erring as well as for the righteous read the indictment. Mercifully hidden from the sharp eyes of the congregation, and from her ironic gaze, he waited, alone in that high pulpit, for her answer. Abigail formally denied the charge.

The second statement was then read aloud:

Caleb Cushman & his wife do Testify & say That we some time since have seen Joseph Benson & Abigail Muxom at our house & their behaviour was uncommon for married people; she was fawning about him & sometimes in his lap or upon his knee & he haleing of her, running his face up to hers, & as we suppose kissing of her or aiming to do so & talking & joacking like young people.

Plymton, Octr. 1750.

There was a stir of consternation in the church, the queer, dead rustling, like autumn leaves, made by gossipy bodies in gossipy clothes. In the house of God, the tidy men watched the squirming children, but the deacons and peeping townsmen watched Mistress Abigail as the minister read words that he had delayed three years to read. Every man wondered why the examiner of souls had held back such damning evidence and had administered communion to the sinner, and called her "Sister." She was very beautiful, men said, and of the minister they thought what righteous minds have always thought when scandal and sin are condoned in the young and gay: Rowland had an eye for a lady. But now that his wife was dead and he was in love with the squire's daughter, he complied with the will of his parishioners, and read aloud the unsworn statements that would condemn the goodwife with whom his name had been linked in gossip. Abigail rose from the forward bench and denied the second charge.

The minister read the final deposition:

Jedidah Swift wife to Eben^r Swift Junr Saith that she was at the house of Edmund Muxom four times the summer past & his wife Abigail Muxom did several times call her child to her & ask the child who its father was, & the child would answer Doctor Jo's at which she would laugh & make sport of.   Wareham, Decem^r. 3. 1750.

The two first statements were sauce for the goose; the third was sauce for the gander. With any luck on the side of righteousness, Abigail was destined to wear the letter A, as Mary Eaton of the Cape had worn it, as other women had been branded in Plymouth and

Massachusetts Colonies. The two first charges were pleasant scandal; the third was matter for grave action. If she had repudiated the lighter accusations, it was obvious that she would deny this one. But Abigail was not obvious. She stated that the last charge was true.

Rowland Thacher, from his cavernous pedestal, asked for the vote of the townsmen. Women were allowed no vote, and without more ado the men convicted the accused, pronouncing her "guilty of immoral Conduct." The congregation waited for the word of their minister; it was his duty to determine her punishment. But Rowland Thacher seemed to lose the thunder that in his sermons inspired men with fear of retribution for sin. He suspended Abigail Muxom from the "communion table" till she "give a Christian satisfaction." The congregation, taken aback, resented this unwonted clemency.

She went out of the meeting house and walked beside the saber-like waves that curved along the shore. Hers was a happy disposition; so she nodded as she passed Deacon Swift's tavern, and there the farmers, bartering mutton and hay for rum, and the tavern roisterers lifted their glasses and toasted first the king, then Mistress Abigail, prettiest, naughtiest, gayest housewife in Agawame.

Rowland married the Widow Fearing, and rapidly increased his family. His salary remained always in arrears. Twelve days before his death, in 1774, it was voted not to allow him anything "for the year past more than his stated salery." As the town had failed to pay his "stated salery," this precaution against generous impulse was unnecessary.

Meanwhile Abigail lived happily in Agawame. Her son grew up and became a likable sailor. Her husband continued to live with her. Joseph Benson continued to visit her. But the scandal never died. She had not paid the penalty of sin; and the townspeople held it against her. They determined, after Mr. Thacher's death, that the new minister should "sweep clean." They chose a spiritual leader who was at the clean-sweeping age. His name was Noble Everitt, and he came directly from Yale College. One of his first actions, as minister, was to appoint a committee "to converse with brethren and sisters who are or may be guilty of public offense according to the rule given in Mat. 18." That committee knew exactly what it wanted: Abigail Muxom was at last to receive punishment overdue some thirty years.

She was an old woman in 1783, with nothing against her save a memory of a minister's baffling leniency, and three dust-worn depositions in the church records. The committee found that John Benson was ready to testify again. After thirty years his memory had improved and he was able to add new details in his remembrance of incidents that had occurred before 1750. His testimony was more damning than it had been in 1753, more circumstantial — for in this world important memories increase their data as one grows old. Hannah "Bessee," of the "garrulous Besse women" was also ready with testimony concerning Abigail's youthful philandering. The old depositions were clearly in the records and could be reread from the pulpit. So in 1783 Abigail Muxom was again summoned to the meeting house. No longer beautiful, she had the hardy open-air look of a Cape woman. Steady work at heavy tasks had left its imprint on her shoulders. The goodmen did not have to rise so often to peer over their pews; they found it easier to remember what she looked like.

As for Abigail, she had lost her sense of the dramatic. Neither she nor the English king were toasted now in the taverns of a newborn nation still bleeding from its birth wound. There was no money to meet taxes, her son, "Lem," was ill, the farm was not providing food for sustenance. This fanatic revival of a long buried scandal seemed to her futile, childish, "trawlin' fer minnews." The nobility of Noble Everitt bored her. He was young; Yale College might not be responsible for him; still, she was glad that her son had not gone there, though it did not matter much as he was like to be drowned at sea. From the mist of thirty years she recalled another voice exhorting her from this same pulpit, a voice more hesitant, a voice that gossip had called "guilty."

No such irksome conscience hampered Noble Everitt, who thundered the new deposition in his "sou'wester" voice:

John Benson of Middleborough testifieth that upwards of 20 years ago he was at the house of Edmund Muxom the husband of said Abigail, sometime in the afternoon before sunset, he saw said Abigail on bed with Joseph Benson, in the easterly part of the house. He also saith that at another time he was at work near Edmund Muxom's house and heard him repeatedly bid his son Lem. go and fetch the horse and on refusal corrected him. Abigail came to the door and said — What do you whip that child for? it is none of yours, upon which John Benson said I always thought so, at which she went into the house and said no more.

April II. 1783.

Hannah Besse testifieth that sometimes about 20 years ago or upward she went to Edmund Muxom's house late in the evening and there saw Abigail his wife on bed by the fire with Joseph Benson.

April II. 1783.

With increasing indignation Abigail listened to the charges. What right had John Benson to make false testimony against his brother Joseph? Why traduce old memories? Life was sufficiently difficult without that. In the presence of the "assembled church" Abigail declared that "the evidences of John Benson and Hannah Besse are false." Again no attorney represented her; no friend spoke for her; there was no cross-examining of the unsworn witness. The church voted that she was "guilty of the charge."

Definite punishment was deferred in the hope that she could be induced to "make a penitent and public confession of her sin." The deacons, who had voted her guilty, labored with her zealously. The women pleaded with her to confess and be forgiven. Abigail continually lost her temper. She called the witnesses "liars"; she described Noble Everitt and the ladies of the parish as "wet-foot turkeys"; the deacons she appears to have regarded as beneath contumely. After some weeks she was summoned for a third time before the assembled church and was publicly "admonished" in a long exhortation by the minister. She sat, proud and defiant, on the forward bench. Steadily she refused to confess her guilt, refused to be drawn into any orgy of the emotions. Day after day she worked in the fields, or washed the clothes, and did her household chores.

Then, from the neighboring towns, six ministers were summoned. They came mounted on six ministerial horses, sleek, fat animals, cemetery nourished, for the ecclesiastics of the early Cape had the privilege of foddering their steeds on graveyard turf. So these mounts were reputed to be familiar with ghosts, to be "fey" horses, and their presence in the graveyards gave rise to many tales of heavily breathing "sperrits," of moving "nottomies" (skeletons) in white, of ghostly Indian giants encountered near the Burying Acre.

The ministers, invited to this inquest upon the defunct romance of

Abigail, were royally entertained at the homes of goodmen. Then, on a day when no man worked, the curious gathered from miles around, and the floor and galleries of the meeting house were packed. Abigail Muxom stood in the presence of the six visiting ministers, while the evidences were read aloud. She denied their truth. In a dramatic appeal, Noble Everitt requested the ministers "to give their opinion what particular immodest conduct our sister is guilty of, and hòw this church ought to proceed with her." The ministers were prompt and unanimous. Her conduct was "forbidden by the 7th commandment" and it was her duty "to make a penitent and public confession of her sin." She refused. Parson Everitt then pronounced her excommunicate. The custom of the wearing of the letter A had passed; but the minister branded her with unforgettable words, described her publicly, in the presence of the large assembly, as "visibly a hardened and impenitent sinner out of the visible Kingdom of Christ, one who ought to be viewed and treated by all good people as a heathen and a publican in imminent danger of eternal perdition."

Abigail, quite alone, went out of the meeting house, and walked beside the thin, curving lips of the sea. She was old and no longer nodded to the roisterers of the town tavern, and they no longer toasted either the king or Abigail's smile. At dusk she went home to Agawame and there, day after day she worked in the fields, or washed the clothes, and did her household chores.

THE TARRING AND FEATHERING OF THE WIDOW NABBY

From Barnstable Harbor, Rendezvous Lane runs south to the King's Highway. In 1776 the Green that is now a small sodded triangle at the debouchment of the lane extended eastward along the highway, forming a parade ground for militia; and on the Green, at the outlet of the lane, near the whipping post and stocks, the Vigilance Committee erected their Liberty Pole.

One sunny morning, not long before the Declaration of Independence, Mistress Abigail Freeman opened the door of her green grocery and oddment shop, then peered toward the gold-tipped Liberty Pole that stood shining in the sun. The "Widow Nabby" shook her fist at this emblem of revolt as she stooped to pick up a small pamphlet thrust under her door. She adjusted square spectacles, carefully hooking them over her ears, where wooden thread bobbins on which she wound "vanitous fore-curls" interfered with the precise alignment of the spectacle wire. "An Indean Dream, drempt on Cape Cod," read Nabby. She laid down the pamphlet and hurried to the fire where steam rose from her black iron water kettle, for not even the most libelous of political or personal gossip could interfere with her morning rite of "samp and brew."

Seated in the ingle with a steaming cup in one hand, the Widow Nabby held the newly discovered pamphlet in the other. Her sharp wits concentrated; the wrinkles between her keen old eyes deepened as she read. Undoubtedly Satan in the pamphlet was her neighbor, Otis Loring, tavern owner, blacksmith and chief Tory of Barnstable. Satan, indeed! The widow sniffed. She held no brief for Otis and to him frequently gave a "piece of her mind"; nor had she any illusions concerning her numskull patriot relatives, such wags as young Nat Freeman, "court'sy nevvy," who was leader of the Ardent Whigs. In the mind of the Widow Abigail only one romantic illusion clung, that of the English king.

After breakfast, Aunt Nabby put on her "Chatterfest shawl" and walked across the Green, past the Liberty Pole. Some young patriots chanced to be within earshot, so she threatened "straightaway to heave thet dead tree up." She entered Loring's tavern, discovered that Otis had also received a copy of the pamphlet, and announced that Satan in the satire was a caricature of the innkeeper himself. Loring had already reached that uncomfortable conclusion, and thereafter the two readers slowly identified first one, then another, of the local Patriots and Tories. When it came to settling upon identity of the author, scant progress was made. The Widow Nabby finally acceded that it must be a Crocker; Josiah, perhaps, who fancied himself as a writer, although his Whiggish sympathies blew now hot, now cold. It could not be Cornelius, Jr., who lived across-lane from Nabby. The lame owner of the rival tavern to Loring's was overcautious, a professed neutral hated by both sides. The one consistent Whig among the Crockers, sensible Captain Samuel, would, so Nabby maintained, have "come out with print-letter sense"; said what he meant to say.

Marked respect existed between these two political enemies, the Widow Abigail Freeman whom no man could down in argument, quick, shrewd, witty, fearless; and Samuel Crocker, captain of the

militia, moderate Whig, with no use for headstrong young "Ardents,"
nor for the old-maidisms of a Vigilance Committee that "snooped" to
discover hidden stores of tea. He even refused permission to his sons
to question young girls concerning their political sentiments, a mental
exercise, in the estimation of Captain Samuel, too "strenewous for
the . . . female mind."

While Nabby and Otis Loring discussed the pamphlet together,
other townsmen were gathering on the Green with more copies of the
"Indean Dream." All men laughed, Whig or Tory, at some of the
shots that struck home, but the laughter petered out in time as personal retorts grew acrimonious. Aunt Nabby glanced out of the window, saw the gathering throng, and bustled out to join in the topic of
the hour. Her voice was high, sharp, clear; in almost no time she had
put all the Whigs to rout. As Timothy Phinney remarked to the retreating Ardents, she was the most "pernitious" enemy that the In-
dependents of Barnstable were likely to encounter "this side o' the
sea."

The Vigilance Committee and the Whigs of known alignment assembled further up the Green in Cornelius Crocker's tavern, there
to rejoice among themselves at Otis Loring's discomfiture in the role
of Satan, and to mock Aunt Nabby's speech. Captain Samuel Crocker
sprang to the widow's defense. Despite coarse innuendo he clung to
his allegiance. She was a grand old warhorse! She was to have her
say!

Young Nat Freeman, razzed mercilessly for his relationship with her,
was told that the Freeman family were unable to control their women.
The joke rankled with Nathaniel who was convinced that Aunt Nabby,
a Freeman by marriage, should have contented herself with a position
as nurse and general helper in one of the Freeman homes. Instead she
insisted upon maintaining a "degraded and raucous independence."
Also, one branch of the family kept shop in Barnstable, having for sale
"sundrie supplies." It was a rankling wound that Cousin Abigail, by a
system of petty barter, had prospered during the late years of depreci-
ated and shifting currency while the other shop, run by men of the
family, barely remained solvent. Finally, her outspoken Toryism
jangled Nathaniel's nerves.

The Vigilance Committee, stirred by the accusations in the pam-

phlet, decided to arrest Otis Loring that afternoon; but when they
went to his blacksmith shop he met them at the doorway and in his
hands he held an iron bar that completely blocked the door. The central portion of the bar was heated to a red glow. "Gentlemen," said
Loring politely, "I am ready for you. Come on." The committee departed without making an arrest and the Widow Nabby accompanied
them, "adding a few remarks." Listening to these, it occurred to Nathaniel that when he had entered the kitchen of the Whig tavern,
earlier in the day, he had seen Aunt Nabby there conferring on
household matters with Eliza Crocker. At once he suspected that she
was a traitor, a spy, an eavesdropper. Hotheaded patriot that he was,
he still had enough wisdom or family pride to keep this suspicion to
himself.

Once more assembled in the Crocker tavern to discuss this newest
Tory defiance, the Ardents and moderate Whigs quarreled among
themselves. To quiet the turmoil and restore amicability, Cornelius
Jr., the tavernkeeper, proposed to treat them all to a free bumper of
rum. "Hot-Jamaica" went down throats which were already far from
dry and precipitated the outbreak that it was designed to avoid. The
Ardents determined to show the Moderates how much in earnest
they were, and, departing, carried with them a section of the Crocker
fence. With wooden fence rails clutched to their hearts they marched
to the western end of the Green, between Loring's tavern and the entrance to Rendezvous Lane. There, presumably, they intended to build
a bonfire beside the Liberty Pole, but the night was darkening and
Nathaniel Freeman, as ever in advance of his compatriots, stumbled
and fell to the ground. Willing hands pulled him upright while other
hands investigated the source of the disaster. Flat on the Green lay
the Liberty Pole; "heaved up" as Aunt Nabby had declared that it
would be. By the aid of lanterns the Ardents discovered that the pole
had been cut at the base.

While insulted patriots partially restored their fallen token of
liberty which, try as they would, persisted in toppling at a drunken
angle, they discussed the probable consequences of an attack upon
Otis Loring. It meant battle, a court examination, possibly heavy
fines. Even if Loring had done the cutting, the real instigator of the
offense was the widow of Rendezvous Lane, who had twice undone

the Whigs in one day. As Captain Sam Crocker remarked, if
King George had only left the war to Nabby Freeman, rebellion
would soon have been quelled.

Up Rendezvous Lane marched the Ardents, led by an angry Nathaniel whose shins were barked and aching, whose family honor was
dimmed. In front of the widow's house they sang the Liberty Song,
and might have gone away quietly if Aunt Nabby had not come to the
window in a ruffled nightdress and a red flannel cap. With a drip candle held aloft, illuminating her lean, long profile, she started to lecture
them anew. Nathaniel went close under the window and addressed her
fondly as aunt. Then, suddenly, he seized her by the shoulders and
hauled her over the window ledge. She came flapping, headfirst, pre-
cipitate. Her nightdress slipped up "scandlus." Her discourse never
ceased.

The patriots hilariously rushed her to the Green. They strung her
up on the leaning pole while her old feet kicked, and her scrawny
limbs battled and twisted. A young blade broke into Loring's blacksmith shop and seized a bucket of tar. Willing confederates heated
it at the bonfire on the Green. Another Ardent crept in at Abigail's
window and confiscated her feather pillaber. Then the ruffled night-
gown of the Widow was torn rudely from her shoulders. The pillaber
was slit and Aunt Nabby cruelly smeared with feathers and tar.

A rail from the Crocker fence stood ready to "ride her." Nabby was
lifted aloft, the rail raised to men's shoulders with her lank body
astride it. One man held her on either side while, with lanterns up-
lifted to light the spectacle, a slow procession started east over the
Green. No one knows, irrefutably, who marched in that company of
Cape Cod men who tarred and feathered a woman, the only occur-
rence of its kind in the annals of the American continent; but every
indication suggests that the men were no ordinary rabble and that
no ordinary woman drove them to such revenge. No feminine weak-
nesses beset her in her ordeal. Around the bobbins of her "fore-curls"
clung a wild feather halo; the quivering of her angular old limbs revealed torture and physical strain. Yet, neither frightened nor pro-
pitiatory, she met violence with tongue-lashings until her voice gave
out. A dozen times they asked her if she would swear to abandon tea,
Toryism, tongue-wagging. A dozen times she refused. When she

could no longer speak, she shook her grotesque head in negation, and slowly the fun died out of the repetitions.

She sagged over at last in a dead faint, and was lifted off the rail. Tradition says that she "came to" for a moment as she fell. Her "court'sy nevvy" leaned down, his conscience troubling him, to ask a belated forgiveness. But Aunt Nabby was beyond answering questions. Her old lips, trembling, whispered, "God save the King."

AUNT BECK'S MUSEUM

Rebecca Blush, descendant of David and Hannah Linnell, lay on her great bed. All day through the house sounded a rumbling like the far presage of storm. "Be that thunder?" questioned Aunt Beck, but the people who came and went in her room were too busy to reply.

Rebecca Blush was eighty-six, and her husband a young seventy. Try as she would to forget their discrepancies of age, she was continually aware of his youth. She rested quietly in the great bed and thought about her husband. Was he closing the windows, downstairs, to keep out the storm? Was he guarding her "Museum" well? Now and again, in the crowding of her thoughts, she became conscious of the sheet folded over her, the "new sheet" carefully unused since her wedding day. She would have to get up and change it. Then, queerly, she forgot bed linen and wondered about Elisha again.

She had made many mistakes in her life, but not so many as Elisha. The Methodists were to blame for his follies. If she did not take care of him they would get his last cent. She summoned him to her bedside, tried to ask about her collection of feathers downstairs, suggested some new places for the storage of beef bones for soapmaking. Docile, yet evasive in his answers, Elisha's eyes glittered with an unnatural excitement. Aunt Beck did not like the look of him. Since he had taken up with Methodists he had grown prodigal of purse, argumentative, and he went from home frequently. She wondered: could Elisha Blush have taken to strong drink?

Thirty years changed him from an honest young shoemaker, who married a woman of forty-six, to a secretive, complaining husband hampered by an old wife. Once he had possessed a gallant quality that died all too soon. Once he had planned a stately house and a sunny garden, and contemplated the ownership of a pair of horses. But Rebecca, from the outset, "knocked out his notions" just as her first husband had cured her of childhood's "tomfoolery."

John Linnell had been married previously to her sister, and when the sister died, Rebecca married John without knowing that it was illegal, by ecclesiastical law, for a man to marry his deceased wife's sister. After John's death, his heirs by former marriages tried to claim his estate to the exclusion of the widowed Rebecca and her daughter. Barnstable relished this scandal. Rebecca, who had been proud in carriage, was suddenly stripped of her position, her good name, her daughter's birthright.

To her Elisha came in sympathy, thought her a fine, upstanding woman, stood ready to give her a name, and to adopt her only daughter, did not even care to wait until the lawsuit was settled. She had scarcely time to think. John was dead, her position changed from widow to mistress, her husband's heirs were claiming his estate, and Elisha was wooing her. Legal action, to her way of thinking, was like "ketchin' smoke in a fish net." Yet life moved faster than lawyers, for before settlement was made, her daughter died, she married Elisha, and the law concerning sisters changed.

A period of stagnation followed, and Rebecca was desirous that nothing should ever again happen to disturb the tenor of her days. When the lawsuit concluded in her favor, she became, once more, a woman of property, and Elisha promptly proposed schemes for the betterment of her death money. She listened to him tolerantly; she was much wiser than he. When she told him that she would attend to her own inheritance, Elisha made no audible protest, but estrangement grew between them. He ceased to be gallant, protecting; became sarcastic and wore an air of aggrieved, suppressed criticism. In response, she emphasized her natural tendency toward economy. She would show Elisha how to run an estate!

Elisha began to air his troubles, to "flacker his wings outside the nest." Barnstable was ready to listen to tales of "Aunt Beck." If he would contribute church money, the Methodists, who were sympathetic, offered to reason with his wife. Owner of extensive tracts of forest, of rich acres of plowed land, she could well afford a comfortable fire to keep Elisha warm.

Aunt Beck listened politely to the Methodist delegation when they visited her home. She inquired as to the amount that Elisha had "given in." Then she ordered them to leave, prophesying that any returning member of the sect should feel the weight of her broom. After their departure she went alone into the east front parlor. Bitterly angry, she waited there for Elisha; yet, as the hours passed, her temper cooled, and again she remembered his youth and inexperience. She was so much older; in time he would settle down.

When Rebecca Blush was carried into the upstairs room to die, she thought bitterly of Elisha's failure to "settle." To him the hours were "easy come, easy go." Yet she, who watched over him and doled out pennies, had made almost as many mistakes. She had loaned money to smooth-tongued borrowers who offered, not sound security, but magnificent return. She had overvalued broken-down possessions. She had lost capital by investing in mortgages on old houses and worn-out land. At first Elisha was inclined to voice a sanctimonious, "I told you so." Later, he made no comment, and her pride would not let her ask why.

One Saturday in November, as Aunt Beck lay dying, a noise like thunder echoed through her gabled house; not the crash of the breaking storm, but a roll, a thud, muffled and distant. She had never heard such a tempest in November; it made her restless of heart.

Proud of her reputation, proud of "Aunt Beck's Museum," she was aware that people traveled for miles to see her strange collections. Elisha might complain of the cold, but rich men and women were glad to sit by her fire of twined faggots and listen to ancient Cornish ballads to which she added a homespun talent, a line here, a change there, till the old songs came close to the listeners as part of the New Cape. The townsfolk brought their children to hear jingles of her composing, or verses altered from English themes. The tunes, the words were all in her head; not one rhyme had been written down. They would perish when she perished, at thought of which sometimes she was sorry; then, perversely, she rejoiced.

While children listened with tense delight, Aunt Beck seemed happy. Seated on a chair by the quick-dying fire, she leaned forward as she sang. Erratic flickers of faggot blaze shone now upon this curiosity, now upon that, in the east front parlor. Elisha shivered and frequently complained of the lack of good chairs to sit upon. The children did not care. They stood, their small mouths agape; stared at her, stared at the room; listened, breathless, to her tales. Some of the daring came alone, without the protection of parents. Often they grew too familiar, fingered the feathers or the broken crockery, or tried to appropriate some small and irresistible article. Then Aunt Beck seized her broomstick, and they fled, screaming, from the door.

Gossip, breezy jokes, parlor anecdote, sly kitchen wit, Aunt Beck knew all that there was to know about the life of the town. She could tell of fraud decked in flowered waistcoats, of virtue parading in vice. When, at last, they lifted her up the stairs and she rested in the great bed under the eaves, the vast stores of memory came crowding upon her too swiftly; through them echoed a rumbling thunder, far off, reverberant. She asked repeatedly: "Be that a tempest?" No one seemed ready to reply.

Elisha padded about the house, in and out of the two front rooms, up the stairs, down the stairs. Was he taking care of her things? Elisha could play traitor to her "Museum." She remembered the incident of the beef bones. For thirty years she had saved bones to make soap, depositing them in her large kitchen fireplace and about the rooms. The hot summer of '20 seemed hideously "close." Windows could not be opened lest air destroy the "Museum" and the sea breeze blow away objects cluttered on tables, hanging from walls and ceilings, piled in heaps on the floor. Elisha fussed and fussed. He would die of apoplexy. He could never endure the odor of beef. He summoned Captain Hall who lived across the street, and who was always spying, always gossiping. The captain also could not endure the odor of the bones. If he had used common sense he should have known that when the heat abated, the "noxious smell" would vanish. Such heat could not last. He and Elisha refused to listen. Other neighbors took up the plea. So the bones were collected from hearth and bedside, from beneath tables, from behind the doors. Captain Hall tried to count the collection, but Rebecca gave him scant opportunity. More than an ox-cart load of them were driven away and dumped in the marsh; and after they were gone Elisha mopped his brow, thanked God, and asked for a dime to "give in" at Methodist meeting.

At eighty-six Rebecca Blush was an old and weary woman. Elisha remained young. At seventy years old one scarcely felt the approach of senile age. Little he knew of the troubles ahead! All youth was thoughtless. She sensed this as he watched her grandniece, Rebecca, named after her. The girl frequented the house as if it were her own. Elisha took her home at night. Elisha walked the woods with her. Grandniece Rebecca, twenty-eight, remained unmarried, and seemed unwilling to take for a husband any one of the friendly village boys. What did her grandniece want of life? During Aunt Beck's last illness, the girl administered broth. But almost immediately after she had delivered the bowl, someone called from below-stairs and young Rebecca disappeared. Aunt Beck forgot to drink broth. She listened to the rumbling storm; a tempest, four days long, in the cold month of November: no wonder she felt heavy and weak.

The townsmen called her untidy, yet no yard in the village was as neat and trim as hers. The grounds looked hand-polished, the grass close clipped, the fences shining, the wood piled in exact design, the chips at the woodblock raked away. No wisp of straw, no scrap of debris bewhiskered outbuilding or barn.

Inside, no house was ever like hers. Aunt Beck tried to recall the thousands of items in each room. If she did not remember and demand restitution, some of her treasures might be lost while she was "resting" upstairs. The east front room, fourteen feet square, contained, besides an old fireplace topped by a broad mantel, a bedstead covered with dirty and ragged clothes. Underneath were boxes overflowing with broken crockery, and old-fashioned saucepans discarded by the modern housewives. Some of the pans were brought from England when the first comers settled the land. In front of the bed, near the center of the room, stood a handsome table, three feet square, receptacle for perishables. On it Aunt Beck laid whatever she thought worth preserving. Once an article was placed there, the "curiosity" could not be removed, for no one dared to meddle with Aunt Beck's property. The perishable curios, in process of time, rotted and changed into a black mold, covering the table with a stratum about an inch in thickness. Elisha pointed out that this mold was no longer a collection of curios, and should be removed for the better preservation of new material. Aunt Beck ignored his arguments. Later, he would understand that though the husk of an object perished, its essence or "sperrit" remained. Thus a broken dish, retained and treasured, was in reality a whole dish. Elisha thought, hearing such talk, that Rebecca had "gone past herself, wit-loose and maundersome."

The east front room became so crowded that the floor, excepting narrow paths between the doors, fireplace, and bed, was entirely covered with crockery, old pots, kettles, pails, and tubs. The walls were completely festooned with old-fahioned costumes, broken bits of furniture, bunches of dried herbs, ropes, old sword blades, garden tools, and farm tools. In the west front room, even Elisha's shoemaker's bench was laden; and from one wall jutted out an antique saddle and pillion. At the time when Samuel Taylor Coleridge, seated by an English hearthside, was reading a shabby volume entitled *Restitution of Decayed Intelligence in Antiquities,* across the ocean an old Cape woman was hoarding antiquities without reason, without discimination, one of the first American collectors to prize objects more for their age than for their intrinsic merit.

The antiquities became a mania. Aunt Beck hid parcels of coin among her rubbish. Light-fingered visitors took advantage of her blind eyes and pilfered her money bags. She accused some of the children of theft, but Elisha seemed so nervous, so flushed and uncomfortable, that a sudden fear beset her, and she said no more about her loss.

She died, Sunday, November 7, and the noise like thunder continued in the low "double" house. She was "laid out" in the upstairs room, and looked peaceful, Elisha said, though he did not go up to see her but once. He was very busy all that day; and when Rebecca was brought down the narrow stairs to the west front room, no trace of her handiwork remained in her home. If she had been able to rise, to change the "new sheet," her last hours would have been fraught with desolate bewilderment. For Elisha played her false. The thunder had not been thunder, only the steady removal and disposal of her treasures, the destruction of "Aunt Beck's Museum."

Young Rebecca, her grandniece, superintended the moving. Elisha readily complied. When Barnstable came to Aunt Beck's funeral, the mourners stared at empty rooms. The Methodist preacher conducted service, and comforted the widower. After the funeral the interior of the house was recleaned and repainted. "Fashionable" furniture appeared in the rooms. Forty-five days after Aunt Beck's death, Elisha "made merry in the Museum." No old ballads were sung by the hearth, no faggots disgraced the fire. For Elisha brought to Aunt Beck's home her young grandniece, Rebecca. He was over seventy, his bride was twenty-nine. For them the tall forests were cut, for them the wood was sold.

Unfortunately, Elisha Blush could not stand the pace. Sometimes he aired his troubles; "flackered his wings outside the nest." He died, a child of seventy-six, without realizing that even as her "Museum" had vanished, so Aunt Beck's inheritance had completely dwindled away.

CYNTHIA GETS HER BONNET

Midnight, no moon; Cynthia Gross leaned forward in the saddle and touched with her warm, capable hand her little mare's neck. The horse knew the way in the darkness and Cynthia gave her rein. The young rider, despite enormous vitality and a calm sense of power, was weary in body and soul. Forcing her horse at breakneck pace, she had ridden fifteen miles that day, to reach a woman believed to be dying in childbirth. She had fought to save mother and child, working with the knowledge and daring that made her the best loved midwife and doctor that the Cape has ever known.

Passing by night over treacherous bog trails, through "Indian Forests," along desolate moors, she frequently had cause for gratitude that her father had taught her the Indian tongue. But before she had practiced for many years, so widely was her skill heralded that those who had no personal knowledge of her recognized the indomitable little horsewoman with her midwife's bundle strapped at the rear of the saddle and her crisp bonnet mounted high on her smoothly coifed head. Every man and woman on the Cape, one might almost say every living creature, wished Cynthia Gross Godspeed. Her ability to alleviate human suffering was almost equaled by her proficiency with injured animals and birds. A broken-winged crow, a lame hen, a blind dog waited at her doorstone; and once in the night her little niece, Miriam, sleeping soundly in the feather poster, was ordered to "lie over" while Aunt Cynthia placed in the "cozy-hole" a tiny, shivering lamb.

Almost a fetish became the belief in her medical prowess; almost a fable the story of her midwifery: five hundred babies brought out of the womb, often in homes of poverty without convenience or resource, and by her capable, cool ministrations, never a mother lost.

As she rode toward home that night, her level eyes peered into the blackness of the highroad. She had won a sharp battle with death, but she ached in every bone.

Wellfleet Methodist Church loomed against the sky. Past the meeting house the mare would turn into the shortcut through the cemetery, then over the hill to Gull Pond, to the farmhouse where Cynthia and her nine sisters lived; all ten of them clear-minded, energetic women, skilled singers and musicians.

Tired as she was, Cynthia remembered her Sunday bonnet with its butterfly bow. After the last Sabbath meeting, when she discovered how the rain was falling, she had hesitated, blushed a little, turned back into the church and deposited her best bonnet in her pew. Bareheaded she had walked home in the mild summer rain, through the Burying Acre, over the hill, past Gull Pond, from whose dark waters the Gross sisters were said to have stolen the color of their eyes.

Nine of the ten sisters were "overweening of bonnets." The tenth refused to wear one. Cynthia, sharer of the family's competitive enthusiasm, decided to retrieve her Sabbath cap before its crisp allurement proved an irresistible temptation to some weak-willed church visitor. In the darkness of clouded midnight, Cynthia dismounted, found the meeting house door open, and felt her way within.

The mare whinnied nervously; but to the young rider, whose life centered in the life of Cape Methodism, every inch of wall and flooring was familiar. Toward the front of the church she groped, slowly counting pews. Entering the "fourth from the front," she saw a white substance againt the bare bench. That would be her Sunday bonnet. Reaching down to "pluck it up," she touched a dead man's face.

"Alas, poor soul," sighed Cynthia Gross, and she felt of the cold features again, to be quite sure that nothing was left to save.

"This must not be our pew," thought she. "I have miscounted in the dark."

So Cynthia entered the next pew and again saw a blurred whiteness, again reached down to it and touched a dead man's face.

Confusing to the mind at midnight! But Cynthia did not think it so. Instead she thought it was sad to be "laid out" without a burying box or a shroud. She surmised that the dead were drowned sailors from some wreck offshore.

"God rest their souls, where is my bonnet?" queried Cynthia anxiously, then perceived a nodding whiteness suspended from the aisle-post. Carefully, not to hurt the bow, Cynthia carried her bonnet outside, folded her night riding cap and thrust it into her saddle-pocket, donned her precious Sabbath headgear, mounted her mare and rode homeward through night's shadowy trail.

Midwatch, no moon; but Aunt Cynthia loitered late in Wellfleet village. Like her sisters who, all nine of them, played musical instruments and "sang like angels," she found life so interesting that occasionally village marketing was allowed to wait. Also, Aunt Cynthia had received news from Uncle John of Hawaii, the uncle who married a royal princess, and whose granddaughter became a queen. Cynthia speculated about John. He was a Young, her mother's brother, and unlike herself and her nine sisters (who were descended from William the Conqueror through the Norman family of La Grasse), John was "off-Cape minded," a condition of brain likely to induce sin.

Swung across her shoulders by a rope, Cynthia had carried a rocking chair on her four mile walk to the village. She intended to have the seat "rushed over," and it had not occurred to her to take her mare on such a local errand. The rushman, gone from home, would not return until after dusk; so Aunt Cynthia "visited around," supped, and waited for his coming. He set to work at first-hour-night and Cynthia, now known as Mistress Atwood, discussed, with pride tempered by reserve, the problems of life in Hawaii.

The rushman before he sprained his back had been a deep-sea sailor. Ladies in "them isles," he remembered, wore grass around the midriff. "Plaited grass?" questioned Cynthia, but the rushman thought it was a fringe.

"No reason why they should not plait it, neat and firm, like Indian baskets. They could have good skirts if they wanted them."

Her fears for Uncle John redoubled. She would have to get the next "Cap'n out" to carry with him some Methodist pamphlets to steady John's mind.

When the chair was done to her liking, she strapped it over her shoulder and started for Gull Pond. A high mist blurred the stars and in the Burying Acre Aunt Cynthia lost her path, became confused, and wandered among the tombstones, striking now one, now another, with the long rockers of the chair. Unseemly to be whacking the stones of the quiet "Judgment Houses," as if knocking for entrance! Also, Cynthia thought of the scars on the tips of her favorite rocker.

Weatherwise, as are all Cape folk, who get cock eyes from keeping one orb trained on the doings of the heavens and the other on the sea, Cynthia recalled that the moon would be up in about an hour's time. " 'Tis quiet here in the Burying Acre, a good place to knit a stint." She put down her chair where the turf was even and sat, rocking back and forth, knitting even rows. "Poor souls," said she, of the unseen dead, " 'tis little they get of pleasure-biding; what with all the weepy women, and the new black wagons. 'Tis a bit mournful and damp here. I should have come visiting before." As if something in the way of entertainment were expected of her (all the Gross sisters were invited to sing wherever they "stopped"), Aunt Cynthia, rocking between rows of tombstones, knitting a "saque" for young Maria, sang in her clear, firm voice: "See Gideon going forth to fight."

A cheerful tune, it suggested action comforting to sailor boys who must find it long waiting for the bright call of Gabriel. After she had finished her song, Aunt Cynthia allowed a decent interval for applause and murmurings. Then she "obleeged" with another: "You touch one string and the whole will ring, Sing Glory Hallelujah!" The tune reminded her of Sister Deborah whose favorite song it was; and also of Maria, the "baby" sister who lived in Provincetown, refused to wear a cap, and was "prideful of her voice." Once when someone remarked to tease her that the same tune was rendered more gracefully by a rival, Maria smoothed her skirts and answered, "But *I* descend from William the Conqueror."

Aunt Cynthia chuckled. Bethia, the "brainy" sister, declared that Maria was an "illogical popinjay" whose wits had been "put in with the bread and took out with the cake." But Cynthia, who defended the "baby," knew that the wellsprings of Maria's response had naught to do with logic. Bethia, for all her "book-larning" (seventy times she read the Bible through, and was an expert on the "Geography of the Heavens" and the "Chronology of the Bible"), had not the curious understanding of human impulses and desires that belonged to Cynthia, perhaps because Bethia had not seen so much of human suffer-

THE TEN GROSS SISTERS OF WELLFLEET, WHO ALL SANG LIKE ANGELS
Doctor Cynthia is standing at the extreme left

ing. She had even reproved Lurania, the eldest, who read only "good" authors and refused to countenance Shakespeare, for quoting from the censured playwright. Lurania answered: "If it wasn't in the Bible it ought to be," and Bethia could not see, thereafter, why Lurania still refused to read Shakespeare. But Aunt Cynthia knew. The reason was not explainable; it was part of Lurania.

The moon peered mistily over the seaward hill. Cynthia rose, pocketed her knitting, and slung the chair over her back. Tombstones now shone gray against the peopled earth below them. Aunt Cynthia regained her path. In the flood of a rising moon she walked over the hill.

Midnight, no moon; mischief was abroad, though, and so was a quaint old lady, her capstrings tied under her chin, her lace house bonnet carried in a small round box in her hand. Her compact body, clothed in rustling mohair, moved slowly through the Burying Acre. The fame of her, the fearlessness, the shrewdness and the wonder, had gone abroad and stirred in youth a certain natural skepticism. Behind a gravestone lurked, waiting, a fearsome form with horns and a tail and a blue aura of sulphur. Knowledge it had of how the sisters believed in apparitions; of how Maria, the youngest, who married a Provincetown captain and lived on the desolate harbor point, had been sorely troubled by ghosts. One day she had lost her sympathy for the scrambling, scratching souls of the departed and she cried in her clear voice, "Get ye gone, Evil Ones!" The "sperrits fled away."

Aunt Cynthia, too, for all her modern notions of medicine, was Methodist at heart and believed in the implications of horns, a tail and sulphur. Her eyes, unequipped with "specs," were not as keen as in youth. So when Greataunt Cynthia, at moonless midnight, taking the shortcut through the cemetery, saw bluefire flash and a sinister phantom emerge from the depths of a crumbling tomb, she queried: "Who might that be?"

"Madam, I am the Devil."

Cynthia paused. Her voice, when she spoke, was warm with the deep compassion of age:

"Alas, poor soul, I pity thee."

Quietly she continued on her way through the shortcut in the Burying Acre.

"WIDDOWS AT VANDUE"

No poorhouses existed in the early days of the colony. When good-men died leaving widows and half-cleared acres, the land, if not self-sustaining, was disposed of by order of the General Court, and the "relicts" were "farmed out." The annual process of selling bereaved wives became known as the "Widow's Vandue." Prices varied yearly, but in 1770 their average value to the towns was £3 per widow, taken as they ran. As a woman grew old and feeble, often she was not profit-able in services rendered. Sometimes at the auctions the towns had difficulty in disposing of such widows at all.

Fortunately for exchequers, "Towne Widdows" seldom attained a ripe old age. They worked too hard; they suffered too constantly from the strain of knowing that as their faculties declined they might be moved from comfortable homes to farms whose owners could only afford to pay the town a small sum for their services. Occasionally the old women were reduced as low as ninepence per annum; whereas a young comely widow brought over £10.

The expenses of a widow's illness always occasioned a "bickerfest." Should the community be required to pay the doctor if the family overworked and underfed their charge? Often such expenses were de-termined in advance, and when a widow exceeded in her needs the amount that the town had voted for possible illness, she was forced to continue without further medical attention, unless bestowed gra-tuitously, until the completion of her "Widdow's yeare."

The evils of this system, horrible in theory, proved less appalling in practice. Throughout colonial New England many wives died young, victims of too frequent childbearing, of overwork at household tasks, or stricken by the prevalent diseases. A comely widow had a good chance of remarriage within the year to an attractive widower, for both men and women believed it wise to console themselves as promptly as possible after a marital loss. Older widows were blessed with sons to care for them, and run their farms. Rich widows provided money to hire labor. Others had kind relatives willing to give them homes.

Nevertheless, even fine women were forced to undergo the humilia-tions of auction. Mistress Lovell appeared at the annual "vandue" in 1776, was "set up by the Selectmen . . . and struck of (f) to Josiah Stevens for to keep one year for the Sum of nine pounds Six shillings

& if She did not live the Year in he to have in that proportion." She lived to appear at eight annual auctions. Her clothes grew shabby with time; but there were no new bonnets and cloaks in the yearly contracts, and the people with whom she worked were unwilling to provide fresh garments. In 1782 Mistress Lovell was officially in need of a shirt. The town voted to buy her a cheap one, expense sixpence; then sold her again. This sale was a "bargain," for the widow was not thriving. Born of gentle English stock, she had not been able to assume the heavy household tasks, the stock-tending required of her. Seven years of servitude broke her in spirit and health.

"Set up" again in 1783, she was transferred to a new home, and in the following September the town elders were summoned to a stormy meeting. The Widow Lovell lay dead in her "poverty box," under the pine trees in the churchyard since her clothes were not considered suitable for a last entrance into the meeting house. Over the coffin a sail-cloth was thrown while the selectmen estimated and bickered. Finally they voted "a winding sheet and a shift for the Widow Lovell, eight shillings."

They were not so generous when it came to the burying of Jane Bumpus, wife of Louis Bumpus, direct descendant of the Sieur Louis Bompasse who came from France to the French colony in Canada, and later migrated southward. When her "furrin" husband died, Jane was placed at "vandue." The town crier announced her auction. The goodmen assembled. Jane was "set up" by a selectman; but instead of a demure, downcast countenance, or a winning, eager smile, Jane faced that meeting squarely, scowled and cried out, "For shame!" The minister ordered her to be quiet, and Mistress Bumpus, pious of heart, reluctantly obeyed the administrat of ecclesiastical law.

A farm owner in need of a "female hand" thought her worth taming. She was "bid in" and carted away to serve her "Widdow's yeare." Of tougher fiber than Mistress Lovell, and with no intention of perishing, Jane took no interest in her success at "vandue." Regularly, every year, she changed homes, falling always to lower estate. Yet she never suffered for clothes. What she needed to keep herself "decent" she appropriated; and if a family protested, she invited them to seek recompense from the deacons and selectmen whom she called her "cruel stepfathers." Capable, ingenious, unfailingly devoted to children, she exerted herself when she pleased, and never to excess.

If smallpox or diphtheria or black fever visited the youth of the community, Jane frequently dismissed herself from a service to which she
was contracted and went to nurse a suffering child until the crisis was
past. She put small value on her own existence; and the children
whom she nursed through illness became unswervingly devoted to her.
They had seen Aunt Jane with her sharp tongue gentle, her keen eyes
quiet, as she battled death.

The selectmen grew to hate her for she understood how to black-
mail them. If she detected a deacon breaking the Sabbath by work on
his woodpile, or an elder meandering home from the tavern on lecture
night, she called on the elder or deacon and suggested that a vote in the
approaching town meeting to allow her some small spending pence
might bring her to feel that she had mistaken a truly charitable man
for a Sabbath offender. Otherwise, she deemed it necessary to rise
and publicly declare in meeting that she was witness to an offense.

In this manner a large number of generous impulses developed
among deacons. The records include many charitable proposals in
behalf of Mistress Bumpus. Unfortunately the bulk of them were
"passed in the negativ."

When she died, the spite of these men who had held small, guilty
hates in their hearts was reflected in the final consideration of "Jane
Bumpus, deceased." The Widow Lovell had had eight shillings to
"rig her for etarnity"; Jane was given no winding sheet, only ninepence voted for a clean shift. A grave was dug in Poverty-corner at
the briary end of the Burying Acre; and as no notice of her funeral
was posted, the minister came alone to the church to read over her
body the service of the dead. To his horror and bewilderment and
to the consternation of the gravedigger, when they two approached
to nail her pine box preparatory to burial, it was discovered to be
empty. Investigation revealed that four of the children whom she had
nursed, all boys under sixteen, had carved a fine oak coffin into which
they laid her tenderly. Then the four of them bore her away to a place
in the woods where they buried her, with such prayers as they knew.
They planted the sod over her with fresh green pines and flowers, and
erected a cross carved with the words:

MISTRESS JEAN BUMPUS
WIFE OF SIR BUMPUS OF FRANCE

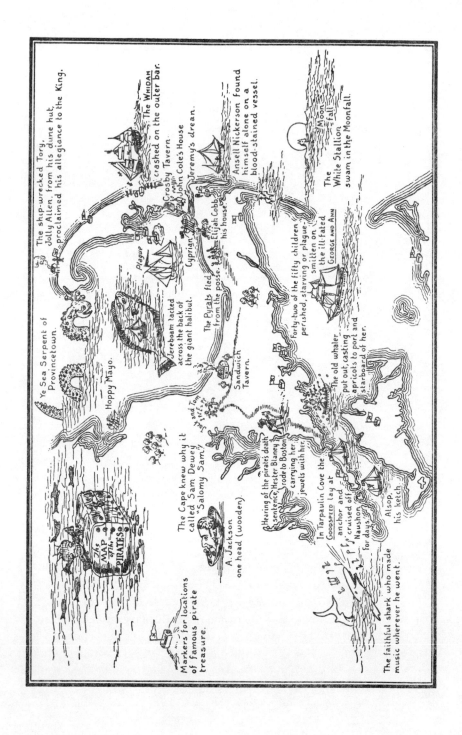

CHAPTER V

PIRATES, MOONCURSING AND
YARNS OF THE SEA

Valleys, tilled, brought forth their grain; bogs, peat and marsh fodder.
Wherever man placed his hand the earth grew tamed and constant. But
the surrounding sea revealed no tilling of waters, although to the beaches
drifted husks of a stormgarnered harvest. The same formless, unmarkable
platform that was cleaved by the black knorrs of Brattahlid, by the birch
or skin canoes of redmen, by the Concord, *the* Half Moone, *the* Mayflower,
the Sparrowhawk, *still obliterates in one tide the wake of the deepest keel.*

1. GENTLEMEN OF THE CUTLASS

"As IN ALL lands where there are many people, there are some theeves,
so in all Seas much frequented, there are some pyrats," wrote Captain
John Smith, "Admirall of New England," one of the first white men
to explore the Narrow Land. He judged rightly of Cape waters, for
the bleak tip of Monomoy, the broad Bay harbor, the Rumsey-voosey
taverns of Tarpaulin Cove and the Province Land constantly experienced the visits of seafaring marauders who buried their gold, so it is
said, on Naushon Island, Squaw Island, Grand Island, Hogg Island,
Lost Billingsgate and Great Island. Every acre of the Cape contains
it, if we may believe the landowners; and for at least a century
treasure-seekers have faithfully repeated the necessary formula,
"There's Money Hid at Money Head," and gone to dig into the sea
cliff of Hogg Island, a region guarded by an armed piratical ghost.

Few fortunes spaded from the earth were displayed to the "Water
Bailies" whose privilege it was to record such finds as belonging to
the king. Since buccaneers were Satan's men, it may be that the old
Cape notion was a true one: that when the pirates sold their souls,
they bargained to carry their sea chests below; and the pieces of eight

and the bars of gold, hot, molten and bubblish, roll down rivers of flame.

In small West Indian harbors pirates "snugged down for wintering," but when mayblossoms crept from under brown leaves on the slopes of old New England hills, or when fleets were sailing for Georges Banks, or when "faraway craft" were "headin' in" from China and the Indies, back to northern waters hurried the pirates, to cruise along green outer shoals, to dodge the sloops of the wary king's men, to "make in at a Randie-voo" for supplies, recruits, and courting talk. Many a gallant buccaneer walked with a maid to Sabbath meeting, more for the look of her two eyes than to learn of the wages of sin. Such a sailor was called "Cousin George" in honor of the king.

THE BLACK BELLAMY

The Black Bellamy came out of the West Country, England, and when he was old enough to know better he staked his fortune on the salvaging of "bags of silver" from a Spanish vessel wrecked in the West Indies. On the way to this doubtful venture he put in at Eastham Harbor and tried to interest Cape men in his scheme; but the Narrow Land knew too many wrecks bleaching their beams off the outer reefs to spend money on an unseen hulk sunk in the Spanish Seas. Her sailors wished the "bonnieman" luck and nodded approval of his tight little sloop, old and "sea-kindly"; for this happened in the spring of 1715 while Samuel Bellamy was staying at Higgins' Tavern in Eastham, not far from the Burying Acre, and near the Minister's Pond.

One evening, to clear his head of the fumes of Sandwich ale and cod muddle, Sam took a stroll through the "Judgment Lot," and as he reached the southern end of it, heard a girl's voice, singing. He traced the song to a circular hollow surrounded by trees, and coming to the edge, saw, below him, a white cloud floating. From the cloud rose a song. He strode downslope, through 'Tarnity Briars, and found that the cloud was a flower apple tree. Under the tree stood Maria Hallett, a drip-rush lanthorn in one hand and blossoms in the other. She was fifteen years old; her hair glistened like corn silk at suncoming; her eyes were the color of hyacinth, like the deeps of Gull Pond. Black Bellamy made masterful love, sailorman love that remembers how a following wind falls short and makes way while it blows. Maria Hallett had never seen a man as handsome as Sam Bellamy; just out of the West Country, his black hair curly, his fortune buckled in his three-cornered pocket, and mighty dreams in his eye. Love was settled between them in no time at all, under the apple tree by the Burying Acre, and Sam sailed away with a promise to Maria that when he returned he would wed her by ring to the words of the Rev. Mr. Treat, and in a sloop, laden with treasure, carry her back to the Spanish Indies, there to be made princess of a West Indian isle.

Maria went home to wait for him, and in time gave birth to a "bonnieman's child" with black eyes and black hair. Maria was afraid to show it. She hid the boy in the Knowles' barn, and crept out there to feed it, but a straw caught in its throat and it died. Before chance came to bury it, Elder John Knowles found the baby, and hid in the hay to catch Maria when she came. A week later the selectmen confined her in Eastham prison, but she proved as wild as Nauset wind, and her wistful eyes and silky hair made her pleadings irresistible to jailors. Time after time she escaped and was caught, for as soon as she won freedom she went to the apple tree hollow, or ran to the Backside to watch for the sails of Bellamy's ship. The sheriffs had only to walk to the high Clay Pounds to discover her, a small figure standing silhouetted against the sea.

After a time the elders grew weary of chastising her, and the townspeople, impressed by her ability to break jail at will, stoned her away from Eastham as a witch. She went north, far from habitation, and with her own hands built a hut on the Backside. From the sand meadow at her doorstone she looked to the east where ships rode like ivory beads on the long blue chain of the Cape's seaway. Below the sand meadow, breakers foamed, eating the tall cliffs, licking the peat strata from which Maria cut fuel. The slow withdrawal of the tides at ebb left unending reaches of sand, over which lights danced and ships seemed to ride.

No woman on the peninsula wove the beautiful patterns that Maria Hallett knew how to draw from her loom. Many fine weavers tried to copy them, but the wools snarled and the designs faltered, so Maria took in weaving in exchange for bread; and because she never lacked for food, and was independent as tidewater, people continued to think her a witch, and said that she danced on Sabbath nights in the hollow by the Burying Acre, and that she had signed a pact with the devil in exchange for young Bellamy's soul.

All this time, in the hot Indies, a young man from the West Country toiled over a waterlogged wreck, spent his last farthing, with never sixpence to show for it, not to mention silver or gold. With him worked a Nantucket sailorman named Paul (or Paulsgrave) Williams, and the two became close friends. Whether or not Sam Bellamy remembered his promise to Maria, he soon grew impatient at the failure of his salvaging, and as a swifter road to wealth, he and Williams decided to turn pirate, or, as they put it, "to go on the account." Bellamy still possessed his sloop, long due at the Sea of Sargossa, but he could sail her, under press of canvas, like a ghost vessel.

During the first weeks of their "piratical undertaking," they fell in with Benjamin Hornygold, a stouthearted buccaneer in command of the *Mary Anne,* and also with Captain Lebous in the sloop *Postillion.* The combined fleet made several rich captures; but Hornygold refused to plunder English vessels, and on this issue Sam saw his chance to foster disaffection among the buccaneers and profit by discontent. When the matter of plundering the king's ships was finally put to vote, only twenty-six pirates were willing to follow Hornygold, while ninety elected Bellamy as their new captain and determined upon a career of swift, relentless looting, with the rapid accumulation of a fortune, and prompt purchase of the king's pardon.

Bellamy and Lebous sailed in concert and off the Virgin Islands took several small vessels. Near Saba they captured the *Sultana,* cut her down into a galley; Bellamy took command of her, and placed Paul Williams in the sloop. For a month in the winter, the fleet refitted on a "maroon island" and in early spring they set sail for the Windward Passage. Between decks on the *Sultana,* bags of money were accumulating, and a good cargo filled her hold; but she was heavy-hulled, slow-footed, and Sam longed for a tall ship so lovely that when her sails gleamed along the white beaches, Cape eyes would widen, and Maria would think it another mirage, till she looked again and saw the young captain, and, later, the silver and gold.

A half gale shot up the Windward Passage and the pirate vessels were scattered. Bellamy and Williams, ready to conduct their own affairs, made no effort to rejoin Lebous; and as dawn whitened the mists to lee-

ward, a ship rose out of tropic darkness, her sails winging like a swan
awakened, the salt dew like fire on her rigging, and a mastlight so high
in the dawn that it looked like the morning star. The *Whidah*, London galley; the "Paradise Bird" men fondly called her, laden with a
cargo of elephants' teeth, gold dust, sugar, indigo, and Jesuit's bark,
had delivered a shipment of slaves to Jamaica, and was making way
under easy sail, homeward bound. To the maintruck, Sam ran up his
pennant, "Death's Head and Bones a-cross," and for three days gave
chase. Any sailor could see that the *Whidah* must outsail the *Sultana*,
yet Bellamy refused to give over pursuit, and Captain Prince of the
London galley seemed to have lost the magic of her, for the hull
dragged, wind slid off the sails, and slowly the pirates gained. The
more Sam saw her the more he longed for her, and was ready to offer
easy terms, if she might be spared battle. Captain Prince, as though
sensing this, fired only her two chase guns as the buccaneers "came
up under her." Then, without further resistance, he lowered the *Whidah*'s flag.

Sam was in no mood to bear ill will to the Londoner. He gave
Prince the *Sultana*, and permitted him to load her with some of his
own cargo, while Paul Williams, a chagrined quartermaster, was commanded to retain the sloop. Bellamy stepped on teakwood decks, awash
with the spume of a night of storm, found his way to the gilded poop
and turned the ship's course north. Twenty thousand pounds were
stored between decks in the new prize, in doubloons, pieces of eight,
gold dust, bars of silver and gold. She carried, likewise, a cargo fit
for the dowry of a princess, and no man knows exactly what Bellamy
intended to do with it, since, instead of making for a glory hole in
the West Indies where treasure was safe, he faced increasing risk of capture by passing north of the Virginia coast, headed for Cape Cod.

Three ships and a snow were captured on this northward passage,
two of the ships plundered and dismissed, one that was leaky sunk;
the snow, manned by men from the *Whidah*, was added to the pirate
fleet. Shortly after her capture, a thunder shower came on. Bellamy
furled his small sails, but the *Whidah*, caught in hurricane winds,
was nearly overset. The wind blew from the northwest, driving the
vessels offshore, "with only the goose-wings of the foresails to scud
with." The storm increased as night fell, and the ship was forced to
"bring her yards aportland." "With Tackles to the Goose Neck of the

Tiler, four Men in the Gun Room, and two at the Wheel," Bellamy
kept her from broaching to.

> The Heavens were cover'd with Sheets of Lightning, which the Sea
> by the Agitation of the saline Particles seem'd to imitate; the Darkness
> of the Night was such, as the Scripture says, as might be felt; the terrible
> hollow roaring of the Winds cou'd be only equalled by the repeated . . .
> incessant Claps of Thunder, sufficient to strike a Dread of the supream
> Being, who commands the Sea and the Winds, one would imagine in
> every Heart.

Triumph had gone to the head of the young, reckless captain;
neither he nor his crew gave thought to prayer or to God's wrath.
With "Blasphemies, Oaths and horrid Imprecations" they tried to
drown the "Uproar of jarring Elements." When thunder blared in
a leaden sky, Sam regretted that he could not "run out his Guns to
return the Salute." When lightning thrust its rapier over a steel-dark
ocean, the sea rover of the West Country lifted his rum pot to drink to
gods "drunk over their Tipple, and . . . gone together by the Ears."
All night the vessels cudded under bare poles. The next morning
the mainmast of the *Whidah* was discovered to be "sprung in the Step."
The men cut it away, and at the same time the mizzen went by the
board. The ship made a "Deal of Water," though by continually man-
ning the pumps the crew kept it from gaining. The wind shifted
"round the Compass" and "made so outrageous and short a Sea, that
they had little Hopes of Safety; it broke upon the Poop, drove in the
Taveril, and wash'd the two Men away from the Wheel who were
saved in the Netting." After four days and three nights of unabated
fury, the wind decreased, the skies cleared, jury-masts were set up, and
the carpenter found that the leak in the bow was occasioned by nothing more serious than oakum spewing from a seam. So the crew "became very jovial" and a strolling player among them suggested that
they enact a play, an idea so joyfully received that he took quill and
ink in hand and provided the seamen with parts. Roles were memo-
rized audibly; Indian and African chests overhauled for "Thracian"
togas and scarves. Then the quarterdeck was cleared for a stage, and
"Alexander the Great" ascended a stalwart throne. Over his tattooed
chest hung "a toger of Eastern sateens," and his words were followed
with rapt attention by a rum-inspired crew. When Alexander lifted

his arm and pointed toward high heaven, the gunner looking up to see what was there, "creak'd his Neck," lost his balance and fell against the bosun. When Alexander the Great wept into a red kerchief from the Indies, the gunner, in excess of sympathy, removed his pea-jacket to wipe away his tears. And when the handsome hero pirate was captured by "Great Alexander" and brought before him in chains, the tense breathing of the audience sounded like the Channel Sea. Alexander, looking with disfavor upon the hero pirate, exclaimed in ringing tones:

> "Know'st thou that Death attends thy Mighty Crimes,
> And thou shalt hang Tomorrow Morn betimes!"

Whereupon the gunner, lost to all sense of reality, leaped upon the quarterdeck stage, to the defense of the hero, and flung at Alexander the Great a "hand-grenade." Equally zealous cronies followed the gunner to the boards. With drawn cutlasses they attacked; and only the voice of Black Bellamy brought knives to the sheath. Alexander had lost his arm, the hero pirate broken his leg, and of the gunner's companions, one lay dead on the deck. Bellamy clapped the more responsive members of the audience into irons, to be court-martialed next day — when the gunner, sober, a tear in his eye, pled for the rights of piracy, and for the honor of his trade. Sam had not the heart to punish him, but forbade that the "Royal Pirate" ever again be enacted upon the *Whidah's* deck.

Coasting near Rhode Island, not long after the court-martial, Bellamy and Williams came upon a Boston sloop commanded by Captain Beer. They captured and plundered this prize and were about to return her to her captain, when the buccaneer crew demanded that she be sunk. "D— my Bl—d," said the Black Bellamy, regretfully, to Captain Beer, "I am sorry they won't let you have your Sloop again, for I scorn to do any one a Mischief, when it is not for my Advantage . . . Tho' . . . you are a sneaking Puppy, and so are all those who will submit to be governed by Laws which rich Men have made for their own Security, for the cowardly Whelps have not the Courage otherwise to defend what they get by their Knavery; . . . Damn them for a Pack of Crafty Rascals, and you, who serve them, for a Parcel of hen-hearted Numskuls."

Captain Beer, who was busy remembering the speech verbatim, answered that his "Conscience would not allow him to break thro' the Laws of God and Man." Bellamy, his lip curling, called Beer a "devilish Concience Rascal." "I am a free Prince," said the West Country rover, "and I have as much Authority to make war on the whole World, as he who has 2 hundred Sail of Ships at Sea, and an Army of 100,000 Men in the Field; and this my Conscience tells me, but there is no arguing with such sniveling Puppies, who allow Superiors to kick them about Deck at Pleasure; and pin their Faith upon a Pimp of a Parson; a Squab, who neither practices nor believes what he puts upon the chuckle-headed Fools he preaches to."

The captain of the Boston sloop was put ashore on Block Island, and about a fortnight later, early in the morning of Friday, April 26, 1717, while the *Whidah* "with King's Ensign and Pendant flying" was halfway between Nantucket Shoals and St. George's Banks, she came up with the pink *Mary Anne,* Andrew Crumstey master. The pink struck colors; a boat was lowered from the *Whidah,* and seven seamen, sent on board, "armed with Musquets, Pistols and Cutlashes," discovered that the prize was laden with sweet Madeira wine. In the afternoon the *Whidah* took a sloop from Virginia, and setting a course northwest by north, the fleet put out lights astern and made sail together. About ten o'clock, the weather thickened, the wind veered east, bringing on a violent "Trapado" (squall of lightning and rain) in which the vessels lost each other. Not long afterward the watch of the *Whidah* sighted "Breakers ahead!" An anchor was let go, but dragged, and black water mountains, rolling astern, bore the ship straight toward that line, on the close-walled horizon, where the sea was capped with a white maelstrom of foam. With breakers ahead, on a lee shore, there was only one chance, and Black Bellamy knew it. She could not ride, so he cut her cable to work her off the coast. Men flew to the yards, their cutlasses out to whip at the gaskets and loosen the mainsail that lashed itself free like a great white whale, fluking — till bitted by sheet and tack. The *Whidah* lurched, wallowed; to windward fought and to windward held, till "Great Hurricanoes" sent her reeling back, smothered with green water. Shock after shock, the rollers groaned over her and passed beyond to unseen cliffs, where they broke, howled, and crept wailing back to the mother sea. With James Lambert, pilot, beside him, for a long half watch Sam fought for the

Whidah; four bells to eight he held her to the wind, but she could not draw ahead. Never free from the menace of the bars, he kept her slim, precise hull afloat and her bowsprit into the wind.

The fight proved a losing one. As the watch changed, she was borne leeward by a wall of water risen against her, a "Sea Vulcanoe" that thrust her before it as she struck on the outer bar. A few moments later, in a tangle of frozen wreckage, her mainmast went by the board. Midnight: eight bells rang faintly beneath storm canvas stiff with frozen spume.

The loss of the *Whidah,* according to a Wellfleet historian was due to the prize snow. The captain of the snow, familiar with the treacherous Backside, had been promised the return of his vessel if he would guide the pirate galley and her consorts into harbor. In the murk of night, he drove inshore and his sloop, of light burden, passed over the sand reef, but the *Whidah,* following, struck heavily.

Sailors say that the wine had run too freely that night, and that Bellamy swore as she struck the bar that he would see Maria Hallett if he had to sail his vessel over the dunes of the Backside to her door. Whether misled by a false pilot, or drunk, or bewitched by Maria, or the recipient of "just retribution" at the hands of "Outraged Deity," before morning Bellamy lost the silver-heeled *Whidah,* the Paradise Bird of the Gold Coast, lost her rich cargo of indigo, elephants' teeth and gold dust, lost 400 money bags locked in chests between decks. She was heavy with guns and worn with storm, and the pound of the surf against the bar was intolerable. She turned bottom up before she broke and her decks fell out, and the guns and gold and much of her cargo may well be lying beneath the iron caboose of her that has been seen at low tide on the bar.

A hundred and one bodies washed ashore from the *Whidah.* Alexander the Great and the rum-drinking gunner; the hero pirate with his leg in a splint; Andrew Crumstey, Irish master of the prize *Mary Anne*; Lambert, the worthless pilot. "Robbin Hood's Men" they had called themselves, this crew who scorned to rob the poor "under Cover of Law," preferring instead to "plunder the Rich" under the "Protection" of their own "Courage." The long waves hurled them against cliffs, then sucked them back in the undersea wash, to hurl them forth once more.

Tom Davis, the carpenter, John Julian, Cape Cod Indian, kept

alive as the sea swept them landward. Somehow they secured a footing on the perilous cliff, climbed out of the smother of combers, and
reached the tableland above — on which stood a lonely hut built by
unskilled hands. In the darkness the two survivors either missed
the house of Maria, or went there to find it deserted; or perhaps she
was nursing a wounded, half-drowned seaman, before whose gaze
they quailed. As soon as day broke they walked inland, two miles, to
the home of Samuel Harding; and after rest and refreshment there,
Davis, accompanied by Harding, returned to the Backside.

The wreckage of the *Whidah* littered the beach for miles. Bodies,
picked up, were laid together on the stubble of Hallett's Meadow; and
on Sunday, April 28, Paul Williams approached in a sloop, and sent a
boat inshore. Perhaps he came to salvage treasure, perhaps to carry
off the wounded man who was hidden in Maria's house. Sunday morning Mr. Justice Doane rode over to inspect the bodies. One he identified as the young West Country captain; and later, in a trench dug by
"Coroner's fellowes," the dead were piled, pirates, forced men and
new-made prisoners, some of the bodies so mutilated that the belief
was current (accepted by Cotton Mather) that the prisoners were murdered on board ship to prevent them, if rescued, from revealing the
secrets of the buccaneers.

Tom Davis, with John Julian and seven pirates from the *Mary
Anne,* were taken to Boston jail. Davis was acquitted as a forced man,
but John Julian never came to trial, for he mysteriously disappeared.
Later, Obed Snow saw him near the hut of Maria, but the seas had
taken toll of his strength and he was near to death. Maria nursed him
at the end, and it may be that he revealed to her the whereabouts of a
hidden cache of treasure; for after that she never wanted for money,
enough for a fine house, servants, and a coach, though Maria cared
for none of the things that gold would buy, save food, fuel, and fair
colors in wool. She wove for herself gowns as lovely and strange in
design as the robes of a princess. Dressed in these she walked and
sang along the high cliffs at night. If she dreamed no longer of a West
Indian island, she seemed to be watching, waiting; and sometimes, in
the starlight of that first summer, she went down to the edge of the sea.

In autumn a tall stranger appeared and stopped at Higgins' Tavern.
His black hair was streaked with white, his dark eyes commanding;
but a deep wound scarred his forehead, and his mind was not always

clear. Once he called the landlord to see a ship sailing over Eastham meadows; again, he stood quietly, moving his hands as though serving his watch at the wheel. Sometimes he became lost to all sense of reality, and sat in the Great Room, his eyes smoldering, yet in them the look of a bewildered child. He had no lack of money; he lived well, with a gold-button coat and lace at the wrist; and there was distinction in his highborn manner and his black curly hair. One lock of it, over the scarred temple, had gone winter white.

He died in the summer of 1720 in the apple tree hollow by the Burying Acre, where he went so often and seemed to be waiting for someone. After he was carried to Higgins' Tavern, a belt of gold was found on his body; and the men who looked at his face in death said that it was brave and young.

A week later young Thankful Knowles, daughter of Elder John Knowles, took her courage in her capable hands and walked across-dune to Hallett's Meadow to get a pattern from Maria. The witch girl was not in her hut, and knowing that she was wont to sit on a ledge by the sea where the *Whidah* lay, Thankful walked to the cliff and peered below. Then she ran, stumbling, breathless, across-dune to the town. For Maria Hallett, dressed in hyacinth blue, with at least a thousand appleblossoms woven over the skirt of her gown, lay stiff on the ledge, her eyes shining, a gash across her white throat and a stained knife in her hand.

THE "PYRATS" AND THE POSSE

"For God's sake let us go down into the Hould and Die together!" said the "pyrats" as the pink, *Mary Anne,* struck in a night of storm. Thomas Fitzgerald, rineteen-year-old mate, stood at the helm; but the Dutchman, Baker, Bellamy's man from the *Whidah,* was in command, one of seven pirates who had taken over the pink as prize. Through the dark and the rain, in stabs of lightning, the breakers flashed wildly; and as Tom Fitzgerald cried out his warning, Baker ordered the headsail trimmed. Before the order could be obeyed, great combers thrust the *Mary Anne* high against an unseen obstacle. The men cut down foremast and mizzen; and as neither boat nor man could live in the frothing maw below them, there was nothing to do but "Die together." So they went into the hold, lighted a sea lantern, and considering it wise to be fortified against cold water and Judgment, they opened a demijohn of Madeira wine (with which the pink was laden), and sat on casks, drinking, while Tom Fitzgerald, in his young Irish voice, the brogue thick and sweet as syrup on his tongue, read aloud for upward of an hour from the *Book of Common Prayer*. The pirates prayed and made fine promises to a God who strongly favored them, for when day spread its kites and skysails over the fighting deck of the ocean, on the "shoare side of the Pink" nothing more dangerous threatened than a strip of dry land.

The ten shipwrecked mariners jumped from the deck of the *Mary Anne*; and Mackonachie, cook, who had not lived fifty-five years in vain, located a chest of sweetmeats and prepared a breakfast, washed down with wine, that brightened the look of the spume-soaked island on which they were stranded.

About ten o'clock in the morning a canoe appeared, headed from the mainland. John Cole and William Smith climbed out on shore, informed the shipwrecked sailors that the land on which they stood was Pochet Island, near the South Parish of Eastham, and offered to convey the mariners to the mainland. A number of trips in the canoe proved necessary, since demijohns and casks of Madeira were carried to ballast boat. Then John Cole invited the unfortunates to rest and refresh themselves at his home in Eastham, a house overlooking the Baywater, and across-tomb from Crosby Tavern. The twelve men, heavily laden with casks, demijohns and other salvage, walked inland from the Backside, and by the time that they reached John Cole's house they were ready to eat and drink again. The rum pot passed merrily, and Alexander Mackonachie, cook, waxed braver with every swallow. Soon he arose and in a fine Irish oration denounced seven of the seamen as pirates, proclaiming them Bellamy's men.

Thomas Baker answered roundly that Bellamy was no pirate, but an English captain with a commission from King George. Simon Van Vorst loyally seconded him, crying with enthusiasm, "Yes, and we will stretch it to the World's end!" Baker then inquired of Cole the way to Rhode Island and when the tired adventurers heard what a long walk lay ahead of them, they were "very dejected," so downhearted that one laid his head on his shiny knees and sobbed till the great salt tears rolled into his leathern boots.

All this time a blue eye, a snub nose and indelible freckles were applied fiercely to the "doorlatch peeper" of the closed door that led from the greatroom into the downstairs chamber. Undoubtedly "Pyrats" were wiping their muddy feet on the rose pattern Turkie Carpet, drinking wine, laughing, sighing, and planning to journey to Rhode Island. John Cole's son, too small to "go a-schoolin'," was not too small to know adventure when he saw it, even through the difficult perspective of the doorlatch peeper. He struggled into his greatcoat, climbed out the bedroom window, threaded his way swiftly among the tombstones in the Burying Acre, and ran, breathless, into the tap-room of Crosby Tavern.

No one there listened to his story or gave it a moment's credence; the men laughed over their mugs of ale and the Crosby girls first offered Johnny a cookie and then threatened to kiss him. Disgusted, he fled from the tavern, retraced his steps through the burying ground, looked through the window of his house, to sustain his own shaken credulity; then, fists clenched, set out in the opposite direction toward the home of that august, terrifying and mighty officer of the law, Mr. Joseph Doane, Justice of the Peace and Representative to the Great and General Court. The mere thought of Mr. Justice Doane tongue-tied Johnny, yet he pulled the knocker on the great front door that was brought by ship from England, and asked to see the justice. Mr. Doane interviewed him briefly, hurriedly summoned deputy sheriff and posse, and started for John Cole's house, young Johnny in the lead.

Now Peter Hoof from Sweden, who could outdrink Sam Bellamy, with only a little more than his usual melancholy to show for it, chanced to direct his mournful gaze to the south window of the great-room, and saw the posse, Johnny and Mr. Doane marching down the road. All ten mariners ran for it, the crew of three belonging to the *Mary Anne* as well as the seven pirates, dodging through the Burying Acre in an attempt to gain Crosby Tavern where, if luck favored them, they might secure mounts. After them ran the sheriff, with the deputy sheriff, Johnny and the posse in concentrated pursuit. The pirates barred the taproom door, but one of the pretty Crosby sisters let the law in at a window. After that there was no fighting, for the sailors declared themselves "perforcst" men, innocent, honorable, and freely told Mr. Justice Doane of the casks and demijohns of Madeira sinfully reposing in the front parlor of John Cole's house. Immediately Mr.

Justice Doane sent over for the demijohns which were clearly the property of the law; and Johnny when he went home a hero, having rescued his father from pirates, received a licking for his pains.

In the tavern the posse rested, to recover from their able exertions. There they sampled the wine from the pink; and that afternoon word also came through of the wreck of the great ship *Whidah,* seven miles to the northward. Mr. Doane at once utilized the Madeira to loosen the tongues of his prisoners, since he needed prompt information concerning Bellamy's gold. Simon Van Vorst told him of "£20,000 laid in bags between Decks"; John Brown of Jamaica told of indigo and elephants' teeth with which the *Whidah* was laden; Hendrick Quintor of Amsterdam had a story of how Sam Bellamy possessed a casket of East Indian jewels taken from Captain Prince. John Shuan, the Frenchman from Nantes, said little, since he spoke no English; and Thomas South, the carpenter, who had been in reality a forced man on the *Whidah,* spoke less and drank less than any of the other men.

Saturday night, in Crosby Tavern, the torches flared on the old oak tables in the taproom, center of news and excitement, while the sun went under the Baywater, leaving a scarlet, herring bone mitten floating in Spool Penny Pond. Mr. Doane decided not to accompany his prisoners on their journey to Barnstable jail, since his duty, in the morning, lay in the direction of the major wreck. He stayed at the tavern, hour after hour, waiting reports of the dead and of wreckage; and when at last he wavered homeward, it was dark — dark comes so soon in April — and he, a man of faultless habit, was more than three hours late for supper, of which he was sharply reminded as he pushed open the great front door that came by ship from England.

In the tavern the posse and their prisoners grew mellow and philosophic, as men do on a Saturday night. Later they went to sleep in the taproom, informal and cozy under the table; but when the fumes of liquor staled and salt mist thickened around the windows, Thomas South waked Simon Van Vorst, Simon waked Peter the Swede, Peter waked Hendrick from Amsterdam and also John Brown of Jamaica; all of them succeeded, with applications of cold water, in arousing Thomas Baker, the leader of their little company, and Shuan from Nantes, who was nothing but a Frenchman and did not understand. The seven decided to set out for Rhode Island somewhat in advance of the posse. Then, for a time they hesitated, conferring about the boy, Fitzgerald, who was none of them, but such a likable Irish lad. Sheriffs, inclined to wreak vengeance on him for the loss of the real pirates, might string him up by the neck. So the seven pirates awakened Tom, invited him to join them; and as he was not yet twenty, and very much afraid of jail, he decided to cast in his lot with them. Then they remembered Mackonachie, the fat cook, fifty-five years old, too old to serve a sentence and be alive at the end of it; and they thought of breakfast on the island, made from the box of sweetmeats; and that left only John Dunavan behind, so they wakened the solemn Dublin boy also. All of them, in the night, while the posse slept under the table, laid whispered plans. Once more in darkness and danger, the sense of destiny, the will to "Die together" grew upon them. They had been welded by a night of storm into queer unity, some of them good men with nothing to fear, some determined upon piratical adventure, a few desiring to turn the corner, and start life anew. All of them except Mackonachie, and Peter Hoof (aged 34), were under thirty. Together, pirates and upright mariners, they crept, bootless, from the common room of the tavern, carrying their heavy footwear by the "eeres," pulling it on over wet feet in the outer chill of the inn yard, then starting down a lonely road.

Past the house of John Cole they went, and knew John for a tolerant man who would neither have encouraged them nor betrayed them. Little Johnny they cursed roundly, and the child, as if sensing their anger, suffered a spell of nerves that night, and had to be taken out of his trundle and put between his father and mother. Mrs. Cole was proud of her son who would, she foresaw, grow up to denounce sin and become a great minister. She confided as much to her husband, John, who groaned and turned in his bed. Johnny failed to see the connection between pirates and the ministry, so he fell asleep, lying on his stomach, because where the whip had fallen he was undoubtedly sore.

Had the pirates scattered and traveled through the forest, or sought small craft along the shores, a few at least might have escaped recapture; but their wits were not what wits should be, suffering as they did from a hangover, and the queer sense of solidarity, of union, persisted among them. They traveled as fast as weary feet could carry them through rutted sand of the King's Highway. They had no mounts and dared procure none, for they were as dirty and haggard as wine, wind and weather could make them, and the farmers at whose doors they might knock would perceive all too readily that here were no ordinary travelers. No farm was sufficiently stocked to mount all of them at once; and should their identity be suspected a post might be ridden back to the tavern to arouse the sleeping guards. So the ten went afoot, though the going was hard, and before noon the posse quietly overtook them. Nobody spoke about an escape, the pirates lest it go against them, and the goodmen of Eastham who represented law felt that the Sabbath should always be a day of silence.

Under a heavy mounted guard the pirates were taken from Barnstable jail to Boston where they remained in a hot, foul prison all that summer of 1717, until Friday, Oct. 18, they were led into Admiralty Court, their spirit broken by long weeks of confinement, the curious union between them gone forever. Penniless flotsam, weak from prison food, dirty with prison dirt, their bronzed young bodies and devil-may-care brains were dulled by the long anxious wait. They were sentenced to death, all but Thomas South; and of course the former crew of the *Mary Anne* were set free, Fitzgerald, Mackonachie, Dunavan; but these three had also served their time in the hot prison and were not friendly toward the others, bitter that innocence should suffer for the crimes of guilt.

In the month after the "six pyrats" were convicted, and while they awaited execution, they were taken to the North Meeting House, where they sat, under guard, on the commoners' bench, their plight to serve as a warning to unruly innocents, godly freemen and men who went down to the sea. Cotton Mather preached about them, and labored with them for the peace of their souls. On the fifteenth of November, they were summoned from jail to stand surrounded by "Mosketeers and sheriffs" while Mr. Vincent, Admiralty Marshal, adjusted his robes, held aloft his "Silver Oare" of office, and then, at a solemn pace, led the procession in the direction of the harbor. The jurisdiction of Admiralty Court ended at high water mark; so these, as other pirates, were hung on a slender strip of shore between ebb and full of the tide. They marched, a rabble milling around them, to "Scarlett's Wharfe" and there, by boat, were conveyed to "Charleston Ferry" where a scaffold had been erected. Cotton Mather took the "sad Walk with them," and when at length they stepped on the scaffold, he stood in the bow of a boat, before them. Bible in hand, black robes gathered around

AT 'BOSTON NECKE' PIRATES WERE HUNG 'WITHIN FLUX AND REFLUX OF THE SEA'

From an early broadside

him, he spoke the last stern words of exhortation and repentance. He was not closely followed. Each prisoner, in his own way, underwent with supreme intensity the last few moments of existence. Thomas Baker, silent, suffered, so his watchers declared, a deep penance of heart. Peter Hoof and Simon Van Vorst, hands clasped, heads thrown back, sang their very souls out in a Dutch hymn that no listener understood save, perhaps, Hendrick Quintor, whose lips moved, but not in song, and no man knows what he tried to say to himself, or God, or the devil. John Brown of Jamaica lost reason in a sudden madness and lashed out violent "Blasphemes and Oathes"; then, suddenly, prayerbook in hand, he took to reading prayers aloud, "not very pertinently chosen," says critical Mr. Mather. John Shuan said nothing at all, spoke no English, and was only a Frenchman who did not understand.

Hempen knots were tied about the six young necks; the scaffold ropes were ready to drop, when John Brown laid aside his book and in a clear voice spoke to the mariners assembled. Sailors he advised to beware of wild and wicked living, and if they fell into the hands of pirates, he warned them to have a care into what countries they came. As if in answer to this bitter reproach, the scaffold dropped, the six men swung; and in a few hours the breaking waves, that had missed them so narrowly once before, came hungrily licking beneath them. The bodies dangled for a long time, grotesques against water and sky, "within Flux and reflux of the Sea."

THE KETCH *Elinor*

Inward bound from the island of Nevis, laden with sugar and indigo, the ketch *Elinor*, William Shortrigs master, edged her way into Nantucket Roads. In her cabin lay a woman, four men and a boy, all ill of the dreaded smallpox. She was short of provisions and medicines; the wind failed, the flood tide was almost spent; so Captain Shortrigs anchored, and with the mate and one seaman set out in the ship's boat for Boston to get aid. The next morning Mr. Thomas Cooper, owner, and Captain Shortrigs, appealed for permission to bring the *Elinor* into harbor; but fear of the spreading "Pox" tied the sympathies of officials, and the two men were informed, on November 22, 1689, that they might not dock the *Elinor*, but that she could be brought up as far as the Castle. Four men were sent down-harbor to fetch her, and twenty-four hours later returned with word that no such vessel lay anchored in the Roads. The town criers at the street corners proclaimed a "Hue and Cry" for the missing craft; while Mr. Cooper hired a sloop and embarked upon a search of neighboring waters.

On board the *Elinor*, when the captain departed, James Thomas, seaman, was left in charge; to assist him, only one young boy. All the other occupants of the ketch were too ill to keep to their feet; and Thomas knew a great fear that death would be among them before doctors and medicine arrived. He did what he could, but there was the entire ship to tend, and the six sufferers struggled to aid one another. At seven o'clock in the evening, Thomas called the boy to turn the glass and mind the pump, since he was busy between decks. Suddenly he heard, alongside, the sound of a boarding party. He had not hoped for aid until morning when the vessel could approach port; but the captain was a kindly man, and Thomas' heart warmed as he realized that the master, in some incredible way, had secured succor. He climbed on deck to welcome the newcomers, was struck on the head with the butt of a musket, his body then forced under the half-deck, the scuttle shut and a tarpaulin drawn over it. When he came to, he found his way to the sufferers in the cabin, who had heard the noise of the boarding party and were sitting up, feebly, their eyes shining at thought of good nursing and supplies. The boy was with his young chum, a lad of thirteen, so ill that he could not raise his head. Thomas had not the heart to tell these stricken yet courageous people exactly what had happened. Still dazed from the heavy blow, he was far from sure himself. He comforted his fear with the knowledge that if the invaders were pirates they would soon rifle the ship and begone, for a leaky ketch, with no provisions and a crew of delirious smallpox patients, would be to no mariner's taste.

Minutes that seemed hours passed before the scuttle was opened and William Coward, leader of the boarding party, descended into the cabin. When he discovered the woman, the four men, the boy, all ill — only Thomas and the second boy untouched by disease — he drew away, but made no comment other than to offer Thomas a chance to join him and his four companions on a trip to England in the ketch, there to dispose favorably of the sugar and indigo. Failing acceptance, Thomas was warned that he would be locked below with the pox sufferers, to watch them struggle with hunger and neglect, perhaps to die himself of the disease. He did not set up for a godly man, but the stark brutality of this proposal shocked him into defiance. He and the boy, who staunchly stood with him, were locked into a foodless and dark cabin, stenching with a foul plague. The armed pirates then cut the gaskets, loosed the sails of the *Elinor* and headed for Cape Cod.

Daylight of the next day, Friday, they anchored in Cape Cod Harbor (Provincetown) and fired a musket to attract the attention of the settlement. A shallop put out to them but refused to sell them any provisions other than a gallon of rum and some biscuits and cheese until the ketch was brought nearer shore, and until such time as extra provisions could be assembled from outlying farms. All that day the ketch remained at anchor in the harbor while the pirates negotiated for food. Unsuccessful in their demands, at midnight, full tide, they got under way and headed toward Barnstable harbor. The *Elinor*, nosing among the bars, ran aground before morning. At ebb tide the armed party despaired of all chance to float her, abandoned ship, and disappeared in the pine woods on shore.

James Thomas had his seaman's knife, and as soon as all was quiet on the ketch, he hacked his way out of the boarded-up cabin. Before the tide rose he plunged into the water, and swimming between bars and wading across them, he made his way to the beach. Far in the distance he caught a glimpse of rising gray smoke and toward it set a course. He had not gone far when he came to a roadway. Down the road, cantering on a great black horse, a woman approached with a scarlet cloak flying at her shoulder. The Atwoods say she was Desire Atwood; the Paines say she was Bethia Paine; the Nickersons say she was Rose Nickerson; in fact there is no family on the Cape, to this day, who does not claim to be related to that woman on the great black horse.

She drew up when she saw James Thomas wet, haggard, well-nigh frozen in the keen November air. He told her the story of the ketch *Elinor,* and of the six souls dying in the cabin, with poor water, no food, no medicines to save them. He mentioned that one was a woman; and when she heard that, the scarlet-cloaked lady took out her purse and thrust money on James Thomas, and explained to him, carefully and clearly, how to reach the house of Mr. Samuel Treat, minister, nurse, doctor, who was never afraid to face disease, and who would come, bringing the requisite supplies, as soon as he was summoned. Then, without further comment, she wheeled her horse and made for the shore, and while Thomas stared after her in wonder, she rode that horse through the November water, over the first bar, swimming him expertly through the deep eddies; over the second bar, again through deep water, until he reached the side of the *Elinor,* where she climbed the Jacob's ladder to the deck while the horse plunged, whinnied, then turned at her order, and slowly swam to the shore.

When James Thomas brought Samuel Treat in a shallop, some four hours later, the two men found the cabin clean and sweet, the cook's galley washed, a warm fire glowing, a pot on the stove, disease-racked bodies washed, broken sores bandaged, fever cooled by "applicashuns." A woman's voice was singing; and in the cabin there was comfort and hope, and occasionally a little laughter. On deck, in the rigging, the ketch *Elinor* flew the strangest signals that ever a ship displayed: one scarlet cloak, drying; one gray woven dress; two homespun hose with scarlet bands ringed around the top of them; six loom-linen petticoats. The rescuers were met by a laughing figure in seaman's jacket and trousers, with a soap sponge in one hand and a ship's pail in the other. The Atwoods say she was Desire Atwood; the Paines say she was Bethia Paine; the Nickersons say she was Rose Nickerson. In fact every Cape family is closely related to the girl who rode her black horse over two bars and three deeps to the rescue of the ketch *Elinor.*

THE SCOURGE OF THE SEA

Ned Low, "Pirot Admirall," delighted in disfiguring the faces of New England captains. He slit their noses, cut off their ears, and hacked them about the bodies. In June, 1723, he appeared off Cape Cod. Horrible tales circulated among seamen in port. Never was sharper watch kept for the glint of unknown sail by day, or strange mastlight in the dark.

The *Greyhound,* man-of-war on the New York station, put out to capture Low, came up with his sloop, the *Fortune,* sailing in company with the pirate schooner, *Ranger,* Harris in command. After a protracted conflict, the *Greyhound* shot down the main yard of the schooner; whereupon Low bore away from his consort, while Harris, witness to his Admiral's treachery, lost courage and called for quarter.

Captain Low, escaping his pursuers, put in for water at Tarpaulin Cove. A few days later, about eighty miles off the Cape, he came upon a whaler with two boats out, one of them at a distance. Nathan Skiff, the captain of the whaler, young, unmarried, a Nantucketer, irritated Low. The pirate, ordering him stripped, cruelly lashed him with a rawhide, slashed off his ears, and when the youthful captain became unconscious, shot him through the head. Three of the whaler's crew succeeded in making an immediate escape in a whaleboat. With a little water and a few biscuits, the three reached Nantucket "beyond all Expectations."

Two days after this capture, Low boarded two whaling sloops out of Plymouth. The master of one vessel was ripped open alive, his heart cut out, roasted. The mate who had served under him was compelled to devour it. The captain of the other vessel was slashed, mauled; his ears cut off were roasted, sprinkled with salt and pepper, and his crew were forced to eat them. Sometime later, this sailing master died of hideous wounds. Sailors from the crews of these two whaling sloops, at least the few who regained shore, reported that Low had on board the *Fortune* £150,000 in gold, silver, coin and plate.

Thomas Calder, a "Pockfretten Scotsman," sailed from Piscataqua and off Nantucket sighted a sloop with sails fluttering, rigging cut, and not one soul on board her. A pipe of wine, with the head knocked in, lay on the deck; several buckets half full of wine stood in the deserted cabin. One of the victims of Low's insane cruelty, the vessel could tell no tale, save her name and port, and no record was ever found of captain or crew. Derelict, she drifted off the Cape until Captain Jacob Waldron towed her to Boston, as "Flotsom taken up on the high Seas."

All manner of rumors startled the Narrow Land. Low was off Nauset; Low was in Tarpaulin Cove; Low had sailed over the Rip and was headed for a land raid at Eastham; he had established a secret base among the dunes of the Province Land. The *Greyhound* and the *Sea Horse* (Boston) were reputed to have captured him, a report soon contradicted by tales of renewed depredations. In Sandwich, the townsmen despaired for the life of young Jonathen Barlow, forced man on Low's vessel, and grandson of the colony Marshal who had so cruelly persecuted Quakers. Jonathen went to sea when he was not quite fourteen and at twenty was an expert ship's carpenter and able seaman. Captured by Low off the Guinea coast, in a Cape sloop looted and sunk by pirates, Barlow, considered too valuable a man to be freed or killed, was forced to serve under Low. He witnessed many ghastly crimes, and when opportunity offered, rendered unobtrusive assistance to Cape sailors victimized by the buccaneers.

Gradually during Barlow's service, Low acquired a large "privateering fleet" including his commodore ship, the *Merry Christmas*, captured off the Guinea coast in the autumn of 1723; the sloop, *Happy Delivery*, Lowther in command; the *Delight*, captained by Francis Farrington Spriggs; and added to these, he kept a constantly changing retinue of minor craft.

When Barlow was first taken he was "treated very barbarously; made to eat candles with the wick"; and his life often threatened. Low knocked out one of his teeth with a pistol, threatening to shoot down his throat "whereupon Barlow fell and was taken up sick which held him three months." After this brutal initiation, the Cape boy quietly accepted his destiny, and because of his good seamanship, was left unmolested. Before the spring of 1724 his allegiance to Low had been assumed and it may well be that Jonathen Barlow would have lived and died a pirate if he had not encountered Matthew Perry, member of an old Cape family, Quakers who "forever were bitter to Barlows"; and if he had not witnessed the "Quartermaster's Quarrel" on board the *Merry Christmas* and joined in the resultant mutiny when Low murdered the sleeping quartermaster. The infamous "Admirall" was thrown into a boat without provisions and set adrift. Captured by a French vessel owned in Martinico, Ned Low, given summary trial, died upon the gallows.

Shipton became captain of the frigate, and Jonathen Barlow continued under him. The pirates went to the Isle of Ruby; found Francis Farrington Spriggs there with the *Delight* "heft down" and in process of a cleaning. Shipton burned the *Merry Christmas* and sailed away in a sloop taken from Captain Jonathan Barney of Newport. Barlow, transferred to Spriggs' vessel, took part in the famous "Ride of St. Christopher" when a Rhode Island ship, with a cargo of horses, was captured. The pirates released the horses, mounted them, and rode around the decks in the moonlight, urging their steeds to full gallop, betting on the races, cursing and howling like devils. The animals, wild with terror, threw their drunken riders and then, in frenzy, plunged into the ocean. The buccaneers, deprived of their sport, took to riding the captured crew; they brutally whipped straining bodies, goaded them with cutlasses, raced them until the human steeds dropped bleeding and exhausted. Those few who survived the torture were subjected to the horrible processes of candle-sweating, in a ceaseless marathon around a flame-encircled mainmast.

Sailing north, Shipton captured the *John and Mary*, plundered her, removed the crew with the exception of the mate, Matthew Perry, and placed on board three pirates and two forced men from the *Delight*, all five invaders double armed. Nicholas Simons of Newport and Jonathen Barlow, Cape man, were the forced men put aboard. The mate of the *John and Mary*, Matthew Perry of Sandwich, whose family had suffered much in the Quaker persecutions led by Jonathen's grandfather, was lashed to the mainmast of the sloop, his hands bound behind him. He and Jonathen looked at each other and smiled. Here was a chance to redress an old wrong. Jonathen secretly unbound the mate, drew Simons into his scheme, and proposed that they three kill the three armed pirates and sail the *John and Mary* back to an English port. Matthew Perry and Simons eagerly assented. Barlow slipped Perry a pistol and the mate started for the steerage where one of the pirates was "rummaging." The Cape Quaker shot at the pirate's back but the pistol missed fire. The buccaneer turned quickly and let fly at Perry who started up the ladder. Simons, in the cabin, heard the snapping of flints and came rushing to the rescue. "In the name of God and His Majesty King George, let us go on with our design," he called. But the pirate's gun had also missed fire and Perry was unharmed. Simons promptly shot the pirate, and cowed another, while Barlow disposed of the third. Then the three "true salvage men" cut the ship's cable and set sail for Newport where they arrived toward the end of January, 1725.

Their stories, printed in the *New England Courant* and the *Boston*

News Letter, brought relief to seafaring communities who rejoiced to hear that the "Scourge of the Seas" had perished. Once again sailors weighed anchor with a chanty on the lips and faith in good fortune. And on the Cape, men smiled to know that an old feud was over. For Jonathen Barlow, anti-Quaker, came into Sandwich with Matthew Perry, Quaker; two brave seamen with the traditional quarrel between their families buried, and deepwater wisdom in their eyes.

THE SECRET OF TARPAULIN COVE

Long Tom Johnson sang a chanty as he heated a pulley over the cook stove of the sloop, *Goodspeed*. When the pulley had reached the right temperature, Tom paused in his aria, wet his finger and thrust the scarred digit against the surface of the iron. A satisfactory sizzling ensued; a peaceful, beatific smile lighted the seaman's countenance. Using the pulley as an improvised flatiron, he pressed the ruffles on the captain's coat. No ordinary seaman's jacket, this braided, be-ruffled garment whose buttons he so carefully polished with a mixture of pork fat and sand! When the ironing was completed, Long Tom, limping grotesquely, climbed to the Great Cabin where Captain Thomas Pound was waiting to put on the coat. Long Tom stood back to admire the effect.

For the first time since he had turned pirate, some two weeks previously, Thomas Pound felt himself a gentleman, dressed in his full uniform as sailing master of His Majesty's frigate, *Rose*. He set his cocked hat on his curls, possessed himself of a £12 note drawn against Mr. Blaney of the Elizabeth Islands, and set out to collect the money. His ship, the *Goodspeed*, lay by in Tarpaulin Cove on the southeast side of Naushon Island. Captain Pound had himself rowed in a skiff to Mr. Blaney's landing, while Long Tom stared after him from the deck of the sloop. Adoration lighted the eyes of the lame sailorman. His gray head was full of schemes for the amassing of a West Indian fortune to benefit this wronged and "bonnie" sea captain, and incidentally to smooth the rough spots for Long Tom himself. His heart was big with gratitude as he remembered that he had been a penniless taverner three weeks before, he who was now mate of the *Goodspeed*. He knew more than he chose to tell about the profession of piracy. As one of the "Three named Thomas," who signed articles in the Bull Tavern, Boston, he became practical guide and counselor to the two very amateur, ardent buccaneers whom he found it in his heart to adore. To be sure, the adulation was slightly tempered when it came to Thomas Hawkins, whose ways were not winning, whose seamanship was obviously inferior to that of Captain Pound.

Protégé of Governor Andros, the hated popish Governor and "Minion of James II," Thomas Pound, Roman Catholic, had turned his back forever on the "rable of Boston Cittie," wharf rats who had boarded the *Rose* while she lay in dock, torn away her sails, dismasted her; and, in a screeching mob dominated by political and religious maniacs, had carried the ship's gear from her unprotected decks to a city square where the masts were consumed in a bonfire.

Captain Pound chanced to be on shore at the burning. Had he been on the poop undoubtedly he would have defended the *Rose* with his cutlass until such time as he was disarmed and trampled underfoot. As soon as he heard of the raid on the *Rose*, he strode angrily to Province House, home of the royal governor, to demand in the name of His Majesty, King James, immediate redress. To his bewilderment, he learned at Province House that Sir Edmund Andros was a prisoner, that King James had fled England, and that "two tow-headed Dutchers," William and Mary, were to ascend the English throne. The Protestant town was in an uproar of celebration. The handsome captain mopped his brow and hurried down to the Bull Tavern where other honest seamen who understood the relative importance of a good ship and a religious controversy might be willing to interpret the new regime.

In the tavern sat Thomas Hawkins and Long Tom Johnson, drinking together. They had so far depleted their beakers that melancholy suffused them. Long Tom wept into his rum pot; Thomas Hawkins drooped like a "lillie"; and Thomas Pound sat watching the two, his heart bitter within him. Long Tom suggested cheerfully that anyone with half an eye (his own vision was none too clear) could see that the town of Boston, teeming with mutinous scoundrels, would soon be forced to release the governor and refit the *Rose*. Thomas Pound, who knew more of Andros than did either of his two companions, surmised that the headstrong, proud governor would never again be acceptable to New England provincials. As for the *Rose,* she would be given to some freshwater sailing master with a psalm-singing face and a hellfire tongue, and no more understanding of that tidy frigate than a woman has of the stars. As night wore on, the bitterness, the sense of no future before him, settled into certitude.

Suddenly Long Tom roused from his drunken torpor. A gleam shot into his eye, and loudly he began to narrate his experiences as a privateer. Lost opportunities for great wealth besieged him, coupled with spacious visions of chances that yet remained for those equipped to prey upon French shipping out of Martinique. Gradually his discourse took the flavor of romance. Thomas Hawkins, who felt himself something of a failure, inasmuch as his endeavors after some years of following the sea had led him only to the possession of a small, half-decked Bermudas boat, listened enviously. Thomas Pound, an acknowledged sea king, seemed not to attend the harangue, yet after Long Tom had concluded his discourse, Pound leaned forward and suggested that the three of them "go on the account." That night they discussed plans, signed articles, and just before dawn made their way quietly out of the public house, down the length of the Old Bull Wharf and into Hawkins' Bermudas boat whose sails they unfurled.

Sunlight found them on the sea road to Cape Cod. Off Race Point they sighted the *Goodspeed,* John Smart master; boarded her, captured her, cajoled or forced the crew to join them, and sent Smart back to Boston in the Bermudas boat, with word to the populace that "they [the pirates] knew ye Gov^t Sloop lay ready but if she came out after them & came up wth them they sh^d find hott work for they w^d die every man before they would betaken."

Smart reached Boston, August 19, 1689. The *Resolution* with a crew of able seamen immediately weighed anchor and cruised along the Cape coast with orders "Strenuously to Endeavor the Suppressing and seizing of all Pirates, Especially one Thomas Hawkins, Pound and others Confederated with them." The *Resolution* strenuously avoided the rounding of Monomoy Point, and as the South Seas and Vineyard Sound were the natural hiding places of piratical craft, the government sloop was obviously not looking for "hott work."

In Tarpaulin Cove (Naushon Island), the *Goodspeed* lay at anchor. Rum huts and water springs conveniently rimmed the shore, and on the moors roamed flocks of sheep, a supper for the stealing. Long Tom sewed busily on a handsome "bloodie flagg" which the pirates "ran up" to the masthead when they espied, on August 27, a brigantine at anchor in "Homes His Hole." They made short work of the brigantine, extracting from her hold 20 half barrels of flour, and a good supply of sugar, rum, and tobacco. A relieved crew forsook the sheep of Naushon; the *Goodspeed* ran to Virginia before a stiff northeaster, and remained in York River for a week. Here Pound acquired a kidnapped Negro and added some young adventurers to his crew. Still there was not sufficient food for the desired voyage to "Corazo," so the *Goodspeed* returned to Tarpaulin Cove and found there a bark captained by William Lord. Sugar was traded for an anchor, and Lord also purchased the Negro, giving in payment a £12 note drawn on Mr. Blaney of the Elizabeth Isles.

The ex-sailing master of the *Rose* needed £12. The shame of it brought a flush to his cheek as he lifted the knocker of the Blaney front door and felt in his waistcoat pocket preparatory to the presentation of the note. The door moved swiftly inward; a small girl stood in the aperture. "Is your father within?" inquired the captain with a low, sweeping bow. He was informed that Mr. Blaney, uncle not father, was "gone from home" but expected to return shortly. Would the stranger care to wait in the greatroom or the garden? The stranger chose the garden and was accompanied into it by young Hester Blaney. Warm September drowsed on shining holly leaves. Bees hung over the flowers. Captain Pound, his hat in his hand, paced narrow, box-bordered paths and conversed with a smiling child. She was quite old, fifteen she informed him, engaged to be married to a "Great Gentleman of Virginia." She had been educated in Boston, was "new come" to her uncle, so the conversation naturally centered about the town.

Thomas Pound told her of the magnificent balls at Province House presided over by Sir Edmund Andros; but he did not mention that the royal governor was now a prisoner of the people. He spoke also of Captain Thomas Hawkins whose four lovely sisters were the toast of all the dandies. She knew the two younger of these gentlewomen, one still unmarried. Pound assured her solemnly that he was in love with all four; but he did not mention that their brother Thomas, at that moment in Tarpaulin Cove, impatiently awaited his fellow conspirator and sufficient provisions to make sail safely to the West Indian Isles. Nor did she mention that the "Great Gentleman" from Virginia was an old man of her uncle's choosing, a man who had seen her but once and who had settled a fortune on her family for the possession of her hand.

When Mr. Blaney came upon them, they were old friends at home in the garden. The host invited his distinguished guest for dinner. A smell of roasting Cape hen mingled with the scents of autumn honeysuckle and marsh aster. Thomas Pound had not had a good meal for two weeks, and the stars were high as he rowed back to the sloop, *Goodspeed*. There he informed an irate Thomas Hawkins, a bewildered Long Tom, that he had failed to collect the note. He did not admit that he had also failed to present it; but he promised that he would return for the money in the morning.

The next day and the next he returned, and while he was gone a small ketch put out from Martha's Vineyard and proved too tempting a morsel for the piratical appetites of Hawkins and Long Tom. They set out in pursuit of the ketch, and the small craft fled back into the Island harbor, with the *Goodspeed* in pursuit. To the amazement of the pirates, inhabitants gathered alongshore and made a show of defending the ketch with guns. Long Tom and Hawkins drew away, but not before the *Goodspeed* had been identified; and the two buccaneers as they made back to Tarpaulin Cove knew that the time had come when their captain must forsake the collecting of his £12 note.

As soon as the ex-sailing master of the *Rose* heard that his companions had exposed themselves to complete identification, he subjected Hawkins and Long Tom to stern reprimand. Long Tom took it in good part, but Thomas Hawkins was angry. After the captain had reironed his ruffles and started once again for the garden of Mr. Blaney's house, Hawkins went ashore at Tarpaulin Cove, to drown his resentment in rum. In the Cove tavern he met an Indian who revealed, under the influence of firewater, the full extent of the danger resultant from pursuit of the ketch. The inhabitants of Martha's Vineyard, not satisfied with their display of martial prowess, had sent a post messenger from Governor Thomas Mayhew of the Island to the Governor of New York. The message, so the Indian declared, had to do with those black fiends of piracy, Thomas Hawkins and Thomas Pound.

Hawkins had no illusions concerning the New York frigates whose crews, unlike the *Resolution*'s, were unacquainted with Pound. He gave the Indian a drink, returned to the *Goodspeed*, and refrained from mentioning to Long Tom the import of his information. Nor did he say anything to Pound when an oddly elated captain came aboard in the late evening and issued orders for an immediate rounding of Monomoy Point.

Over the Rip the *Goodspeed* found her way by moonlight. The next morning she cruised along the Backside, and the following day, off Race Point, Hawkins went ashore with a boat's crew. Making some excuse to the men he strode inland, over the dunes. The men waited patiently until dusk, then rowed back to the sloop to report his desertion. Pound seemed perplexed. Nevertheless he retained his curious elation and Long Tom eyed him suspiciously.

The *Goodspeed* encountered half a dozen small craft on Nauset Sea. These were boarded and looted of whatever provisions they possessed, but Pound, unsatisfied, continually discussed a return to the Cove. After three days of aimless cruising, he took the *Goodspeed* over the shoals, through the Sound to Homes His Hole. The sloop, *Brothers Adventure*, Boston bound, loaded with provisions, was coming out of the Hole. The pirates captured her and put aboard the *Goodspeed* thirty-seven barrels of pork, three of beef, and an abundant supply of peas, Indian corn, butter and cheese.

Long Tom contemplated these edibles complacently. At last the pirates had supplies necessary for a southern voyage, and the lame mate, who suspected Thomas Hawkins of treachery, longed to be clear of Cape waters. To his consternation, Pound reanchored in Tarpaulin Cove and issued commands that the rigging be overhauled. Long Tom protested. His captain, he knew, was well aware that the crew had done nothing for four weeks but overhaul rigging. The sloop was as ready as seamanship could make her.

Despite his disgust, for two days the *Goodspeed* waited in the Cove. On the evening of the second day Pound returned to the ship from a visit to Mr. Blaney. To the delight of the impatient crew and the profound relief of Long Tom, the captain announced that at the turn of the tide on the following night they would up-anchor. In preparation the captain demanded that his cabin be swept and shining. Long Tom, peering in, discovered a bunch of "autumn posies." At

sight of them he sickened; but his speculations were cut short by a
shout from the man on lookout: an armed sloop approached off the
anchorage.

Less than two weeks had elapsed since Hawkins and Long Tom
had chased the small ketch into Martha's Vineyard harbor, but the
messenger had ridden post and Captain Samuel Pease, late commander of the Duke of Courtland's ship, *Fortune,* had volunteered to
go to sea at once in pursuit of the pirates. He was given the sloop
Mary, with a crew of twenty able seamen; supplied with a barrel of
powder, fifty pounds of small shot, cartridge papers and match. He
was asked to "prevent ye sheding of blood as much as may bee."

The *Mary* drew abreast of Woods Hole, October 4, in the morning. An Indian in a canoe paddled out from shore and brought information to Pease that the pirates were anchored in Tarpaulin Cove.
A stiff south-southeast wind was blowing. The *Mary* ran up her
"King's Jack"; and as she came within range of the *Goodspeed*'s guns,
Captain Pease ordered a great gun to be fired "thwart her fore foot."
In reply Long Tom climbed to the masthead of the *Goodspeed* and
nailed aloft his "bloodie flagg." Pound stood on the quarterdeck
"with his naked sword in his hand flourishing." Pease called to him
to strike to the King of England. "Come aboard, you Doggs," answered Pound, "and I will strike you presently." He had no long
shot, so his men stood by him with their guns in their hands, and
when Pound gave a signal, the pirates let fly a volley. Pease maneu-
vered his ship to leeward "because the wind blew so hard." Long Tom
mistook this action for surrender, and the pirates "gave severall
Shouts." Fast firing continued, as rapidly as the two ships' companies
could load. A bullet entered Captain Pound's side, another lodged
in his arm. Long Tom, struck in the jaw, presented a grisly appearance as he drew his cutlass in readiness to repel the boarding party.
Before a hand to hand struggle began, Pease called to the pirate captain, bidding him yield, offering good quarter. "Ai yee dogs,"
Pound replied through clenched teeth, "we will give you quarter
by and by." As he spoke his body slumped heavily to the boards.
Long Tom, "blubbering," carried him below.

At about the same time, Captain Pease, shot through the arm, side,
and thigh, suffering from loss of blood, was carried from the deck of
the *Mary.* Benjamin Gallop, lieutenant, took his place and opposed

the command of Long Tom. Gallop led a boarding party. Long Tom and his men put up a fierce defense against them. The two forces "went to club it," knocking each other down with the butt ends of muskets. Ultimately Gallop's men "queld" the pirates, "killing four and wounding twelve, two remaining pretty well."

The stiff breeze strengthened into a half gale. Doctors were essential for wounded men, so the *Mary*, with fourteen prisoners aboard, shaped her course for Rhode Island. There the wounded were lodged on shore while surgeons extracted bullets and sewed up cutlass holes. The eleventh day of October, Pease put his prisoners on board the *Mary* and set sail for Boston. Scarcely had he cleared harbor when he "was taken with bleeding afresh." The sloop came to anchor and Pease was removed to shore, where he died the next morning and was buried in the town of Newport. On the night of his burial the *Mary* sailed, arriving in Boston Saturday, October 18, 1689.

Thomas Pound, Long Tom Johnson, and their twelve comrades were escorted to the new stone jail where the first face that greeted them wore a familiar melancholy. Thomas Hawkins, last seen amid the Cape dunes, now a fellow prisoner, tried to justify his desertion by a long yarn to which Pound listened doubtfully. Long Tom, whose natural charms had not been augmented by the shot in his jaw, sneered as he heard Hawkins claim that as soon as he knew himself to be recognized, he had deserted in an attempt to save them. But when the Boston pirate came to that part of his saga which pertained to Cape Cod, Long Tom was comforted, for scarcely had Hawkins been lost to sight behind the dunes before he was seized by Nauset fishermen who deftly relieved him of all his gold and precious possessions, and "ware" he said, "a pasel of Roughes." Forlornly he wandered, until Captain Loper, Portuguese whaler and oysterman, found him, conveyed him to Boston and, distrusting his story, turned him over to the magistrates.

For three months all the pirates languished in Boston prison. Their "treasure," including the sloop, was appraised at £209.4.6. The widow and four children of Captain Pease, who had given his life to capture the *Goodspeed*, were also "in a poor and low condition." The General Court passed a bill providing for a collection in all the Boston meeting houses for their relief. The wounded pirates were doctored by Thomas Larkin, bill to the government £21.10.0.

Pound had "Severall bones Taken Oute." Long Tom underwent an operation on his jaw. Buck, another of the pirates, had seven holes in one arm. A sailor named Griffin lost an eye and an ear.

Hawkins, who had been incarcerated some days before Pound and his crew were captured, was examined by the aged Governor Brad-street, and came to trial on January 9, 1690. Found guilty of piracy he was condemned to die. Pound and his confederates were brought to trial January 17. The ex-sailing master of the *Rose*, guilty of felony, piracy, murder, was condemned to be "hanged by the neck until he be dead." The four sisters of Thomas Hawkins, two of them married to magistrates, used their influence to obtain their brother's release. Appeals to Judge Sewall and Cotton Mather led to a visit by these two dignitaries to the imprisoned men. Sewall signed the peti-tion for Hawkins, and the governor granted the reprieve so tardily that the noose was around the captain's neck as he stood on the scaf-fold, February 20, ready to be "turned off." Carried by special rider, the order reached the sheriff; the rope was unfastened, and Hawkins went free. "Which gave great disgust to the people; I fear it was ill done," wrote Sewall, adding, "I rashly sign'd, hoping so great an inconvenience would not have followed. Let not God impute Sin."

On payment by each pirate of twenty marks (£13.6.8.) the other buccaneers were released, with the exception of Captain Pound and Long Tom Johnson.

Roman Catholic, friend of the detested ex-governor; there was no one left in that expurgated city to speak for Thomas Pound. But word of his sentence reached Cape Cod, even as far as the Elizabeth Isles, and a girl who had waited one entire night for a cavalier who never came, mounted her horse, rode for the city, with a box of jewels strapped to her saddle and an uncle's curse behind her. Just four days before the sunrise when Thomas Pound was condemned to meet death, Hester Blaney started her ride. Journey-bated, travel-stained, she dismounted at the door of Hannah Hawkins' house in Boston. Hannah's husband, the magistrate, impressed by her heroic ride and by his wife's supplications, intervened for Pound. As the old records explain, at the instance of "sundry Women of Quality" Thomas Pound's sentence was respited.

During the first months of 1690, the acting governor refitted the

Rose and toward the end of April she sailed for England, carrying as passengers Hawkins and Pound. So many pirates infested the seas that she lay for a month in Piscataqua awaiting convoy. Despite this delay and the safeguard of the convoy, off Cape Sable the *Rose* encountered a warlike French "Pirot." A fight ensued in which Pound distinguished himself and Hawkins was killed. The *Rose* gave battle royal. The "tops" of her assailant were full of "Grenadiers and Fuzes" which fell like "Piggeins," while "Multitudes of his (the Frenchman's) Men lay Slaughtered on his Decks."

Arrived in London, Pound wrote a long letter to Sir Edmund Andros and published "A New Mapp of New England" which served as a basis for other charts for nearly fifty years. The charge of piracy was dismissed and as captain of the *Sally Rose*, one of the sauciest frigates in the Royal Navy, Captain Pound put in at Virginia where he was much entertained and gave a famous "Ship's Ball" for the young wife of a "Great Gentleman of Virginia."

Meanwhile, where was Long Tom who had ironed the ruffles and polished the buttons of the captain's coat? He had no fair sisters, no ladies of quality, to plead his case with the magistrates; and the populace of Boston, cheated of many hangings, watched him "turned off" one cold winter's day. He swung by the neck near the sea that he loved, his gaze directed eastward toward the rising sun and the frigate, *Rose*, preparing for her ocean voyage.

2. "Mooncussin'"

The Moon Curser is generally taken for any Link-Boy; but particularly he is one that waits at some Corner of Lincolns-Inn-Fields with a Link in his hand, who under the pretence of Lighting you over the Fields, being late and few stiring, shall Light you into a Pack of Rogues that wait for the comming of this Setter, and so they will all joyne in the Robbery.
Richard Head's *Canting Academy,* 1673, p. 101.

At haggard sea corners of old Cape Cod men held lanthorns high in the black nights of the seventeenth and eighteenth centuries. They swung the discs in a wide arc as though directing pilotless ships over Nauset Sea. Many a hemp-and-salt shipmaster mistook these swaying signals for mastlights of other craft, turned to follow them, and ran on hidden bars. Such misfortune only occurred when no moon whitened the dunes that loom along that waterline, when no decisive starlight sharpened the shadow between tall Clay Pounds to the northward and the foam-spreckled edges of the sea. "Mooncussers" was the name bestowed on these human harpies, who fed on the spoils of such moonless disaster, who filched a lucrative plunder from the unchartable, shifting shoals of Race Point, Nauset, and Monomoy.

A few wise inhabitants put their hands into their pockets to contribute toward "Government Beacons," whereupon certain God-fearing puritans advanced sharp arguments against the "policy of beaconing," a device designed to "injure the wrecking business." Yet these same puritans risked their lives again and again to rescue sailors as well as cargoes and ribbed hulls and wreck-iron from fishing sloops, snows, pinks, Bermudas boats, broad-winged East Indiamen, deeply laden yawls and ketches that were "Poundin' up" on the offshore bars. After initial salvage had been completed and flotsam had been gathered from spume-wet beaches, the goodmen buried drowned sail-orboys while churchbells rang and prayerbooks lay open and salt tears glazed the eyes.

In up-Cape towns such as Sandwich and Barnstable, whose harbors face Baywater, freemen expressed disgust at the "dirty doings" down Nauset way, to which the wreckmasters of Monomoy and Nauset replied by mentioning "green grape cankers itchin' the tongues" of envious "up-Capers."

With the growing trade of a young nation, so many ships perished along that "White Graveyard of the Atlantic" that link-boys were not necessary to lure unwary wanderers into a pack of rogues. The term *mooncursing* gradually lost its older connotation. With no implication of false lights it was used, in the nineteenth century, to indicate all those who practiced beachcombing or salvage. But in 1717 the old derisive, condemnatory aspect of the word still clung to it, though without the precise implication of "luring lights." So a hostile Cape took pleasure in bestowing the title "King of the Mooncursers" on Captain Cyprian Southack, brave mariner, skilled mapmaker, when he came at the behest of the Royal Governor to court "fickell salvedge," after word had reached Boston of the Black Bellamy's death.

CYPRIAN IN THE RAIN

Cyprian Southack sat in the cabin of the sloop, *Nathaniel,* and chewed his pen. He was suffering from the throes of composing an official communication, while rain beat against the porthole and Cyprian's back felt chilly. He wrote to Governor Shute:

Cape Cod Harbour, May (5?) 1717

Maye itt Pleass Your Excellency

Sir, may 2 at I After noon I Came to Anchor here, finding Serveral Vessells, Visseted them and on board one of them found a Yung man boling to the Ship the Pirritt Took 26 April in South Channell, Saileing from Nantaskett the day before at 3 After noon. April 26 Pirritt Ship Took a Sloop in South Channell, Lading with West India Goods, Sloop or Master I no not as Yett. at 7 After noon the Pirrett Ship with her Tender, being a Snow a bout Ninty Tuns they Took in Latitude 26, 15 Days agoe, maned with 15 of Pirritts men, wine Ship and Sloop all to Gather Standing to the Northward. at 12 Night the Pirritt Ship and wine Ship Run a Shore, the Snow and Sloop Gott Off Shore, being Sen the Next morning in the Offen.

Sir, 29 April Came to Anchor sum Distance from the Pirritt Rack Ship, a Very Great Sloop. After Sending his boat to the Pirrit Rack Thay Came to Saile and Chassed several of Our fishing Vessells, then stod in to Sea which I believe to be his Cunsatte.

May 2 at 2 After noon I sent Mr. Little and Mr. Cuttler to the Rack. they Got their that Night and Capt watch till I Came the Next morning. at my Coming their I found the Rack all to Pices, North and South, Distance from one a Nother 4 Miles. Sir, whear shee Strock first I se one Anchor at Low water, sea being so Great Ever sence I have ben here, Can not Come to se what maye be their for Riches, nor aney of her Guns. she is a ship a bout Three hundred tuns. she was very fine ship.

Here Cyprian paused in his narrative to muse, as a seaman will when he writes the requiem of the living vessel. In harbor the seas were choppy; the wind blew a "frisking gail"; the *Nathaniel* bobbed at anchor. But Cyprian's thoughts were not with this hired sloop in whose cabin he sat, nor for the moment with the governor to whom he wrote. Like all poets and lovers of beauty, men who follow the sea pay tribute to their calling. Cyprian paused as he fashioned the words: *She was very fine ship.*

For nineteen years Captain Southack had been in command of the "Province Galley." Sea captain and pilot, he had also commanded

a vessel under Sir Hovenden Walker in the expedition against Que-
bec (1711). Walker stayed at Southack's house during the admiral's
long detention in Boston, and Sir Hovenden took pleasure in com-
plimenting his host on maps drawn with such care and precision that
many men of New England considered Southack the most noted mapmaker of his time. In England the king honored him for his map of
"Newfoundland, Nova Scotia, and the St. Lawrence region." So it
was as a man of authority and experience that this valiant captain
dropped anchor in Cape Cod Harbor in search of such salvage from
the *Whidah* as his ingenuity might wrest from the waves, or from His
Majesty's "Loveing subiects" who had already kindly collected much
property of the Crown.

Cyprian expected to be entertained, perhaps a little feted, in that
long peninsula of well stocked larders where the garnerings of the
four seas were brought under the gray roofs. He anticipated inform-
ing pioneer farmers and longshore sailors of life at the Court, and
of his famous interview with "Great King William" who had bestowed
on him a chain "of £50." Confined to the local coasts for the last
nineteen years, never before chancing to make harbor at the Cape, to
his surprise he found himself in a community of men who had traveled from early youth, who were still traveling; a community with a
constantly increasing number of sea captains who often took their
wives, even their young children, when they "viaged across the Atlan-
tick."

To the Boston captain the inhabitants seemed unresponsive, hostile. Justice Doane's wife gave him a "plum Posset" to soothe his
"soar throte"; and the justice loaned him an "Indie-kachoo bandanie"
(West Indian bandana) at a time when Cyprian took to sneezing
unexpectedly. But with the exception of these small courtesies, he
received neither kindness nor cooperation. Rain continued day
and night. Thick, low-lying layers of cloud sagged along the beaches
like ghouls of dead sandbars. When Cyprian put into Cape Cod Harbor, May 2, after-seas following the great storm were so high that
he could not round Race Point. A man of resource, he promptly
devised a way to outwit time and the elements. Through every
finger of every inlet spring tides were surging, and on the edge of
the South Parish of Eastham (now Orleans) a sluggish stream met
the bay; another one emptied into the ocean at the head of Town

Cove. These two streams, with two adjacent ponds for their head-waters, provided a potential cross-Cape canal. Cyprian hired a whale-boat, and "geer." At four o'clock in the morning, May 3, he started to cross from the Bay to the Backside, carrying salvaging tools from the *Nathaniel* to the site of the "Pirritt Rack."

All Cape Cod remembers that voyage when a whaleboat manned by nine men first crossed the Narrow Land. It is said that the penin-sula resented this careless making of an island and put the land's curse on the men, who "came to bad ends." On the Bay side, the women of the South Parish watched from the banks of Boat River Meadow; on the ocean side, they lined the banks of Jeremy's Drean. They cheered and laughed and mocked a little at this determined, slightly pompous seadog who was come in the name of the Royal Governor to take what no off-Cape man could hope to take, the Cape's God-given heritage from the sea. Cyprian's men now rowed, now pushed, now punted the heavily laden whaleboat. The walls of Jeremy's Drean came close; cattails smacked the faces of the crew, reeds brushed their arms. But the sea was with them; it flooded the Drean until pale meadows were all awash, and the sweet smell of mayflower mingled with marsh salt.

Cyprian posted notices on three church doors in the villages, to demand that all salvage from the *Whidah* be submitted to the Crown, and to make formal declaration of his right to search private houses for treasure not voluntarily submitted. Loiterers gathered around the meeting house doors. The Boston captain was surprised at the ease with which goodmen could read, at polite townsmen who com-mented pleasantly on Cyprian's spelling but seemed benignly un-aware that this peremptory order to disgorge pertained to them. He wondered who had taught the Indians, even the native women and children; then heard of the Reverend Samuel Treat, who died in the Great Storm, that winter (1717). He marveled that one man could mold the culture of so various a multitude, be comforter and companion to the lonely university men of Cambridge and Oxford, strong minds self-exiled for their faith, and at the same time be con-stant instructor and missionary to proud alien natives, and teacher to children who had never known the books and schools of "Ould England."

At the end of three days spent in vain appeals for "the Crown's salvedge," and in even vainer contemplation of the *Whidah*'s in-accessible caboose, Cyprian returned for a night to the *Nathaniel,* and wrote to Governor Shute:

> all that I Can find saved Out of her (the Whidah) is her Cables and som of her sailes, Cut all to Pices by the Inhabitances here. their has ben at this Rack Two hundred men at Least Plundring of her. sum saye they Gott Riches Out of the sand but I Can not find them as yett. Sir, what I shall Gett to Gather will be to the Value of Two hundred Pounds. If Your Excellency Pleass to send the sloop to Billingsgatt for itt, is Carted Over Land to that Place. . . . If their be aney News by the Pirritts at boston whear the money is, I humbley Desier Your Excellency menets of what Place in the ship itt was in, for I am in Great hops. whare the Anchors are the money is I fancy, and weather Per mett I have Got a whale boat to fish for itt and Things for that service.

The captain sealed his letter and sat staring at the blurred silver of the porthole. He opened the port and looked toward the long gray land with sullen waters surrounding it, gray clouds dripping over it. Then he spoke softly to himself. In a few well-chosen words he consigned to a destination that sandy peninsula and all the people upon it.

That day Cyprian interviewed the coroner. Samuel Freeman had done a "deal o' diggin'" to bury the many pirate bodies and he "figgered" that the hard labor was worth £83. As Cyprian had so far gathered together £82, it was something of a blow to have the "Curnors Jurey Putt a stop" upon it for the expenses of the burial. Cyprian lost his temper, told Samuel Freeman what he thought of him; to which the "Curnor" responded with a deprecating tut-tut and a seaward look of the eyes. Thoroughly disgusted, the Boston captain clambered into his whaleboat. Once more he was rowed out to the bar. Not the sharpest of eyes could see through the turgid waves that were roiled with sand. At "Low Watter" the slim finger of the *Whidah*'s great anchor beckoned, and it seemed to Cyprian's fevered imagination a pledge of treasure below.

Two days later the captain, with a cold in his chest and a mean cough, went into the bedroom of the Doane House (whose great front door came by ship from England), and indicted a bitter communication to the Governor:

Eastham May the 8, 1717

Maye itt Pleass Your Excellency

Sir, Captt. Gorham, Mr Little, Mr. Cuttler and Mr Russell, Gentt'men that I have Deputed, have Rid at Least Thirty miles a moung the Inhabtances, whome I have had Information of ther being at the Pirate Rack, and have Gott Concernable Riches out of her. the fist men that want Doun to the Rack with the English man that was Saved out of the Rack, I shall Mention their Names to Your Excellency in Order for a Warrant to me for bringing them for boston before Your Excellency, or as You Pleass, Sir, for all thes Pepol are very stife and will not one [own] Nothing of what they Gott, on the Rack.

Here Cyprian hesitated. When he started to make a list of offenders, he realized that he was thirsting to arrest the entire population. Common sense assured him that he could never march the lot of them to the stone jail in Boston. They were all incredibly irritating; so was the insistent beckoning of that hazy anchor where the decks of the *Whidah* had fallen out; so, for that matter, was the ceaseless rain which the "inhabitances" assured him was unparalleled in Cape history. Then Cyprian remembered his news about the coroner. He dipped his quill deep in the ink and expressed himself again:

Sir, I am of the mind that the Curner and Jurey should have nothing for buering aney of thes men After they New them to be Pirats, and they had bured but Thirteen before they new them to be Pirats. as Your Excellency Pleass, I humbley Desier Your Excellency Orders to this Afare. the Curner name is Samuel freeman for his stoping aney of the Rack Goods for Paye is very hard.

Here the poor captain began to feel sorry for himself. Altogether the whole experience was hard. He hoped the governor realized how hard it had been to force that whaleboat across Cape Cod. The attitude with which the inhabitants met his proclamations was hard. His cold proved a hard one. Even his bed was hard. It rained hard throughout the week; and the sand-thick waters over the wreck with their vague temptation to "Great hops" made defeat hard to accept. Hardest of all had been the extraction of £82 from the "stife Pepol"; to have the coroner "Putt a stop" on it was more than Cyprian could endure.

He did not know that while he was writing, the sloop, *Swan*, under orders from the governor, was sailing to Cape Cod, to bring in triumph back to Boston the noble captain and the pirate treasure. The *Swan*, boarded by Paul Williams, Bellamy's "Cunsatte," and robbed of stores to the amount over which Cyprian was mourning, £83, came safely to the Bay harbor. Captain Southack loaded her with those few dilapidated items not claimed forcibly by the "Curner's Jurey." Then he sailed back to the civilized town of Boston where in due course an advertisement appeared in the *Boston News Letter* to the effect that "two Anchors, two Great Guns and some Jonk that came from the Wreck Whido" would be sold at "Publick Vendue" by Mr. Ambrose Vincent, Admiralty Marshal, who combined in one person the aspects of drum major for all executions (carrying at the head of processions his "Silver Oare of Office") and, in time unoccupied by the pageantry of beheading criminals, served as auctioneer.

Cyprian went down to the Crown Coffee House on the "Long Wharffe," Boston, to inspect the "Jonk." He also was running an advertisement in the *News Letter*, a far more satisfactory way of picking up a penny than trying to squeeze it from the tightwads of Cape Cod:

> To be sold by Capt. Cyprian Southack at his Hill, Sand for plaistering, or for Brick-work, at One Shilling a Cart Load, Mould Two shillings a Cart Load, and Gravel Three Pence a Cart Load: There being Two very good Cartways to fetch it, one over against the Bowling Green, the other by Mr. William Young the Glazier's House.

This small quotation tells us much about the captain. For one thing, it bears striking evidence against the claims of certain Cape Codders that the *King of the Mooncursers* possessed himself of Bellamy's fortune, bought himself a "Creole mistress" and sailed away to England to take tea on the terrace with the Royal Family. Selling gravel for threepence the cartload seems hardly in keeping with so debonair a destiny. If the captain had a Creole mistress (in 1717!), where did he acquire her, in Boston or Cape Cod? Where did he keep her? "Oh," said Old Hut Dyer and the yarners of the Lyars' Bench, "he kep' her *very dark*." Which you may believe or not; the author suggests doubting it; but at least it proves that on the long peninsula that was rudely, ruthlessly made into a temporary island by this bluff, determined seafarer, the "stife Pepol" took no liking to a man who wore a king's chain, who tried to take from these children of the sea their one inviolate heritage; a man who needed more than gold, or "plum Posset," or a Creole mistress, one pocket dictionary.

THE WHITE STALLION

The slender sandspit of Monomoy extends from the landward cliff of Chatham some seven miles to sea; as eerie, isolated, gleaming a bar as ever shone back at the moon. Along that shore the bony ribs of wrecks burrow in drift sand, like skeletons of dinosaurs peering with bolt-rusty eyes at the interfurrowing waves. Years ago a white horse sank to the fetlocks, plowing his way through drifts of "singing sand." A light like a star gleamed in his mane, another swung at the saddle. His broad flanks loomed like a sail against the starless water. He swayed as he walked, nodding his head, for a long pull through sand drags at the muscles and causes a certain pitching of the body. Many vessels followed him, "the false mirage of Monomoy"; many hulks lie buried in the sand that were once led like winged chariots at the heel of the mooncurser's stallion.

Who owned him? Nobody knows. Nobody tells if he does know. But one night when the wind blew a northeast gale and cold spume frothed at the crests of waves, a light was hung on the stallion's mane, and he was driven over hissing sand by a cruel spider of a master, one who had caught many shining sails like moths in a foggy web.

The wind blew full gale that night! The roof of the church rose from its walls and flapped away like a crane; then settled down, tidily, where the shingles were worn on the roof of the Widow Atwood's house. " 'Tis the will of God made manifest," said the widow, and sent her nephew up to nail the new roof fast. In that gale the arms were ripped off the windmill of the Atkins Brothers, and the bell on the Hill of Storms rolled down into an open grave. No one dared to pluck the bell forth until the clapper was detached. If one peal resounded under the earth it might rouse the dead for judgment before their lawful time.

Black fields of clouds hung over the sky. No rain fell. Hurricane waves beat up the beach, and not a vessel that could find port was out to risk the seas. Yet the white stallion and his master fought their way up and down the spinning sands of Monomoy. The mooncurser rode his horse till the wind ate through his thin black doublet; then he dismounted and "sand-shuffled" on the lee side of the stallion. The tide, running as never before, knifed its way through the spit; then roared down Stage Harbor Channel like a gang of yelling whale-men broken loose with "three-winter money," making for Mother Thornton's Tavern down New Bedford way.

In two places the stormy sea bit through Monomoy sands. A fast dwindling island was left between these two channels, and on the is-land stood master and horse. Three men on the landward cliff saw them, but no boat could have been launched, nor could have survived the flood of onrushing water. Clouds parted to reveal a thin cirrus scudding through the upper air. The white stallion pawed at the sand, then stood still, trembling. The spider man mounted his horse, and as the last inch of footing crumbled, he called against the roar-ing wind, a shriek devoured by the sea. At that moment the moon came dazzling through the scud. Lunar madness seized the stallion. Wildly neighing, he breasted the tide, swimming in the center of the moonfall. The rider's body, swept away, came to rest two days later on Stage Harbor shore. But the white stallion swam on — on into mountains of ocean. He still swims beyond the Rip, and when the moon comes out may be seen close to the pointed prows of ships, his white mane gleaming as he guides them over the bars.

The sands lie, an unbroken expanse, on the long sea spit of Mo-nomoy. The red rust eyes of the wrecks keep baleful watch to sea.

3. YARNS OF THE SEA

"TALL TALES"

Uncle Eliakim Pierce and Uncle Eleazar Mayo went into the wreck-ing business together. On the beach they put up a tent in which to keep gear and "strippings." Through the center of this tent they pegged off a line. All goods on one side belonged to Uncle Elia-kim, all goods on the other side were the property of Eleazar. At first the two wrecking partners were "confidin'," inclined to swap salvage not included in their contracts, but in time the rivalries of their profession grew upon them. Eliakim became embittered if Eleazar stripped ship ahead of him or appropriated anything that Eliakim craved.

One twilight a thick fog settled over the bars. The two wreckers agreed to sleep, that night, in their tent, a scheme by which they succeeded many times in establishing priority of salvage claim. Despite the fog, the air was warm, and before he rolled into his blanket Eliakim decided to cool his feet in the surf. He strolled down-beach and waded along the water's edge until his foot became entangled in a rough obstacle. Leaning down to extricate himself, he discovered a length of rope. Eliakim needed a boat mooring; but he thought of his contract with Eleazar for the fair division of flotsam. If this rope were cut in half, it would not make a mooring. He concluded not to tell Eleazar where he had acquired his prize.

Pulled up-beach, the rope dragged heavily, suggesting great length. He turned to haul, hand over hand, casting the slack behind him; and he hauled and he hauled till his arms grew weary. Never had beachraker "come acrost" a finer length of rope. When at last he pulled in the end, he turned around to coil the slack. Except for the meager yard in his hands, no rope remained.

Now Uncle Eleazar, when Eliakim did not return from "keel-cooling," wandered out to find him and concealed by mist stood behind his unsuspecting partner. While Eliakim pulled, Eleazar coiled. When he had enough for a boat mooring, he took out his knife, severed the rope, and quietly, enshrouded in haze, he made his way back to the tent.

Later, Eliakim returned. He laid himself down without comment, but in the morning the first object that his eyes beheld was an "anchor-road" in a neat coil, stacked beside the tent wall in Eleazar's territory. Observing his partner's fixed gaze, Eleazar "let on" that yonder lay a rope.

Eliakim reached over and felt of the rope's end. He complimented Eleazar on the good quality of hemp. Then he strolled outside the tent to wash up for breakfast, sneaked around to the opposite wall and seized upon a rope's end that protruded from under the canvas as if it had been pushed beneath it. Very quietly Uncle Eliakim hauled rope, but this time as he hauled he coiled. When he had completed his task, he entered the tent with a coil on his arm and "let on" to Eleazar that he had acquired an anchor-road.

Eleazar peered into the tent corner. *His* rope was gone! But as Uncle Eliakim said, the devil must have stolen it, since during the time the theft occurred, no one was in the hut but Eleazar himself.

Down to the dunes came deepwater captains to buy ship's gear of the two wreckers, to sit on the golden, painted chairs from the fancy ship of Spain. The captains smoked and yarned a little: Captain Zeke had been fighting pirate junks in the Chinese Sea; Captain Ed had been "hurricanoed" in the "yellow Indies"; Captain Isaiah had "met up with" a princess in a South Pacific Isle. The eyes of Eliakim glistened with unwinking wonder; the jaw of Eleazar loosened at the hinges; but after the captains had finished telling of phantom frigates and speaking whales and elephants bugling with their ears, Eleazar cleared his throat and dropped signal to Eliakim, or Eliakim flicked an eyelid as sign to Eleazar, and one or the other of them spun a yarn for the deepwater captains. "Tarpaulin tarradiddles," the old sailors called such yarns. We call them tall stories today.

The captains sprawled over salvage goods or tilted back the golden chairs from the fancy ship of Spain. Outside the tent, water gurgled, innocent as a teething babe, and the reefs were rigged in lupine blue, shot with green, cockled into halfmoons, spreading their "eyes" in the sunlight like a peacock's tail.

The Flying   All "eddicated seafarin' men" have heard of the ship
Spouse   built from designs of a Cornishman, the frigate that
scraped off Dover Cliff, trying to wedge through the Channel. Young sailors went into the shrouds of her and came down with long white beards on them; and one of her discarded jackstays, sunk into the London mud, made "Piccalilly Circus."

The New Peninsula built such a ship under direction of Asey Shiverick. She was so tall that sailors took their wives when they went up to furl the toproyals. Later they sent down their grandsons to report that orders had been filled.

The Dover cliff was a thornberry scratch compared with what befell Cape Cod when the *Flying Spouse,* as she was christened, tried to turn around in the Bay. She could not make it, could not come "nigh to it," so Asey sawed off her flying jib boom at the cap. That took three years. Still she could not make it, so he sawed off her Dolphin striker and her whisker boom. That took five years. Still she could not make it so he sawed off her jib boom and her bowsprit. Hard sawing and Sunday work, that took him ten years. Then he put her helm down hard and swung her till her nose knocked, whacking Billingsgate Island, plunging it under water. After that, Asey thought: how about taking her out stern first? So he cleared her neatly, but by that time the good meadows of Billingsgate, all owned by ministers, had disappeared in the Bay. The pirates up by Wellfleet had buried their gold on Billingsgate Island, and they lost a "deal of treasure."

Asey's ship was rigged with sheets so heavy that no gang could haul them. A team of mules was put aboard, and with this and that, so many mules were required to work ship that no room was left in the hold for cargo. She was nothing but a fancyman's dream. Yet Asey was so proud of her that he bet Captain Obed Paine of Eastham that the *Flying Spouse* could sail to Ireland, there and back in six days and rest upon the seventh. Obed took Asey up, and went along to see fair play. The mules hauled anchor on a Monday.

For all her size the *Flying Spouse* was no faster than the wind blows, so Obed was sure that Asey could never get her to Ireland and return in a matter of six days. What he forgot when he made his reckonings, was that her bow, when her stern was three days out, would be wedged tight into Queenstown Harbor and likely to get stuck there.

"You're a right smart sailorman, Asey," said Obed, when the ship reached Ireland, Wednesday night, "but how're y' goint' pull 'er out an' swing 'er aroun', Asey?"

Captain Shiverick grinned. "God save King George!" he yelled, jumping on the foredeck. "God save England! Horray for Parlyment!"

The Irish were that mad they pushed the prow of the *Flying Spouse* so hard out of Queenstown Harbor that she shot backward across the Atlantic into the Clay Pounds. Broke them up with a blow from her counter, scarred them, cracked them; all in strips they are, grooved by her stern timbers.

Saturday night at six o'clock Obed shook hands with Asey, and he handed over his old woman's recipe for quahog fritters, due-money on the bet. Asey ate fritters on Sunday morning — bad ballast amidships — and that night he gave orders to scuttle the *Flying Spouse*.

The Sea Serpent From the quiet waters of Herring Cove emerged *of Provincetown* the serpent of Provincetown, disturbed from prehistoric dreams by an earthquake in the sea. She spouted a jet fifty feet in the air before she appeared above water, and the town crier hid in a plumberry bush as out of the cove she came.

Up rose her head; as large it looked "as a two hundred gallon cask," convex on the upper side and concave on the under. Up rose her body, twelve feet thick, with scales like the head of a fish barrel, colored "green, red and blue." She opened her mouth in a wide smile, disclosing four rows of ivory teeth. Her six eyes on "moveable projections" protruded three feet from her head, and she looked "before, behind and sidewise," all at the same time. Three of her eyes were a shining green; three were ominous red. The town crier forgot to remember how these colors were placed, whether to port and starboard of her, or whether crisscross, landlubberly.

The sea serpent of Provincetown rose out of Herring Cove. She undulated over the dunes, keeping her head thirty feet in the air. Her V-shaped tail dragged after her, the base of it studded with bony scales "shaped like the teeth of a mowing machine." Underbrush and tough scrub pines were cut off by it neatly; the stubs had a burned, sulphurous look as if seared by a hot iron.

The serpent entered Pasture Pond, and when she reached the center, she dived headfirst like a duck. As the tip of her tail went under, water began to recede from the shore. Lower and lower sank the waterline, until a deep hole was disclosed in the pond center. Sounding leads were lowered down the hole, two or three hundred fathoms. No bottom was found.

I, George Washington Ready, do testify that the foregoing statement is correct. It is a true description of the serpent as she appeared to me on that morning, and I was not unduly excited by liquor or otherwise.
(signed) George W. Ready
[Town Crier]

The Lyars'   Old Hutta Dyer, "Prince of Yarners," stretched out his
Bench   legs, thrust his cob through his whiskers and made
himself comfortable on the Lyars' Bench that overlooked the sea.
There he sat through the long summer "noonings," his gray eyes
somnolent, his expression mild, mournful; but let a cat so much as
spread its tail or a ship lift her maintruck over the horizon, and Hut
Dyer saw that cat, shivered and "smelt trouble"; saw that sail and by
some process outside of human deduction "reco'nised 'ship." His constitution needed a "deal o' rest." This he obtained, as he fished the
Backside, by half-hitching his line around his big toe. When he felt a
nibble he waked a "leetle," hauled line and brought up a bluefish.

Once a squidhound bass bit the hook and ran to sea with the line
in his stomach and Hut Dyer in tow. That was a ride. Hut moved
fast, almost as fast as the squidhound bass. Soon Hut's toe began to
hurt him, so he folded himself together, got a handhold on the line
and began hauling in. By and by he and the bass met face to face.
They were a long way from home, so Hut talked fast and friendly,
and promised to let bygones be bygones if the bass would tow him
to shore. The squidhound was no shark, only a "leetle" playful. He
towed Hut to the beach again, and Hut held nothing against him;
for he baked him and ate him, just like a bluefish with pickle and
Dennis salt.

Hut Dyer was as kind as that to almost any animal. Shearjashub
and Bathsheba, his oxen (named after the Bourne family because
they were all slow and stubborn), had bogwater dispositions, neither
of them cheerful; and when the two swayed together, swinging their
heads, slow and mournful, and Hut up aloft swinging his head to be
"soci'ble," the sight would make a Nantucket whaleman weep. Only
three things ever make a Nantucketer woeful. One is when a Cape
man brings home the ambergris; one is when an Island girl marries a
"cod-faced peninsula-man"; the third is when the Nantucketer meets
Hut Dyer swaying his head in rhythm with his oxen, all three of them
rolling along like a three-ply junk on the China Sea. The Nantucket
whaleman seeing a sight like that lays down his head on the tattoo
of his mother and weeps like a broken comber.

Hut Dyer never discouraged Shear and Sheba, his oxen. One day he
hitched them with traces made of new rawhide and drove them into

the back lot to gather winter wood. When he started for home, the load was so heavy that it stuck while the traces stretched. Longer and longer they grew as the oxen plodded ahead. Hut never mentioned the matter to Shear and Sheba lest they feel disheartened, and the "beasts-o-burden" ambled peacefully into Hut's barn. By that time the graces were thin as ribbons and the load was still up in the back lot. Old Hut told the oxen not to worry, just to wait for the Lord; and that night Hut left the barn door open. The weather turned cold; the traces shrank; and when he went out in the morning, there was his load of wood come down from the back lot in the night and standing inside his barn.

Hut Dyer owned a handsome weathervane but was too kindhearted to oil it; afraid he might fall off the roof, injure himself and be an expense on the town. He made a slingshot out of green rawhide and a forked ash bough. When the vane needed a "leetle" reminder that the wind was shifting, Hut took a pebble and slingshot the vane till it pointed in the way that the wind blew. This Hut found out by wetting his finger. Sometimes it took him two hours or more, knocking that vane with pebbles, but he never "give up" till it pointed dead true, "the airy-most vane in Truro."

"One fer the   "One fer the Arkyologists," said Captain John Flan-
Arkyologists"   ders of Sippican as he told the yarn of the last Cape whaler. You cannot find any more Cape whalers. Neither can you find Sippican.

"Durin the blockade before the War [1812] the brig *Nautilus* come home from a viage. I don't know nothin bout the trip nor how she dodged the men-o-war that was standin off-and-on, but I heered the story from my grandther and I know that the brig was full of ile. Prime sparm, right through, and nary a drop scorched in the tryin-out. But business was shot to pieces, so the owners jest laid the brig up. Longside their dock she lay, and they run out chains to the wooden bollards, sent down her upper masts, unslung the spars and stowed everythin away in the riggin-loft. In time, the bollards chafed; so they set stone posts down in the fillin of the pier which was dirt and stone, built like most Cape piers, with only the chafin-spiles of wood.

"The war was fought and won. Then some whalers, fitted out,

were sent to sea again. But the owners of the *Nautilus* had died and the wrangle over their leavins kep the brig tied up for years. When the tangle fin'lly got straight, the only livin heirs was two-three fellers that had gone out West and couldn't be located nohow. So the court appointed a feller to keep tract of the prop'ty and make expenses if he could. A kind of a white-livered feller he was, from inshore. He didn't even know that a whaler was layin alongside.

"When a vessel idles fer a long time, she begins to go back. Bein mostly of a veg'table nater, she goes veget'ble agen; fer no kind of veg'tation ever loses all the life that's in it, no matter what. So the seagrass grew fathoms long on the old brig's bottom; and the deck seams opened up; and dust blew in and, fust thing you knew, grass sprouted from the seams and stood up a couple of feet high on deck and on top of the deckhouses. More dust and sand blew in, betwixt the brig and the dock; and fin'lly all the space filled in until it was solid earth. The dock grew over with grass too, till the moorin chains were buried deep in sward. All this took gen'rations, unnerstand, and by that time the brig was so covered with green growin things that nobody would have guessed that she was a whaler. Nobody was left to remember her when she was in commission.

"Now the masts, made out of Norway pine, standin in the mixture of bilge-water and ile began to sprout. What with all the changes they had seen and the sort of stuff they was soakin in, they grew a soft, smooth bark, and limbs put out nearly the whole ship's length. Aside from bein unusual straight, they looked like any tree.

"I dunno how long she laid there, but the whalin business died away cept for a few craft sailin from New Bedford, and those that went into the Arctic from West Coast ports. Out in Pennsylvanie some fellers struck min'ral ile and the story got afloat that ile might be found anywheres, if the soil and bottom was right. A lot of smart-alecks went around with hand-drills lookin fer deposits in every beach hummock and sheep pasture; so nobody paid any attention when a feller showed up at Sippican and begun to bore around the old whale-dock. Nobody watched him as he sunk little holes, and fin'lly he walked out onto the cur'ous little point of land with the two straight trees in the middle of it. He begun to bore there. When he hauled up that drill from bout fifteen-sixteen feet down, looked at it and smelt it, he let out a yell you could hear on Nantucket. 'Ile!'

he yelled. 'Ile, by Judas!' He had drilled right into the old cargo and didn't know the diff'ence between whale ile and ker'sene.

"Waal, he located and secured his claim, set up a watchman, and ordered ile riggin. It come, all manner of heavy gear that was stacked up on the wharf. Some parts was late showin up so the feller couldn't set up his riggin fer a space. A good thing, too, fer heres what happened!

"Twas September, ruther late, and we got the Line Gale. It breezed out of the nothe-east and kep risin til a hurricaine was blowin. The sea made up higher than ary man has ever seen it round this place; and bime-by there rolled up a reg'ler tidal wave that come rolling in, past the island, gittin higher and higher, curlin, featherin, risin, so high that it shut off the wind from the folks that watched it from the shore. It hit the old whale dock, and went clean over it.

"A little mite of life was left in the old brig yet. When she felt that comber, she riz, and she riz until her old chains parted. And when that sea run back agen, she went along with it, the most cur'ous lookin craft that ever sailed the ocean.

"Jest like a little floatin island, she was all covered with grass and nettles, with two straight trees amidships, full of green leaves and loaded down with ripe, yellow apricots. I fergot to menshun that apricots is what the masts fin'lly bore on em. So she went pitchin and rollin across-bay, shakin showers of leaves out of the branches, and heavin them apricots to port and starboard.

"If a man could have got an anchor over and saved her, she would have been worth a fortune to the Arkyologists. But all hands were too upsot. Besides, the sea was so bad that they couldn't have done it nohow.

"Slowly she drifted out with the swell, sagged back and forth in the wind, and fin'lly come down with a thump on the ledge, where she jest fell apart like a rotten punkin. Tussocks of sward, broken timbers, ile casks floated in all directions. Folks picked em up."

How to Tack a   Up among the hills to the northward of Punkhorn,
Square-Rigger   there is a place called "The Wilderness." Old-timers shiver at the mention of it, for "back in Seventeen Hundred, sometime," says Captain Enoch Appleby, "a feller rigged up a set of sema-

phore signals on that hill. He had others, here and there, within sight of each another, and by this means Marthas Vineyard, Nantucket, and Cape Cod was all geared up to Boston. Ships comin in from sea could be reported at Nantucket or the Vineyard, and the news signalled acrost to the Cape and so-on along the line, till the Boston owners knew all about it, days before the ships got in. Twas a grand invention, no mistake, and saved time and money.

"A big, tall pole was set up with two arms on it that could be raised and lowered with ropes and tackles. One arm up and one down, meant 'ship.' Both arms up meant 'brig.' And so-on, with signals for letters so's they could spell out words.

"In them days, as all hands know, the Cape was the breedin-place of sailors. A boy that didn't show int'rest in sea-farin waant regarded as a citizen in the makin; and when some old capt'n had a son er grandson who didn't take to ships and shippin real handy, it would pretty nigh drive the old cuss crazy. He'd do almost anything to inspire the boy with a desire to git to sea.

"Now Capt'n John Dias, who had sailed master of almost everything under sail, had a grandson, risin a dozen year old, who didn't skursely know that a boat was holler. The old man talked to him by the hour, tryin to larn him the things he'd ought to larn; but it seemed nothin soaked into that boy's head. Each lesson left the old man more ragged than ever.

"Over to the woodlot, one day in early winter, they two was choppin wood; and the old man tried to tell the boy how to tack a square-rigger. Twaant no use at all. Lookin up, Capt'n Dias noticed the ship-signal up on the hill. Twas one of the days when it waant in use. 'Come here, you!' sezze, 'I'll show you how tis done!'

"So up the hill they went. The old man cleared away the falls and halliards. 'Now then,' sezze, 'here's the way you do it. When the mate sings out: *Leggo yore lee braces!* you cast off here and let her run. When he says: *Down with your fore-tack!* you haul up here; and when he says: *Leggo and haul!* then, by Godfrey, you cast off both sides, slack away on one, haul the other, and do it lively! Unnerstand?'

"Now while the old man had been doin all this, he had been workin them telegraph arms up, down, sideways, like a streak-o-litenin. He never give it a thought, neither; and when he thought the boy had got the lesson haaf-way larnt, he went back to his wood-choppin. One er two parts of the process waant quite clear to the boy.

"Twas towards night that the folks alongshore noticed boats a-comin from the Islands, comin fast; chock full of men, they was. All hands landed; and most of the male popullation from the Vineyard and Nantucket was there. 'Where's the fightin?' they wanted to know.

" 'Fightin? We haint heerd about fightin!'

" 'You mean to tell that war haint broke loose agen? That the British and Injuns haint burnin and slayin?'

" 'Nary a burn ner a slayin', furs we know.'

"Bout that time a bunch on hoss-back come ridin up from inshore. Loaded down with guns like the Islanders, they asked the same questions.

" 'What ails you fellers, anyhow?' demanded the Cape folks. 'What do you mean by showin up ready fer war?'

" 'The ship's telegraph!' they all yelled. 'It said that war had broke loose, that Wareham was burnt flat, that British men-o-war was in the bay, shellin everything from Cape Ann southerds, with Injuns scalpin all hands. Where's that war? that's what we waant ter know!'

"There waant much that they could do to an old man and a boy; but those Islanders were certainly sore agin the ship's telegraph. They marched up the hill, and hauled the pole up by the roots, singin out: 'War, eh? War, be blowed!' They smashed that pole to kindlin-wood, singin out: 'Injuns in Wareham!'

"Then they got madder and madder. They knocked down trees, as big as barrels, whole gangs tacklin one tree and haulin it down. 'Injuns!' they yelled. Down come a hemlock. 'Men-o-war!' they bellowed. Up flew an oak. Waal, they kep this up till every man dropped from exhaustion, and then the fury of their anger sort of run down. There waant no more telegraph, ner woods, ner even a hill left; jest a trampled place, several acres over, the ground all dug into pits, and covered with busted trees. From that time on thar waant no more telegraph, and when electric'ty come along the Island folks kicked about bein hooked to the Cape agen. Long ago most Island folks was related to Cape folks by marriage, but not a dozen tie-ups has occurred in the centuries since that telegraph; and every time boats from the Cape and the Islands meet on the grounds fer fishin, the Islanders yell: 'War's declared! Haul yore wind!' Matters haint none too friendly."

The Saucer-   Whiskery as a "porkypine," tanned to the color of an
Back Halibut   old leather boot, Jereboam Thacher of Provincetown,
longshore fisherman, looked old enough to have fished in the flood.
One leg, missing from the knee joint, was pieced out with the loom of
an oar.

"How did I lose my leg?" asked he. "It's a tale that would turn your
hair gray. I don't often tell about it, for folks won't believe me. Haint
nobody left these days that kin remember what the fishin was like when
I was a young feller. But I'm tellin you life was different when a man
could walk alongshore with a pitchfork and load up an oxcart with
squiteague, and when the cod schooled right in to the rocks and laid
there for days. In them times the lobsters used to crawl in on the
marshes and bed down for the winter as soon as the weather cooled up,
and men dug em out by the bushel along in Januwary — Febuwary.

"Twas a halibut took my leg off, although the critter didn't mean no
harm. Used to be a lot of em around inshore in them days, big fellers,
shaped like a sole or a flounder, broad, with both eyes on one side of
their heads; spotted light and dark brown on the back and dead white
underneath. Only place they git em now is well offshore, but in them
days they used to run right in to the beach. And they run from twenty-
five pound weight up to, waal, no man ever knew how big the biggest
one was. They get em now that run to three-four hundred pound.

"There was bigger ones than that when I was young.

"A halibut is a bottom fish, but there's times when they come up.
They'll skitter acrost-water, jump out clean, and then there's times
when they'll lay almost awash, with their sides and fins curled up like
a saucer. Jest lay there. What for? The Lord only knows.

"Waal, this day, I had run off-shore into the bay, haulin lobster-pots,
doin a little hand-linin and managin to git a hundred er two pounds
of lobsters and bout as many fish. I was runnin right along under sail
in my smack-boat, makin good time before a light southerly that was
blowin, and glad of it, too, because the fog was makin. I must have
been three mile from land when all to oncst I fetched up solid. Pretty
nigh capsized. Figgered 'twas a piece of driftin wreck, and I went for-
rad to shove clear and look for damage, but it waant a wreck at all. It
looked like bottom, but no bottom that I ever seen before. Besides,
there was forty foot of water there.

"I got clear, put her on the other tack and stood off, wonderin about it. I run on for mebbe twenty minutes, then tacked inshore and bingo! I was aground agen! Bout six times I hit before I fin'lly tuk in that there was somethin between me and home. What it was I couldn't tell, but it was there. And then, jest as I was pushin off the last time, I noticed a flurry some fathoms ahead of me, and I see somethin big break water, a oval brown thing that opened and shet. It was a head, but, Godfreys, what a head! I could see two eyes, twice the length of a whaleboat oar apart. Lookin around they was.

"Bimeby I reelized what the eyes belonged to. A halibut! Layin awash. And I had been sailin acrost his saucer-back for nigh on an hour!

"Things didn't look too good to me, but I waant real worried. How to git clear, that was the question. Fin'lly I figgered that I'd run on to his fin agen, climb out, stand on it, and hang onto my boat, which might be lightened enough to ride over. I trimmed aft my sheet and headed for where I knew his side laid. I miscalkerlated some, and hit it before expected, hit it hardish, too. Then I passed the slack of my halliards round me, and jumped over the bow. Something hit my knee, and I never felt sech pain before. I crawled over the gunnel, more dead than alive, saw that my leg was bleedin bad, and wound a line tight around it. Then I took an oar, and dizzy with pain, I tried to shove the boat over. As she moved ahead, and went clear, I saw what had done the damage:

"I had struck that fish solid and started up a couple of scales. There they laid, four foot acrost, standin half on edge, sharp as a meat-axe, hard as flint. I had stumbled onto the edge of one, and later, when some of the bunch picked me up, they found that my leg was so nigh cut off that they had to finish the job."

"We Old Men"   Back in the seventeen hundreds lived two ancient sailor-men, Jack Taffril who sailed on the *Mary Ann,* Tom Staysil who sailed on the *Nancy.* Whenever they made the home port, the old salts met in Sandwich Tavern, and after a round or two of rum they swapped the "logs" of their voyages. Whatever the waves or the whales or the mate had done to Jack Taffril, the waves and the whales and the "murderish mate" had done Tom Staysil one better.

Once Jack came home from sea and told how porpoises followed ship till a sailor spilled a pail of red paint over the side. All the porpoises ate that paint. All of them turned red.

But that same voyage Tom Staysil, given a bottle of rum by the mate and suspicioning that it was poison, poured the firewater over the taffrail. A shark alongside opened his mouth and received a dose of grog. Was that shark happy? Was that shark faithful? It followed the *Nancy* around the Horn, and west to the island of Tahiti.

Now at Tahiti sailors go ashore "to git their eddication," and when Tom no longer appeared, leaning over the ship's rail to pour out a share of his rum, the faithful shark "took to worritin'." Likewise the shark grew thirsty, so he slowly cruised around the shoreline looking for his old friend, Tom. By and by he found him, sitting on a sea cliff singing tunes to a Yoo-hoo Lady decked out in floral ornaments and playing on a twang-stringer. The shark stuck his snout over the cliff, opened his mouth, and bared his teeth like a long white row of tombstones.

Tom picked the twang-stringer off the Yoo-hoo and cast it down the shark's throat, where it sunk athwartships and stuck in the gullet. Every time the shark swallowed, his palate swept across the cords of that Yoo-hoo love fiddle. Thereafter the faithful shark made music wherever he went.

On the next voyage, Jack Taffril was capsized from a stove-in boat. He landed on a whale's back and held to the driven harpoon. With perilous speed he rode the whale, above seas and below seas, till the great mammal bled, weakened, drifted. No. 2 boat rescued Jack.

That was the year in which Tom Staysil took an oar in a whaleboat out to strike a killer! The plunging brute came under the keel and smashed the boat to driftwood. Tom, still clinging to an oar, was taken between gaping jaws; swallowed by the whale. Once inside, Tom struck his flint, looked around and thought about Jonah. He tickled the ribs of the killer for a time but the whale would not cough up. Then Tom drew out his knife and thrust it in the killer's heart. Two hours later, while the pious seaman was reading his pocket Bible by whale oil taper, the mammal sighed, floated on the ocean, and Tom climbed aloft.

He peered out through a picket fence of white whale's teeth. A full gale beat the waves skyward. Icebergs clung to the killer's whiskers. Glaciers floated on the sea. Tom went below where the weather was warmer, cut a hole in the stern of the whale, stuck his oar through;

then he sculled and he sculled, till he sculled that killer to Fairhaven.

A year later Jack Taffril was captured by the cannibals. Stripped, trussed, ready for the kettle, he decided to die like a Christian. He raised his voice in a psalm:

> "And I shall be like to ye tree
>   Implanted by ye rivers,
> That in my season yield my fruits
>   Unlike ye leaf that withers."

Jack sang valiantly. The cannibals rejoiced. They appeased their hunger with missionary men, and the chief kept Jack beside him to sing during council meetings. Jack married a cannibal lady and lived like a king till the captain of the *Mary Ann*, needing an able seaman, paid for him with ransom.

Tom Staysil likewise was captured, off the African coast. The head cook felt him all over, then decided not to boil him. They called him Very Tough Meat.

Very Tough Meat became a slave and was driven by a lash to work all day for the chief's nine wives. Living inland from the coast, he despaired of ever seeing Sandwich again, but decided to die like a hero. So, to restore his dolorous spirits, he lifted his voice in song. All nine wives came out of the mud hut, and listened to him gravely. Then they summoned the chief. The chief summoned the council; the council summoned the tribe. Soon the whole village stood listening to Tom Staysil's song.

Before he had finished, the chief placed a firm hand on his shoulder. Holding a whip in the other hand, he directed the singer to the coast. As Very Tough Meat departed, the Africans gave him a rousing cheer. And not only did the great chief lead him to the waterfront, he even insisted on signaling a vessel and placing Tom aboard. So careful was he of Tom's voice that if the appreciative seaman so much as opened his mouth, the chief struck it with a thong.

At this point in the tavern log, Jack and Tom sang the psalms that saved them from slavery or death in a boiling kettle. But mine host of the tavern dealt with them as the chief had dealt with Tom. He led them firmly out of the taproom, starting them toward Fairhaven. Hand in hand, singing sweet songs, they journeyed down the highroad.

Now back in the eighteen hundreds lived two ancient wreckers, and their names, as you have heard before, were Eleazar and Eliakim, and they knew all the lost stories about Jack Taffril and Tom Staysil, as many yarns as there were sailors putting in to port. But bitter words raged between the wreckers, for Eleazar claimed that Eliakim had lost his sea wits and that the yarns that he told about Jack Taffril rightfully belonged to Tom. Whereas Eliakim claimed that Eleazar had soured his brains "till they come to a curdle," and that all the yarns that he told about Tom belonged by rights to Jack.

The line that was pegged through the tent on the sands where the two old men "bided," became a sort of no-man's-land across which battle thundered. Yet as dusk gentled the barren dune country, Eliakim lighted a tallow and drew from an ancient sea chest a tattered pamphlet rescued from a ship, a "snack" of salvage that he would not trade for a boat or a Spanish pearl. In his slow drawl he read the words: "Great Frost of January, 1608"; then, running his horny finger down-page, he stopped at a worn passage:

> We old men are old chronicles, and when our tongues go they are not clocks to tell only the time present, but large books unclasped; and our speeches, like leaves turned over and over, discover wonders that are long since past.

"TRUE TALES"

"The earth is sinking under us; the sea is rising over us. Captain Isaac is bringing a new ram's horn back from Boston town."

Thrusting his staff in front of him to test the vanishing crust of the earth, Nathaniel Coleman, simple boy, felt his way down South Road, doffing his hat with its colored feathers to "em'nant sperrits takin' the air." What was deepwater truth to him was not truth to Captain Isaac Bacon, at that moment racing his packet, the *Somerset,* to Boston, passing the *Polly* off the Castle, and the *Nancy* still in the Roads. A rat gnawed a hole through the planking on the starboard side of the packet; the side under water "on the Boston tack." The *Somerset* filled so fast that the pumps failed to free her. Captain Isaac swiftly jibed, swinging both fore and main booms to port, heeling her over and bringing the hole above the waterline. Then he made a plug, let himself down over the side and drove the plug into the rat hole. Heading again for Boston, his caulking proved successful. He defeated the *Polly* and the *Nancy*, racing to "beat the Boston market" with early onions bunched in green bulrushes.

Purchasers for the West Indian trade objected to this bunching. "Gentlemen," affirmed Captain Isaac, "these be 'Tarnity Onions. They keep to all etarnity." But one week later the West Indian buyers were forced to throw them over the side.

Home to Barnstable sailed the *Somerset*, unfailingly bringing a trinket to simple Nat who waved his staff with a ram's horn topping it, and felt his way protestingly over the receding earth.

Longshore "codderies," such as those of Captain Isaac (who would skin a toad for its "sparm ile"); witless chants of simple folk, such as those of Nathaniel Coleman; or great adventures — shipwrecks, massacres, mutinies, plagues, piracies — whether the tales are ocean sagas or old fishermen's "dildrams," there are as many "true yarns of the sea" as there have been men on the Cape.

Three tales, widely known, are repeated year after year, three tales that to Cape minds verify the recurrent adage about truth that is stranger than fiction. One is a story of murder, one is a story of war, the third is a seaman's audacious prank that set the nation smiling. Sometimes tersely narrated, "shipshape, Bristol fashion," sometimes at a snail's gallop; all too often they lost the charm of the old hearthtellings when the poverty kettle sang up the crane, and the tea was seasoned with Methody cream (liquor), and the cat thrummed by the fire.

The Trial of   Ansell Nickerson slung himself over the stern of the
Ansell Nickerson   *Abigail* and "held with his Hands by the Taffarill, with his Feet on the Moulding under the Cabin Windows." His cousin, Thomas, master of the schooner; his cousin, Sparrow, the mate; Elisha Newcomb who had married the sister of the captain, and William Kent, ship's boy, remained upon the deck. But Ansell concealed himself. He did not like the look of four boats filled with armed men, a boarding party putting out in the night from a topsail schooner and heading for the *Abigail*. They were, he suspected, king's men come to impress sailors. Cousins Sparrow and Elisha might be ready to accept impressment,

but Ansell, a "New Country Whig with rebell notions," had no desire to undergo enforced service to the Crown.

Four boats illumined by sea lanterns drew alongside the schooner, and after a colloquy, men boarded the *Abigail*. Cut off from any clear knowledge of what might be taking place on the deck, Ansell heard cries, sounds of a scuffle, three distinct splashes in the water; then a cheer and a noise like a barrel rolling along the boards. A few moments later someone shouted a toast.

The hidden sailor winced. The only barrel of rum on board was a cask of fine Jamaica, purchased by him from his yearly wage, when the crew of the *Abigail* received three years' pay in Boston, just before they set sail for Chatham. Was Cousin Thomas permitting "Crowners" to regale themselves with his "prime Jamackie," his one, small "comershal adventure?" Perhaps Sparrow and Elisha, the two men most likely to be impressed, thought the opening of his cask fair punishment for "skulking." Ansell started to climb to the deck to remonstrate, then bethought himself in time. Having lost his barrel of rum, why lose his liberty? He readjusted his hold on the taffrail, but his footing continued insecure. Chill mid-November wind sucked through his sea jacket; his hands felt stiff and raw. He wondered how long he might be forced to maintain this precarious position, while his cousins, who at least had not betrayed him, feasted on his liquor.

As sounds of revelry increased, a disquieting suspicion assailed him. If the boarding party were not king's men, they might be "privateers of the bloodie flagg." Then, sooner or later, they would find him. Reassuring himself, he smiled at such womanish fancies. No pirates lurked in North Atlantic waters in the civilized year, 1772. His wits were as dazed as a duck in thunder!

A murmur of voices became audible as men descended into the cabin. Ansell listened for Cape talk, for Cousin Thomas Nickerson's "nor-west booming," for William's shrill treble. He overheard an unfamiliar voice suggesting that the *Abigail* be burned. Another speaker urged hasty departure, a plea loudly seconded. Shortly thereafter, the voices died away; the cabin door closed.

Four lighted boats pulled clear of the *Abigail*, and headed toward the topsail schooner. The rhythmic dipping of their oars intermingled with the thud and slap of waves against the hull. Complete silence on the deck suggested that no prize crew manned the Chatham craft, and Ansell wondered why his cousins failed to summon him from hiding. Slowly, cautiously, he hauled himself up by the taffrail and saw, with the first pale light of dawn, fresh stains of blood on the boards, and a disordered deck that gave mute evidence of a battle that had raged across it. Dully he noted that his barrel of rum had been opened and almost emptied. He called aloud the names of his cousins as he hurried into the cabin. No response was audible. With increasing excitement he searched from bow to stern. No other living being remained aboard the schooner, *Abigail*. The bleeding bodies of captain and crew apparently had been thrown overboard, and the vessel, her canvas filling, drove steadily through a pale sea, as if conscious of her destination.

Ansell, who had never attempted to study navigation, also understood little of the control of sails. Outward bound from Boston, he was aware that Captain Nickerson had expected to make Chatham in the afternoon; but the entire coast was so dotted with reefs and bars that the Chatham sailor abandoned hope of taking the craft into her home port. He set the wheel, went below, found distress signals and mounted them to the best of his remembrance. Then he stood staring at the fringed horizons of day.

Captain Joseph Doane of Chatham, Boston bound, discerned a schooner, her course wayward, her distress signals incorrectly mounted. The captain drew abreast. He recognized a home port vessel and saw one man rise from the deck to wave in frantic excitement. At once Doane put off in a boat, reassured Ansell, inspected the decks and the broken money chests and conveyed the *Abigail* to Chatham where the schooner's one surviving seaman was required to repeat his story over and over: first to the leading townsmen; later to the sheriff; then to the mothers of William Kent and of Thomas and Sparrow Nickerson; finally to Elisha Newcomb's young wife, sister of the captain and mate. In this one disaster she had lost her husband and her two brothers, and she sat all day in the greatroom, mending Elisha's sea jacket, and nodding, murmuring. The women whispered that she stayed too long in the mourning trance, that her wits would never return.

Ansell also narrated his adventure to Squire Bacon of Barnstable who forwarded an account of it to Province House in Boston. Terror invaded New England ports. Seamen required strong liquid stimulus before they put out to sea. Were pirates in northern waters? Were king's men murdering colonists? The governor summoned Admiral Montague who reported that all Boston craft had been "snugged down" for the winter; but the *Lively,* frigate, was immediately fitted for sea, and put out twenty-four hours after word had reached Montague of the tragic murders off Chatham. Posts, express, to the governor of Rhode Island brought forth His Majesty's ships from Newport. For weeks government frigates combed the sea, searching for a topsail schooner, while authorities in every port and every "cove for watering" maintained a vigilant watch.

No trace appeared of a vessel answering young Nickerson's description. No news of further depredations or of forced impressment reached Province House; so the governor issued instructions that Ansell Nickerson of Cape Cod be brought under guard to Boston. There he was examined by the chief magistrate, by Admiral Montague, by the lieutenant governor, by the secretary commissioners. Highnoon, Sunday, November 22, 1772, suspected of murdering three of his relatives and possibly the ship's boy as well, he was committed to Boston jail "in order for his Trial."

Bitter political issues centered about his guilt or innocence. Tories swore that he had perpetrated a horrible, inhuman crime, and that rebel Whigs were attempting to hang the suspicion of it around the necks of His Majesty's seamen, so alienating wavering Tory sentiment in America and fanning to a white heat Whig hatred of the Crown.

A tragic, innocent figure, declared the ardent Whigs, describing Ansell as another victim of King George's methods for subjugating his colonists. If the accused were condemned to die by a pack of "Tory Admiral's Men" (Admiralty Court), the shame and stigma of such a false trial would rest forever at the doors of freeborn Americans. Other brave sailors and merchantmen might be slain by dastardly, armed cowards, decked out in "gilt coats" and murdering their countrymen.

Ansell petitioned that his trial be delayed, he to remain "confin'd in Gaol" while harbors and shipping records were searched for evidences of piratical craft. Meanwhile anti-Tories fixed on the crew of His Majesty's schooner, *Halifax,* commanded by Lieutenant Crespin, as perpetrator of the crime. A stiff denial appeared in the *News Letter*:

If you think it will afford any Satisfaction to the good People of the
Province, you will be pleased to insert, in your next Paper from un-
doubted authority, that the Admiral received Dispatches from the said
Lieut. Crespin, Commander of said Schooner, dated from House and
Peck Island in Casco-Bay the 29th ult. all well.

For nearly eight months Ansell remained in Boston jail, but during
that time no pirates appeared on the Atlantic seaboard. Wednesday,
July 28, 1773, the prisoner was brought to trial. The examination of
witnesses for the Crown lasted from Wednesday until Friday. Then
Samuel Fitch, Advocate General, "applied the Evidences on the
Crown Side and closed the case for the king.

Two young advocates, Whigs of promising caliber, John Adams and
Josiah Quincy, Jr., advanced to the bar, to present the cause of the prisoner. They had very little evidence to offer other than character witnesses and the direct testimony of the accused; but their wit and wisdom
stirred the court and they conducted their case with dramatic speed.
They opened it Wednesday morning, closed the defense Thursday
afternoon. The court gave the prisoner a chance to "express any
further Evidence that he might wish to Offer." Ansell regretted the
absense of certain witnesses, then spoke briefly in his own defense. "If
I lose my life," he concluded, "I am innocent of the Crime laid to my
Charge."

The courtroom was cleared. For two hours and a half eight admiralty judges debated. At the conclusion of the debate the prisoner
was recalled. The president spoke, after a pause, addressing Ansell
directly:

The Court have considered of your Case, and they do not think that
the Evidence offered . . . is sufficient to support the Charge alledged
against you in the Information and therefore adjudge you NOT
GUILTY.

"Thus ended a Trial," declared the *Boston News Letter*, "for the
most surprising Event which has happened in this, and perhaps any
other Age of the World." Four of the judges "were for Acquittal, and
four for Condemnation."

As to what actually occurred on the *Abigail* no man has ever been
sure. Somewhat later, John Adams, who pleaded Ansell's innocency,

wrote in his diary: "This was and remains still a mysterious transaction. I know not to this day what judgement to form of his Guilt or innocence."

Jolly Dick Rag-
gett Loses a Prize   This is the story of how Hoppy Mayo ringed the noses of the king's Jack Tars while the British were rocking their barnacle cradles in Cape Cod Bay. Jolly Dick Raggett led the king's fleet, a man who had fought in all seven oceans and had no heart for shelling villages where girls were pretty, rum was hot, and men followed the sea. Dick Raggett was born in Cornwall, like many a Cape Cod man, and but for the muddling of his wits in a college would have fought on the side of freedom.

Hoppy Mayo and Winslow Knowles, captured with their whaleboat while running the blockade between Eastham and Boston, were ushered into Jolly Dick's quarters on board the ship-o'-the-line, *Spencer,* manned by three hundred Liverpool "no-nauts" with queues down their necks and buttons to their chins and several letters left out of the alphabet because their brains had not the power to master *H* or *G*.

"One of the prisoners," said Captain Raggett, "will be sent on shore to raise a ransom." Then he added, "What cargo was taken aboard the whaleboat?"

Now Hoppy Mayo and Winslow Knowles, two deepwater captains who had been waiting for President Madison to give them a catboat with which to sink the *Spencer,* had been "recreatin'" by running a whaleboat, cargoing odds and ends, around the Bay to Boston. The odds and ends, on the day of their capture, were two barrels of rum.

"Where is this rum?" inquired Dick Raggett.

"On board the prize schooner, Sir," answered his lieutenant — Fotheringay was the name. Just like his name he was; and to get rid of him, Jolly Dick had put him in charge of a prize schooner, a Marblehead fishing craft captured in the Bay. In this vessel Fotheringay went hunting whaleboats, and one morning sighted a blockade runner edging along the coast. He fired the brass cannon mounted on the schooner's deck. With his two prisoners put aboard, he raced back to Provincetown, as proud of his capture as if he had sunk Mr. Madison's navy which was about as popular on the Cape as Mr. Madison's war [1812].

Winslow Knowles, sent back to Eastham, summoned a meeting of the Committee on Safety and broke the news that Hoppy Mayo was about

to be incarcerated in Dartmoor Prison, England, unless gold was forthcoming to pay a ransom to the British.

The chief sources of Cape revenue had been tied up for months. Shipping rotted at the docks; crops had proved a failure; and the Committee
on Safety sent back word that time was necessary for the raising of
money.

On board the *Spencer* Jolly Dick Raggett, with a practiced seaman's
respect for the walking sandbars of the Cape, began to swap yarns of
them with Hoppy Mayo, and always Hoppy's stories ended with some
account of his successful mastery of offshore channels and shoals. A ship
might approach within shelling distance of any Cape town, he averred,
if the pilot knew the right tides and "deeps."

Jolly Dick, whose craft had been floating like useless corks in Provincetown Harbor, his guns unable to reach Sandwich, Barnstable,
Eastham, or any of the defiant villages, decided to induce Hoppy to
guide the prize schooner through the channels. No valuable vessel
could be sent on such an errand; for Hoppy, although he accepted the
bribe, might prove a false pilot, and Jolly Dick, though a trusting soul,
was not an off-Cape fool.

He and Hoppy fancied each other, thick as thieves and about as trustworthy. Each thought the other well baited, and as Hoppy drank Jolly
Dick under the table, his blue eyes smiled.

The next day the prize schooner, still loaded with two casks of rum
taken from the whaleboat, pulled clear of Provincetown Harbor.
Hoppy, for a sum of gold, had agreed to pilot her, bringing Lieutenant
Fotheringay, twenty-three British seamen, three brass cannons and
twenty-three rifles within shelling distance of his native town.

While the vessel put off up the Bay, Hoppy introduced the "bosun"
to the hogsheads of Jamaica rum originally his own property but now a
prize capture. The finest rum, Hoppy declared, that had ever been
served in Snow's Tavern, Boston! The "bosun" yearned to sample it
and went to find his bunkmate who was adept at broaching a cask in a
way that left no outer traces. Six men returned with the "bosun" and
pronounced the liquor unexcelled. Four of them went back for their
bunkies and reappeared, a few minutes later, with all of the men off
duty.

Hoppy raised his pannikin to toast the English king. Cornish sailors,
he maintained, should never be fighting peninsula men who had no

use for Madison's war and whose hearts were always friendly. While amiability was at its height, he even offered to carry to the deck three noggins of rum as a treat for the men on watch. As he departed he firmly fastened down the hatches.

Swiftly making his way to the captain's cabin, he crept in where fire-arms were stacked and dropped the twenty-three rifles that he found there into the Bay. Then, quietly, he armed himself with a pair of the captain's brass mounted pistols, made his way aft, overpowered the unsuspecting helmsman and reset the schooner's course.

Less than twenty minutes later the vessel grounded heavily. Lieu-tenant Fotheringay hurried on deck and was stopped by two brass mounted pistols held by a menacing stranger. A stern voice com-manded the Britisher to raise his hands over his head.

Neatly Hoppy disarmed the lieutenant and tied him to the rail. The second officer, coming to the rescue, was also disarmed and bound, while pandemonium broke loose in the hold as the shut-in seamen dis-covered their predicament and tried to force the hatches.

Obed Knowles of Eastham, strolling along his Bayside meadow, in-spected the water with a spyglass and discerned a Marblehead schooner driving head on across-bar. With an ebbing tide such a course meant certain disaster, so Obed hurried back to town to collect a rescue party. Some fifty citizens of Eastham waded out to the Marbleheader which was perched high and dry. They were not a little surprised to find there the erstwhile prisoner, Hoppy Mayo, in control of His Majesty's ship with three brass cannons and twenty-three seamen — twenty-one of them at the moment roaring imprecations in the hold.

Hoppy's prisoners were marched to Eastham jail where the Com-mittee on Safety fed them for two days, and then concluded that pris-oners of war were an off-Cape luxury. Lieutenant Fotheringay and his men, released, were invited to walk toward Provincetown, to reboard their ship.

Jolly Dick groaned when he saw young Fotheringay back again on the *Spencer;* but the honor of England must be avenged, so the British commander landed an armed contingent on the Bayside. They marched, while the townsmen cheered, up the road to Hoppy's house where they thrust bayonet holes in his bed while Hoppy hid in the swamp.

The Head of   "Dewey, if ye'll do it, I'll give ye a hundred dollars."
Andrew Jackson   "Done," answered Sam Worthington Dewey, onetime singing master in the town of Falmouth, school committeeman,
later captain of the brig *Falcon,* just back from a voyage to Pernam-
buco. Tied up at Old Central Wharf, Boston, her bobbing masts
loomed alongside, and the cries of longshoremen unloading her cargo
stabbed the sultry morning air.

That night, July 22, 1834, Captain Sam, armed with gimlet and saw,
rowed his flatbottomed skiff from Battery Wharf to the Navy Yard
where the frigate, *Constitution,* retimbered, refitted, manned by her entire crew, creaked hawsers at the dock. A thunderstorm brooded over
the Bay and as Sam approached the old frigate, the summer darkness
was shredded by flashes of clear light. These revealed a manrope dangling from the ship's side. Sam's lip curled in contempt. "Slipshod, jus'
like Jesse," he muttered, wasting no love on Captain Jesse Elliott, Commandant of the Yard.

To the rope Sam made fast the painter of his skiff. The scuppers, directly above him, he failed to notice as he clambered up the side and
made his way through a gundeck porthole. Sentries, "thick as a her-
rin' run" trod the boards heavily. Captain Jesse, recipient of threatening letters and handbills, had determined to protect the frigate against
a possible raid. So every foot of the deck was patrolled by marine
guards. "Mil'tary pop-alongs," thought Sam disapprovingly. What
kind of way was that for a man to move along a deck!

The lightning that revealed the pop-alongs served also to expose
Captain Sam, as stealthily he made his way forward and climbed
through the bridle port under the bowsprit. On the spar deck the or-
bit of a sentry passed within four feet of him. Sam kept "still as a
buryin' box" until the marine guard retreated. Then the Falmouth
sea captain made sure of firm footing on the bobstay. A few moments
later he reached into his pocket, drew forth his gimlet and bored ruthlessly into the "brains" of the handsome new figurehead whose strong
features, illumined by flares, wore a look of implacable martyrdom.
"Dern yer hide," said Samuel Dewey, as he used the gimlet for a handhold. During fortuitous rumbles of thunder he plied his saw with fervor.

The storm broke. Thick waves of rain, crested with a spume of white hail, beat against Sam, soaked through his seaman's jacket and well-nigh blinded his eyes; but his saw bit wood along the chin-line of the figurehead and he kept his right arm swinging. At length, with an ominous crackling, the handsome head severed itself from the "stock-collared" neck. Sam pulled out a huge handkerchief, passed it around his own neck and fastened it to the gimlet that was still firmly imbedded in the wooden head. Much depended on the loyal service of this West Indian "bandanie," for with his trophy dangling before him, like an elephantine pendant, he cautiously edged backward and safely regained the spar deck. If need arose both hands could be freed at once, a wise precaution since rain put a gloss on the slippery planks and the shiny paint of the figurehead felt like spun grease in his fingers. "Lookee, Salomy," said Sam to himself, "here is no place for hornpipin' "; and he laughed as he tiptoed through the wash left by the retreating tempest. Once on the gun deck, he heaved a sigh, half relief, half regret, then slowly lowered himself out of the port through which he had entered.

Dropping into his skiff he landed in the center of a sizable fish pond; for the scuppers, freshly cleaned, had poured their offering of collected rainwater directly into his boat. Before he could succeed in bailing her, Sam feared that his weight, added to that of the heavy head, might submerge the skiff. He clung by his knees to the ship's rope, untied the "bandanie," and laid the painted head in the bow. A long owlish face stared up at him; glimmers of receding lightning played across its forehead. Still hanging with his weight on the manrope, Sam took off his cap and used it as a precarious bailer. The eyes of the severed head watched steadily; eyes that gleamed into momentary life, then faded in the darkness. Sam put his wet cap back on his head, and while water ran oozily down his neck, he leaned over and turned the face till the blank eyes stared toward the thwarts. Then he returned in peace to his bailing and when the water in the skiff had been reduced within the margin of safety, he cut loose and drifted out of earshot before he leaned on his oars.

July 23, 1834, found Boston in an uproar. Every citizen advanced his own theory concerning the decapitation of the new figurehead of the *Constitution*, done in the likeness of President Andrew Jackson. Captain Jesse Elliott, Commandant of the Yard, swore that the Navy would avenge this insult to the Chief Executive; to the Navy Department; to the commandant himself, who had authorized the figurehead as a compliment to Old Hickory.

All that day and the next day Whig merchants and sea captains paid calls at the "West End House" of Henry Lincoln, staid senior partner of the firm of H. and W. Lincoln, "Cape traders and shipowners." A few of the more privileged of these guests were escorted down to the wine cellars where the cover of a champagne basket, lifted, exposed a round object at which observers gazed with attention. Slapping each other on the back they evinced a joy more than commensurate with normal appreciation of even the most rare of vintages.

A few days later, invitations for a dinner were issued to certain Boston Whigs, a feast presided over by Parker Pierce. William Lincoln presented to Sam Dewey one hundred dollars, and, curiously, the *pièce* of that dinner remained all untasted. Like John the Baptist's head it reposed "upon a garnished charger."

Captain Sam pocketed his money and the next day took passage to Battery Wharf, New York. There he was met by a contingent of gentlemen who insisted on carrying his portmanteau; and a few days later invitations were issued for a New York dinner presided over by Daniel Webster, Cape fisherman, who made a stirring speech addressed to a pair of wooden eyes.

Next, Sam, who was "seeing the world," took passage for "Philadelphy." Again he was met by an elated escort, again he appeared at a sea-minded dinner, presided over by Nicholas Biddle. At Philadelphia Sam received something of a send-off. His hundred dollars were almost gone and his next destination was the national Capitol. Arrived at Washington, with money saved for passage back to the Old Central Wharf, he yet took the precaution of conserving pence by walking, his ditty bag slung over his shoulder, from the tavern to the offices of the Department of State. There, Secretary McLane relieved Captain Sam of his burden, giving him in return a slip of paper:

Received of Samuel Worthington Dewey one head of President Jackson (wooden), property of the Government of the United States.

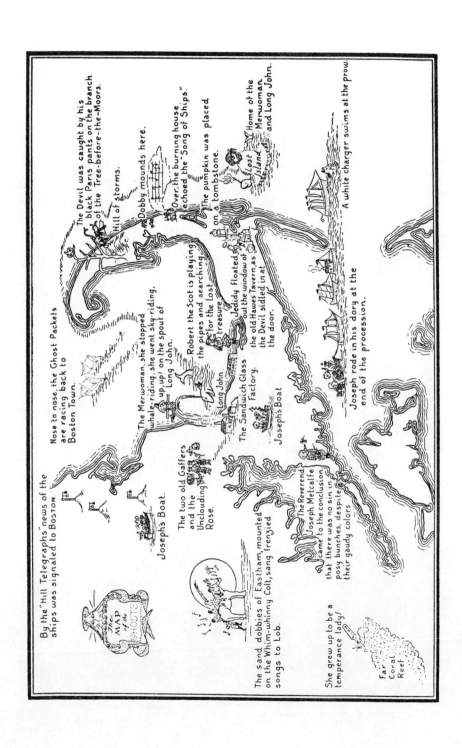

GHOSTS WHO STILL WALK
THE NARROW LAND

In a land where a live man fades from view, a ghost, poor soul, has but little chance of being noticed at all. Yet sometimes Cape men walking in the salt fog have been taken for ghosts; similarly it may be that Cape ghosts are taken for men. Once, one was considered to have carried this joke too far. He came home from sea and lived a lifetime with nobody the wiser, even redied and was buried like a respectable corpse. A week after his demise, his executors discovered, in examining his papers, that he had perished ten years before in Lisbon, leaving to mourn him a Portuguese wife and eight Portuguese children. For a decade he had carried in his pocket his own death certificate, while his ghost married a Falmouth girl who bore him a lusty son. Very few peninsulas have phantoms as able as that one; it takes a seafaring community to produce the vital stock.

Home of mist and mirage, phantasmagoria itself, the silver peninsula, like a slender clipper, cleaves the Atlantic where fog banks roll; and caught in these, the decks of the moors become like a ship's bow in fog watch, tense, overquiet; the pine tree rigging grows rime-edged, cold-fingered and clammy. Sometimes a shrouding born of icebergs, sometimes thick vapors from the Gulf Stream drift over hills and marshes, and the Cape passes suddenly from bright hours of horizoned certitude into cloud immersion so deep, so impenetrable, that ship or forest or ghost or man, life is all shadowy doubt.

The land has lost many children who once were young and fair. In consequence, the living evince an unfailing gentleness toward even the unnamed dead. Pioneering conditions in the first years, large families, inability to cope with diseases, resulted in a shocking infant mortality. Later, when the sea trade became the center of prosperity, the young, eager to embark and thoroughly bred in the stormy moods of Mother Carey, too easily found shippers willing to "sign them." Yet many of these youthful mariners, given up for lost, have come home again, and Cape mothers cannot fail to believe in miracles of survival.

They remember the story of young David Snow and his father who were captured by a British frigate when the boy was fifteen, and incarcerated in Dartmoor prison, England. While the prisoners thumped their logs in a lively courtyard dance, David and his father, with fourteen other men, escaped from jail. The fugitives made their way to Plymouth, stole a raft, seized a ship, reached France, appealed to Franklin and secured passage to

*America. The ship landed them in the far south and they tramped their
way north. Seven years after they had disappeared, they came home to the
Cape, one foggy night, and the mother of David, seeing a dearly familiar
face, yet that of a grown man, fainted, for she thought her boy a ghost.*

*So a Cape sailor, shanghaied and forced to row Benedict Arnold's barge,
believed himself branded as a traitor, thought it necessary to run away,
and was mourned as dead until he reappeared, forty-eight years afterward,
and was taken for a "vision." Nor does the Cape forget the men who returned to their own funerals. A ship's crew sailed away and were caught
in the harbor ice of a northern port, in the days before regular posts were
run to bring back word of them. The spring thaws came and went. The
crew did not return. The townspeople assembled in the meeting house
to hear their funeral service. Suddenly a noise outside disturbed the congregation, and the crew, who had gone from house to house and found no
member of their families at home, filed into church to discover what the
sermon was about.*

*Many a ship's apprentice has come home for his doughnuts and had
sense enough to remain "at the for'ard end of a breaker," yet if all the
Cape boys who have gone to sea and never returned, save in a mist or a
dream, were to take hands and caper over the beaches in the moonlight,
old sailors claim that the line of them would rim the peninsula twice
around, as they are reputed to do on All Saints' Eve, horn-piping, clog-
stepping, playing ringtoss and knucklebone and, shades of Cotton Mather,
post office as well! Young, merry sailors, deeply loved, grudgingly lost,
awaited with unceasing hope! How shall a Cape man shudder or call them
ghosts? The old name for a drowned sailor comes better to the tongue,
Jack-in-the-Mists, bronzed, merry, walking the trails in the moonlight, up-
Cape to take ship on a whaler out of Fairhaven; down-Cape to Provincetown to join the fishing fleets in spring.*

*Three old whalemen sat, one day, in a deserted tavern. Blue fog crept
in at the eaves and blinked around the candles. The first old man lifted his
glass and sang to the winter night:*

> *"O my young hellion ran away*
> *And now he's raking Ould Davey's hay*
> *Down in the green meadows o' Baffin's Bay,*
>> *Way, hey,*
>> *Hi-lee-o."*

The three old men took up the theme:

> *"Young feller, young feller, come home at will*
> *And you may have the gold in the till*
> *And the box hid under the apple-tree hill,*
>> *Way, hey,*
>> *Hi-lee-o."*

*Outside the tavern a jolly voice caught up the refrain, perhaps a boy taking
the road to his ship, since no one entered the taproom although the voice
rang clear:*

"O I carried that till along o' me,
And the box from under the apple-tree;
We're all in the bottom o' Baffin's Sea,
Way, hey,
Hi-lee-o."

THE DEACON BRINGS THE SACRAMENTAL WINE

WIND BUFFETED the gray walls and howled around the windows of the first meeting house in Truro; but to Deacon Collins who helped split the oak, who stirred punch and flip for the "raising," this House of God on the Hill of Storms was the apotheosis of desire. Each member of the parish had been permitted to build his own pew according to his architectural fancies, or the number of pence in his purse. Although Deacon Collins owned a "square-box," cost £3. s.10. d.6., the outer posts of the structure carved from a ship's knees, he chose to sit apart from his family on the Deacons' Bench at the foot of the pulpit, where he craned his neck and cricked his back in an attempt to detect those lost in the insolent sin of slumber.

As he grew older he found it hard to climb on foot up the long Hill of Storms, the highest point on the Lower Peninsula, overlooking the wide Bay, glimpsing the eastward sea. To convey him to Sabbath Meeting, he purchased an old gray horse, and on the first Sunday of the month, Communion Sunday, he always started many hours before service began. At the saddlebow dangled a jug of sacramental wine. As he passed the groups of pedestrians who moved, antlike over huge anthills, he bowed in formal Sabbath salutation, but later, toward the end of his journey, an obsession came over him, and too perturbed to know or to see those in his way, he beat the old nag into a wheezy lope, urging her uphill at a pace unsuitable for either steed or rider. Of no avail the "forehandedness" with which he left the house. Of no avail the calm reassurances spoken by his tall sons, and by his "dilling dawters." Before the goodman had ridden far, fear shone in his eye. Time was passing, unconscionable hours! Never was nag so slow in pace; and he, the deacon, was failing his God. On the Hill of Storms, Parson stood ready to administer communion, without the sacred wine!

The old mare resented her master's increasing tension; then caught, as animals have a way of doing, the urgent mood of the rider. As she broke into a lope, the wine splashed in the jug at her side; the sacred supper of the Lord thrummed like mulling ale.

"Take your good leisure, Deacon," cried the churchgoers. "We shall not be there this half-watch. The mare blows. Ease her down."

But the deacon did not hear them. His wide hat, his wide knee-breeches, his thin old legs flapped. He made a comic figure and the young maids snickered. The horse, too, had a ludicrous way of jerking her fat flanks. As one watched from the rear, it seemed as though the mare was coming apart, the forward half of her running due south, the hind half, south by east.

One Sabbath in early spring, first flowers were laid on the graves and the people trod lightly in the Burying Acre, for the young of the land were away on the wild and foggy Georges Banks. They were fishing the catch that would be brought home, come mid-summer, salted, and taken for selling to Spain, the Indies, Europe, perhaps even to China to trade for spices, opium and tea. Often in the Burying Acre new white stones appeared in spring, with no bodies sleeping in the turf beneath them; and on the stones a young life-span was recorded, for a lost son of whom word had been relayed home from the Banks.

Mayblossom Sabbath, as the day was called, brought a deep sense of responsibility to Deacon Collins; but it brought only delight to one boy of Truro who could not go with the fishing fleets in spring. Silas Rich had given promise of becoming a great seamaster, a slip of a boy who night after night sat by the fire studying navigation. As soon as he could handle an oar he sailed boats in the Bay. When he was ten, the usual age to "sign on for a first-timer," he embarked on his father's sloop, and during that voyage the fishing boats were overtaken by the Seven Ways Gale (in which the wind seven different times shifted quarter). In the afterblow the mast of Henry Rich's vessel went by the board and his son, Silas, caught in tangled rigging, was dashed against the gunwale, then dragged into the sea. He clung fiercely to a broken halyard and his father risked life to save him. Half dead, the boy was carried into the cabin, wine poured between his lips. Many hours later he awakened, to look upward with black, bewildered eyes. Some part of the ship's gear had struck him on the head. His fair hair was clotted with blood; his clear brain dimmed.

He lost also certain powers of locomotion; and home he came with no memory of his waiting mother, and with only a grasshopper sort of a body that doubled and hitched as it moved. No asylums on the Lower Cape cared for such incurables and Silas became a responsibility to the whole community. If townsmen met him wandering vaguely on the moors, they guided him home, answering with patience his endless, childlike questions about ships, waves, sailing clouds and countless grains of sand.

He always went to church on Sunday, where he sat motionless, never making noise or commotion and, unlike strangers, the community were neither oversympathetic nor afraid. Such "bafflements" had come to strong men as well as boys. Always some tragedy returned with the fishing fleet: a sailor with his foot frozen off; a lad with a bruised and broken hand that never might pull ropes again; or a boy who returned only as a name to be spoken from the high pulpit on the Hill of Storms. A white stone, carved for him, would be placed in the Remembering Acre where no bodies rested.

Silas' thoughts, of a Sabbath, centered about Deacon Collins who, despite his obsession, was a shrewd and kindly man. He never failed of a word to Silas who looked for him, waited for him, and even shared the deacon's sense of a delayed and mighty marathon. "Ride-away, ride!" exhorted the "oddlin' boy," cheering the old horse on. "Good day," replied the deacon, "God be with thee, Silas."

One Mayblossom Sabbath, when the able young men were gone to fish the Banks, chanced to be Communion Day, and Deacon Collins strapped to his saddle the demijohn of Canary, clambered aloft, shook the reins. As the old mare started, mist blurred a golden sun.

Up two headlands and down they passed to the foot of the Hill of Storms. There, as ever, the conviction seized the deacon that he and the horse had fallen into a trance-like slumber while unknown hours passed. The wine was not in readiness. The good Lord awaited it. Despair clutched at the old man's throat as he looked up the Hill. Lashing his mount with a hazel switch that stung her thick old sides, he forced her pace; her muscles tightened, her long back strained upward, the wine jug beat sharply against her leathery hide.

He wheedled her with cajolery, stung her with abuse. She flicked back her ears and soon goodman and horse were immersed in fog that lay along the Coombs. The people heard the deacon's cries, smiled, drew aside to let him pass; but Silas was moving in a yonderly dream and did not remember to turn from the path as the hooves that sank in sloshing sand drew nearer. The old mare, blind in one eye, charged against the boy. The deacon knew that Silas fell, but, lost in his mad obsession, he continued up the hill. Silas could pick himself up; church laggards would attend to him. A moment's delay of the Lord's servitor and the Son of God would turn in disgust from an empty communion table.

The gray mare, frightened by the collision with Silas, wheezed, wallowed, leaped. Deacon Collins clung to the saddle with one hand, with the other he steadied the sacred wine.

When the top of the hill was attained, it was necessary to pass around the outskirts of the Burying Acre to reach the church. Ordinarily the old nag knew where to carry her rider, but on Mayblossom Sabbath, horse and man were shaken with mutual frenzy. The deacon belabored the mare with his whip and she plunged recklessly across tombstones, over graves where the dark earth, brought by ship from more fertile country, had been seeded to bring forth green turf. The wide hooves of the frantic horse trampled the first flowers, dug scars in the mounds. Hitting dizzily against tombstones, the mare zigzagged, reared, bucked, stumbled, to the church door. The deacon sprang from the saddle, seized the wine and ran into the church. None of the congregation had arrived as yet. The minister and the gravedigger were putting the benches square.

Goodmen carried the body of Silas into the meeting house. They laid him in the forward pew. At the time of his death he was only twelve years old. He had not grown since he was ten, and as there was no hope for his mind after the accident on his father's sloop, it was perhaps as well for Silas that the mare's hoof struck his temple.

All through the service, Goodman Collins sat on the Deacons' Bench, below the pulpit, directly in front of the forward pew. He watched Silas' face. Mercifully, the eyes were closed; the expression no longer drawn nor vague, but strong and clear in death. Then the obsession of his own importance fell away from the deacon. So, too, waned his desire to know who sinned in the Lord's House. After service, the minister held aloft the jug of Canary wine for sacrament. Deacon Collins rose, passed through the aisle, walked out the door. Before he departed he leaned for a moment over Silas. Men and women, prim, reticent, turned their heads away.

The old man led his mare slowly down the hill. The horse wheezed and choked. She knew that her day was done, so she whinnied and rubbed her head against the Deacon's arm.

He never again partook of the Lord's Communion. When the goodmen went to church he came and stood by the door. As soon as the sermon was over, he hurried into the Burying Acre; often knelt for long hours beside a new grave. After communion he spoke with the participants who clasped his hand and still called him deacon. The Cape had seen too much of trouble not to be wise with its men.

When he died he was buried on the Hill of Storms, and those who remember the story declare that the marks of the gray mare's hooves never disappeared from the graves until after the deacon's death. And now, though the goodman rests in heaven, so ill-content is he with this one remembered folly, that the first Sunday in the month you may see him, if the moon is out at midnight. If it is not, you may hear him as he reaches the Hill of Storms. Back and forth among the graves he rides. The old horse wheezes. The wine splashes in the jug. When at last the deacon finds an ancient, weatherworn tombstone, he dismounts, kneels, prays until the time of cock-waking. Then, in the mist called the pride-of-the-dawn, he mounts his faithful old gray mare and away they ride to spend another month in the green meadows of heaven.

SAND DOBBIES OF EASTHAM

A horse from Whitby, Yorkshire, was shipped in a sailing vessel to Boston in New England. Hidden in the horse's mane lurked two stable fairies, long-nosed goblins with flapping ears, red caps and button-up North Country reefers. The two stole feed from a nose-bag, slept in the ship's hold, and when the vessel came to port in the Round Head Country of America, the stable elves disembarked. They found themselves in the town of Boston and wandered up the Old Bull Wharf to the innyard of the Bull Tavern. There they heard that they were the first dobbies to reach New England. Alarmed at this news, since stable elves are gregarious, lodging in burrows in a hay loft or in dobby mounds on the moors, the two decided to take counsel with a broad-backed horse in the sixpenny stalls, who argued that if a vessel sailed from Whitby and docked in the Americas at Bull Wharf, Boston, that a vessel sailing from Bull Wharf would dock at Whitby, England. The dobbies saw the force of this reasoning and when they heard that the broad-backed horse was to make an ocean voyage, they concealed themselves in his mane. A few hours later, the horse was blindfolded, and after much difficulty induced to board a sloop.

For two days wind from the east battered the vessel. She wallowed, she rolled through crisscross water. When she reached Eastham harbor the frightened dobbies scurried ashore, and made inquiries for the road to Yorkshire. Three horses stabled in Crosby Tavern were questioned and all made the same reply: was Yorkshire Backside or Bay? The stable elves despaired. Something was wrong, they felt, in a land where equines were simple between the ears, where barns were not thatched, where goblin feet sank up to the knees in a white, unglued earth. Relieved to hear of seaward moors that wore whiskers of yellow broom, the two goblins filled their patch pockets with oats from the bins of Crosby Tavern, tucked their long ears under their caps, and journeyed with the broad-backed horse across-village, over-dune, till they came to Nauset Sea. Stars slept under tucked-in blankets of cloud. Wind moved athwart waves.

To the infinite terror of the elves, a lantern was hung in the mane of the horse. Up and down the beach they went, horse, fairies and master, until, toward dawn, an offshore vessel grounded, signaling for aid. Then the horse was led inland, hitched to a wooden stake driven into the sand, and as sun-coming warmed his body, the little night goblins, day-drowsy, were lulled into deep slumber. At top-hour-light the horse grew hungry, shook his head and whinnied. The dobbies rolled out of their nests, slid down his neck, and still dreaming, curled up in the sand. All day they slept quietly while the broad-backed horse trudged toward the north to try his luck at the foot of the Clay Pounds.

Dusk awakened the goblins, alone in a desert of arid sand. A pale moon shone over them. Bald dunes, like risen sea giants, peered beneath shagged marram-grass eyebrows over a waste of waters. The two dobbies offered prayer to Lob, master of magic, then burrowed bravely into a sandhill as though it were a bundle of hay. After they had fashioned a moor mound, they looked about them for food, and discovered kelp bulbs, succulent and salty, strewn along the great beach. Searching inland, they found clusters of waxberry, delicate to the palate. With these they stayed their stomachs, then climbed to the crest of the highest dome to take measure of the land. Westward the hills

THE MARSHES OF OLD NAUSET

were darkened by the barbarous, unthatched village of Eastham. Eastward lay the sea. North and south for more miles than any dobby could hope to traverse, loomed moor and bog and dune and moor, an unending wilderness. "Better bide here," said the older dobby, "here we have food and a house."

They wandered back to their burrow, carefully built on the duneside, but wind had been blowing the unglued earth; sand blocked the hole. "This will not do!" said the littler dobby, of an ingenious mind. He traveled inland while his mate kept watch over the mound, and in an hour returned with a sprig of spicy bayberrry tilted over his shoulder. The goblins planted this green slip; kept the root watered from below; and in less time than mortal would believe, a waxberry bush flourished. Spreading its branches to protect the entrance to the dobby mound, it distracted by the glint of its shiny leaves the keen gaze of fishermen and mooncussers who were often puzzled by a wisp of white emerging from a dune bush. Could an offshore wind be mixing, with no filly-tail clouds in the sky, no spume bonnets on the waves? It did not occur to the Nausetmen, at least not for a long time, that the wisp of white was not blowing sand but smoke drifting from a tiny chimney, perhaps signaling a roast berry feast, for the little people kept all manner of fete days.

The two dobbies grew round and fat on a diet of salted kelp and bayberries. They planted dobby eggs in the sand and when the moon shone white on these, bright-eyed baby goblins popped out, rolled, capered, turned up the toes of their flat little feet, spread their ears like sails to catch the wind, and coasted down-dune, up-along and down-dune, with the dobby ancients in pursuit. As soon as the elder dobbies caught their offspring, they took them into the burrows to dress and educate, for each dobby baby was equipped, when he was born, with a red cap and a patchpocket reefer neatly folded in the upper drawer of the egg.

The young were not instructed in stable knowledge of Yorkshire, nor in the art of dobby riding; yet if a horse scuffled alongshore the youngsters felt a curious excitement. They came out of their burrows to cheer, and as fewer and fewer grew the visits of lighted mounts pacing the beaches, a great loneliness and longing afflicted the sand dobby people. After sunset, wild young dobbies disappeared inland, to reappear at dawn with flushed cheeks, glittering eyes, a wide, swaggering gait.

Farmers of Eastham who sought their barns at first-hour-light were mystified to discover their horses blown, spavined, bloodshot of eye, ears flat back and in vile equine temper. An iron horseshoe over the door, even witch hemp tied to the night bridle, brought no alleviation. Then old Captain Snow, who was born on the rim of the Wolds in Yorkshire, remembered a trick his grandfather told him. The captain searched till he found a stone with a hole through the center of it. This he called St. Godric's Stone, and suspended it on a string over his mare's head. After that, all was peaceful in Captain Snow's stable. No more grain disappeared from the bins; the mare, sleek, fat, unwearied, whinnied a friendly "howdy-due" when the captain entered her stall.

Other farmers adopted the device. Dobbies came home from nocturnal excursions, their eyes sulky, their footsteps dragging, and nothing new to report to the babies who were always waiting, hoping to be led astray. Gradually lethargy of spirit overcame the community. Goblins refused to come out of their mounds even at full of the moon. Then a young elf with a duck's feather in his cap — not quite as tall he stood as that duck's feather — decided that a horse was essential to the happiness of Dobby Land. The goblin dug a carrot, chanted an elf rune over the double tail of it, and armed with this delicacy journeyed across-marsh till he reached Eastham Pasture. Pitiably inexperienced when it came to choosing a horse: "The first fellow who comes from pasture when I hold out this carrot," he argued, "will be a Robin-nip-the-daisy."

The Whim-whinny Colt of Captain Snow saw a succulent two-tailed carrot protruding through the pasture bars. She arched her neck; she bucked and stiffened, full of beans and "sky-falutin'." "Ahoy!" called the sand dobby. "Take a look, little horse!" The colt teetered on her skewed hindlegs, then tilted to her forelegs. She nosed toward the carrot. "Will ye take Lob for you master?" queried the dune goblin.

"Nay, nay," breathed the little colt, flinging her hindlegs skyward.

"Yea, yea," wheedled the dobby. "Little horse, taste of the carrot." The Whim-whinny Colt of Captain Snow took the carrot between her teeth; the dobby leaped on her back.

"Run to the dunes, little horse," he chanted; and the young mare could do nothing but obey, for once a dobby mounts a horse, the will of the steed is as bogwater. A dobby rides like a king.

The colt fled through Eastham Marshes, picking her path as the dobby directed. Triumphantly he brought her to the edge of the seaward sand. She arched her sleek little neck, she pranced. The dobbies came out to see her, swung their caps high, cheered, chanted, forgot all melancholy. Half a dozen of them sprang to her back and away she ran along the beach while elves tumbled, elves shrieked, elves roared with laughter. They slid, they clung on her smooth small flanks. One of them swung by her tail. At first she galloped like any colt showing her heels to the moon. But later she became dreird and elfshot. Her speed increased till her mane stood on end. Her tail streamed out like a comet. Wilder she grew as the night grew darker. Anyone seeing the Whim-whinny Colt could foresee that she would madden by dawn.

Inside a burrow sat a dobby sage, his head cupped in his hands. Now and again he pulled his ears trying to remember what his grandame had told him of the way in which elf heroes of old saved stolen horses from madness. "By the moon's last ray, sprinkle berry leaves pounded into an elf-potion over the dancing hooves." "That is not quite right," sighed the dobby wiseman; "but the colt will be taken from us tomorrow and St. Godric's Stone hung over her ears, unless I save her by a philtre." The sage prepared a waxberry potion and crept out of the dobby mound just before moonfall. He stuck a grain of sand in each eye to keep him wide awake. Swiftly the little colt whirled, red-eyed, frothing like a wave. On her back rode frenzied cobolds singing songs to Lob. As the moon dropped into the marshes, the dobby sage, watching his chance, leaped between the colt's flying hooves and applied to all four of them a trickle of elf brew.

The mare paused, shivered, quieted; the madness was drawn out of her. Up from the sand crept a waxy mist over her forelegs, over her hindlegs, over her glossy hide. Soon she was coated with blueish waxberry, almost as translucent as dawn. Mortal eyes could not discern of her more than a blue shadow.

The dobby sage tumbled down, overcome with day-slumber, unable to crawl back to the shelter of his burrow. The invisible pony nuzzled him, shied, galloped away. She ran back to Captain Snow's pasture, but those of her kind, no longer friendly, bared their teeth and nipped at her flanks, and the colt, at moon-up, fled to the dunes where her goblin friends, hopefully waiting, were gathered on a mound. As she came, they cheered and sang; five or six of them jumped on her back and away she galloped to the sailcloth sand pulled crisp and taut by unfurling of waves.

The dobby sage did not live to see the effects of his waxberry potion. He shriveled up in the sun's hot rays, and blew away like a leaf. But his elfbrew works very well. Not only has it saved the colt from madness, and insured invisibility; in addition the bayberry wax protects the pony from effects of growth or weathering. Like the hair wreaths and the wax flowers that still repose in greatrooms, the Whim-whinny Colt of Captain Snow is preserved for sand dobby posterity. In spongy fogs, or glamorous moontime, those who walk the great beach hear the beat of tiny hooves, hear cries like belated sandpipers, and frequently they step aside with a sense of something galloping past, pixie, goblin, cobold, bargeist; something mischievous and moon-touched. If they carry St. Godric's Stone and look quickly, they may descry a red cap, a duck's feather, a flapping ear, a sparkle of small, sharp eyes. Lest they be turned to moon-gossoons, best recite the dobby charm that begins:

> "Benedicitee!
> Do you see what I see?"

If they have no holed stone and cannot seem to find one, they may ask any Cape Cod boy. The intuitive wisdom of the young bids them collect such trophies, though often without knowledge of who elf-bitten St. Godric was, or what the holes are good for.

ROBERT THE SCOT

"The law enacted about minister's maintenance is a wicked, devilish law. The Devil sat at the stone when it was enacted." Captain Matthew Fuller, first regular physician of Barnstable, able, indiscreet, contentious, roared forth his disgust. "Fifty shillings fine for impudence," decreed cold-hearted Governor Hinckley. The two men glared at each other. They were permanently at odds.

Beside his master stood Robert the Scot, a North Country madman with naked knees and a chess-checker petticoat. Wherever Matthew Fuller went, Robert formed a bodyguard, a combination of adjutant, chemist and personal servant.

Two weeks after this fine, Governor Hinckley ate whilks and was seized with ominous cramps. Matthew Fuller, summoned in a hurry, left Rob holding his horse at the governor's door, and found Hinckley doubled piteously over a ladderback chair. The governor refused to tell Matthew all his "simptomes," only admitted what was all too obvious, that his innards smote him like a knife. Matthew called Robert the Scot and ordered him to repair to the kitchens and mix a mild emetic. This the doctor administered. Suffering from its effect, sudden and thorough, Thomas Hinckley lost his pain, his dignity and his temper. His sense of grievance settled on Robert who had, he declared, threatened in tavern to beat the governor's brains out. Between spasms, Hinckley proclaimed that the Scotsman had instead administered a poison, an obvious death-dealing potion of which His Excellency "perished."

Matthew Fuller seemed satisfied with the effect of the dose. Cautioning the governor to eat mush and milk porridge, he departed, followed by the huge hairy servitor who attended him with a dog's devotion, an apothecary's precision and a king's pride.

Governor Hinckley undraped himself from the ladderback chair. He was assisted into what he vowed was to be his deathbed; and despite a rapid recovery, clung to the belief that the Scottish servant of the captain had attempted to poison him, and that Matthew Fuller, Quaker dog, had departed to let him die. Only the direct interference of God, with whom Hinckley was intimate, had spared him for further usefulness upon a licentious planet.

Matthew Fuller, clever physician, man of wealth, given to eccentricities, frequently became embroiled in disputes. Uncomfortably forthright in speech, in addition he insisted upon the constant presence beside him of a man who mocked the Lord by wearing a folded petticoat, and shattered the mind by music drawn from an instrument resembling a giant snail bloated in *rigor mortis*. Furthermore, Captain Fuller carried in his pocket a number of unset gems. These he loved to pluck forth and hold in his hand, allowing light to facet them in splendor. When he was appointed Surgeon General to the forces of Plymouth and Massachusetts Colonies (1673), he traveled on horseback for many miles through the forests, accompanied by the devoted Robert carrying, among other effects, a box of costly jewels. Vanitous!

A lust of the flesh! The ministers of that oversupervised colony rebuked him fiercely. Matthew smiled and bade them keep their thoughts "on a leash within door."

During the war against King Philip, Captain Fuller saved the lives of many fighters. His notions of surgery and of post-operative care involved the Dutch baking of linen before it might be applied to a wound. Amazing luck followed this eccentricity. Wounds frequently failed to fester; patients recovered in record time.

In 1678 Matthew Fuller died, and in his will he left to his heirs, among his personal effects, a box of "Pearls, precious stones and Diamonds, at a guess £200." A fortune in jewels, this, in a colony where such items, if existent, were almost never recorded. A few days after his death, the jewels disappeared. Robert the Scot, who had been with his captain during the deathwatch, was promptly charged with the theft. Governor Hinckley summoned Robert, who had not slept for three weeks, whose eyes were red and heavy, whose look was sullen as he stood before the magistrates and listened to the charge. The governor pointed out to him the peculiarly suspicious circumstances: Robert alone had been the captain's body servant; to him alone had been intrusted the care of the box of gems. Now, when the lawful heirs required it, all he could say was that the jewels had disappeared. Thomas Hinckley looked at the accused with narrowed eyes of suspicion, and let it be inferred that for years this huge taciturn servant had been Matthew Fuller's evil genius.

No proof of guilt permitted the governor to condemn his prisoner; but the accusation was left hanging, and Robert the Scot was so constituted that grief choked him, and he could not swallow food. His great body dwindled in substance. In an amazingly short time after the decease of Captain Fuller, Robert, a victim of grief and starvation, died alone in the night. Toward the end, delirium overtook him, and he searched in the most absurd, unlikely places for the missing treasure; searched with fevered intensity. No man's denial stayed him.

Deep snow covered the ground at the time of his funeral and the neighbors who carried his great-boned corpse found it impossible, bearing this burden, to reach the Burying Acre. They buried Robert on the northeastern slope of Scorton Hill, digging a shallow grave beneath the snow. Unhallowed earth covered him, a hard couch for such as he who had been grimly devout; and ever since then his spirit has refused to await quietly Gabriel's summons. Before the dead rise from their tombs, before the sheep and the goats are divided, Robert the Scot is determined to find and restore the lost jewels. Seated in the grove, on moonlight nights, he pauses occasionally in this search to play on that terrible music box shaped like a swollen snail. In crossing Scorton Hill by night, one must not be astonished at the dregging (dirging) of the bagpipes, at the sound of following footsteps, at a man's tragic sobs.

When nearly two hundred years had passed after the death of Robert, another captain took pity on that restless grave. Two hundred years is long to mourn without compassionate comrades. Thinking so, Captain Oliver Chase placed two stones over the faithful servant's resting place, one at the head, one at the foot, and hoped that their heft might weigh Robert down a little, or at least make him aware that another age discounts the arraignment and suspicions of Governor Hinckley.

It has never proved an easy task to change the habits of a Highlandman; not to mention the even more determined ways of an established Scottish ghost. Though Scorton Hill erode to the sea and fishes swim over Rob's bonnet, though barnacles grow on the handsome tombstones, Robert will walk in the moon's pallor or the sea's green twilight, and pipe and search the whole night through. He may even fail to hear Gabriel's summons, so bent is he on finding the "Pearls, precious stones and Diamonds, at a guess £200."

THE MERWOMAN AND THE FINBACK WHALE

Long John, a finback whale, lived in the sea not far from Lost Island, and while all other whales were caught by the Truro Seed-Corners, Long John, harpoon shy, succeeded in escaping. Likewise he evaded the charms of the merwoman of Lost Island who coaxed him with fish coddle, kelp cakes, and flattery. The big finback curveted, blew and when temptation came too near, dived under the island, coming up on the opposite shore. Mischief twinkled in his small eyes, flickered along his tail. When the merwitch begged for a ride on his back, Long John blew bubbles at her, chuckled, and departed.

Contrary is the nature of woman whether with heels or a fishtail.

The boon denied her becomes heart's desire; and the merwitch soon lost interest in flipperdancing, in sewing frills on kelp bonnets; even forgot to contemplate mirrored pools where her mica scales, her green hair, her fish-shaped eyes, her square white teeth gleamed back at her pleasantly. Once she had delighted in manipulating a ship's pump that fell topside-turvy in the sea bottom. Instead of sucking water up, the pump sucked water down. But as Long John continued to flout her, even this toy became neglected. She spent her days fashioning a greenweed harness of Sargossa Sea rope, herringbone stitched, barnacle tufted. With this, if she succeeded in catching John, she intended to bridle him smartly.

What with tears, bribes and a thwart temper, that merwoman grew to be a deep-sea nuisance. Lobsters and crabs sighed when they thought about her, for her singing never meant happiness; nor did she render, as they well knew, any tidewater psalms. Also they ruefully recalled the time when she tried to make them hold Long John by sitting on his horizontal tail. One, two, three, jump! they all caught hold at once. Then they took a ride, dizzying, dazzling, spun up, spun down, spun over and roundabout, until one by one they lost hold and sank into the mud bottom. A long claw walk it proved, back to the shores of Lost Island where the merwoman sat, scowling.

One moonlight night the water witch swam up-coast to Truro. Out on a coomb sat Ichabod Paddock, the great whalemaster, who was later sent from the mainland to teach frail minded islanders (of the Vineyard and Nantucket) how to catch a fish. Ichabod was spread over the edge of Truro Coomb, looking for a ship due to bring him death money from England. He heard a faint ripple, saw cockled silver, and the merwoman looked up and smiled.

"Howdy-due," said Ichabod.

"Ev'nin'," said the merwoman. Then she tucked down to business and told him how Long John was living at Lost Island. She would give, she declared, a rope of pearls to the man who killed that whale. Ichabod had no pearl hanker; especially with death money due by ship from England! As it was, he feared the minister might nominate him deacon, or Miranda Paddock might stop his going to sea. He thanked the merlady courteously, but declined her offer.

Then she promised him corals, and assorted treasure chests, even to the "twelve foot copperbox" known to be full of gold bars, sunken off

Monomoy. Ichabod was chary. The gems, he suspected, would all be flawed ones, and as for the gold, she did not look to him like a girl that gives away money.

Next the sea woman proffered love. She held out white arms, looked "thwartships at him with a slant-eye," sang a mer-chanty. Ichabod felt "langerfied" yet he remembered how she was constructed, both legs locked up in a fishtail. Being a practical man, Ichabod declined love.

After that she pestered him until he could sympathize with the worn look on the faces of Lost Island crabs. So, man-fashion, he decided to get himself some peace by granting her desire and something more besides. "Tell Long John," said he to her, "that Ichabod Paddock, master whalesman, will never draw harpoon against him if he will take you on his head and ride you once around-Cape."

The merwoman hurried back to Lost Island. She took two squid-hound bass as witnesses to Ichabod's statement; and when Long John heard of the whaleman's promise, he was relieved of a long-concealed terror. Before Ichabod could change his mind, the great finback permitted the merwoman to bridle him with a weed rope. "Git aboard," said he to her, "there's a cozy little berth up for'ard." Graceful as a lily, her green hair flying, her mica scales a-glitter, the merwoman sat his bows, and so busy was she unpacking her ditty bag that she did not notice how Long John winked his eye at the lobsters.

Up-coast, past Nauset beach, they floated; Long John docile as a shrimp. Now and then he even tacked, pretending that he was a frigate. The moon rose up. The sea witch sang. Long John would not "jine chorus." At the Peaked Hill Bars he put down his helm and came about into the broad Bay, swimming the length of it toward the harbor opposite Sandwich. "Good measure, John," applauded the merwoman who was usually soft-tongued when the ducks were flying her way. Suddenly the finback took to swimming under water, straight toward shore. Then he rose and spouted high, a jet handsome as the "fountings of Vair Sally." Up, up, up with the spout shot the merwoman. She stopped whale-riding. She went sky-riding, sailing plumb to landward, over dunes, over roofs, over Sandwich town. "Look to your cock-beavers," sang out the goodmen seeing no cloud but receiving a salt-wetting. The whole sky flashed with moon glitter and out of it dropped one silver splinter that fell like a meteor into Sandwich Pond.

There the merwoman has lived ever since, bottled up, out of mis-

chief. Sulkier and sulkier she grows since no one takes her back to
Lost Island. She is nothing but a pale ghost now, the shining mica of
her scales gone dune-white with age. She skulks low in the pond bottom, sometimes singing a mer-song, feeble and woe-silly. Her brains
were always "noddlin' ones" and have not improved with time.

Long John spouts off the sunken reefs of Lost Island. He is pale
anyway, so age has scarcely changed him. He squirmed out of the
greenweed harness, back in Sandwich Bay. Great ropes of it line the
shore, a broken and shabby weed. Any man may own a piece of the
merwoman's bridle.

A SONG OF SHIPS

On Eastham Plain a square house with a French box roof stands ten-
antless, a weary house with dead trees crumbling around it. In aspect
completely lost to the pulse of life, yet not of ancient lineage, the house
is reputed to be tenanted by ghosts. To its comparative modernity an
old story has been attached, that once was told of another home built
on Eastham Plain.

In the early part of the eighteenth century, a young theological stu-
dent came to Nauset. He had curly brown hair, dark eyes and was a
great searcher after sin. He was clever, too, in finding it where no one
had thought to look before, in the wanton ways of the young. Many
a laughing maid he admonished to look to God, abstain from levity,
fasten her calamanco higher, and refrain from showing her shoe.
When the time came for this boy to be ordained, he made a journey
via Barnstable, Sandwich, Plymouth and Boston to the outermost
town of Cambridge where once stood a college designed for the making of ministers, an institution now fallen into secular decline. The
boy, named Barnabas, received his ordination and a few weeks later
returned to the Cape to await a calling suitable to the display of talents
in theology.

With him came a young wife, quickly wooed, promptly won, in the
regions of Harvard College; a girl whose father, a "furrin doctor," had
lived in the Dutchlands of the Rhine. She was beautiful, showed her
shoe, loosely tied her necker-linen. A roving eye could distinguish
clearly the dimple in her foreneck; and it took no perspicacity at all to
see how Barnabas loved her. Her mother, daughter of a Boston magis-

trate, had named the newborn baby, Remember, in the hope that the word would recall to the child a mother destined to die before her baby was three years old.

A handsome pair, Barnabas and Remember, walking some ten miles of a Sunday, to hear Old Man Treat discourse on hellfire and damnation. The Eastham parson had exhausted his strength by work among Indian converts. Townsmen whispered that young Barnabas hesitated to accept another parish because before long he would be replacing Old Man Treat. An immediate settlement was not essential to the young theologian, born of titled South Country stock, a wealthy family given to feasting, fighting and lusts of the flesh. They were inclined to pay well to keep Barnabas away from home, but they would have been agreeably surprised at sight of his wife, Remember, who had off-Cape manners, spoke languages and, of all outlandish accomplishments, played the fiddle like a man. Enjoyed it too, despite solemn warnings that her shoulders would soon be uneven, her two arms of two sizes unlike and uncomely!

None of these horrors affronted the eyes of pious Eastham observers, whereas the tunes Remember played frequently affronted their ears: tunes to make the foot tap, the body warm, the senses swirl, and a great variety of doubtful emotions chase themselves through the brain. Strangest of all sounded one song with the sea in it, and the hearts of men, a tune that Remember made herself and called the "Song of Ships."

Never a psalm tune slipped along the bright strings of the fiddle that would not discourse with God, nor the angels, nor utter prayers for men. It was too old and wise, she said, to bother with theology. Nice talk for a parson's wife, living in Eastham colony! Old Mr. Treat, consulted, suggested that she was with child no doubt, and given to cradle fancies. "Bide a year," counseled Old Man Treat. "When Barnabas' son is born, she will have something more soft than hollow wood to tuck under her chin."

The winter passed, the spring came, and Remember had no baby, nor did she seem to want one. Older goodwives visited her with anxious prescriptions and advice. Remember thanked them gently, but often failed to attend their words and could never correctly repeat them. The townspeople began to feel sorry for serious, young Barnabas. In summer deacons traveled up-Cape to interview him as a possible mentor for their meeting houses. They came away with roses in their lappets and a palpable dreaminess of the eye. Most of them wisely enough dispelled the languor by a glass of Sandwich ale before returning to their wives; and reported to the elders that Barnabas exhibited profound knowledge of doctrine and not much wisdom in dealing with the wages of sin.

Old Mr. Treat, fond of Barnabas, knew with the clarity of age that money and no chance for service were hazardous to character. Not able to sit long in saddle without rheumatic stiffenings, the old minister proposed that the young man aid him by undertaking visits to faraway parishioners. Barnabas accepted eagerly, and away he rode, long days at a time, to succor the ill and guide the perplexed, while Remember, left at home, was not without company. Three sea captains sat by the hour in Barnabas' greatroom, and listened to the violin tunes and to the lovely "Song of Ships." It was even said that dancing went on while the young master was gone. This he hotly denied, when for his good it was discussed openly in tavern.

One day as he rode homeward, cold, saddle-weary, he chanced, before entering by door, to gaze in at the window. Red flames of "fat-pine" were roaring up the chimney. By their light he saw a sailor seated in the ingle, with a violin tucked under his chin. The room throbbed to a jig tune. Whirling madly in front of the fire, her hair flying, her gown leaping above her anklebone, the minister's wife danced the Square Jig with a sailor captain. Barnabas edged away from the window. At the crunch of his step on the path, the music stopped, and as he crossed the doorstone he saw his wife, her cheeks pink, bent over her loom linen. The captain who had danced with her stared out of the window.

That night while Remember quietly slept, Barnabas went down-ladder and with his two hands broke her small, dark violin into a hundred pieces. In the morning Remember found them lying by the hearth, and gathered a few of the fragments to keep in her rosewood box.

If words had been shattered between these two, their tension might have broken, and he have sorrowed and she have sorrowed and the trouble ended in a compromise infused with the normal self-pity peculiar to the marital state. But she was proud and he was proud, and no children sickened of croup, nor swallowed pins, nor by other urgent infant dynamics united parents responsible for their young. All that winter Barnabas continued his sickbed visits. Three times, as he approached his house, he heard a fiddle playing, distinct, sweet, mocking, as only his wife could play. The first time, tiptoeing to the window he peered in curiously. Flames were low on the wide hearth. No one stirred in the room. The second time, he did not wait to reach the window. He raced down the path, flung open the door and found Remember gazing into the fire, her white hands empty in her lap. The droop of her shoulders smote Barnabas' heart.

The third time that he heard the fiddle, on a crisp, winter night, thin snow frosted the earth and he stopped in the path to listen. From the greatroom came music, first a laughing tune, then a low, sobbing story told in vibrant chords. Suddenly, with change of key, the music welled forth into the "Song of Ships." Cadences rippled like waves, floated, surged, swayed. Barnabas closed his eyes. Out under the cold young moon he saw a frigate, slim, delicate, riding beneath the stars. The tune changed, coarsened; it sang the ways of sailors. Barnabas felt his face burn, and he beheld the evils of the world: the snake in the garden, the canker in the rose, the damned in their eternal tomb. He strode into the greatroom where Remember stood looking gravely into the face of a sea captain whose brows were drawn in a frown.

"Wife," said Barnabas, "give to me that Instrument of Satan!" The girl started, shrugged her shoulders. " 'Tis only the sin that sings in thy soul," she made unwifely answer.

The minister searched the house until dawn, but he found no fiddle, found only a lost page from a sermon and a great weariness of the heart.

The next morning he wrote a letter to relatives in England and by ship received an order on a money-changer of Boston. He journeyed to town without his wife, and returning, announced his intention to build a house away from all worldly distractions, there to devote his life to the solving of certain theological problems. By ship from Boston came a collection of short iron rods. By ship from England came assorted boxes which were carted away unopened from a sloop in Eastham harbor. On a plain to the north of the township, a plain as flat and desolate as any western prairie, the minister built his house. No habitation eased the eyes; nothing rested the mind with confidence, or strengthened the soul like the sea. At all the windows the short iron bars were fastened securely, and a strange new lock was put upon the door. These precautions, the minister explained, would prevent mooncursers and pirates from removing the fine house furnishings sent from Devonshire, England.

When all was complete in the house, the minister mounted Remember on a postilion behind him. Out of Eastham town they rode, plowing through miles of the sea pine country, along sandy trackings. After dusk they came to the house and Barnabas carried Remember over the well-made doorstone. That night she was happy. In the darkness, she did not see that no dwellings were near them, nor did she notice the bars. The rooms were paneled, like English rooms, and contained fine silver, old chests, and treasures of family lineage. Remember's heart rose with wonder at the riches and the beauty. She laughed with a new delight. But Barnabas seemed not to hear her. He sat with his head buried in his arms, and spoke no word except to give necessary orders to his old Indian servant.

At dawn he departed for parish visiting, and as he went he fastened the new lock on the door. Old Mr. Treat was dying of palsy and Barnabas had been asked to take over many of the minister's duties, so he rode far and returned late, and all that day, in the house on the plain, Remember beat her fists against the bars on the windows, hurled her body against the locked door. By sunfall she knew herself to be a prisoner whose utmost cries would bring her no aid.

At night no word of her new knowledge passed Remember's lips. Barnabas read the Bible. Outside the house, the Nauset wind howled like a witches' Sabbath. Not many miles beyond, toward the dunes, the possessed girl, Maria Hallett, was known to have built a hut. Sometimes, it was said in the village, Maria grew angry with her familiars when they would not do her bidding. Then she forbade them shelter, and they moaned and roamed Eastham plain, seeking a refuge, shrieking forth their anger.

As soon as the three sea captains heard of the plight of Remember, they took opportunity, while Barnabas was away, to ride north with an extra horse, Chips, the carpenter, and plenty of frigate gear. They overpowered the Indian servant, bandaged his eyes, and in little more than three hours, Chips made a tidy, scarcely discernible opening behind shelves in the kitchen. A neater means of entrance and exit no one could desire, although the going was narrow for a hoop or a quilted petticoat. To the consternation of the captains, Remember refused to leave with them, or even to make use of the hidden runaway hole. Each man of them offered her his heart, his ship, his loyal safe-conduct. The minister's wife declined these offers. The fire was bright, she said; the rooms were warm and beautiful; soon she would be content. The captains rode away in dudgeon, pledging romantic homage, swearing too, that before the year was out, if Barnabas did not awaken to his crime they would wring his neck, minister or no. Furthermore, each of them took an unvoiced vow to search the shops, at the first foreign port of call, for a small dark violin.

For three years Remember lived in the barred house on Eastham Plain. Now and again goodwives took the long ride over the moors, carrying with them elderberry wine, or plumberry jam or journey cake. The elders reasoned with Barnabas, insisting that so lonely and exposed a location was no place for a young wife. Dangers of pirates, mooncursers, "wild Nausetmen" were involved; but Barnabas replied that the house was staunchly protected with iron bars against the incoming of strangers, and that his Indian servant, who alone besides himself held a key, had strict orders to admit no one without Barnabas' foreknowledge. The elders looked at one another. They determined to select an off-Cape minister to keep their souls out of hell.

No man ever saw Barnabas approach his house after dusk, so no man learned, until it was too late, of the tragic delusion that obsessed him. Every night, as he neared his home, he heard a violin playing. Lights flared from the windows, at least a hundred candles flamed. Invariably he urged his horse to the gallop and raced from the highway over the plain. Louder and louder as he came sounded the violin. Feet tapped and shuffled in a dance, but always as Barnabas reached the door, the music stopped, a woman screamed, the high, laughter-choked screaming of one half courting, half denying, swift and wanton passion.

Barnabas tore open the door. The flames leaped in the chimney. Remember sat with her white hands empty; she was watching the lonely hearth.

One night the young minister could stand his wife's deceit no longer. He broke down, sobbed like a child and knelt at Remember's feet. He begged her not to torture him, to dance if she must, to play the fiddle, to wanton as she listed; but to do these things in open sin, not to conceal them with magical cunning like a demon or a witch. Remember laughed. She looked at him and asked if he had heard as he approached the new, wilder ending to the lovely "Song of Ships."

The first snow of winter (1718) coated the sea pines on the plain, making them look like Rhine goblins with hoary beards and crooked shapes, recalling to Remember fairy tales told by her German father.

During that first snow Barnabas murdered his wife, and left her body in the house that was known as Barnabas' Folly. Before he fled he set a torch to the paneled walls, then mounted and rode toward Eastham village, to make confession of his crime. As he turned to look back, tree goblins danced around the funeral pyre of the girl who played in death as in life the mysterious "Song of Ships." The "new wilder ending" rang in Barnabas' ears. His horse reared, stumbled, fell, and would not rise again. The "Song of Ships" sang over the two, horse and maddened rider, sang over the red, rising conflagration of the plain.

Barnabas forsook his horse and ran steadily southward. When he reached Higgins' Tavern his strength was almost spent. Dawn had not come; no one was astir; embers slept on the hearth. The minister crept in at the door and lighted a candle in the taproom. He took paper and quill and wrote a long, distraught confession. In it he told of the dancing, of the perpetual deception, of his wife's unwillingness to deny the music and the revelry, or to forgo it, or even to temper it, or to keep it after his coming. He described his perpetual unavailing search through that barred house, for fiddle and dancers; described his wife lying as she was left, in the high bed in the upper chamber, dead by his hand. He told, too, of his flight to Eastham with the "Song of Ships" surrounding him, while the sea pines capered on the plain.

Barnabas finished his confession, with its final short and stern self-condemnation to death. He left the paper on the taproom table and opened the door as dawn lifted. Below the tavern a small pond reflected the morning sky. There Barnabas ended his tortures in waters white-rimmed and clear.

No upright timber of his house remained when the townsmen reached the plain. A smoky sunken area contained charred corner-stones, chimney stones and iron window bars. These bars have since proved useful made into cranes for hearthkettles. In many of the old houses they still continue their service, the iron rusted and worn with time, the hooked ends crumbling; but few of the users know that these were the bars that once held confined the minister's wife, Remember.

The body of Barnabas, recovered from the Minister's Pond, lies buried in the old cemetery west of Higgins' Tavern. The paper on the taproom table was given to the new parson who read it carefully, folded it, consigned it to the flames. In his records he wrote very little that was scandalous, so we only read there of the untimely decease of Barnabas and Remember; she by fire, he by drowning; both of them, as the minister said, "too yonge to dye."

THE BUNDLING MARSH

Jack-in-the-Mist met Will-o'-the-Lantern down by Pochetty Marsh. "Quit wavin' your lights at me," said Jack, "you mooncussin' bogey. I ain't no maunderin' sloop."

"Nobody's wavin' no lights at you. I'm waitin' here for a Boston Lass what come by packet yestereven to visit Greataunt Doane. Kind of flighty by mind, she be, but smooth in the build as a sandglass, reefed in amidships."

"I might look on her," said Jack. "How many bells is she due by?"

"She ain't due by bells."

Jack-in-the-Mist unbuttoned his jacket and fingered its silver topbutton. "Look," said he to Will-o'-the-Lantern. "Silver it be, from Spanish bully-ones (bullion). Down to m' watery grave it went. Look alive, Willie! I'll trade you the Button for the Lass."

" 'Tis uncommon shiny. What would you want of the greatniece of Abyssinia Doane?"

"Aw, ware's your manners?" said Jack. "Askin' sech questions!"

"Have it your own way," said Will. "I'll trade the Lass for the Button."

Jack-in-the-Mist stood by Pochetty Marsh, his seaman's cap in his brown hand, as the Boston Lass went by.

"Good evenin', Missie," said Jack. "Could you be givin' a man his welcome?" He stooped down and kissed her on her soft, red lips.

"The mist is cool on my cheek," said the Lass. "Down here I'm getting a Cape-complexion to dazzle the beaux at home."

"Come, pretty," said Jack-in-the-Mist, slipping his arm about her waist. "I'll show you a merry trick or two, fit to welcome a sailor."

"The marsh mist creeps about my new mulberry gown. A little strange, the feel of the mist, but I like it much," said the Boston Lass, and wondered whether to run back to Greataunt Doane and put on her storm cloak, or whether to circle the edge of the bog and pluck a wild rose mallow. Very beautiful seemed the mallow, closed and pink in the closing dusk. "I'll pluck the flower while I see it," said the Lass, "and then return for my cloak."

"Step this way," said Jack-in-the-Mist, "we'll plight our troth in mangle-brew."

"The salt that stings my lips is warm! Quare doings are in this marsh!" The Boston Lass entered the bog, holding her quilted petticoat high, above her anklebone!

"Did you never hear tell," said Jack-in-the-Mist, "of the ancient custom of bundlin'? A fine, upstandin' way of love; though, come to think on it, upstandin's not the word. It's a way of larnin' whether two crafts ride easy at one moorin'. Missie, soft is the bed of reeds, with a centre-board of blackberry thorn. There's Friend Will, has a silver button to his cap, like Mr. Sheriff Doane. He'll light us, proper and conventual with a bundlin' cradle."

"The footing is treacherous, smooth and slippery." The Boston Lass moved among the reeds, and reached toward the sleeping mallow.

"Take it easy, easy, lass. The bells will be ringin' for you an' me, in Osborn's church in South Parish. There's a fine Irish parson, now, understan's men an' women; though they do say O' Man Stone will throw him out of parish for it. Easy, m' darlin', easy."

The Boston Lass fell down, and the windy reeds bowed over her. Damp soaked through her gown. The wild rose mallow in her hand crushed heavily against her. She took her time to find good footing, clambering out of the bog. Her tidy dress hung crumpled and torn, darkened by black marsh mud. She hurried back to Greataunt Doane who was bound to a chair and an ivory cane. Greataunt looked at the girl, gasped, pounded the hearth with her cane. Then she spoke words that she should not have learned from the son who was born to be a sailor.

"What's to peeve at?" answered the girl, "I've prettier gowns at home." Nevertheless, child of her time, she mended the tear and cleansed the silk and donned the mulberry dress again as the stars came over the bogwater.

With his knees tucked under his chin, Will-o'-the-Lantern sat on a turtle. He chuckled and drank mangle-brew.

"What's so funny?" said Jack-in-the-Mist. "She was worth shippin' to China for! I ain't grudgin' you the button."

"A silver button for nothin' at all, nothin', nothin', nothin'. She ain't saw you, ain't never loved you. She was only a Boston Lass, not Cape Canny."

"Aunt," said a girl in a mulberry gown, while the burning pine logs rosied her cheeks, "Aunt, I'll never marry."

"Fol-de-roddle! Silly maid's talk! You'll marry this twelvemonth."

"No, not I," said the Boston Lass. "Down in the marsh it came on me, I was not meant for love."

JEDIDY AND THE DEVIL

"I got to be gittin' m' ghost-legs on," said Captain Jedidy Cole as he rose from his Burying Box, opened one eye and saw the devil coming down Captain's Row. "I got to be sailin' along o' the tide. Good-bye, Sairy Ann. I'll see you, come Judgment. Don't fill m' boots with no sea-farin' men, and keep the harpoons shiny."

"Here I be, Jedidy," said the devil, just outside the door.

"Gimme ten minutes' start," pleaded the captain, "ten minutes and m' bowie knife."

"You don't desarve it," said the devil, "but on account you're a marryin' man; four times, ain't it, Jedidy? One in Hongkong and two in Cadiz — I don't rightly place the third."

"She was a error," admitted the captain. "She wa'n't our kind."

"Son," said the devil, "I was always tender-hearted of you. I'll give you ten minutes and your bowie knife; but it ain't no use, poor old Jedidy. I kin run faster than a cooncat scootin' and you ain't hardly got your ghost-legs on."

"You leave me be," said Jedidy. "You made your bargain. I don't say you don't desarve me. Faithful you bin, and steadfast persued me, ever since I was knee-high. But ten minutes and a bowie knife it is; ten minutes I'll take."

"Light up your binnacles and set your course," directed the devil. "I'm countin' up to ten."

Jedidy Cole blew out four corpse candles, and tucked them under his grave bonnet. Then he speeded over to the pumpkin field, cut four pumpkins by the stumps, ripped off a reefing yard of shroud and quick as any yardsman knotted together three of the pumpkins in a bundle over his shoulder. He took his bowie knife, cut two eyes, a nose and a grinning mouth in the fourth pumpkin, stuck it on top of a picket in the fence and went down to the Hawes Tavern to get a rum bracer for his ghost-legs.

By and by the devil, who was slow at numbers, counted as far as ten. He looked up. "Hie, Cap'n," he called, "I see you hidin' in the bean-field yonder. Grin now. You won't grin long! I'm a-comin' after you!" As he drew alongside of the pumpkin he grew more talkative. "Lookie, Jedidy," he confided to the pumpkin, "I never did approve of you givin' out three grams of grog a day, and orange after codmuddle." His voice, being infernal, penetrated to distances. Old Jedidy, who was used to having the devil right at his elbow, heard that insult, down in Hawes Tavern, forgot he was dead, and spoke right up just as he used to do when his soul was safe in his body.

"Drat your hide," swore Jedidy. "You're makin' me out a freshwater Cap'n."

"Yo-ho-noddle," sung the devil, "I might have knowed you'd be down in thet Tavern." He turned to the pumpkin. "Beg pardon, Sir," said he, "I took you for somebuddy wiser."

"Ever sence I bin dead," Jedidy chided himself, "I bin actin' nitwit, like a fust mate. Here I wasted one good punkin, and only three left-over."

"Watch me, I'm a-comin'," yelled the devil, who always thought him-self the whole crow's nest and the ship's clock as well.

Captain Jedidy whipped out his bowie and pulled a corpse drip from under his bonnet. Swift as a hawk dropping after fish, he carved a pumpkin from his pack. Two eyes, a nose, a mouth, he made, then skewered the face on the up-spike of the chairback in the tavern. He lit the drip inside the pumpkin and chucked it under the whiskers. "Now I'll be movin' on," said he. "You let the Old Man have his way. Don't you go interruptin' him."

Jedidy cloud-floated through the window; the devil sidled through the door. The devil sat down beside the pumpkin, drank a round of ale and told his listener all that they two were going to do when they got home. Fifth drink around, the devil grew suspicious. It wasn't natural for Jedidy not to be answering back. So the devil decided to bait him a little. "Down home," said he, "I got your two wives from Cadiz, waiting to communicate." The pumpkin said nothing. But old Jedidy who was making his way from Chatham to Orleans, going fast on his new ghost-legs, was so used to listening to whatever the devil had to say that he heard him, way back in Hawes Tavern, telling about the ladies from Cadiz.

"Drat your hide, thet's a lie," roared Jedidy. "One of them wives went into a nun-house. She's salted down fer heaven."

"Yo-ho-noddle," sung the devil, "I thought you was unnaturel silent. But never you mind, I'm a-comin' after you up there in Eastham South Parish. I'll be a-treadin' sternwater before you port your helm."

"Now I've done it," sighed Old Jedidy, who was resting in Treat's Burying Lot. "Wasted another punkin." He drew out his bowie knife, carved a face, lit it with a corpse candle, and set the pumpkin on top of an urn-shaped stone. "You bide there," said Jedidy, "and don't go answerin' questions."

In no time at all the devil arrived in Eastham South Parish where he came upon the pumpkin sitting on top of a white tombstone in Old Man Treat's Burying Acre.

"Jedidy," said the devil to the pumpkin, "you make a fine spook. Your figger has curves to it. You ain't a-tall the barrel you was."

When Jedidy overheard that, while he was scuttling through North Parish, he nearly yelled back an answer; then chuckled to himself. "This time, Old Feller," said he, "you're not a-goin' to ketch me. There's only one drip behin' m' ear; one punkin left-over." He made fast time along Nauset Plain and ran into Wellfleet while the devil wasted blandishments on the pumpkin's tombstone figure. By and by the devil, getting playful, poked his friend in the ribs. "Ai-ouch!" yelled the Old Man, sucking his finger ruefully. "You're as hard as nails, Old Jedidy, just like you always was. What keeps your muscle up?"

Way past Wellfleet, Old Jedidy thought he'd die of a chuckle-spasm. "Lan' sakes," he giggled, "I use Jamaica Rum. Thet sulphur you drink keeps a man lack-a-daisy."

Far off he was, but the devil heard as the devil always hears when anyone speaks to him directly.

"Looky, you lan'-lummox," he swore, abusing the pumpkin on the tombstone, "you go unner groun' till Judgment. This ain't your watch." As he spoke, he gave the tombstone a shove. The pumpkin rolled down, broke on the ground. The candle guttered out.

"Hell's bells," said the devil, impressed. "Kin I destroy the Lord's deceased like thet?" He swung his bright cloak wide and handsome and in a run-o-bluefish hurry started for Wellfleet Village to catch Old Jedidy.

"Sufferin' Scat," groaned the anxious captain as he lighted his last candle, "I'm down to m' boat-rations now." He climbed up the Tree-before-the-Moors, the last big oak, north of Wellfleet, and lodged the lighted pumpkin face on the skysail yard of the oak. Then he climbed down and hurried on, and in no time, the devil was alongside the tree. "Howdy-doo," said he, craning his neck, "I see you hidin' on the top-boom, Jedidy. Come down, or I'll be after you." The pumpkin did not move. The devil was loath to climb a tree, for while he had his feet in the sand he felt more or less secure, but the air was angel moorings. Any cloud-floating or tree-climbing up in the direction of heaven made the devil sick.

"Aw, come down, Jedidy," he coaxed. "I'll let you have another rum-hot before we go home."

The lighted face in the tree did not stir. The wide mouth grinned. "Yo-ho-noddle," sung the devil, formal and dignified. "Watch me git you!" He swarmed up the ratlines, passed the main yard, passed the topsail yard, passed the topgallant yard, passed the toproyals; clear up he climbed to the skysail yard of the Wellfleet Oak. As he reached toward the smiling pumpkin, he slipped; the lighted face rolled to the ground; the devil swung by his pants.

"Ha-ha," roared Jedidy, over past Truro. "Lookit you goin' up to Heaven!" For the Tree-before-the-Moors stood gaunt against the sky and, Jedidy, far away, could see the devil swinging.

"So thet's where you be," said the squirming devil. "Wait till I open up m' hind hip pocket and get m' flint undid." No sooner said than accomplished. The devil set his black Paris pants afire, burned himself free of the oak tree branch, dropped to the ground and smothered the fire by sitting down on it sudden. Then he loosened a drawstring. His handsome cloak swung down a little further behind him, and off he set after Jedidy who was racing into Provincetown with his bier bonnet gone, and his grave jacket torn into strips. In no time at all the devil was behind him.

"I give up," said Old Jedidy. "You're a habit with me, just like likker. It ain't in me to git away from you."

"Lead on, mate," continued Jedidy. "I'll be goin' wherever you take me."

"Lead on?" said the devil, perplexed. "Ain't we got to Provincetown? Ain't we to home?"

THE BOAT THAT FAIN WOULD LIVE ON LAND

The Reverend Joseph Metcalfe "viaged" from Falmouth to Dedham. Before he embarked on this perilous journey he visited Caleb Gifford to announce a welcome legacy and discuss the purchase of a boat. The Reverend Joseph, father of one son and ten daughters, never before had enjoyed money to spend. Generously he relinquished £60 in arrears on his salary, a stipend that the new little town of Falmouth had not been able to pay.

Joseph informed Caleb that he always had wanted a boat, "in which," said the eager, innocent dominie, "to take mine ease on the deep." Caleb regarded him with astonishment not unmingled with fear. The Reverend Joseph was as seagoing as a buttercup. Moreover, Caleb was shocked: a minister "taking his ease!" What had ease to do with parsons, or with boats, "worritin' critters" necessary to some pursuits but never allied to pleasure. Joseph exhibited his legacy, "figgers wrote down on a paper"; and Caleb decided, if Parson Metcalfe was ready to pay good shillings and pence, that he was not one to let another man "horn in" on the trade.

The minister returned from Dedham and the collecting of his legacy one Saturday afternoon. While passing through the town of Boston he had purchased a new wig, and "covered" with this, he made his appearance at Caleb Gifford's door. Caleb led him down to the shore where an apple-cheeked dory bobbed at its mooring, a craft that had known far better days, but Caleb saw no sense in wasting seaworthy timber on "Parson's folly."

As Mr. Metcalfe looked at this boat pride shone in his eye. He scanned the horizon where the sun was reddening the "minnew-ripples" of the fairway. On such a calm night, in such a boat, a man might voyage far.

When he returned to the parsonage, he found three goodwives waiting. A pressing problem of moral delinquency occupied their minds. Were colored flowers vanitous? Were colored flowers worldly? And what about plucked posies? Might flowers appear in church or did their gaudy hues suggest the adornment of godless women? The Reverend Metcalfe, genial soul, who had just come into his world's estate, was in no mood to chasten nor condemn the radiant gifts of earth. Flowers, he opined, were a sign of God and might be plucked in posy bunches. With this reply the three women departed, unconvinced, but with their minds distracted by the minister's new wig.

They spread word of parson's adornment and by meeting hour of the next day, Sunday, the whole village goggled at the dominie's "Boston vanitie." The Reverend Metcalfe took a text about Joseph who was a fisherman, but felt no deepening response in his auditors although he was vaguely conscious of his flock's unwavering gaze. In the "nooning," before second service, the secular status of flowers came up for a reconsideration and then Joseph discovered that the problem hinged, not on posy bunches, but on his own garden plot. It was thought he spent overmuch time there, time that might be far better expended on parish visits or sermon making. At heart devoutly humble, eager to please his congregation, he would, he declared, abandon his garden; devote to his people all hours — except those, he added quickly, in which he looked forward to "meeting his Maker at sea." This was news to the parish. Caleb, desiring no competition, had abstained from mentioning his negotiations with the minister. Joseph, his round face beaming with pride, made known his purchase; then settled the matter of posy bunches by appointing a "Ladies Delegation" to search the Bible for "light." He would call, he said, "on Monday-morrow" at the house of Deacon and Goodwife Jenkins, there to study the "Bible-findings" and reach a final conclusion.

The next afternoon as he set forth, he turned to look back at his posy plot. Summer roses were "taking the brease" and the "hiehocks" swayed. His practiced eye caught a gleam of weeds sprung up during his visit to Boston. He stopped to right a sagging moss rose; then straightened, remembering his promise. Weeds were to choke these flowers of his; the dry earth wither them to dust.

Joseph walked slowly down the lane and paused at the deacon's door. Goodwives in the greatroom gabbled so fast that they did not see him. No longer intent on their Bible-findings, they were wagging their tongues, every garrulous one of them, about his "Vanitie Wig." "Not expressed in fancy, neat, not gaudy," he had felt very pleased with this purchase that covered his scanty hair. He spoke aloud from the doorway, effectively silencing chatter. Would the goodwives be better pleased if he ceased to wear any wig? They turned in confusion but answered his question frankly. "No wig? Scand'lous! An insult to the sacred office!" Would they prefer that he put on his old wig "mouldy and gnawed by silver boter-flies"? The goodwives' souls revolted. "Then let us alter the new one until it ceases to offend." This solution met prompt response. Joseph removed his Boston wig and handed it to Goodwife Jenkins who clipped the lush and sinful locks, then passed it on to Goodwife Hatch who clipped it yet more closely. "Cut out of plumb, galley-west," a product of erratic fervor, it soon lost "unaform-acie" as each one of the "Ladies Delegation" snipped and pulled to her taste. The last goodwife, returning the peruke, remarked that to wear any wig at all was to break the second commandment. Joseph could stand no more. The wig, said he, was now so unlike "anything that is in Heaven above or in the earth beneath, or in the water under the earth," that to it no law of God nor man could rightly be applied.

He clapped the relic on his head and sorrowfully returned to his home. There he found three elders waiting in the matter of the sea-going boat. They stared, puzzled, at his galley-west wig, then stated their business plainly. God willing, the three elders stood ready to supply Joseph, his one son and his nine surviving "datters," with adequate servings of fish. The parson hastened to reassure them, declaring that he did not desire nor expect to fish from his dory; all that he wanted was *a seagoing boat in which to take his ease.* The elders looked at one another. Then they reminded Joseph that ministers should not be seeking ease; that the sea was a restless, fluctuant platform; that certain poor widows might benefit much by the money expended for the boat.

Joseph promised the elders to dispose of his "legacie purchas" and in the evening he walked down-lane to notify Caleb. At the foot of the

lane, in a little harbor, the dory tugged at her mooring. Joseph removed his moccasins and waded in to get her. He laid his hand on her
side; he touched her thwarts and rowlocks. She rubbed her nose
against his coat and Joseph looked across-Sound toward the shadow of
"Mayhew's Island" where a sloop rode and the sun descended over the
"minnew-ripple."

During the night a violent tempest, a "thund'rous storme" long remembered, swept the whole South Shore. Houses were blown from
their cellars; trees toppled, were shunted inland; ships were wrecked
in the Sound. All night Joseph prayed for the safety of his people, for
their stock, their crops, their shipping. Toward dawn, he heard a
sharp knock at his door. He rose from his knees to answer the summons. Holding his lanthorn high he peered into the darkness, drew
his hand over his eyes then looked out again. A long heavy object
leaned against the doorstone. In the storm the seagoing boat had journeyed the length of the lane.

The good minister entered his study and wrote in his commonplace
book:

August, 1723 —
I have bin tempted to persue the sea sence I was borne. Yit may natt
be. Yett have I pruf of the Lord's haboring no wrath, for this nite in
storme cam to me my bote that fain would live on land.

In the morning Joseph rode out to care for his stricken people. When
he returned at nightfall his "datters" had shoved the dory into the front
yard. Blown sand completely covered the parson's flower garden. But
some kind hand rescued his uprooted rose trees and thrust them for
safe keeping into the seagoing boat. Absentmindedly Joseph straightened the dory, straightened the plants that were placed in her, and covered the roots with soil. Tuesday-morrow he would bid his daughters
deliver them to some goodwife who had lost her flowers in the storm.

While he slept, exhausted by his long day of "service," death crept
in for a bedfellow and "embraced the Reverend Joseph Metcalfe,
aged forty-two." In the morning when the deacons came, the roses
were blooming in the seagoing boat that stood in a sandy yard.

The dory was old; her timbers rotten. Caleb did not haul her back
to the shore. Instead he stood and "looked on her," and thought how
Joseph had loved posies; how he had never used his legacy.

And after the funeral other men "looked on her" and returned to beautify her by the planting of "slips." Even the three doubting good-wives brought some godless pansies.

"Joseph's Boat," the townsmen called the dory, and every summer they filled and seeded her; for they had not known until he left them how much they thought of Joseph Metcalfe, who preached short sermons and gave long counsels, who managed to "rear up" one son and nine daughters with almost no money at all.

Old dories were plentiful; the good brown earth was scarce. Never had flowers flourished so gaily, thrived in droughts, preserved their soil, as they had in Joseph's boat. Towns where good topsoil was lacking adopted the strange device. Other boats were dragged on shore, filled with earth, planted with "greenerie." When sailors came home from sea these skiffs were "striped up good."

In the Burying Acre in Falmouth no tombstone has ever been placed over Joseph's body; but Joseph's Boats are in every town, and on the due date of the "thund'rous storme" the Reverend Metcalfe is said to return to inspect his "landgoing" dories.

THE GLASS GAFFER OF SANDWICH

The two old men who were always together sat opposite each other on nail kegs in the Sandwich Glass Factory. They had huge gray whiskers, wore long aprons of blue and white ticking, and on their heads crackled square turbans designed from paper bags. All day they chipped off flakes of thin glass that adhered to the openings of lamps. Dressed identically, bearded similarly, the two chipmasters resembled a pair of giant twins, only to be differentiated by the iron spectacles which one of them wore well down on his nose.

They knew everything worth knowing about the art of glassmaking, so distinguished a profession that long ago in France it was open only to the sons of noblemen. They told stories of crystal bells that rang the hour, of ruby-glass flowers that opened when the sun shone on them and gave forth sweet perfume, of glass ships with the rigging and spars wrought of spun silver. Sometimes they whispered of a cloudy rose that, held in a woman's hand, unclouded to reveal virginity. Anyone would think to hear them talk that such wonders were true!

Sandwich boys trained as "rosin monkeys," seated on stools beside the glory hole, discussed the tarradiddles of the chipmasters, and threw pulverized rosin into the fire, using small shovel-like scoops. Later the rosin was superseded by coal tar, then by crude petroleum; but the tales of the two old men were never superseded, for no one else could recount so well stories of Venice glass. Rosin monkeys gossiped about it with mold boys, who resembled English chimney sweeps, grimy with smoke from the glowing furnaces. Perched like small black imps on wooden boxes, before them lay molds of heavy black iron in two hinged sections with the exterior design of the blown glass objects cut out of the mold. The mold boys waited, ready whenever gaffers ordered it, to seize the mold by its two iron handles and open or close it according to directions. Smoked like herrings, solemn mites, they shook their heads in sensible doubt of the rose and the ship and the crystal bell. They felt themselves to be connoisseurs in the matter of blown glass. Yet the tales of the chipmasters were no stranger than the stories of tanned sailors, older brothers who were vague about Venice, but very much interested in the unclouding rose.

The gaffers of the Sandwich Factory were off-Cape "furriners." Gaffer Matthews, a huge, rotund Englishman, made the tiniest of wineglasses. Gaffer Lutz of Germany wrought gypsy kettles of flintglass wound about by a shining ruby-glass thread. Gaffer Lovett worked on large thick dishes, and Edward Swan, artist and designer, painted flowers and fruits on vases, plates and lamps.

Around the circumference of the furnace a series of circular holes gave access to flames roaring up the chimney. The irons of the gaffers, as each article took shape, were reheated in these glory holes, keeping the glass malleable; and at such times the mold boys or rosin monkeys questioned the foreign gaffers about the stories of the chipmasters. The older men smiled and shook their heads, or, intent on their irons, showed no interest in the marvels of Venice glass. But Gaffer Bonique, the Frenchman who made "odds and ends," who could copy anything with unfailing precision, was the friend of the two old chipmasters and their staunch defender. Of course it was true, he maintained, the roses and ships and flowers.

In the middle of the nineteenth century the Annual Glassmakers Ball in Sandwich was the greatest event of the year. Usually a masquerade as it used to be in France, original costumes were designed for the Ball. Fantastic dresses and cloaks were decorated with glass flowers sewn on patiently. In those days the Cape prospered, and its captains were bringing back to the peninsula the riches of the seven seas. The workmen in the factory sent to Boston for their clothes, paying as much as a hundred dollars for an overcoat, twenty dollars for a pair of high kid boots, and for their wives and daughters, French velvet at twenty dollars the yard. The whole week was a gala one. The two shifts at the factory exhibited to visitors the skill of the best gaffers. But the art of the actual soon paled before the wagging of tongues. Over the nail kegs guests lingered to listen while the two chipmen told of miraculous glass.

During the week of the Glassmakers Ball, Gaffer Bonique, female shy, fled into the woods, or into what was left of the woods, for the forests for miles around the factory had been sacrificed as fuel to keep the furnaces hot. The whole land had a shorn look; but as between a tree and a Bleeding Heart Goblet, every Cape citizen preferred the goblet and was willing to pay for it with the tree.

During Bonique's absence, the chipmasters seized the opportunity to make him into a hero. "Yes," said they, nodding together, "Gaffer Bonique has a history." Of course they were pledged not to reveal it; but surely the listeners had heard of the Revolution in France. Sons of dukes, even a king's son had been brought to the Cape by the merciful connivance of sea captains. Gaffer Bonique with the French name, and the fine chiseling of brow and nostril; anyone could see, to look on him, that he was no ordinary man! Sometimes the chipmen varied their discourse, and remarked how a great strategist had advised the young Napoleon, teaching him all the secrets of military genius. What did the thankless emperor do after achieving an empire by following his master's advice, but exile this teacher! Gaffer Bonique knew a great deal about military strategy. Visitors could decide for themselves. Occasionally the chipmen whispered the story of an Acadian exile who managed to conceal a hoard of gold at the time when sixty Acadians came in boats to Buzzards Bay and asked to have their vessels carried across-peninsula to the Bayside. Refused their request, kept as prisoners to do service on the farms of goodmen, one of them hid his rich inheritance, and the descendant of this unfortunate still held a clue to the treasure. He spent his days in the forest collecting this gold.

When the hour of the masquerade came, great ladies and kings and clowns went trooping through the streets. Fiddles scraped, "base vials" throbbed in the new, wicked tunes to which a lady and a man danced always together, without the old precautionary groupings of the square "figgers." A special form of powdery glass had been prepared in the factory, and was dusted over the costumes and into the hair of the masqueraders. The two chipmen, their fierce gray beards new-combed and bristling, crowded their widening bodies into velvet knee breeches and scarlet brocaded coats. For long since had tarnished the bright gold on braided lappets; but the brocade kept its stiffening, the velvet its thick dark pile. Away they whirled in the Cape Square-shuffle and the Sailor's Minuet. How they could dance, and how they could tell of blue glass bears, rose glass boxes, shiny eyes of crystal dolphins; and of a strange secret process, known only to the two of them, whereby the blue of Nauset Sea was about to be caught and held forever in the stem of a goblet of wine!

Rosin monkeys and mold boys, out long after bedtime, fell asleep on the benches. Masks were off, farewells were whispered, and at last in the quiet box-like houses the tired dancers slept. The two chipmen went home together to fold away their knee breeches and scatter tobacco leaves into the chest where the scarlet coats were stored. As they laid out their blue ticking aprons and paper caps for the morning's work, the stars paled in a wide sky and the night wore into dawn.

Meanwhile where was the son of the nobleman of France? The descendant of the Acadian exile? Napoleon's senior strategist? Gaffer Bonique, dressed in the white brocade of a Bourbon, with a ribbon across his breast and a jeweled star hanging from it, had started for the Glassmakers Ball. But no one ever remembered seeing Bonique arrive, although the chipmasters kept special watch among the masks. In the street a young, gallant figure had been seen lantern in hand, bowing like a courtier, never lifting his mask. Some men claimed that his dazzling costume moved in the crowd, before the music started, bowing over the small hand of a foreign lady. Then mysteriously the figure disappeared, not to return until red dawn lighted a deserted highway. While gaffers, rosin monkeys, mold boys slept the sleep of the pleasure-weary, a straight gallant courtier of France passed down the old King's Road, and rapped with a white and golden cane at the doors of certain village houses; a strange figure in the half-dawn, walking Sandwich streets.

When at last the glassmakers, sleepy-eyed and reminiscent, assembled on their benches adjacent to the fire, Gaffer Bonique in his old gray homespun with wide "petticoat trowsers," was bending over his iron. He seemed to know all that had happened at the Annual Ball. At least he never asked about it; but some of the townsmen, who remarked that his white brocade fitted him with a precision and distinction entirely alien to the usual masquerader, vowed that during the ceremony he who had been cheated of his birthright relived a life of ceremonies of which the miming of the Glassmakers Ball was only a faint caricature. Discussing this, the old chipmen muttered into their beards. They nodded until their caps crackled like brown autumn leaves.

The coming of American labor unions destroyed Sandwich Factory, debased the art of noblemen into a trade with rules and hours and queer regulations that broke the hearts of the old gaffers, and of the owners who shattered the molds and let the glory holes grow dark. Never, in the fashioning of modern glass for wages and hours by banded workmen, shall the earlier work be duplicated precisely. But long before the factory closed and the molds were twisted and broken, death darkened the eyes of the two old chipmen and of the cleverest glass master of Sandwich, the Frenchman, Gaffer Bonique.

On the anniversary of the Ball, excitement still stirs the old town. Ghosts of fair ladies, of troubadours and jesters, walk the quiet streets, and dance to the scraping of fiddles and the throb of "base vials." Except for a few of the ghost-minded people, the world does not see these dancers; but almost any wary listener may detect an unusual rustling in the old houses at night; or wandering through the street may hear, far away and "wisterly," the lilting of the fiddles.

At dawn something more definite occurs, in the nature of a phantom parade. A slender figure in glittering white, transparent as glass, comes down the street, knocking at the village doors with a white and golden cane. A tall, gallant, debonair ghost; any romantic girl would take him for a lover in a dream. After him walk two old men, very belligerent, very possessive. Great gray beards bristle over their breasts, and they wear blue ticking aprons, and brown paper hats on their heads. One would think that the figure before them, the final triumph of the glassmakers' art, was a puppet of their creating, like the crystal bells that ring the hour, the ruby-glass flowers that open in the sun, and the cloudy rose that unclouds when placed in a woman's hand.

THE PROCESSION OF THE LOST SHIPS

Midsummer Eve, "Jack's night"; the ships rise slowly; scarcely a cross-ripple breaks the rhythm of the sea. The first to appear are the April Sailers, the *Volutia*, the *Brutus*, the *Ulysses*, Crowninshield East Indiamen that perished in an April storm. They hover like white birds over Peaked Hill Bars; and when the snow falls late in spring, the old salts nod together. "Thar be the white sails," they mutter, "thar be the three April Sailers goin' to the Last Port."

Midsummer Eve; and the *Sparrowhawk* that once dislodged her moldering beams from the turf of Old Ship Meadow, now slides, the phantom of her, out of Pilgrim Hall, Plymouth; and off she sails for the Outer Cape where once she rode in on a tidal wave, settling her weary hull in the fields that grew up to be Nauset Town.

Framed from the Cape's own timber, little trim packets appear in the Bay, to decide in one last race which is the fastest sailer: the *Charming Betty*, the *Sarah*, the *Winged Hunter*, the *Leading Wind*, the *Post Boy of Truro*, "fitted out in mahogany with silk draps at the ports." The *Commodore Hull* of Yarmouth pulls over Hinckley Bar. Neck and neck she raced the fast *Mail* of Barnstable, while the *Northern Light* of Provincetown rounds the Point, returning from the "Wilde Straits of Magellan" where she was wrecked after her life as Cape packet was done.

Slowly up the ghost-poles run phantom flags to notify Southsiders that the packets are again in port. Then the old races are rerun; old rivalries resumed; old ballads are resung to their haunting tunes:

> The *Commodore Hull* she sails so dull
> She makes her crew look sour;
> The *Eagle Flight* is out of sight
> In less than half an hour;
> But the bold old *Emerald* takes delight
> To beat the *Commodore* and the *Flight*.

John's Night is Sailorman's Eve. Into the waters of Cape bays the whaling fleets come home; the Seed Corners are back in Truro; Elisha

THE WRECK OF THE *JASON*, DECEMBER 5, 1893

One of the Phantom Fleet, the lost ships that, on Midsummer Eve, are said to
rise from the sea and sail again

Doane's bobtailed blubber-ships rock, bewitched, in Wellfleet harbor, and the "Old Woman of Nauset Sea" is whistling up a storm. The schooners built for Elijah Swift, who first captured the live oak trade and then "adventured in whaling," sail into Falmouth Bay. The old *Status Ante Bellum* arrives, built to defy a British embargo. Elijah himself sailed on her, and when he was captured by an English ship, and his sloop ordered to Halifax, he "shewed his white heels in the night." Elijah "took to ships" and he took to green trees, preferring both ships and trees of oak. When a fire destroyed his barn and threatened to burn down his house, while the townsmen relayed buckets of pond water to save his dwelling, Elijah bent his energies on saving his "old oak tree."

"I could build me another house," said the shipmaster, "but 'twould take too long to grow another tree."

His name-sloop, its figurehead "spittin' image" of the owner, even to the patch on his eye, returns from her grave on a coral reef. Captain David Nye commands her, who attempted, after the sloop struck, to swim ashore with a "lady passenger" strapped to his back. By the rope that had been tied around him, his crew hauled him back to the vessel where he was revived with difficulty. The "lady passenger" perished. But on Midsummer Eve he returns again with the lost lady and her newborn baby. Shipwrecked on a coral reef, the infant was kept alive for days by feedings of port wine from a bottle. She was the lass who later grew up to become a great temperance lady.

The *William Penn,* built by Abner Hinckley, and "wisht onlucky" by Quakers (she had too much Sunday work in her), returns from the Island of Whytbotask where she perished in a gale. Luckless she sailed, with murder and plague on board; lucklessly she went under. But when from the Island of Whytbotask she comes again for "Jack's Eve," her pennants are flying, her decks piled high, and from Quaker Hill the hats are waving. The Sunday work has been washed out of her; she is doubly welcome home.

The *Awashonks* and the *Hobomok,* stout old whaling craft, tie up at Falmouth dock. Captain Prince Coffin and Silas Jones walk up the path together. Young Bowman crosses the road to pluck a hatful of huckleberries — the kind that ripen on John's Eve. They all turn to welcome the *Uncas,* back from Baffin's Bay:

A greasy ship and a smiling crew,
And ambergris, each man his lay,
And a house to build and a maid to woo,
Back in Falmouth Town.

Midsummer Eve, once called Johnsmas; in the sea towers watchers stand and signals are passing to Boston Port of the clippers sailing home. The Cape's famous captains command them, the tallest, loveliest wind-driven vessels that the world has ever known. Burgess is back in the *Whirlwind* and Baker in the *Flying Dragon;* Sears is commanding the *Wild Hunter;* Jenkins, the jolly *Raven.* Crowell is master of the *Robin Hood* and Hallett races the *Phantom.* Moonraking sails, pointed prows, lifting hulls ride over the waves; such craft the sea never knew before, nor will it know them again.

The *Northern Light,* with Captain Hatch, comes around the Horn from 'Frisco, and she is the fastest sailer that ever made that voyage. Under her bowsprit a "full-length" angel holds a golden torch toward heaven, and Captain Hatch, like a jolly schoolboy, waves his hat as he comes up-Sound, to signal "Great Aunt Mary."

Only one ship moved by steam returns to Jack's Rendezvous. The *Pacific* emerges from an unknown grave in the stormy North Atlantic. At her wheel stands Asa Eldredge of Yarmouth who still holds the record for the fastest passage ever made by sail across the Atlantic from New York to Liverpool. Captain Asey drove the *Red Jacket,* extreme clipper, through snow, hail and rain from dock to dock in thirteen days and one hour, "logging" four hundred and thirteen miles in one day of the passage.

Commander of packets, later commodore of clippers, Captain Asey looked ahead of his time. He became the Cape's pioneer in steam, and the old sailing masters mocked him for deserting such "wind-flowers" as the *Red Jacket,* to sail the "pugnosed, dirty fleet" put out by John Collins. Yet in their hearts the old men wondered: what if Asey knew?

When his steamer was lost at sea and never spar or boat of her, or body floated the water, or drifted to any shore, the sea masters who had snarled at his "treachery" bowed their heads in sorrow. They were too old to try steam: "You can't teach an old seadog any hot-water tricks." But they knew their master in Asa Eldredge and they spoke it out foursquarely.

He leads the fleet on John's Eve and chooses to command not the

Red Jacket that follows like a silver pup at his heels, but the smoke-begrimed old *Pacific* by which he forged that rare bond, a link between steam and sail.

"Marcy Mist" blurs the sea on the Cape's Midsummer Eve. It blurs the eyes as the wrecks come up, Cape vessels and "furrin" craft sufficient to wall the cliffs from Peaked Hill Bars to Monomoy; five hundred recorded wrecks in sixteen years of the mid-century, countless hundreds before that, far too many since. The *Paradise Bird,* the slim-hulled *Whidah,* comes up from her grave off Wellfleet Bar. Sam Bellamy and Maria are aboard her, and the rum-drinking gunner and the hero pirate and a hundred other sailors including those who swung by their necks at "Admiralty Galloes, Boston."

Cyprian Southack in a wheezy whaleboat drifts over Jeremy's Drean. Ghostly cheers echo from the banks as his "cedar-bowl" sails through the walls of a house; while the *Somerset,* British Ship-of-the-Line, wrenches her timbers out of northern dunes, and with the *Ajax* drops anchor in the waters of Cape Cod Harbor. The *Nina* backs out of the Province post office, into which she sailed on a wintry gale and dispatched a letter to her owners; and a phantom girl of Tarpaulin Cove awaits the coming of a handsome seaman dressed in His Majesty's uniform. Away they sail on the sloop *Goodspeed* to a West Indian isle.

Built by Cape shipwrights, the prairie schooners with sailcloth covers and knee-construction, once drawn by oxen over high mountains, come creaking slowly home. Wagons scarred by Indian arrows, or burned, or left by the desert trails, on Midsummer Eve they are driven again by the Cape sons and daughters who sent no word to anxious parents waiting by Narrow Land hearths, dreading far more the prairie seas than the farthest reaches of ocean.

The vessels form in a long procession out on the old seaway. From under a bayberry mound on the dunes red caps nod, bright eyes peer toward the east where the ships from the south and the ships from the north slowly converge, falling into line like marchers in the old quadrilles. From sober-light to suncoming lost vessels convene. They speak each other; they flash their signals; and the "tailship of all" is a fat-cheeked dory "laden with variant posies" on which reclines the Reverend Joseph Metcalfe of Falmouth, who doffs his galleywest wig, as he passes, to the "Ladies' Delegation" watching from the shore.

With the deepening of the dawn star a change is felt, a summons comes like a low-toned bell. A white courser rises. His mane gleaming, his great eyes flashing, he swims to the prow of the lead vessel, and over the Rip he glides. After him follow the Phantom Fleet, "taking the bone in their teeth" on the Rip, skirting the reefs of Lost Island, following the last sea trail of Maushop. Silver trumpets of dawn lift high to welcome the knorrs of Brattahlid, the slim canoes of Pocanok where a lame crow sits at the helm and a green-eyed princess slumbers; to welcome the wrecks and the pirates, the "Bankers," the whalers, the clippers; bugling over the Narrow Land the dawn sea's reveille.

The key is severed from the lock, the peninsula sundered from the mainland. Tall cliffs crumble at the onslaught of the ocean, and the core of the land narrows, save for a lonely sea-spit lengthening to southward, a few dune islands shaping to the north. Yet the second 'Kingdome of Cornishmen' has broadened into a nation. The English tongue is spoken there; the Lord and Lucifer walk there; and life, they say, is a Giant Cycle that comes, goes and returns again.

APPENDIX

APPENDIX

ABBREVIATIONS USED

Freeman: Frederick Freeman, *History of Cape Cod.* (Boston, 1858-60.)

Otis: Amos Otis, *Genealogical Notes of Barnstable Families.* (Barnstable, 1888.)

Kittredge: Henry C. Kittredge, *History of Cape Cod.* (Houghton Mifflin Company, 1930.)

Bangs: Mary Rogers Bangs, *Old Cape Cod.* (Houghton Mifflin Company, 1931.)

Tarbell: Arthur Wilson Tarbell, *Cape Cod Ahoy!* (The Gorham Press, 1932.)

Mass. Hist.
Soc. Coll.: *Massachusetts Historical Society Collections.*

Patriot: files of *The Barnstable Patriot.*

Register: files of *The Yarmouth Register.*

Swift: Charles F. Swift, *Cape Cod, The Right Arm of Massachusetts.* (Yarmouth, 1897.)

Pratt: Enoch Pratt, *A Comprehensive History, Ecclesiastical and Civil, of Eastham, Wellfleet, and Orleans, etc.* (Yarmouth, 1844.)

T. R.: Town Records.

O. T.: Oral Traditions.

CHAPTER I. MIRAGE ON THE DUNES

The three principal accounts of the Vinland voyages are contained in three manuscripts in Copenhagen, known to scholars as the *Flatey*

Book, Hauk's Book, and *A. M. 557.* The three accounts conflict sharply. Edward F. Gray, in *Leif Eriksson, Discoverer of America* (Oxford Press, 1930), makes a careful study of the three versions. Upon his findings this chapter is based, although I do not go so far as to accept historically the exact locations assigned by Mr. Gray to the Norse settlements.

The "human interest" has been extracted from the three manuscripts, following in general the so-called "Greenland version." Conflicts have been arbitrarily eliminated. All quoted conversations or descriptions are taken from A. W. Reeves' definitive translation of the manuscripts, *The Finding of Wineland the Good* (Clarendon Press, Oxford, 1890). In a few instances unessential expletives, connectives or short phrases have been omitted from the quoted matter (conversational), since the Reeves translation, carefully following the original, suffers from its redundancy.

For the two songs of Thorhall the Hunter, I have used my own translation. Reeves' poetic rendition of the songs varies considerably from his literal translations. These I have attempted to approximate in verse.

For an eighteenth-century account of "honey dew" in New England, see *New York Magazine or Literary Repository,* July, 1791, pp. 378-79.

CHAPTER II. THE DEATH OF THE GIANT

1. The Ancient Traditions

Supplied, as the text indicates, by Chief Red Shell of Mashpee, Mass.

2. Tales of the Praying Indians

Collected from the Bulletins and Reports of the Bureau of American Ethnology; from the Proceedings and Collections of the Mass. Hist. Soc., from the *New Eng. Hist. and Gen. Register;* from F. G. Speck, *Territorial Subdivisions of the Massachusetts, Wampanoag and Nauset Indians* (Indian Notes; pub. Museum Am. Indian), Vol. VII; from H. F. Norton, *Martha's Vineyard* (Hartford, 1923); from *The Barnstable Patriot,* and from oral traditions collected by me from residents of Mashpee. Special sources are listed under individual legends.

How the Devil Threw a Rattlesnake: Patriot. A version of this tale is mentioned by Speck; O. T.

How the Devil Met a Chickadee Bird: Patriot. A version of this tale is included in Agnes Edwards, *Cape Cod, etc.* (Houghton Mifflin Company, 1918). The tale as narrated depends in large part for its flavor upon oral accounts. One "old inhabitant" remembered the jingle concerning Bourne because she used to "skip rope to it" when she was little.

How the Devil Built a Bridge: This, although it is told in one of its more sophisticated versions, undoubtedly goes back to a primitive original. See Speck, *Territorial Subdivisions, etc.*

Squant the Sea-woman: A composite from many fragments dealing with Squant (Granny Squannit or Squonanit, the Sea-woman) and Maushop the Giant. The story of Maushop's visit to the Island is mentioned, in differing versions, by Freeman, Bangs, Kittredge, Tarbell, Swift. Less familiar aspects of this legend have been collected from Daniel Wing, *West Yarmouth Houses* (Register Press, Yarmouthport, 1915); the *Patriot;* oral accounts ascribed originally to Captain Loring Fuller, South Yarmouth; and oral accounts collected by me from residents of Mashpee, Barnstable, and Martha's Vineyard Island.

The Princess and the Magic Bowl: Patriot; Register; Tarbell. A poem on Chief Sagam and Princess Scargo was published in the *Cape Cod Magazine.*

The Corn Cob Doll: O. T. Version followed is that of Mrs. Frederick Gardner, Mashpee, Mass.

The Screecham Sisters: O. T. Version followed is that of Mrs. Gardner, Mashpee, Mass. A legend of Hannah Screecham, very different in content (she is called the Lady Hannah and is not an Indian) is included in Frank Stockton, *Buccaneers and Pirates of Our Coast* (The Macmillan Co., 1922), pp. 296-98.

Geesukquand, the Sun Spirit: A well-known Mashpee story. Version of Mrs. Gardner followed.

The Water-Being of Pau Wah Pond: from a paper entitled *The Indian Legend of Potonamequoit,* by John Kenrick; contributed by his son, John Kenrick, South Orleans, Mass.

The Song of Whales: This legend in part suggests a primitive origin.

It either parallels or copies a Micmac Tale of Glooskap included in *Algonquin Legends of New England*, Charles G. Leland (Houghton, Mifflin and Company, 1885), pp. 31-35. The version that I have put together from fragments includes material from the *Patriot*, the *Register*, the Micmac tale recorded by Leland, and from modern oral traditions, especially the tale as told by the late Mrs. Eleanor Hicks of Mashpee.

The Last of Granny Squannit: O. T. A number of versions of this are extant in Mashpee today. Version followed is that of Mrs. Gardner, who received it from her husband's grandmother.

3. Tales of the Historians

The Uninhabited Island: 3 Mass. Hist. Soc. Coll., VIII. The majority of the quotations are taken from John Brereton's account of the voyage of Gosnold and Gilbert. See also *Original Narratives of Early American History* (Chas. Scribner's Sons, 1906), Vol. III, pp. 325-40. Shakespeare, *The Tempest*. The resemblances between Brereton's account and the Island of Prospero were first pointed out by E. E. Hale.

Baked Bread and Arrows: Voyages of Samuel de Champlain (Prince Soc. Ed., Boston, 1880). All quotations are taken from the Prince Soc. translation, with the exception of the Call of the Watch, which is given in the original French.

The Death of Tisquantum: All general historians of the Cape mention Tisquantum's death. The version of his life followed by this interpretation is that of C. F. Adams, *Three Episodes of Massachusetts History* (2d ed., Boston and New York, 1892), Vol. I, Chap. III, supplemented by William Bradford: *History of Plymouth Plantation* (Mass. Hist. Soc., 1912).

CHAPTER III. MEN OF GOD AND THE PRIMITIVE EARTH

The Missionizing Zealots

The White Sachem of Mashpee: H. S. B. Dykes, *Hist. of Rich. Bourne and Some of His Descendants*, Cleveland, 1919-20; M. F. Ayer, *Rich. Bourne, Missionary to the Mashpee Indians*, New Eng. Hist. and Gen. Reg., Vol. LXII, p. 139 ff. Quotations from

MS. letters of Rich. Bourne in Boston Public Library, also from
H. S. B. Dykes, *Hist. of Rich. Bourne, etc.* The concluding verse
and the legend of the cranberry are taken from oral tradition,
Mashpee.

The Arc of Crystal: Pratt; Otis; Freeman; MS. letters in Boston Public Library; Eastham T. R.

"Amorous Mr. Bachiler": A. Lewis and J. R. Newhall, *History of Lynn*
(Lynn, Mass., 1865); Otis; G. E. Emery, *A Man of Mark, etc.*
(Lynn, 1882); J. R. Newhall, *History of Lynn* (Lynn, 1883).

Andrew Hallett: Otis. His ample and remarkably minute study of
early Cape life, as exemplified by the household of Andrew Hallett, Jr., has been the primary source for this interpretation. Andrew Hallett, after his death, became to the people of the Cape the
typical example of a prosperous and wise goodman. Some of the
detail concerning Mehitabel has come down only as oral tradition.
While this study of the family makes no claim to historical accuracy, it does attempt to record the atmosphere of piety, tolerance and simplicity typical of many of the Old Comers, and
attempts also to "set the scene" carefully. The psalm sung by
Mehitabel is from the *Bay Psalm Book* (facsimile ed. W. Eames,
the New Eng. Soc., N.Y., 1903), Psalm LXIX. Town and church
records have also contributed many bits of information incorporated into the text.

The "Arraignment of Blood": George Bishop, *New England Judged by
the Spirit of the Lord* (Lond., 1703); George Keith, *Call of People
of New England to Repent* (Lond., 1691); Rev. C. B. Perry, *The
Perrys of Rhode Island* (New York, 1913); Otis; Freeman.

"Perfidious Cows": Quotations from Bishop and Keith (see under *"The
Arraignment of Blood"* for full titles); MS. letters of Thomas
Walley (Worcester Antiquarian Society and Boston Public Library); Otis; Freeman; O. T.

The Assembly of Saints: Otis; Freeman; all available church records
of churches that benefited by the Hersey Legacy.

Exiles from Bourneland

Benjamin Bourne: B. F. Bourne, *The Captive in Patagonia or Life
Among the Giants* (Boston, 1853). All quotations taken from this
book, with the exception of the boast concerning his Cape king-

dom. That formula was given to me by an old Cape sailor who claimed that it was typical of the harangues used to impress natives when whalemen landed "among heathen."

Sylvanus Bourne: H. S. B. Dykes, *Hist. of Rich. Bourne, etc.* (Cleveland, 1919-20). Quotations are taken from the letters of Sylvanus Bourne included in Mrs. Dykes' book.

Ansel Bourne: A. S. Comings, *A Narrative of the Wonderful Facts in the Case of Ansel Bourne* (Fall River, Mass., 1877). In the interpretation of this story much oral tradition has been accepted, not all of it clearly pertaining to Ansel Bourne, but typical of the particular form of religious hysteria common to Cape Cod, as to other parts of New England, during the decades of the Revival Meetings and Temperance Pledges. The conversations are imaginary. Ansel Bourne's denial of God, his affliction, the restoration of sight, speech and hearing, 18 days later, in a chapel at Westerly, are included in the pamphlet by A. S. Comings. The mental processes leading to Ansel's denial of God are interpreted, following similar traditional tales. Ansel's words at the time when his senses were restored are quoted from A. S. Comings' account.

CHAPTER IV. WITCHES, GOODWIVES, WIDOWS FOR SALE

1. Riders of the Broom

Ould Betty: W. R. Bliss, *The Old Colony Town, etc.* (Houghton, Mifflin and Company, 1893), pp. 105-06. The story as given by Mr. Bliss has been followed as to plot. Added details taken from O. T.

The Witch Sisters of Buzzards Bay: ibid., pp. 106-07. Enlarged from oral accounts. The term "Jenkin's hens" was also applied to other old maids.

Captain Sylvanus and the Witch of Truro: Shebnah Rich, *Truro, Cape Cod, or Landmarks and Seamarks* (Boston, 1884), p. 184. A few details added from O. T. The "Red-heeled Witch" was, presumably, the lady encountered by Captain Rich.

Goodie Hallett Who Lived in a Whale: Michael Fitzgerald, *MS. Notes,* also in his *1812, a Tale of Cape Cod* (Register Press, Yarmouthport, 1912), in which she appears as an old woman with Indian blood. Shebnah Rich mentions her witchcraft as an existent tradition but is not aware of her name.

The Sailor and the Doughnuts: Boston Herald, Feb. 6, 1919. Gives the story as reported by the grandson of one of the bewitched sailor's shipmates. G. L. Kittredge in *Witchcraft in Old and New England* (Harv. Univ. Press, 1929) mentions the story (p. 219) and says in a note: "I heard a version of this story forty-odd years ago from an old Provincetown man, a native of Truro" (p. 528). The oral capacities of the goat, a familiar of Goodie Hallett, are taken from *MS. Notes* of Fitzgerald and from O. T. Goodie apparently possessed, as familiars, an imp, a goat, and a cat, all with linguistic facilities.

Deborah Burden, Weaver of Spells: W. R. Bliss, *The Old Colony Town, etc.,* pp. 108-11.

Liza Tower Hill of the Luminous Forest: Otis, pp. 10-11, 37-38, 99-103, 122-25. G. L. Kittredge in *Witchcraft in Old and New England,* pp. 20-21. Complaint against Eliz. Lewis in East Parish church records, Oct. 28, 1771. Account of dancing on the water, from Michael Fitzgerald, *MS. Notes.* Story of Benj. Goodspeed and the death of Liza contributed by Mrs. S. Alexander Hinckley, Hyannis. See also prize essay, "Story of Tower Hill," by Abbie Bodfish, *Hyannis Patriot,* Jan. 5, 1933.

The Witchcraft Cases: Plymouth Colony Records. All general historians.

2. Goodwives and Widows

The Three Hinckley Roses: O. T. In the Boston Public Library, a broadside, signed M. T., laments the deaths of Hannah, Samuel and Elisabeth. The elegy does not follow the oral tradition; Hannah, apparently, dying first, and no mention made of the final exhortation made by Elisabeth. For another story, typical of the "pious deaths" of Cape children, see the account of Priscilla Thornton of Yarmouth, in Cotton Mather's *Magnalia Christi Americana* (Hartford, 1820. 1st Amer. from Lond. ed.), Vol. II, pp. 418-19.

The Double Trial of Abigail: W. R. Bliss, *Colonial Times on Buzzards Bay* (Houghton, Mifflin and Company, 1888), pp. 100-14. Quoted extracts from Wareham town records and church records, taken from W. R. Bliss.

The Tarring and Feathering of the Widow Nabby: All general historians of the Cape record some version of this tale. Freeman describes the widow as a Whig tarred and feathered by Tories. I have followed Otis' highly circumstantial account (see Kittredge, p. 115, who also accepts the tale as Otis tells it). In considering the episode from a historical viewpoint, the fine if impetuous character of Nathaniel Freeman should be kept in mind. O. T. makes him the villain of the story, but we have no historical proof that he was even present on the night when Abigail was punished. If he, a doctor and a gentleman, led the Whigs, the "tarring" was nominal, the escapade little more than a lark and the old woman perhaps a bit roughly treated, but probably not made to suffer severely.

Aunt Beck's Museum: Follows Otis closely, pp. 93-98.

Cynthia Gets Her Bonnet: Zion Herald, Sept. 24, 1918; A. P. Palmer, *A Brief History of the Methodist Episcopal Church, Wellfleet* (Boston, 1877), *Appendix: Gross Family;* O. T. derived from a number of the descendants of the Gross family, especially Miss Evelyn Rich (daughter of the historian, Shebnah Rich); and Mr. and Mrs. Theodore Swift.

"Widdows at Vandue": W. R. Bliss, *Colonial Times on Buzzards Bay,* pp. 64-65. All available town records and church records searched for items. Jane or "Geen" Bump (us) is mentioned by Bliss. Otis notes her ancestry. The story of the wooden cross rests entirely upon oral tradition. I have searched diligently and without success for her "forest grave," said still to exist. But those who have "heerd tell" of its exact location, near Falmouth, seem never to have seen it themselves. I suspect that it is either destroyed or apocryphal.

CHAPTER V. PIRATES, MOONCURSING AND YARNS
OF THE SEA

1. Gentlemen of the Cutlass

Quotation from Captain John Smith, *Travels and Works* (Arber and Bradley, Edinburgh, 1910), Vol. II, p. 913.

The Black Bellamy: All general historians of the Cape mention the wreck of the *Whidah.* In this account, the story of Bellamy as pirate follows Dow and Edmonds, *Pirates of the New Eng. Coast*

(Salem, 1923). The story of Maria Hallett is taken from Eastham
and Orleans traditions, and from the *MS. Notes* of Michael Fitzgerald which describe both accounts of her, that of an old witch,
that of a young girl. C. M. Skinner, *Myths and Legends of Our
Own Land* (Philadelphia, 1896), Vol. I, pp. 309-10, "The Wild
Man of Cape Cod," describes the return of the deranged pirate,
but paints him as a ferocious lunatic. Fitzgerald follows the same
tradition in *1812, A Tale of Cape Cod,* but has Bellamy murder
Maria Hallett. I have adopted the more pacific finale to the tale
as more in keeping with the character of Bellamy as revealed by
the early accounts. See also, *Boston Sunday Globe,* Oct. 22, 1916,
Boston News Letter (issues for year 1717-18 in collection of Mass.
Hist. Soc.). Also Mass. State Archives, Vol. 51, 63; Captain Charles
Johnson, *History of the Pirates* (Lond., 1724, 1726, 1762); *The
Lives and Bloody Exploits of the Most Noted Pirates, etc.* (Hart-
ford, 1837).

*The "Pyrats" and the Posse: The Trials of Eight Persons Indited for
Piracy of Whom Two were Acquitted and the Rest Found Guilty*
(Boston, 1718). Pamphlet, Mass. Hist. Soc., Boston; Pratt; Michael
Fitzgerald, *1812, A Tale, etc.,* also *MS. Notes.* The details of the
flight to the Crosby Tavern, the capture there, and the ensuing
night follow O. T.

The Ketch Elinor: Dow and Edmonds, *Pirates of the New Eng. Coast,*
pp. 32-33. The account of a woman who rode her horse across
deeps and bars to the rescue of plague-stricken victims of piratical
barbarity is a frequently recounted tale on the Cape. The identi-
ties of the woman and of the vessel have been lost. Finding the
story of the ketch *Elinor,* which exactly coincides with the situation necessary to the oral tradition, I have arbitrarily given the
tradition this setting that seems to best fit it of all historical accounts of Cape shipwreck known to me. The pirates who took
possession of the ketch were William Coward, Peleg Heath,
Thomas Story, Christopher Knight. They were sentenced to be
hanged, Jan. 27, 1690. Coward was hanged; the others were re-
prieved.

The Scourge of the Sea: Dow and Edmonds, *Pirates of the New Eng.
Coast,* pp. 141-217. Account of Jonathen Barlow in *Boston News
Letter,* June 27, 1723; also Oct. 15, 1724; *New Eng. Courant,* June

17, 1723. See also *Boston News Letter,* Feb. 11, 1725; *New Eng. Courant,* Feb. 8, 1725.

The Secret of Tarpaulin Cove: Dow and Edmonds, *Pirates, etc.,* Chapter IV; Mass. Archives, Vol. XXXV, leaf 10a; Suffolk Court Files, No. 2539:9; *Diary of Samuel Sewall* (Mass. Hist. Soc.), Vol. I, p. 310. The story of Hester Blaney may or may not be founded upon fact. The only supporting proof that I have come upon is the order of release, at the instance of "sundry Ladies of Quality."

2. "*Mooncussin'* "

Cyprian in the Rain: Cyprian Southack's letters are in Mass. State Archives, Vol. LI, pp. 287, 287a, 289, 289a. See also J. F. Jameson, *Privateering and Piracy, etc.* (edited under the auspices of the Colonial Dames of America, New York, 1923), pp. 290-93, 299-300. All general historians of the Cape mention the crossing of the Cape in a whaleboat.

The White Stallion: O. T., esp. Charles Kendrick, Chatham, Mass.; Otis; *Patriot.* False lights, the luring of vessels to disaster, in fact all that is connected with the earlier idea of "mooncussin'," remain entirely within the confines of folklore. I know of no historical evidence whatsoever to support the assumption that any vessel was ever wrecked by false lights on Cape Cod. Nevertheless the tradition is widespread and persistent. Almost every old sailor will tell some yarn concerning it. "*Mooncussin'* " is now the local phrase for predatory salvaging.

3. Yarns of the Sea

"*Tall Tales*"

The Flying Spouse: Based upon the English yarn, but embroidered in true Cape fashion. Ship also called *The Flying Daisy* and *The Flying Mate.* O. T., esp. the late Capt. Robert P. Reynard, Fall River, Mass.

The Sea Serpent of Provincetown: H. A. Jennings, *Provincetown, or Odds and Ends from the Tip End* (Yarmouthport (?), 1890), pp. 172-75. A photograph shows G. W. Ready "seeing the serpent." See also *Patriot,* Sept. 11, 1830.

The Lyars' Bench: See Shebnah Rich, *Truro, etc.;* O. T. Countless variations of these anecdotes exist, esp. on the lower Cape.

"One fer the Arkyologists": written and contributed by Joseph C. Allen, editor of the *Edgartown Gazette,* Martha's Vineyard Island.

How to Tack a Square-Rigger: ibid.

The Saucer-Back Halibut: ibid.

"We Old Men": A number of brief references to Jack and Tom may be found interspersed among sea news and stories in early files of the *Patriot*; O. T. used for this version, esp. C. A. Howes, Chatham, Mass.; Capt. Robert Soper, Provincetown.

"True Tales"

The Trial of Ansell Nickerson: General historians mention this case briefly, often incorrectly. Information used here taken from *The Mass. Gazette and Boston News Letter,* Nov. 19, Nov. 26, Dec. 10, Dec. 17, 1772; Aug. 12, 1773. See also *Boston Evening Post,* Nov. 23, 1772; T. Hutchinson, *Hist. Province of Mass. Bay,* Vol. III, p. 419; C. F. Adams, *Life and Works of John Adams* (Charles C. Little and James Brown, Boston, 1850), Vol. II, p. 224, footnote. See also *Diary of John Adams* (in same volume), p. 304.

Jolly Dick Raggett Loses a Prize: All general historians; esp. Pratt; M. Fitzgerald, *1812, A Tale, etc.,* tells the story in great detail. O. T. followed in certain details given to me by the descendants of Captain Mayo.

The Head of Andrew Jackson: Follows the Cape versions as told by Theodate Geoffrey, *Suckanesset: A History of Falmouth* (Falmouth Pub. Co., 1930), pp. 61-72. Histories of the *Constitution* also tell the story (esp. E. N. Snow and H. A. Gosnell). A figurehead, owned by W. B. Leeds, believed to be the original Jackson figurehead, was exhibited in the Amer. Folk-Sculpture Exhibit, Newark Museum, Newark, N.J., 1932. A photograph of the figurehead appeared in the *New York Times,* Jan. 14, 1932.

CHAPTER VI. GHOSTS WHO STILL WALK THE NARROW LAND

The Deacon Brings the Sacramental Wine: Shebnah Rich, *Truro Old and New, etc.,* mentions the deacon's ride but does not tell the story of Silas which I have taken from O. T., Truro.

Sand Dobbies of Eastham: M. Fitzgerald, *MS. Notes,* chief source. He gives as his sources, "Caps. Snow & Knowles," whom I have not been able to identify. Fitzgerald is my only source for the use of the word "Dobbies." A number of old residents recall that they were told stories when they were young of the "goblins in the dunes" or of the "Little People." Several of these accounts reveal that the storytellers had confused or combined tales of the Indian pukwudgees with earlier English pixie and goblin lore. The little wild horse, galloping along the beach, and ridden by goblins or devils, is a well-known tradition on the Cape. This account has been built up from many fragments of O. T.

Robert the Scot: Follows Otis, pp. 380-81. Details added from O. T.

The Merwoman and the Finback Whale: An expurgated sailor's yarn. O. T. Obviously related to the Indian tales of Squant the Sea-woman. Ichabod Paddock was a real whalemaster. See Shebnah Rich, *Truro, etc.,* p. 111.

A Song of Ships: O. T. Many versions exist of this tale, now associated with a ruined house on Eastham Plain, a house that has not burned down. Therefore, later versions omit the fire. Eastham T. R. do not reveal the full name of Barnabas.

The Bundling Marsh: O. T.; see H. R. Stiles, *History of Bundling.* The account, expurgated, from a seaman's version of no slight iniquity. Bundling was associated with the Rev. Samuel Osborn of Eastham, who was said to have favored it as a custom. Falling into the marshes and quicksands was accounted for, in early days, by claims that the men were lured by bog witches, or sea witches. Women were lured by devils, or desired by ghosts. Women so used were supposed to be unsuitable for marriage.

Jedidy and the Devil: O. T. Many variants. Always the flight ends in Provincetown, and the conclusion is the same; but different captains and different towns are used for the starting point. Probably of late origin.

The Boat That Fain Would Live on Land: Kittredge and Freeman tell the story of the wig. The scrap from his diary was given to me as "copied." I have been unable to find the diary. The story of Joseph's boats seems to have no written source, rests entirely upon O. T. The death of Joseph Metcalfe, the night after the great storm, is "apocryphal." Apparently, he was taken ill then, but did not die until in the winter. According to Falmouth records, deceased Dec. 24, 1723.

The Glass Gaffer of Sandwich: Details of the gaffers taken from Bangs

Burgess, *History of Sandwich Glass* (Libr. of Cape Cod, Hist. and Gen., Yarmouthport, 1925); the story of the gaffer who knocks at the doors at dawn is O. T. Many variants.

The Procession of the Lost Ships: Information taken from general historians, esp. Kittredge; also shipping records: New Bedford, Boston, Falmouth, Eastham; also Theodate Geoffrey, *Suckanesset, etc.* Also O. T.